Creating Microsoft® Access 2000 Solutions: A Power User's Guide

Gordon Padwick

A Division of Macmillan USA
201 West 103rd St., Indianapolis, Indiana, 46290 USA

Creating Microsoft® Access 2000 Solutions: A Power User's Guide

Copyright © 2000 by Sams Publishing

International Standard Book Number: 0-672-31894-6

Library of Congress Catalog Card Number: 99-068160

Printed in the United States of America

First Printing: May 2000

02   01   00   4   3   2   1

Trademarks

Warning and Disclaimer

PUBLISHER
Brad Jones

ACQUISITIONS EDITOR
Danielle Bird

DEVELOPMENT EDITOR
Tom Cirtin

MANAGING EDITOR
Lisa Wilson

PROJECT EDITOR
Paul Schneider

COPY EDITOR
Mike Henry

INDEXER
Aamir Burki

PROOFREADERS
Jill Mazurczyk
Maryann Steinhart

TECHNICAL EDITOR
Kai Soder

TEAM COORDINATOR
Meggo Barthlow

COVER AND INTERIOR DESIGNER
Anne Jones

COPYWRITER
Eric Borgert

EDITORIAL ASSISTANT
Angela Boley

PRODUCTION
Ayanna Lacey
Heather Hiatt Miller
Stacey Richwine-DeRome

Contents at a Glance

Contents

About the Author

Gordon Padwick is a consultant who specializes in Microsoft Office applications and Visual Basic. In addition to training and supporting Office users, Gordon develops custom applications based on the Office suite. He has been working with computers for more years than he cares to remember in engineering, management, support, and marketing positions, and has been using Windows since Microsoft introduced it some 12 years ago.

He is a graduate of London University and has completed postgraduate studies in computer science and communications. Gordon is the author of numerous other books including *Building Integrated Office Applications*, *Special Edition Using Microsoft Outlook 97*, *Using Microsoft Outlook 98*, and *Special Edition Using Microsoft Outlook 2000*, all published by Que, and of *Programming Microsoft Outlook 2000*, published by Sams Publishing.

About the Technical Editor

Kai Soder currently works for New Horizons Computer Learning Center in Indianapolis, IN as a Technical Trainer. When time permits, he consults with clients on development solutions utilizing Microsoft Office, Visual Studio, and SQL. He is a Microsoft Certified Trainer, Microsoft Certified Solution Developer, and a Certified Lotus Specialist. He enjoys road trips, camping, and spending time with his son Stefan.

Dedication

To Kathy, my wife, inspiration, and best friend.

Acknowledgments

Writing the acknowledgments for a new book is one of my favorite tasks—for two reasons: It's close to the last thing to be written for the book, so I can heave a huge sigh of relief that the project is almost complete. Also, it's my opportunity to look back over the last few months and gratefully remember the people who have helped me write the book.

Readers of this book owe a big vote of thanks to technical editor Kai Soder. Kai carefully checked what I had written for technical accuracy and pointed out more errors than I care to admit. He also made many suggestions for improving the clarity of my writing.

I offer my thanks to the many Sams people who have given me their support and encouragement. Among them are Danielle Bird, Acquisitions Editor, Tom Cirtin, Development Editor, Brad Jones, Associate Publisher, and Paul Schneider, Project Editor. My thanks also go to the many other Sams people, whose names I don't know, who have worked behind the scenes to create the printed book you're reading.

The many illustrations of what you can expect to see on your screen were captured with Collage Complete. Thank you, Nancy and Neil Rosenburg of Inner Media for providing Collage Complete—it has to be one of the most bug-free and user-friendly applications I've ever worked with.

As always, I want to acknowledge my gratitude to my wife, Kathy, for her support and patience while I've been writing this book. She's been willing to put up with me spending most of evenings and weekends pounding away at my computer. Her encouragement has made it possible for me to write this book.

—Gordon Padwick, March 2000

Tell Us What You Think!

As the reader of this book, *you* are our most important critic and commentator. We value your opinion and want to know what we're doing right, what we could do better, what areas you'd like to see us publish in, and any other words of wisdom you're willing to pass our way.

As a Publisher for Sams, I welcome your comments. You can fax, email, or write me directly to let me know what you did or didn't like about this book—as well as what we can do to make our books stronger.

Please note that I cannot help you with technical problems related to the topic of this book, and that due to the high volume of mail I receive, I might not be able to reply to every message.

When you write, please be sure to include this book's title and author as well as your name and phone or fax number. I will carefully review your comments and share them with the author and editors who worked on the book.

Fax: 317-581-4770

Email: adv_prog@mcp.com

Mail: Brad Jones
           Sams Publishing
           201 West 103rd Street
           Indianapolis, IN 46290 USA

Introduction

This book is about using Access 2000 to create customized applications for converting raw data into useful information.

In addition to being the world's most popular desktop database management system, Access is a versatile development tool. You can use Access out-of-the-box to store and retrieve data, but Access can do much more than that. Beyond what's immediately available, you can use wizards to begin customizing Access. You can go much further by taking advantage of macros and the Visual Basic for Applications (VBA) programming language that give you detailed control of every aspect of what Access can do.

You shouldn't be overwhelmed with all that Access can do. Just take it one step at a time. Begin expanding your Access horizons by taking advantage of wizards. Then, look into the possibilities of using macros. From there, convert your macros into VBA code and modify that code to suit your specific needs. Once you have a handle on that, you're probably ready to write VBA code from scratch, simple at first but, as you gain experience, gradually more sophisticated.

As you progress through the chapters of this book, you'll learn, step-by-step, how to use Access, not just as a database management system, but as a means to create useful information. The topics covered in this book include

- Organizing your data efficiently in linked tables
- Creating forms for fast and accurate data input
- Designing reports that convert raw data into meaningful information
- Incorporating data from other sources into an Access-based application
- Sharing an Access-based application with other people

Who Should Read This Book

This book is intended for you if you're an Access power user who wants to take the next step—to begin developing applications based on Access 2000. The book assumes you have considerable experience in using Access 2000 interactively. That is, you've created tables, queries, forms, and reports by using the built-in wizards, and by opening menus, and choosing items in those menus. Now you're ready for more of what Access has to offer.

Building on your present knowledge, and sometimes reminding you about things you're somewhat familiar with, this book provides what you need to know to begin creating professional-level applications.

This book emphasizes extending the basic functionality of Access by taking advantage of the programming capabilities built into Access. Although the book pays some attention to using macros, it mainly encourages you to use the Visual Basic for Applications (VBA) programming environment that Access shares with other Office 2000 applications.

If you have some previous experience with using Visual Basic or even BASIC in the past, you'll easily understand how you can enhance an Access-based application with VBA code. Even if you have little or no previous programming experience, with some work you should be able to take advantage of the techniques described in this book.

How This Book Is Organized

This book consists of 20 chapters grouped in five parts; three appendixes; and a glossary.

Part I: Planning and Application Design

Part I contains four chapters that deal with the basics of access applications. Chapter 1, "Planning Successful Access Applications," primarily stresses the importance of creating optimized tables for storing your data. The chapter also draws your attention to what's new in Access 2000, contains advice about documenting applications, and reviews some database terminology.

Chapter 2, "The Anatomy of an Access Application," reviews the structure of Access applications. Chapter 3, "Storing Your Data Efficiently," covers the organization of tables and the importance of choosing the appropriate data types for each element of data. The chapter also shows how to index tables to speed up data access and how to establish relationships between tables.

Chapter 4, "Creating Information Out of Data," starts by showing how to manipulate data in tables and then proceeds to describe the use of queries to organize information. The chapter also provides an introduction to using crosstab queries to analyze numerical information.

Part II: Using Forms to Enter and Display Data

Part II contains three chapters about using Access forms for controlling the Access user interface and for convenient data entry and display. Chapter 5, "Making Your Forms Smarter," tells you how to create a form that displays automatically when Access starts and how to use that form to display other forms. The chapter also describes how to create a form to use for entering data in tables and for displaying information based on data in tables.

Chapter 6, "Making Data Input Fast and Accurate," describes several things you can do to simplify using forms for data entry. The chapter also shows how to automatically check the validity of data that's entered. Chapter 7, "Enhancing Your Application with Pictures and

Other Graphics," deals with graphics such as lines, rectangles, and pictures used as design elements and also with displaying graphics based on table data in forms and reports.

Part III: Finding and Printing Information

Part III contains two chapters, primarily about presenting useful information. Chapter 8, "Creating Informative Reports," contains many suggestions about creating various types of reports, including reports that summarize information. The chapter also shows how to create charts that illustrate data. Chapter 9, "Finding Records in a Database," shows how to use forms to display individual data records and how to find specific data.

Part IV: Accessing External Data and Applications

Part IV contains three chapters. Chapter 10, "Using External Data in an Access Application," shows how you can combine data from various sources into Access applications. The chapter also shows how you can export selected data from Access into other applications. Chapter 11, "Using Object Models Within the Office Environment," presents an introduction to the Access object model so that you can gain detailed control of Access. The chapter also shows how object models can be used to combine the capabilities of various Office applications.

Chapter 12, "Accessing Data," describes how to use ActiveX Data Objects (ADO), the default method of working with data in Access 2000. The chapter also covers Data Access Objects (DAO), the method of working with data used by previous versions of Access and still available in Access 2000.

Part V: Getting More Out of Access

Part V contains eight chapters that show you how to expand your horizons. Chapter 13, "Taking More Control of Access," is where you start working seriously with Visual Basic for Applications. This chapter shows how to create procedures that respond to events and how to cope with errors that might occur when an application runs. Chapter 14, "Making Access Applications Easy to Use," focuses on the way you can create interfaces that keep the people who use your applications informed about what's going on and how you can customize menus and toolbars.

Chapter 15, "Calculating Values and Making Decisions," describes how you can use the many operators built into Access to perform calculations and make decisions. Chapter 16, "Maintaining a Healthy Application," deals with compacting and repairing databases as well as backing up and archiving data.

Chapter 17, "Extending Access to the Web," deals with several topics related to making your Access applications Internet-aware. Among other things, the chapter shows how you can make information available to people who use a Web browser. Chapter 18, "Making Your Application Secure," shows how you can restrict access to your application and to its data.

Chapter 19, "Increasing the Capabilities of an Access Application," introduces the Microsoft Data Engine (MSDE), a desktop version of SQL Server, and shows how to use it to increase an application's capabilities. Chapter 20, "Sharing an Application with Other People," covers sharing information by way of a LAN and also distributing Access applications for use by people who don't have Access installed on their computers.

Appendixes and Glossary

Appendix A, "Visual Basic for Applications Primer," is a quick introduction to Visual Basic for Applications (VBA). This appendix is intended to get you started with using VBA. Appendix B, "SQL Primer," is a quick introduction to the SQL language that Access uses to interact with databases. Appendix C, "Information Resources for Access 2000," contains a list of books for further reading on Access and related topics and a selection of Internet sources. The Glossary contains definitions of words and phrases you'll come across while using Access.

Web Site References

You'll find many Web site addresses (URLs) mentioned in this book. All these addresses were correct at the time the book was written, but by the time you read the book, some addresses might have changed. In many cases, a site's owner sets up a mechanism that automatically redirects you to the new URL, but that isn't always the case. I apologize for any inconvenience changed URLs cause, but hope you understand such changes are completely out of my control.

Author's Final Comment

As I always do in the books I write, I invite readers to send me their suggestions, comments, and questions. Send email to me at gpadwick@earthlink.net. I value the messages I receive and try to answer all of them. Although it's gratifying when people tell me they've found one of my books useful (some do), I also appreciate comments and questions that prompt me to think about things I've previously missed.

I hope you enjoy and benefit from this book.

—*Gordon Padwick*

Planning and Application Design

IN THIS PART

Planning Successful Access Applications

IN THIS CHAPTER

As I explained in the Introduction, this book builds on your knowledge of Access 2000 so that you can create more advanced applications than those you've probably previously created. I assume you've been using Access for a while and know your way around Access menus, toolbars, and most of the dialog boxes, and you've created some tables, queries, forms, and reports that you and, perhaps, other people use to manage information. You might have used macros or Visual Basic for Applications to enhance what Access can do, but I don't assume that.

Previously, you might have created smaller applications and were able to get away without doing much planning before you got started. After reading this book, though, you'll be ready to start creating larger, more complex Access-based applications. You'll find it pays to spend time planning what you want to achieve before you even open Access. If you don't give planning the attention it deserves, development is unnecessarily difficult and time-consuming, and the resulting application probably won't meet expectations.

This chapter provides advice about planning Access-based applications. The chapter contains advice about planning an application that completely satisfies users' needs, designing tables for storing your raw data efficiently, thinking about a proposed application in terms of how it will be used, and creating documentation that simplifies ongoing updating of an application.

Understanding Database Terminology

This book mostly uses the words you'll see while using Access for database components. However, more advanced books tend to use the more formal words in which database theory is described. For example, this book uses the word *record* to refer to all the data about an item in a table. More formal books use the words *row* or *tuple*.

The glossary at the end of this book defines many of the more formal database words. That should help you interpret information about databases you come across in other sources.

Understanding the Importance of Planning

I can't overemphasize the importance of devoting time to planning an application before you get down to the details of designing it. Each hour you spend in planning will save you several hours of work while you design the application and many more hours of work while you modify the application to satisfy users' needs.

Your initial planning activities involve completely understanding what people expect the application to do. After that, you have to plan the structure of the application so that it works efficiently. Human nature being what it is, some people think they can dispense with planning and just let things evolve. That doesn't work! If you take that approach, you'll find yourself reworking the details of your application time after time.

On the other hand, some people feel they have to plan everything down to the last detail before they start designing. Again, that doesn't work. Planning to that detail takes so much time that the need for the application is likely to have disappeared before design starts.

The trick is to do enough, but not too much, planning. Do enough planning to be confident you know what has to be done. Don't do so much planning that design never starts. This chapter describes an approach to planning that should help you reach a good compromise.

Aspects of Planning an Access Application

The purpose of an Access-based application is to provide information. You should have a well-defined set of objectives about what information a new application is expected to provide and how people will interact with the application before you start any design work.

Some people think of Access as a means of storing data in an organized manner. Although that's true, it puts the emphasis in the wrong place. You should think of Access as a means of providing information. The reason for storing data is so that you can subsequently retrieve information based on the stored data. Your goal should be to create an application that provides the information people need.

Applications can be categorized in several ways, one of which is whether the application is intended to replace an existing process, or whether it's to do something new. Each of these categories presents its own set of challenges.

If the application is replacing an existing process, whether it's manual or computer-based, take the time to study what people are used to doing. Try to make it possible for people to work with the new application in much the same way as they are currently working. For example, forms displayed by your application should be as similar as possible to the forms displayed by the current application or the paper forms people currently work with. The more you make the new application appear immediately familiar to users, the more readily will those users accept the new application and the faster will they become skilled in its use.

The major challenge in creating a completely new application is to understand what it's supposed to do. One important technique for determining this is to perform a *needs analysis*: Meet individually with all the key people who will be using the application and ask them to describe what they need. After doing that, you should gather everyone together in a meeting, possibly a series of meetings, in which you present the conclusions you've reached from the individual discussions and let people tell you what you have right and where you're wrong. The aim is to reach a consensus so that you and the future users all know and agree on what's expected.

Whether you're planning to create an application that replaces what's already in use, or something completely new, rest assured that the people who will use your application don't know, or can't tell you, all they initially need and certainly don't know exactly what they will need in the future. For that reason, rely heavily on your own judgment: As you plan and subsequently design the application, try to anticipate what people might need. Leave doors open so that enhancements can easily be made. Try to avoid design decisions that will make it difficult to add enhancements. This doesn't obviate the need for a formal and well-structured needs analysis, but it allows for filling in the gaps when unforeseen requirements arise.

Here's one example of what I have in mind. Suppose you're creating an application that records contacts a salesperson has with a client. The initial requirement might state that each salesperson has only one person to contact at a client company. Don't believe that! Sometime in the future, a salesperson will have two or more people to contact within a client company. Design your application so that multiple contacts within a company are possible with only minor changes to the application.

On the other hand, there's no significant problem in handling names of persons within a specific country or culture. In the United States, for example, it's quite acceptable to address a communication to a person using just the first and last name. I'm not, in any way, offended to receive mail addressed simply to Gordon Padwick. In other countries, though, people expect to receive mail addressed to them to have their names prefixed by a courtesy title and suffixed by any degrees they've earned, professional memberships, and position in society. When planning a database application that may refer to people, keep in mind the need to provide fields in your tables for these types of data items and also to use these fields where appropriate in forms and reports.

This example of a contacts database provides just a taste of the types of considerations that go into planning a successful application. After defining the purpose of the application in some considerable detail, you can start planning the reports and forms that will be needed.

Planning Reports and Forms

The most important thing to consider when planning an application is what information you want to get out of that application—how information on forms is displayed on users' screens, and how information is presented in printed reports. If the application is to be used by several or many people, make sure that you completely understand what each person is expecting.

You can use a word processor to create dummy reports to show potential users of the application what they can expect. Ask them whether these reports are what they need. You'll get much better feedback in this way than by simply asking people what reports they need. Modify the dummy reports according to the responses you receive and ask for comments on these revised reports. Repeat this process until you have everyone's agreement.

Don't expect one set of reports to suit everyone. If you're creating an application for a sales company for example, the reports needed by managers, buyers, and individual sales people are likely to be different. Make sure that each group agrees to the final set of dummy reports.

NOTE

When designing reports, bear in mind the size of paper on which users will print reports. If all users work in the United States, you should usually assume the use of letter-size paper (8-1/2 by 11 inches); don't assume users have access to other paper sizes unless you're sure that's the case. If some users work outside the United States, you should assume people use either letter-size or the international A4 size of paper (210 by 297 millimeters)—somewhat narrower and longer than letter-size.

Bear in mind, also, that most printers have a minimum margin size. It's usually safe to assume minimum margins of half an inch for all four edges. Even that's not enough for all printers.

In the same way, get every user's buy-in on the forms the application will display on screens. Initially, you can make sketches of forms for people to evaluate. Before your planning is complete, though, you should use Access to create dummy forms. These dummy forms should have all the boxes, buttons, and other elements that will be part of the final application, even though they're not functional. Some of these forms will be used for displaying information; others will be used for data input. As for reports, make sure that each potential user agrees to the forms that you propose before you move on from planning to begin creating the application.

NOTE

As a power user, you might have a 17-inch or larger, high-definition monitor. But many people who use your application won't be so lucky, particularly those who work with laptop computers. Take care to design forms that can be adequately displayed on the smallest, lowest-resolution screens any user might have.

Keep your forms as simple and uncluttered as possible. If you need to display a lot of information on a form, consider having two or more forms with an easy way, such as buttons, to switch between forms.

There are two basic reasons for going through this sometimes time-consuming process of getting agreement on reports and forms:

- As a result of the process, you have a firm idea of what the application should do
- When the application is released to users, you can't be accused of not meeting users' requirements

Planning Tables

After getting everyone's agreement on what information the application is expected to produce on displayed forms and printed reports, you can begin to consider how the application will store data. As you know, an Access application stores data in one or more tables, each table containing separate fields for each item of data.

Each report and form primarily contains information based on data in the application's tables. Knowing what's to be in forms and reports, you can decide what fields need to be in your tables. This list of fields is known as a data dictionary. Table 1.1 shows a preliminary data dictionary for the Book application that accompanies this book.

NOTE

Forms and reports can also contain information that's not derived from data in tables. For example, reports usually contain the date and time the information was printed, obtained from the computer's internal clock. Reports can also contain other computer-based information such as the current user's name. You don't need fields in tables for this type of data.

TABLE 1.1   Book Application Preliminary Data Dictionary

Field	Description
Book Title	Title of book
Author	Author's name
Publisher	Publisher's name
Imprint	Publisher's imprint (if any)
Address	Publisher's street address
City	Publisher's city
State	Publisher's state
Postal Code	Publisher's postal code
Country	Publisher's country

Field	Description
Phone	Publisher's phone number
Web	Publisher's Web address
Information	Additional information about publisher
ISBN	Book ISBN number
Category	Book category
Publication Date	Book publication date
Price	Cover price
Acquired	Date book acquired
Paperback	Paperback or hard cover
Information	Additional information about book

You could, but shouldn't, go ahead from here and create a table that contains all these fields. Before going any further, you need to optimize the proposed fields and decide whether the fields should all be in one table or distributed in two or more tables, a process known as normalization.

Refining Fields

One of the principles of good database design is that each field in a table should contain only one item of information. The data dictionary shown in Table 1.1 doesn't comply with this rule. Take the proposed Author field, for example. Each book author has a first and last name, and possibly a middle name or initial as well. As the field stands, it could contain two or three items of information. If you have just one field for the three elements of a name, you'll subsequently run into problems if you want to display or print an author's name as Gwen T Summers in one place and as Summers, Gwen in another. By replacing the single Author field with the three fields, you can avoid this type of problem.

> **TIP**
>
> Don't unnecessarily create several fields if one is sufficient. For example, if your complete definition of the application shows that you always display an author's name in the form Summers, Gwen, there's no need to have separate fields for first and last names. However, needs do change. So, in this particular case, you should probably have separate fields even if the definition doesn't require them.
>
> *continues*

A street address field is probably a better example. Street addresses for single-family residences in the United States have three components, such as 123 Green Street, or four components, such as 123 Green Street #321 for apartments and condominiums. For most purposes, all these components are used as one data item and can safely be included in a single field. However, if your application is to be used for creating delivery routes, you should create three separate fields, one for the address number, one for the street name, and one for the apartment or condominium number.

If the application is to be used for delivery routes that include commercial addresses, the address might well include a floor number and an office number.

These examples should convince you how important it is to understand the information to be provided by the application before you get started with detailed design of that application.

Managing addresses in a database application can become quite complex. If you're only concerned with addresses in North America, you have to deal with only one set of address conventions. Remember, though, that it might be necessary to use a post office box or other delivery box to address certain types of mail, whereas it's necessary to use a complete street address for delivery by independent delivery services. While planning your tables, and while designing other parts of your application, if addressing or delivery routing is required, you have to take all aspects of addressing into account. This becomes even more complex if you're dealing with countries that each have their own ways of specifying addresses.

You should revise the preliminary data dictionary to make sure that each proposed field contains only one data item. There's one exception to this; the preliminary data dictionary for the Book application contains a field for additional data about publishers and another for additional data about books. Many of your tables will contain a similar field. These fields are for any additional data that doesn't fit into the other fields. In many Access-based applications, it's impractical to have individual fields for every possible item of information. To solve this problem, it's usual to have a field (often known as a memo field) that can be used for any data.

Be aware that it's difficult to manipulate data in a memo field, so use that type of field only for data that won't be manipulated. Suppose you don't have a field for book publication date and plan to enter that information in a memo field. Subsequently, you'll run into severe problems if you want to create a list of books published during a certain year. Remember what you read earlier in this chapter about deciding what type of information your application needs to provide before getting into detailed design. If you know users want to retrieve specific types of information, you'll know what individual fields are needed in your tables.

Another rule about good design is that all fields should be independent. The data dictionary in Table 1.1 does satisfy this rule. In another case, though, you might have an application that tracks sales. The data dictionary for this application would probably include separate Price and Quantity fields. You might be tempted to include another field for Total Price that would include price multiplied by quantity. You shouldn't normally do that because that would violate the rule of field independence. Instead of having a field for the total price, the application should calculate the total price when it's required.

There are good reasons for avoiding dependent fields. One reason is that dependent fields make your tables unnecessarily large. Perhaps a more important reason is that, if you do have dependent fields, your application must correct those fields when any change is made to the fields on which they depend, an unnecessary complication.

As the saying goes, "All rules are made to be broken." That's particularly true for the rule about avoiding dependent fields in tables. In practice, this rule is quite often broken, but only when there's a good reason to do so. In the case of large, shared database applications, the existence of dependent fields can enhance performance. Your objective should be to follow the rules of good table design, but to be prepared to break those rules if there is a good reason to do so.

TIP

You're not entirely on your own when it comes to creating efficient tables. After you've created your tables, you can use the Table Analyzer Wizard in Access to get help. With your application open, choose Tools, move the pointer onto Analyze, and choose Table to open the wizard, which provides advice about how you can optimize your tables.

Having determined which fields you actually need, now you need to consider what type of data belongs in each field—whether each field will contain text, a number, a date, or something else. In the case of fields that will contain text or a number, you have to decide how many text characters to allow space for, or how large the number can be. You'll find specific information about this in the section "Choosing Data Types" in Chapter 3, "Storing Your Data Efficiently."

Using Multiple Tables

After you've revised your data dictionary to have a final list of fields, you next need to consider whether those fields will all be in one table, or whether they should be distributed among two or more tables.

Another principle of good database design is that each table should contain fields containing data about one type of thing. The data dictionary shown in Table 1.1 doesn't adhere to this rule—some of its fields contain data about books, and other fields contain data about publishers. You should put the fields that contain data about books in one table and fields containing data about publishers in another table. If you also wanted to have data about authors, fields for that would go into a third table.

It's easy to see why placing data about books and data about publishers in separate tables is beneficial. If you have data about five books from the same publisher, all the publisher data would be repeated for each book. One obvious disadvantage of this is that the space required to store the data is unnecessarily large. Another disadvantage is that if some data about the publisher changes (such as the phone number), that data has to be corrected for each book.

After you've created separate tables for books and publishers, you can relate each book to a publisher so that the forms and reports can include information about books, including information about the appropriate publisher. Also, any change made to the data about a publisher is available when the application provides information about a specific book. You can find specific information about creating relationships between tables in "Managing Relationships Between Tables" in Chapter 3.

The two revised tables you get after applying these rules to the preliminary data dictionary shown in Table 1.1 are shown in Tables 1.2 and 1.3.

TABLE 1.2   Book Table for the Book Application

Field	Description
Book Title	Title of book
Author	Author's name
Publisher Index	Link to Index field in Publisher table
ISBN	Book ISBN number
Category	Book category
Publication Date	Book publication date
Price	Cover price
Acquired	Date book acquired
Paperback	Paperback or hard cover
Information	Additional information about book

TABLE 1.3   Publisher Table for Book Application

Field	Description
Index	Publisher index
Publisher	Publisher's name
Imprint	Publisher's imprint (if any)
Address	Publisher's street address
City	Publisher's city
State	Publisher's state
Postal Code	Publisher's postal code
Country	Publisher's country
Phone	Publisher's phone number
Web	Publisher's Web address
Information	Additional information about publisher

Notice that all publisher data has been moved from the Book table to the Publisher table, and has been replaced by a single Publisher Index field. Also notice that the Publisher table now contains an Index field. The Index field in the Publisher table will eventually contain a unique number for each book. The Publisher Index field in the Book table contains a number for each book to identify the appropriate publisher.

Planning the Application's Environment

An Access-based application can exist in various environments such as

- Entirely on a single user's computer
- With data stored in tables running under Access on one computer, and accessed by users each of whom works at a separate computer
- With data stored on a server, such as SQL Server, and accessed by users each of whom works at a separate computer

The first possibility is the simplest and is suitable for applications in which individual people keep track of their own activities or possessions.

The second and third possibilities are those you're most likely to encounter. These involve data sharing and require you to take account of security and the likelihood of conflicts between people who might simultaneously work with the same data.

This chapter isn't the place to describe how you can take care of the problems that can arise when data is shared. You'll find information about this in the section "Choosing a Database Configuration" in Chapter 10, "Using External Data in an Access Application." Chapter 18, "Making Your Application Secure," deals with security issues.

The main point here is to prompt you to define how your application will be configured and used before you start its detailed design. It's much more efficient to do that than to design for a single-user environment and subsequently have to go back and redesign it for a multiuser environment.

Taking Advantage of What's New in Access 2000

An important part of the planning process is to gain an up-to-date understanding of the tools you will employ. In this case, that means becoming familiar with what you don't already know about Access and, particularly, much of what's new in Access 2000.

If your previous experience is with Access 97 or an even older version of Access, you should become familiar with what's new and improved in Access 2000 before you start work on a new application. In saying that, I'm assuming that the people who will use your application will have Access 2000, of course. Don't rely on what's new in Access 2000 if users will have a previous Access version.

Finding Out What's New

To find out what's new in Access 2000, with Access open and running an application, choose Help, Microsoft Access Help, and select the Index tab in the left pane. Enter What's New in the Type Keywords box and choose Search to display the What's New About Microsoft Access 2000 topic, shown in Figure 1.1.

Installing Access 2000 Help

When you perform a standard installation of Office 2000, including Access 2000, Access Help is automatically installed. It's not necessarily installed if you perform a nonstandard installation.

If Help is not available, you can install it from the Office 2000 CD-ROM by choosing Add/Remove Programs in the Windows Control Panel. Choose Add or Remove Features to list the installed Office components and to install Help.

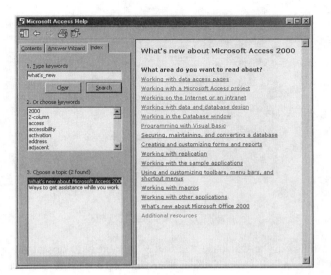

FIGURE 1.1

The topic lists 14 areas of information.

I suggest you open each of the subtopics in the What's New About Microsoft Access 2000 topic in turn and at least scan the information in each of them so that you know what's available. Some of the subtopics describe entirely new Access capabilities, such as Data Access Pages—which are Web pages you can use to manipulate information in an Access database—and Access projects that provide efficient access to SQL Server databases.

Other subtopics provide information about improvements to previously existing Access capabilities. The What's New About Working with Data and Database design subtopic, for example, describes several improvements of this type. One of the most significant points mentioned there is ActiveX Data Objects (ADO) which you can now use instead of, or together with, Data Access Objects (DAO) to access data. Chapter 12, "Accessing Data," contains introductory information about ADO as well as the differences between ADO and DAO. Microsoft recommends you use ADO for all new Access-based applications.

When you first use Access 2000, you'll immediately notice the new Database window, such as that shown in Figure 1.2.

Instead of the multitabbed dialog box in previous Access versions, the Database window now contains a more convenient Objects bar, similar to that first introduced in Outlook 97. Click an object name in the Objects bar at the left to display a list in the pane on the right, such as the one shown in Figure 1.2.

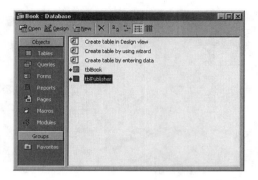

FIGURE 1.2

The new Database window contains expanded capabilities.

Among other new things in the Database window is the ability to organize database objects in groups. Although this capability won't affect your finished application as users will see it, it can help to simplify the development process. The Working in the Database Window subtopic summarizes what's new in the Database window.

Although you probably don't think of yourself as a programmer, sooner or later while you're creating Access-based applications, you'll find yourself taking advantage of at least some of what Visual Basic for Applications (VBA) has to offer. Much has improved in this area since previous Access versions. You can find information about this in the Programming with Visual Basic subtopic.

The remaining subtopics in What's New About Microsoft Access 2000 are no less significant. Take a look at them all.

Accessing Access 2000 Help

The previous section pointed out the value of one particular topic in Access 2000 Help. When you open Microsoft Access Help, you'll notice that it's somewhat different from Help in previous Access versions. There are enormous information recourses freely available to you in Help so, if you're not already familiar with its structure, it's worth taking some time to gain that familiarity. Before getting down to the details of planning your Access-based application, you should become familiar with the help Access provides. (See "Installing Access 2000 Help" in the preceding section if Help isn't available.)

If you've used another Office 2000 application, you're probably already familiar with how Help works. When you choose Help, Microsoft Access Help, you see a window such as that previously shown in Figure 1.1. In the left pane, you can select one of three tabs:

- Index, and then enter a word to see whether that word exists in the index. As you enter characters, Access attempts to match those characters with its index. If it's successful, the Or Choose Keywords list displays topics that match what you entered. Choose any topic to display that topic in the right pane.

- Answer Wizard, and then enter a question. After you've entered the question, choose Search. Access displays a list of topics that possibly answer your question in the Select Topic to Display box. Select any topic to display that topic in the right pane.

- Contents, to display a list of "books" as shown in Figure 1.3. You can expand each book by clicking the + at the left of its name to display the names of chapters within that book. Then you can click the name of a chapter to see the topics within that chapter. Finally, click a topic to see that topic displayed in the right pane.

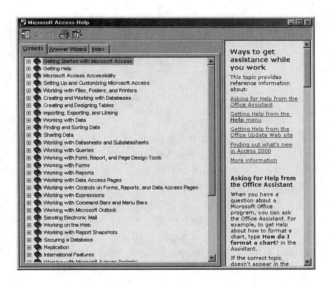

FIGURE 1.3

This is part of the list of books in the Access 2000 Help system.

Microsoft Access Help provides information about most aspects of using Access, including writing VBA code to enhance the application that you're developing. Even more extensive help about using VBA is available in another Help file. To access that help

1. Start Access and open any database, such as the Northwind database.

2. In the Database window's Objects bar, choose Forms and then choose New to display the New Form dialog box.

3. Choose OK to open a new form in Design view.

4. Choose View, Code to display the Visual Basic Editor (VBE) window.

5. Choose Help, Microsoft Visual Basic Help to open the VBA help resource. At that time, you might see a message stating, "This feature is not currently installed." If that happens, see the note following these steps. If Visual Basic Help is available, it's displayed. Select the Contents tab to see the list of books available, as shown in Figure 1.4.

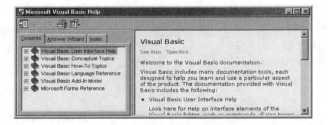

FIGURE 1.4
You can open any of the books listed here to get detailed information about Visual Basic for Applications.

Installing VBA Help

If, when you attempt to open Visual Basic Help, you see a message stating, "This feature is not currently available," you need to install it. Open the Windows Control Panel and choose Add/Remove Programs. In the Install/Uninstall tab, select Microsoft Office 2000, and then choose Add/Remove.

After a short delay, the Microsoft Office 2000 Maintenance Mode window is displayed. Select Add or Remove Features. In the list of Microsoft Office components, expand the Office Tools list. The last item in that list is Visual Basic Help. Set that to Run from My Computer, and then choose Update Now. You're prompted to insert the Office 2000 CD-ROM or, if your installation is from a network source, you're prompted to specify that source. After Visual Basic Help is installed in this manner, you'll be able to use it.

Whereas the programming topics in Microsoft Access Help are Access-specific, the topics in Visual Basic help are more extensive, but apply to Office components in general, not just to Access.

Accessing the Microsoft Information Resources

If you can't find what you need in the Access Help system, many other sources of help are available, one of the greatest of which is the FAQs & Highlights for Access 2000 site. You can reach this site at

`http://support.microsoft.com/directory/`

With that page displayed, select FAQs by Product, then select Access 2000.

This page contains frequently updated hyperlinks to information about Access 2000. You can also click Searchable Knowledge Base to access the Microsoft Knowledge Base in which you can search for articles about Access and other Microsoft products.

When there, you see a Web page in which you can choose Access 2000 as the Microsoft product about which you want to get information. Then, you can ask a question in the My Question Is box. The Knowledge Base responds by offering up to 200 articles that contain information relevant to what you asked. You can select any article to see it in detail and then, if you want, print that article.

TIP

I recommend that you save all Knowledge Base articles you find interesting and useful so that you can easily refer to them later. Either print copies of the articles to keep handy, or save the articles on disk.

Don't limit yourself to choosing information about Access 2000. You can also choose Access 97 as the product about which you want to receive information. Much of the information available about Access 97 applies also to Access 2000.

There are many other sources of information about using Access. The Microsoft Knowledge Base article Q226118 "Programming Resources for Visual Basic for Applications" lists sources of information about Visual Basic for Applications.

Documenting Your Application

Although documentation isn't strictly within the subject of planning your application, part of the planning in your own mind should be to be meticulous about providing information to users and to people (yourself included) who might subsequently be responsible for maintaining the application you create.

Discipline yourself to add this documentation while you're creating an application. If you put off documentation until later, it's probable you'll never get around to it. Even if you do attempt documentation at a later time, by then you're likely to have forgotten some of the essential facts.

Providing Information for Users

People who use your application should always know what's going on. You should commit yourself to providing well thought out

- Labels for the controls in your forms and reports
- ScreenTips displayed when a user points onto menu items, tools in your toolbars, and controls on your forms
- Text that appears in the status bar
- Message boxes

TIP

Don't overdo the use of message boxes because they interrupt the flow of an application. Provide just enough message boxes to keep users informed.

In addition to the information people see while they're using the application, users need some printed material to which they can refer. At the least, the printed pages should tell people what computer facilities are required—such things as

- The type of processor and the recommended minimum speed
- How much memory is needed
- The disk space required to install the application
- The minimum specifications for a monitor or other display device
- Any other hardware that is recommended or required

The printed pages should also tell people how to install the application.

Most people will find an overall description of the purpose of the application very helpful. Include scenarios that illustrate its use.

If labels or other words and phrases users see on your forms and reports might not be familiar to everyone, a glossary of terms would be appreciated by many people.

TIP

A few well-presented printed pages add a level of professionalism to an application that increases people's confidence in it, and helps to enhance your image.

Providing Information for Developers

No application is ever completely finished. You, or someone else, will have to revisit it from time to time to keep it up to date. The documentation you provide at the time you create an application will be invaluable when that application has to be updated. It should include the following elements:

- Descriptions of all the fields in your tables
- Descriptions of the purpose and use of all queries
- Comments describing the purpose of all actions in your macros
- Comments describing the purpose of all variables declared within modules
- Comments describing the purpose of all procedures
- Comments describing the purpose of all blocks of code within your procedures

You might not fully understand all these elements at this time. Keep them in mind, nevertheless, and refer back to them as you development your application.

Using the Access Documenter

At various stages in the development of an application, and definitely when it's completed, you use the Access Documenter to create printed documentation. To use the Documenter, open an application, choose Tools, move the pointer onto Analyze, and choose Documenter to display the dialog box shown in Figure 1.5.

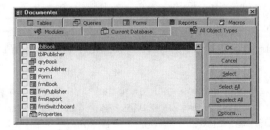

FIGURE 1.5

The Documenter dialog box is shown here with the All Object Types tab selected.

You can select which of the application's objects you want to document, or to completely document the application, choose Select All. Then choose Options to display the dialog box shown in Figure 1.6.

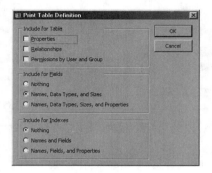

FIGURE 1.6
Use this dialog box to specify how much documentation you want to create.

Choose OK to prepare the documentation for printing. Depending on the size and complexity of your application, this might take several minutes. Finally, print the documentation.

Summary

It's important to plan an application before you start detailed work on it. It's equally important not to spend so much time planning that you never get around to actually designing the application.

Planning involves, first, completely understanding users' needs. Second, planning involves designing the structure of the application that will satisfy those needs. The most important aspect of the structure of an Access-based application is the tables in which the application's raw data will be stored. The structure of these tables depends on what users want to see in forms and reports generated by the application.

Your detailed work in designing an application depends on how it will be used—by a single user or by multiple users who share data. Have this clearly in your mind while you create the application.

Before you start creating an application, make sure that you understand your tools. The principal tool assumed in this book is Access 2000. Make sure that you understand what's available in Access 2000 before you start designing your application.

Be as helpful as you can to people who will use your application by providing adequate printed information about how to install and use it. Also, be helpful to people who might have to maintain your application by being meticulous about providing detailed documentation within the application.

The Anatomy of an Access Application

IN THIS CHAPTER

This book assumes you've been working with Access for quite a while, so you're probably fairly familiar with many aspects of the anatomy, or structure, of Access Applications. However, there might be some things you don't know or don't know in sufficient detail.

This chapter is intended to provide an overall perspective of what's available to you in Access 2000. It describes the components of Access 2000 and how they relate, but doesn't have much to say about how you can use those components. The remaining chapters of this book contain information about using the components.

Compatibility with Earlier Versions of Access

Historically, each version of Access has been incompatible with previous versions. Although you could convert an Access application created in one version of Access so that it could be used in the next version, once you did that, you could no longer use the application with the original Access version. This created a problem for organizations in which some people used one version of Access, and others used the preceding version.

Access 2000 makes it easier to deal with this problem. An application created in, or converted to, Access 2000 can't be used with Access 97. However, you can save an Access 2000 application so that it can be used with Access 97.

The chapter starts with an overview of Access's object structure. Depending on the level to which you want to go in understanding Access, you might want to pay a lot of attention, or little attention, to that information. If you choose to ignore the overview now, you might find it useful to return to it later.

Subsequent sections provide an overall perspective of the principal components of an Access application. The chapter also contains an introduction to the Book application that accompanies this book.

Understanding Access's Object Structure

You're going to come across the word *object* frequently in this book as well as in other sources of information about using Access to create applications. I'm not going to attempt a formal definition of what an object is here for two reasons:

- You don't need a formal definition in order to work with Access.
- I would get myself into a lot of trouble from purists if I did attempt such a definition.

Instead, I'll write somewhat informally about objects as far as Access is concerned. What's important to know is that an object has *properties* and *methods*, and can respond to *events*. These terms are defined in the following sections.

> **NOTE**
>
> The information in this section about the object structure isn't something you need to understand thoroughly. However, if you're puzzled about how Access works, you might want to refer back to this section to get help about what's going on.

Access, as well as each of the other Office applications, is an interrelated set of software structures, each of which is known as an *object*. The things you see and work with in Access are all objects. Each table, form, report, and so on is an object. The entire set of objects and how those objects interact is known as the object model.

Some objects are automatically created and exist when you open Access. Other objects don't exist until you create them. For example, when you create a new form, that form contains a Detail section, which is an object. At that time, the Detail section contains no objects. You can select an icon in the Toolbox and then trace out a rectangle in the Detail section to create an object in that section. That's just one of the ways you can create an object.

Some objects can contain other objects. A form, for example, contains sections and each of those sections can contain controls such as text boxes and command buttons. These are all objects.

An object can contain many objects of the same type. A form, for example, can contain many controls. The object model automatically creates a collection that's an object containing a related set of objects. The Controls collection for a form contains all the control objects on the form.

An Object Has Properties

Each object has characteristics known as properties that define its nature. A form, for example, has a certain width, is displayed with a specific type of border, and contains certain elements such as scroll bars and navigation buttons. These are some of a form's properties.

One of the most-used properties of a Collection object is Count, which contains the number of objects in the collection.

An Object Has Methods

Most objects have built-in capabilities, known as methods. A *method* is something an object can do or what you can do with an object.

A Form object, for example, has a Requery method that updates data displayed on the form from an underlying data source.

An Object Can Respond to Events

Many objects can respond to events. Loosely speaking, an event is something that happens. Opening a form to display it is an event, as is closing a form. Pointing onto a form and clicking the primary mouse button is an event; clicking the secondary mouse button is also an event, but a different one. Pressing a key on the keyboard is also an event.

Access responds to some events automatically. You can customize what Access does when an event occurs by providing macros and Visual Basic for Applications (VBA) procedures that respond to events.

The Database Window

The Database window, such as the one shown in Figure 2.1, is what you first see when you begin to create a new Access application. Depending on how an existing Access application is set up, you might also see a window like this when you start an Access application.

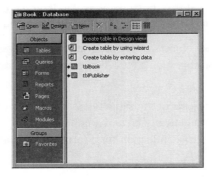

FIGURE 2.1

The Database window provides access to the components of an Access database.

The Objects bar at the left contains a list of object types. You can click one of the object names in the bar to see a list of objects of that type in the right pane and also to create new objects of that type.

By default, the Database window shows the List view that just displays object names. To show more detailed information, click the Details button—the right-most icon in the window's toolbar—to see a detailed view of the Database window, such as the one shown in Figure 2.2.

The Detail view of the Database window shows each object's name, a description of each object (if you provided a description), the date and time the object was most recently modified, the date and time the object was originally created, and the type of the object.

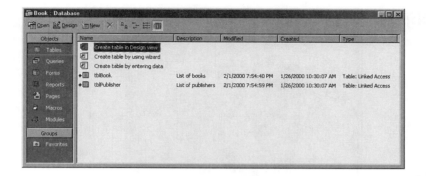

FIGURE 2.2

The Detail view of a Database window shows more information about objects.

Tables

As described in Chapter 1, "Planning Successful Access Applications," tables are where Access stores raw data. Although a simple Access application may only have a single table, most applications have several tables. The section "Planning Tables" in Chapter 1 explains why most applications have several tables.

To display an existing table, open the Database window for an Access application and select Tables in the Objects bar to display a list of tables in the right pane. Select one of the tables and then choose Open to display that table. To create a new table, with Tables selected in the Objects bar, choose New.

As mentioned in the preceding section, you can provide a description for a table. To do so, select a table name in the Database window, and then choose View, Properties. Access displays the dialog box shown in Figure 2.3.

The Properties dialog box displays such read-only properties as the name and type of the table, the date and time the table was created, the data and time the table was last modified, and the name of the table's owner. You can use the Description box to enter a description of the table. The description you enter here is the description that's displayed in the Database window for which you have selected the Details view.

You can check the Attributes check box at the bottom left if you don't want the table name to be displayed in the Database window. After doing that, to again display the table name in the Database window, choose Tools, Options and, in the View tab, check Hidden Objects.

The two check boxes at the bottom right have to do with database replication, a subject that isn't covered in this book.

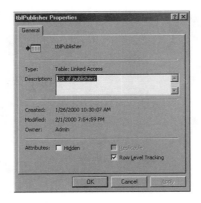

FIGURE 2.3

This dialog box displays a table's properties, some of which you can change.

You can visualize a table as a grid in which each row contains data about an item and each column contains a specific type of data about those items. Figure 2.4 shows part of a table that stores data about books.

BookID	Title	First Name	Middle Name	Last Name	Publisher ID
1	Special Edition Using Microsoft Access 95	Roger		Jennings	13
2	ENIAC	Scott		McCartney	1
3	Teach Yourself Microsoft Access 2000 in 21 Day	Paul		Cassell	14
4	Access 2000 Programming from the Ground Up	Whil		Hentzen	4
5	Inside ODBC	Kyle		Geiger	2
6	A Man In Full	Tom		Wolfe	15
7	Turn of the Century	Kurt		Andersen	9
8	An American Life	Ronald		Reagan	12
9	Writer's Guide to Editors, Publishers, and Literar	Jeff		Herman	107
10	What I Saw at the Revolution	Peggy		Noonan	9
11	Accidental Empires	Robert	X	Cringely	69
12	Primary Colors			Anonymous	9
13	Not That You Asked	Andrew	A.	Rooney	9
14	Word for Word	Andrew	A.	Rooney	93
15	Sweet and Sour	Andrew	A.	Rooney	93
16	The Way Things Ought To Be	Rush		Limbaugh	92
17	The Mint	T.	E.	Lawrence	90
18	The Road Ahead	Bill		Gates	95
19	Heart Sounds	Martha	Weinman	Lear	12
20	Papillon	Henri		Charriere	102
21	Pieces of My Mind	Andrew	A.	Rooney	94
22	Texas	James	A.	Michener	9
23	Carribbean	James	A.	Michener	9

Record: 1 of 40

FIGURE 2.4

This is how Access displays a typical table.

A table can contain up to 255 columns, also known as fields. There is no limit to the number of rows in a table other than that imposed by the limit of one gigabyte for the total disk space occupied by the table. For additional information about a table's specifications, see the Help topic "Microsoft Access Specifications" and select the subtopic "Read About Access Database Table Specifications."

Figure 2.4 shows a table in Table view in which you can see the contents of the table. To see, or modify, the design of a table, choose View, Design View to display the Design view, such as the one shown in Figure 2.5.

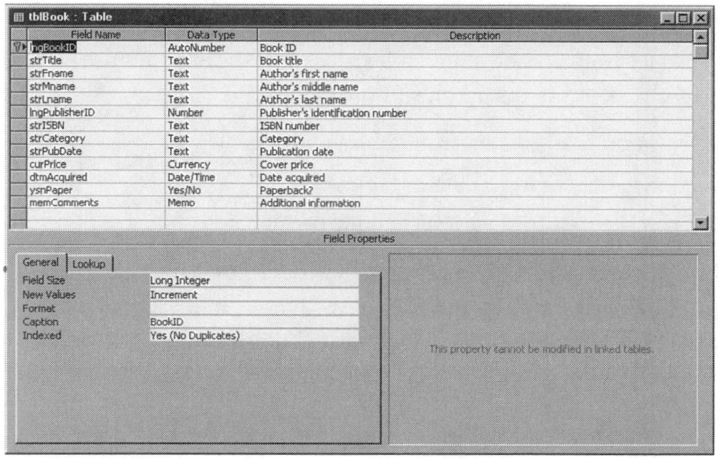

FIGURE 2.5
Design view shows a list of the fields in a table and information about those fields.

Each field has a data type that determines the type of data it can store, whether the data is text, a number, a date, and so on. See the section "Choosing Data Types" in Chapter 3, "Storing Your Data Efficiently," for detailed information about data types. Each field also has a number of properties that control such factors as its size, default value, and any restrictions on the data it can store. Refer to the section "Setting Field Properties" in Chapter 3 for detailed information about field properties.

When a database contains two or more tables, a relationship can exist between those tables. For example, the Book application that accompanies this book contains two tables, one containing data about books and the other containing information about publishers. The tables are related so that data about each book is related to data about that book's publisher.

NOTE

A relationship doesn't have to be established between tables. Instead, a query can be used to create temporary relationships, as described in the next section.

As explained in the section "Using Multiple Tables" in Chapter 1, efficient data design dictates that each table should contain data about only one type of thing. After you create your tables, you can use the Table Analyzer Wizard to check whether your tables adhere to this rule. If they don't, the wizard suggests how you can correct the problem. Choose Tools, move the pointer onto Analyze, and choose Table to open the Table Analyzer Wizard.

Queries

A query requests data from one or more tables, analyzes data from those tables, or performs an action on tables. Access offers three kinds of queries:

- Select queries that request data from tables
- Crosstab queries that analyze data in tables
- Action queries that perform various actions on tables

You can see the design of a query and create a new query by using the Query Design window. To display the design of an existing query, choose Queries in the Database window's Objects bar, select one of the available queries listed in the Database window's right pane, and choose Design. Access displays the Design view of a query, such as the one shown in Figure 2.6.

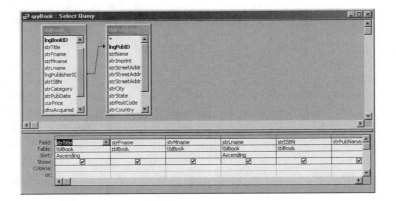

FIGURE 2.6
This is a typical Query Design window.

A Query Design window has two panes. The top pane contains lists of fields in selected tables. The bottom pane, known as the Query By Example (QBE) grid, is where you construct a query.

Using Select Queries

To create a select query, drag the names of fields from tables in the upper pane into the top row of the QBE grid. The name of the table from which each field is obtained is automatically displayed in the second row.

When you run a query, it creates a recordset, otherwise known as a result set, that contains records from the table with just those fields specified in the top row of the QBE grid. You can specify the sort order, ascending or descending, for the recordset based on one or more fields. You can also specify criteria that must be satisfied in order for records to be included in the recordset.

Instead of specifying criteria within the QBE grid, you can specify a request for criteria. This results in what is called a parameter query. A parameter query isn't an additional type of query, it's a special form of one of the basic three types of queries. When you run a parameter query, Access asks you to supply a parameter (a value to be used in a criterion). After you supply the value, the query runs just as though you had entered a criterion into the QBE grid.

A recordset is very similar to a table and can be used as a table. Whereas a table contains data that's saved in a disk file, a recordset is a temporary table in memory. You can use recordsets to provide information displayed on forms or printed in reports. You can also use fields in a recordset in another QBE grid to create a subsidiary recordset.

Using Crosstab Queries

Crosstab queries summarize data in spreadsheet format. You use a QBE grid somewhat similar to the one in Figure 2.6 to create a crosstab query. Refer to the section "Analyzing Numeric Information" in Chapter 4, "Creating Information Out of Data," for a detailed example of creating a crosstab query.

In addition to creating a spreadsheet analysis of data, a crosstab query can also be used to create a variety of charts and graphs that help to interpret data.

Using Action Queries

There are four types of action queries:

- Append queries that append selected records from one or more tables into another table
- Delete queries that delete selected records from tables
- Make-table queries that create a new table and add records from existing tables into it
- Update queries that change data in existing tables

All these types of queries can save you a lot of time and effort because you can use them to work on many records at a time, rather than working with individual records. For example, suppose you have a table that contains data about people that includes data about the companies those people work for. If a company's phone number changes, you can easily create an update query that changes the phone number for all the people employed by that company. That's much easier than changing records individually. After you create a query, you can save it so that it's available for subsequent use.

What Makes Queries Work?

The QBE grid is a visual tool that provides an easy way to create queries. The grid itself, though, doesn't control what a query does. Access uses the information in the QBE grid to create program code using the Structured Query Language (SQL). When you run a query, in reality it's the SQL code that runs to do what you've defined in the QBE grid. If you want to see the SQL code created from a particular QBE grid, choose View, SQL View.

In many cases, you don't need to be concerned with SQL code or even know that it exists. However, when you work with some advanced Access applications, you'll find the QBE grid can't do exactly what you want. In that case, you can use the QBE grid to create a query that's similar to what you want, display the corresponding SQL code, and tweak that code to suit your requirements. Also, in advanced applications, it might be necessary to create a query within VBA code, rather than to create it graphically in the QBE grid. In that case, you can initially create the query in the QBE grid, display the corresponding SQL code, and copy that code into a VBA procedure.

Creating Relationships in Queries

As mentioned in the section "Tables" previously in this chapter, you don't necessarily have to create relationships between tables themselves. Instead, you can use a query to create a temporary relationship between tables at the time a query runs. Do so by dragging from a field in one table to a field in another table in the upper pane of the Query Design window. After you do that, the Query Design window shows the relationship between the two tables by a line connecting the two fields. If the two tables contain a field with the same name, Access automatically creates a relationship between the tables based on those fields.

You can modify the type of relationship by double-clicking the line that connects the two tables. This is explained in the section "Modifying the Join Properties" in Chapter 4.

Modifying Query Properties

Like other Access objects, queries have several properties. To see these properties, click an unoccupied spot in the Query Design window's upper pane, and then choose View, Properties to see the Property sheet shown in Figure 2.7.

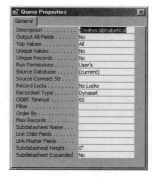

FIGURE 2.7
This Property sheet shows the default properties of a query.

By default, the Description property is empty. You can enter text for that property so that you subsequently know the purpose of each query. In many cases, you won't need to change the other properties. To find out what these properties do, place the insertion point into a property box and then press F1 to display a Help topic that explains the property. Access provides Help for almost all the query properties, but Help is missing for two of them.

Forms and Reports

Forms are used to display information based on data in tables, and also to enter information to be stored in tables. You can, as explained previously in the "Tables" section of this chapter, directly display data in tables and also directly enter information into tables. However, unless the data you're dealing with is tabular in nature, it's much easier to display and enter data in forms.

In many ways, *reports* are quite similar to forms. One essential difference is that forms are intended to be displayed on a screen, whereas reports are intended to be printed. Another difference is that reports have a provision for a page header and footer in which you can place controls that print information on every page of a report. You work with reports in much the same way that you work with forms.

Displaying a Form

To display a form, select Forms in the Database window's Objects bar to display a list of available forms in the window's right pane. Select a form and then choose Open. Figure 2.8 shows a typical form.

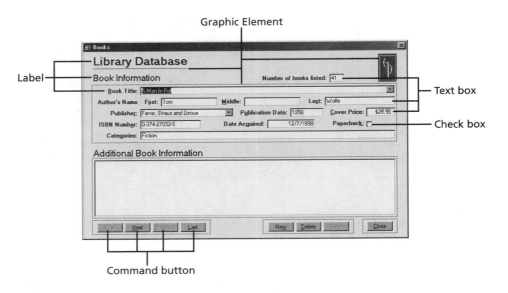

FIGURE 2.8

This is a form from the Book application.

A form is something you design, not something that Access provides automatically (although Access does contain wizards that help you to design forms). You start the design of a form with an empty rectangular box. It's up to you to decide what goes into that box.

The form shown in Figure 2.8 contains elements that are typical of those in many forms. Each of the elements on a form is known as a control. The types of controls on this form are

- Labels—Labels are text that explains the purpose of controls that contain data, provide a title for a form, and sometimes provide instructions for users.

- Text Boxes—Text boxes display information derived from data in an application's tables and can also be used to enter data to be stored in tables. Some text boxes can be used to display other information as, in Figure 2.8, the text box that displays the number of books listed.

- Command Buttons—Command buttons are used to control what an application does. Users can click a command button to cause something to happen. What happens is determined by a macro or VBA code.

- Graphic Elements—A form can contain several types of graphic elements, the simplest of which are lines and rectangles used to make the form easy to understand. A form can also contain a logo that helps to identify the application. Both these types of graphic elements are independent of the information displayed by the form. When tables contain fields in which separate graphic items are stored for each record, the graphic displayed on the form depends on which record is being displayed.

> **NOTE**
>
> The four types of controls explained here are by no means all that can be displayed on a form. They are just those most often seen on forms.

The information displayed in text boxes and certain other types of controls on a form is derived from data in tables. Although a form can directly display what's in one or more tables, it's usual to create a query that assembles data from tables, and then use that query to supply information for a form.

When a form displays information derived from a table or query, the form is said to be bound to the table or query. Binding a form to a table or query in this way works quite well for fairly simple Access applications. However, that technique has limitations that make it unsuitable for more sophisticated applications. For those purposes, it's more common to use a database engine to connect the controls on a form to the underlying data, in order to gain a great deal more control over how a form handles data. The subsequent section "Database Engines" in this chapter provides introductory information about the Jet database engine and the Microsoft Data Engine that are part of Access.

Designing a Form

You can design a form that's bound to a table or query so that its controls can directly display the data in the table's or query's fields. Alternatively, you can design an unbound form and subsequently use a database engine to determine what's displayed in the form's controls.

There are several ways to start designing a form. In each case, select Forms in the Database window's Objects bar, and then choose New to display the New Form dialog box. There, you can choose to

- Use a wizard to help you create a new form
- Use one of the AutoForms to help you create specific kinds of forms
- Use Design view to create a form from scratch

Because this book is written for Access power users, I assume you're already familiar with using wizards and AutoForms, so only designing a form from scratch is covered here.

If you specify a table or query as the basis of a new form, the new form is automatically bound to that table or query. When you choose OK, Access displays a Design view of a form that contains a Field List and the Toolbox as shown in Figure 2.9. If the Field List and Toolbox are not initially displayed, you can display them from the View menu.

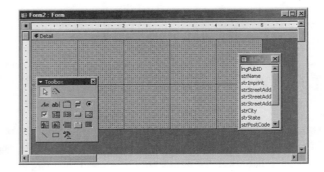

FIGURE 2.9

The Design view of a bound form initially appears like this.

At this point, all you have to do to place controls on the form is to drag them from the field list onto the form. Each field is displayed on the form with a label that contains the name for that field as you defined it in the underlying table.

You can place other controls on the form by selecting an icon in the Toolbox and then outlining a space for that control on the form. A control you place this way isn't bound to any field in a table. If you want to bind it to a field, you can do so by opening the control's Property sheet and setting the Control Source property, or by writing VBA code that binds the control to a field.

If you don't specify a table or query when you create a new form, that form is unbound. Consequently, the Field List for that form contains no fields. The only way to place controls on an unbound form is by way of the Toolbox.

Setting a Form's Properties

A form has many properties that you can set from the form's Property sheet. To display a form's Property sheet, click the small square at the left of the form's horizontal ruler, and then choose View, Properties. You can use the Property sheet to see the form's default properties and to set properties.

Each of the controls on a form has its own set of properties. To display these properties, select a control, and then choose View, Properties. The Property sheet's title bar contains the name of the selected control.

Data Access Pages

Data Access Pages (DAP) are Web pages you can use to access data in an Access or SQL Server database. You can create Data Access Pages for viewing, editing, and entering data into the database tables. You can also create Data Access Pages that display information based on tables, similar to Access reports.

From within Access, you can create a Data Access Page that's saved in .htm format. You, and other people, can subsequently display that page from within Access or, without having Access installed, use Internet Explorer 5.0 to display and edit the page.

Macros

A macro is a recorded sequence of actions that Access can perform. Once you've created a macro, you only have to run that macro for those actions to take place.

Macros in Access differ significantly from macros in some other Office application. In Excel and Word, for example, you can turn on the macro recorder and then manually perform a sequence as actions. While you work, the macro recorder records your actions as a macro. You can subsequently perform the same actions by running the macro.

Access doesn't have a macro recorder, so you can't create a macro by recording your actions. Instead, Access has a macro window in which you can create a list of actions. To create an Access macro, choose Macros in the Database window and then choose New. Access displays the Macro window shown in Figure 2.10.

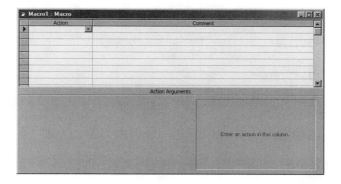

FIGURE 2.10
You can create a list of actions in this window.

Click the button at the right end of the Actions column to display a list of available actions and select the action you want to have in the macro. You can create one action after another in this manner.

Macros provide one way you can add functionality to an Access-based application, but they have significant limitations. Although you might want to include some macros in applications you develop, you'll find that you need to step deeper into Access by creating VBA code in modules.

Access has the ability to automatically convert a macro into VBA code. This means you can create a prototype of an application using macros and then, when you're ready to go beyond what macros can do, convert those macros into VBA code to add the final touches.

Modules

Modules come to your rescue if you want to become an Access virtuoso. Modules contain VBA code you can use to finely tailor Access to do what you need. There are three types of modules:

- Class modules—Class modules contain VBA code that responds to events. For example, clicking a button on a form triggers an event procedure that consists of VBA code within the form's class module.

- Standard modules—Standard modules contain VBA procedures that aren't directly related to a form or report, but can be called from any event procedure.

- Property modules—Property modules are used to create custom properties for objects, a subject that isn't covered in this book.

As you progress through this book, you'll see many examples of VBA code in modules.

Database Engines

Database engines provide links between an application and its data. Since Access was first introduced, it has used the Microsoft Jet database engine for this purpose. Access 2000 is supplied with a second database engine—the Microsoft Data Engine (MSDE).

The basic function of a database engine is to read and write data, but the two database engines you can use with Access do much more. The capabilities of these database engines include

- Interpreting and optimizing queries
- Providing security
- Maintaining referential integrity
- Transaction processing
- Accessing remote data

If you don't understand the significance of one or more of these capabilities, don't be concerned at this point. What is important is you understand that a database engine does much more than just read and write data.

The Jet Database Engine

The Jet database engine is a tool for storing and manipulating data that's automatically installed with Access. When you're working with simple Access applications, Jet works behind the scenes and you don't need to know it exists. However, when you get into more sophisticated applications, you need to take explicit advantage of at least some of Jet's capabilities by writing VBA code.

Jet is a database engine you can use on your desktop computer for small to medium-sized applications. In addition to interacting with data in tables within an Access .mdb file, Jet can also interact with data in

- dBASE files
- Excel workbooks
- HTML tables
- Lotus 1-2-3 spreadsheets
- ODBC-supported databases from such companies as Informix, Oracle, and Sybase
- Outlook folders
- SQL Server databases
- Tabular text files

2

THE ANATOMY
OF AN ACCESS
APPLICATION

> **NOTE**
>
> ODBC is an abbreviation for Open Database Connectivity, a technology that uses drivers to communicate between various types of databases.

The Jet database engine supplied with Access 2000 is version 4.0, which provides significant enhancements over previous versions.

The Microsoft Data Engine

The Microsoft Data Engine (MSDE), available for Access 2000 but not for previous versions of Access, provides local data storage that's compatible with SQL Server version 7.0. The MSDE isn't installed automatically with Access, but has to be installed separately. By using the MSDE, you can create Access-based front ends for an SQL Server database on your desktop computer without having access to SQL Server. You can also use MSDE as a server for a small workgroup.

To use MSDE, you create a front end as an Access Data Project. This contains forms, reports, and other application objects, but not tables or select queries, and is saved as a file with .adp as its extension. Tables and select queries are stored in the MSDE; stored procedures replace action queries.

Working with the Book Application

The Book application supplied with this book is a fairly typical small Access application that keeps track of a collection of books. It consists of tables, queries, forms, and reports. Some VBA code controls what the forms do. You can use the Book application as a model on which to base an application that keeps track of many types of things for personal or business use.

The application is referred to frequently in the remaining chapters of this book. Take a few minutes to look at the application now, so that you'll be prepared to understand the references to it as they occur. By the time you've finished reading this book, you'll be able create applications like this as well as considerably more complex ones.

The remaining pages of this chapter give you a quick look at some of the features of the Book application.

Installing the Book Application

By default, the Book application is installed on your C: drive in a folder named AccessApp. You can install it in a different folder if you prefer. The application consists of these two files:

- Book.mdb—The application's front end (user interface)
- BookData.mdb—The application's data tables

Open the Samples folder on the CD-ROM, select the Samples folder, and choose Install. A dialog box states that the application is about to be installed in a folder named C:\AccessApp and that the folder will be automatically created if it doesn't already exist. You can replace the default drive and folder name if you want. Choose OK to complete the installation.

Tables in the Book Application

The application's tables are in the BookData.mdb file. The table named tblBook contains data about books and the table named tblPublisher contains data about publishers. The fields in tblBook are listed in Table 2.1; the fields in tblPublisher are listed in Table 2.2.

TABLE 2.1 Fields in the Book Table

Field	Description
lngBookID	Book ID
strTitle	Book title
strFname	Author's first name
strMname	Author's middle name
strLname	Author's last name
lngPublisherID	Publisher's identification number
strISBN	ISBN number
strCategory	Category
strPubDate	Publication date
curPrice	Cover price
dtmAcquired	Date acquired
ysnPaper	Paperback?
memComments	Additional information

TABLE 2.2 Fields in the Publisher Table

Field	Description
lngPubID	Publisher's identification number
strName	Publisher's name
strImprint	Publisher's imprint
strStreetAddress1	Street address (first line)
strStreetAddress2	Street address (second line)
strStreetAddress3	Street address (third line)
strCity	City name
strState	State or province abbreviation
strPostCode	Postal code
strCountry	Country
strPhone	Principal phone number
strWeb	Web site address
memComment	Additional information

The table and field names each have a three-letter prefix to indicate what type of object each is. This is consistent with the naming convention described in the section "Creating Fields That Suit Your Requirements" of Chapter 3. The field named lngPublisher ID in the Book table provides a link to the field with the same name in the Publisher table.

> **NOTE**
>
> Some books are published under a name called an imprint that's different from the publisher's actual name. That's the reason for the field named strImprint in the Book table.

Notice that the Publisher form contains three fields for the street address. Although most street addresses consist of only one line, some have two or even three lines.

Forms in the Book Application

The application contains five forms. When you open the application, the Switchboard form shown in Figure 2.11 appears first.

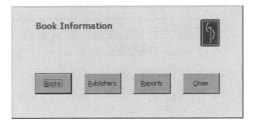

FIGURE 2.11

The Switchboard contains buttons you can click to select various parts of the application.

Notice that the four buttons in the Switchboard each have the initial character underlined to designate it as a hot key. You can click a button or, alternatively, hold down Alt while pressing the hot key to open another form. A ScreenTip is provided for each button.

The Switchboard form also contains a small logo at the top right. This logo was created in a graphics application, actually in CorelDRAW, and then inserted. You can find information about importing graphics objects into a form in Chapter 7, "Enhancing Your Application with Pictures and Other Graphics." The same logo is incorporated into the application's other forms to give a sense of consistency.

Looking at Books

Click the Books button to see information about books in the form shown previously in Figure 2.8.

This form derives most of its information from a query named qryBook that sorts books into alphabetical order by title. Most of the data in the query comes from the Book table, but that table is related to the Publisher table to get the publisher's name. When the form opens, it displays information about the first book in this alphabetical list.

Figure 2.6, earlier in this chapter, shows the Design view of the query that provides the information displayed by the Book form.

You can see information about other books in two ways. One way is to click the buttons at the bottom left of the form to select the first, next, previous, and last book in the list. Notice that when information about the first book is displayed, the First and Previous buttons are disabled because you are already seeing information about the first book and there is no previous book. Likewise, if you click the Last button to display information about the last book, the Last and Next buttons are disabled.

Enabling buttons when it makes sense to use them, and disabling buttons when it doesn't make sense to use them, helps people to use an application, so it's something you should learn how to do. It doesn't come automatically when you place buttons on a form. You have to write a small amount of Visual Basic for Applications (VBA) code to make it happen. This code is described in the section "Understanding How the Buttons Work" in Chapter 9, "Finding Records in a Database."

Instead of using the buttons at the bottom of the form to display information about one book after another, you can choose books from a list. Notice that the Book Title box near the top of the form is a combo box. Click the button at its right end to open a list of books. Scroll down the list if necessary, and select a book. When you do that, the form displays information about the book you selected.

You can use this form to enter information about a new book by clicking the New button. When you do that, the information displayed in all the boxes in the form is erased. At that point, you can enter information into the boxes and then click the Save button to save information about a new book.

You can also edit existing information. Click the box that contains the text you want to change and then edit that text in the normal manner. Click Save to save the changes.

If you discard a book in your collection, you can display information about that book by using one of the methods previously described, and then clicking the Delete button. You're asked to confirm that you want to delete the information about that book. Click Yes to confirm the deletion. When you do that, the information about that book is permanently deleted from the Book table.

In addition to showing information about books, the Book Information form also contains a box at the top that displays the total number of books in your database. It does this by quickly counting the number of records in the Books table.

After you've finished working with the Book Information form, choose Close to return to the Switchboard.

Looking at Publishers

In the Switchboard, choose Publishers to display a form that displays information about individual book publishers, as shown in Figure 2.12.

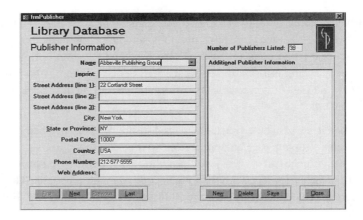

FIGURE 2.12

This form displays information about individual book publishers.

The Publisher Information form derives its information from the query shown in Figure 2.13.

The query sorts the information in the Publisher table, first on the publisher's name and then on the imprint name.

This form works in much the same way as the Book Information form. The form opens showing information about the first publisher in the alphabetized list. You can display information about other publishers by clicking the buttons at the bottom left of the form. You can also open the Name combo box to display the beginning of a list of publishers, scroll down to find a specific publisher, and select that publisher's name to display detailed information.

You can click New to display a form with blank boxes if you want to create information about a new publisher. After you enter that information, click Save to save the information about that publisher in the Publisher table. You can also display information about a publisher and then click Delete to delete information about that publisher from your database.

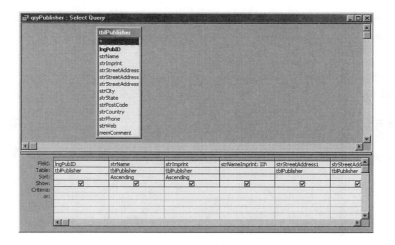

FIGURE 2.13

This query is based entirely on the Publisher table.

Just like the Book Information form, the Publisher Information form displays the number of publishers in your database.

When you finish working with the Publisher Information form, choose Close to return to the Switchboard.

Creating Reports

To choose a report you want to print, click Reports in the Switchboard.

Summary

Access is an object-based application, each object having properties and methods, and being able to respond to events.

Raw data is saved in tables. Queries are used to select data from those tables for display on forms and to print in reports. In addition, queries can be used to analyze data and to perform actions on tables.

Data Access Pages can be used to work with Access data by way of the Internet or an intranet using Windows Explorer.

You can use macros to automate an Access application to a limited extent. VBA code in modules provides much greater control of Access.

A database engine provides links between an application's front end and the data with which the application works. Two database engines are available for use with Access: Jet and the Microsoft Data Engine.

The sample application supplied on this book's CD-ROM illustrates many of the topics covered in subsequent chapters.

Storing Your Data Efficiently

IN THIS CHAPTER

The purpose of an Access application is to retrieve data and present that data in an organized manner; in other words, to present data as useful information. The manner in which data is stored has a significant effect on how much effort it takes to create an application that can present information in the way that people need, and on how the application can be enhanced to satisfy changing needs. For that reason, it's important to think carefully about how data is stored before you get into the details of how an application works.

As described in detail in Chapter 1, "Planning Successful Access Applications," designing an application starts with identifying users' needs, particularly what information users expect the application to provide. When you've done that, you know what data the application should store. Then you're ready to start designing the tables in which Access stores data.

Understanding the Importance of Organizing Your Data Tables

As you know, Access stores data in tables. Although you can use tables as a means to enter and examine data, you won't normally do so. Instead you'll create forms to be used for entering data and examining data previously entered; you'll create reports to print organized information based on the data in your tables.

Simple applications based on Access contain everything within one file: tables, queries, forms, reports, macros, and Visual Basic for Applications (VBA) code. It's usually better to have two, and sometimes more than two, files. One file contains queries, forms, reports, macros, and VBA code. This file, sometimes called the *front end*, contains what makes the application work. The second file contains only tables.

> **NOTE**
>
> Although Access can use data in many formats, only the native Access format is considered in this chapter. Refer to Chapter 10, "Using External Data in an Access Application," for information about using Access with data in formats created by other database applications.

Suppose you have a small business and you want to create an Access application that provides information about all the items you purchase. The results of your initial survey of the information users need from the application might include

- Printing reports showing all items for which you have less than a minimum inventory level in stock
- Printing reports showing all items on order but not received

- Displaying names, addresses, and phone numbers of specific suppliers
- Printing reports showing items used in specific products

Creating Fields That Suit Your Requirements

Having decided what information you want the application to supply, you're ready to start identifying the fields in which you'll store data. An inexperienced application designer might create an Access table containing fields such as those shown in Figure 3.1.

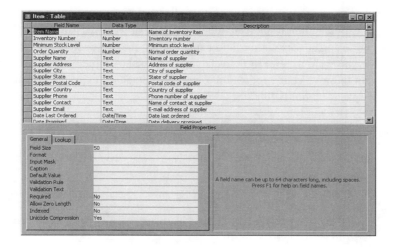

FIGURE 3.1

The Design view of an Access table shows a list of fields the table contains.

The table design shown in Figure 3.1 has a number of problems. These problems are identified and solved in the following sections of this chapter.

Making Fields Independent

One of the rules of good table design is that no field in a table should be calculated from other fields. For example, if you're creating a table that contains information about orders received for products, you'll probably have one field for product unit prices and another for the number of products ordered. You *shouldn't* create a field for total cost that would contain the unit price multiplied by the number ordered because that field depends on the values in other fields. In fact, Access doesn't allow you to create a field in a table that contains a value calculated from the value in other fields.

3

STORING YOUR
DATA EFFICIENTLY

Instead of providing a means to create calculated fields in tables, Access provides a different mechanism: Select Queries, as explained in Chapter 4, "Creating Information out of Data."

Giving Fields Meaningful Names

The left column in Design view of a table contains names for each field. The field names should not be too long, but should be long enough to be descriptive. Although field names can consist of up to 64 characters (including spaces), most field names are usually no longer than about 15 characters.

Although field names can contain spaces, most application designers prefer not to use spaces. Instead, they use capitalization to indicate the beginnings of words, as shown in Figure 3.2. One reason for not using spaces within field names is that the presence of spaces adds some complexity when you want to refer to fields from VBA code. Another reason is that you might subsequently want to move your application to another database environment, which might not allow the use of spaces within field names.

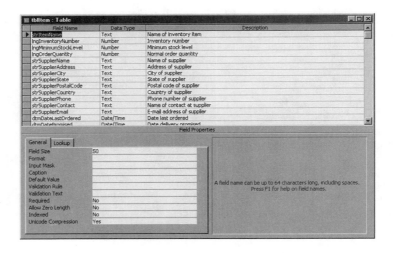

FIGURE 3.2
The Design view of a table shown here contains field names without spaces.

Using a Naming Convention for Field Names

A naming convention is a way of identifying fields and other named objects in such a way that the nature of the object is clear from its name. The naming convention used in this book uses a prefix before each name, as shown in Figure 3.2. The prefixes used for field names are listed in Table 3.1.

TABLE 3.1 Naming Convention Prefixes for Field Names

Data Type	Prefix
Byte	byt
Counter	lng
Currency	cur
Date/Time	dtm
Decimal	dec
Double	dbl
Integer	int
Long	lng
Memo	mem
OLE Object	ole
Single	sng
Text	str
Yes/No	ysn

NOTE

Some of the data types listed in the left column of Table 3.1 are not listed in the next section. That's because fields of Number type are identified by a prefix that indicates the size of the number those fields can hold. You can find information about this in the section "Setting Field Properties," subsequently in this chapter.

You'll find frequent references to this naming convention throughout this book, particularly where VBA code is covered.

If you look at Access applications designed by other people, you might see

- A naming convention very similar to the one described here. Some people use the same style of naming convention, but with different prefixes. For example, you'll sometimes see "dte" used as a prefix for names of Date/Time field names.

- A naming convention that mainly uses single-character prefixes for names. Microsoft publications sometimes use this type of convention.

- No naming convention used. You can find many examples of this in the Northwind database supplied with Access.

I strongly recommend you adopt the naming convention used in this book. An exception to this is if a different naming convention is already in use within your organization; in that case, use that one.

Choosing Data Types

Each field in an Access table is suitable for a specific type of data, such as text, numbers, dates, and times. One of the ways you can make your Access application more efficient is by choosing the appropriate data type for each field. By default, when you design a table, Access proposes Text for each data type. Don't accept that default unless it's the correct type for a field.

To select a different data type, move the insertion point into the Data Type column in the row for a specific field and click the button that appears at the right end of the column to show the list of data types. Table 3.2 is a guide for selecting a data type for each field.

TABLE 3.2 Access Data Types

Data Type	Usage
Text	Alphanumeric data up to a maximum of 255 characters per field. Use this data type for numeric information, such as postal codes, that isn't used in calculations.
Memo	Alphanumeric data that may contain more than 255 characters, up to a maximum of 65,535 characters.
Number	Numeric data, other than currency, to be used in calculations. The properties of a Number field can be set to eight different types of numbers, as explained in the next section.
Date/Time	Dates and times. Dates in these fields must include month, day, and year, so you can't use this data type for dates such as birthdays for which you might not know the year. When you display dates in Date/Time fields, Access uses a date format appropriate for your location, as set in Regional Settings in the Windows Control Panel.
Currency	Currency values. When you display values in Currency fields, Access uses the currency symbol appropriate for your location, as set in Regional Settings in the Windows Control Panel.
AutoNumber	Fields in which Access automatically gives records consecutive or random numbers. Access enters a unique number in these fields for each record.
Yes/No	Fields that contain only one of two values representing Yes or No, True or False, or On or Off.

Data Type	Usage
OLE Object	Fields that contain links to other files or embedded files. These files may contain documents created in other Office or Office-compatible applications, graphics objects, sound objects, and so on.
Hyperlink	Fields that contain hyperlinks to documents and files on the Web, on an intranet, on a network, or on a local storage device.

Although you can also select Lookup Wizard, this isn't a data type. Instead it enables you to specify a Lookup table for values available to be entered into a field. Refer to Chapter 6, "Making Data Input Fast and Accurate," for information about Lookup tables.

One reason for being careful to choose appropriate data types is that Access handles data items differently according to their type. When you get to enhancing your application with VBA code, you'll find your task is greatly simplified if you have correctly chosen data types.

Another benefit of choosing appropriate data types is that, together with choosing appropriate properties for data types (described in the next section), it minimizes the size of tables. Smaller tables occupy less disk space and require less time to be sent by way of a network or the Internet. Also, Access applications run faster with smaller tables.

Setting Field Properties

Access displays a list of field properties in the Design view of a table. Click anywhere in a field row to display the properties of that field, as shown in Figure 3.3.

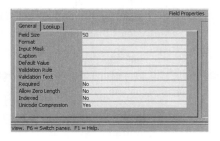

FIGURE 3.3

A Text field has the default properties shown here.

Each data type has a different set of field properties. In general, you can change default properties and enter values for properties that are initially undefined. The following sections describe only some of the available properties in detail. Other properties are covered in various chapters of this book.

Setting Text Field Properties

By default, the Field Size property is 50. That means that each record contains a field large enough to hold 50 characters, even if the field contains fewer than 50 characters. It also means that the field can never hold more than 50 characters.

You should change this property to something that's appropriate. For example, if you need a field for five-digit postal codes, change the property to 5 in order to minimize the size of your table. Likewise, if you need a field for organization names, increase the size of the field so that it's large enough for the longest organization name you can imagine being entered, and even somewhat larger than that to be on the safe side.

You can use the Format property to control how Access displays and prints data that's stored in a field. This property has no effect on how Access stores data.

You can use the Input Mask property to simplify and control data entry. Like the Format property, this property doesn't affect how Access stores data. Refer to Chapter 6 for information about this property.

The Caption property controls how field names appear when you display a table in Datasheet view. It also controls how field names appear when you create forms and reports based on tables. If you leave this property empty, Access uses the field names you created in Design view. Enter the field name you want to be displayed in this property. This is particularly useful when you've named fields using a naming convention and you want to have more friendly names appear on your forms and reports.

The Default Value property determines the value Access automatically enters into fields. For example, if you have an application that supplies names and addresses, it's likely that most of your contacts are in your own country. By setting the default value of the Country field to USA (or wherever you live), you don't have to enter that value for each record. Where necessary, though, you can change the default value in specific records.

The Validation Rule and Validation Text properties are used to check the validity of data entered into a field. Chapter 6 describes the use of these properties.

The Required and Allow Zero Length properties enable you to control how Access handles blank fields in a table. By default, the Required property is set to No, meaning that Access will allow you to create records with nothing entered in the field. In most cases, that's what you probably want to do. However, there usually are fields for which data is required. The Book application, described in Chapter 2, "The Anatomy of an Access Application," is a case in point. You probably don't want Access to allow creation of book records in which the Title field is empty. For fields of this type, change the default value to Yes.

> **NOTE**
>
> When you leave a field blank, Access inserts a special value known as *Null* in that field. You can use the Null value in much the same way as other values. For example, you can search a table to find records in which specific fields contain Null.

With the Allow Zero Length property set to its default value of No and the Required property set to Yes, Access won't permit entry of a zero-length string in the field. With the Allow Zero Length property set to Yes and the Required property set to Yes, Access will allow entry of a zero-length string by entering two quotation marks ("") with nothing between them.

The Indexed property is No by default. The subject of indexing is covered in the section "Indexing Tables to Speed Up Your Application" later in this chapter.

Unlike its predecessors, Access 2000 normally saves alphanumeric characters in Unicode format that requires two bytes per character. By default, the Unicode Compression property for text fields is set to Yes so that Access compresses Unicode if you're using a character set for which this is possible. You can change the property to No, but you shouldn't normally do that.

> **NOTE**
>
> If you develop applications for international use, including regions in which the language requires Unicode, you'll have to pay close attention to the significance of Unicode compression.

Setting Number Properties

The most important property of a Number field is its Field Size. You choose a field size by selecting the size of number the field is able to contain, as listed in Table 3.3. Avoid choosing a size that's larger than necessary.

TABLE 3.3   Available Number Types

Field Size	Bytes Occupied	Number Range
Byte	1	0 to 255
Integer	2	-32,786 to +32,767
Long Integer	4	-2,147,483,648 to +2,147,483,648
Single	4	Negative values: -3.402823E38 to -1.401298E-45 Positive values: 1.401298E-45 to 3.402823E38
Double	8	Negative values: -1.79769313486232E308 to -4.94065645841247E-324 Positive values: 4.94065645841247E-324 to 1.79769313486232E308
Decimal	12	With no decimal point: +/-79,228,162,514,264,337,593,543,950,335 With 28 places to the right of a decimal point: +/-7.9228162514264337593543950335
Replication ID	16	Provides a Globally Unique IDentifier (GUID) for use by the data synchronization process

You can use the Format and Decimal Places properties to control how Access displays numerical values, as explained in Chapter 6.

The remaining properties for Number fields are the same as those for Text fields and are explained in the previous section.

Setting Date/Time Properties

Use the Format property to select a format for what's to be saved in a Date/Time field. You can select one of the available preset formats or you can define a custom format. To select one of the preset formats, click the arrow at the right end of the Format property row. Access displays the available formats. (Refer to Chapter 6 for information about creating a custom Date/Time format.)

The remaining properties for Date/Time fields are the same as those for Text fields. Refer to the previous section, "Setting Text Field Properties," for information about these properties.

Setting Currency Properties

By default, the Format property for Currency fields is set to Currency. With the Currency property selected, Access uses the Regional Settings property selected in the Windows Control Panel to format values in Currency fields. As described in the preceding section about Date/Time properties, you can select from a list of available formats and you can create your own formats.

The remaining properties for Currency fields are the same as those for Text fields.

Setting AutoNumber Properties

Access uses an AutoNumber field to automatically enter a unique number for every record.

The default value of the Field Size property is Long Integer, thus allowing more than two billion uniquely numbered records in a table. The only other value available is Replication ID, a subject that's beyond the scope of this book.

The default value of the New Values property is Increment. With that value chosen, each new record has an AutoNumber field containing a value one greater than the previously entered record. Instead of Increment, you can select Random, in which case Access randomly creates values for each new record.

CAUTION

When you delete records from a table, Access does not recover incremented AutoNumber values assigned to those records. Keep this in mind when creating relationships with other tables.

AutoNumber fields also have Format, Caption, and Indexed properties that are the same as those previously described for Text fields.

Setting Yes/No Properties

The default Format property for Yes/No fields is Yes/No. You can also select True/False or On/Off, and you can create custom pairs of values.

By default, Yes/No fields are displayed as check boxes. In that case, the Format property has no effect—all you see is a checked or unchecked box. However, if you bind a text box control on a form to a Yes/No field in a table, the pair of values you choose for the Yes/No field's Format property appear on the form.

> **NOTE**
>
> When a control on a form is bound to a field in a table, the control displays the contents of the field.

The remaining properties for Yes/No fields are the same as corresponding properties for Text fields.

Setting OLE Object Properties

OLE Object fields have only two properties: Caption and Required. These properties are the same as the corresponding properties in Text fields.

Setting Hyperlink Properties

Hyperlink fields have most of the same properties as Text fields. After you've created a Hyperlink field in a table, you enter a hyperlink address that has up to four parts, separating one part from the next by a number-sign character. These four parts are

- DisplayText—The text that's displayed in a field
- Address—An absolute or relative path to a document or a URL
- SubAddress—A location within a file or page
- ScreenTip—The text that's displayed when you point onto the field and pause

See "Examples of Hyperlink Fields" in Access online help for specific examples.

Using the Lookup Wizard

The one remaining choice in the drop-down list of data types is Lookup Wizard. This isn't a data type but is a way for you to get help when connecting a Text field to a lookup table. Refer to Chapter 6 for information about this.

Making Your Intentions Clear by Including Field Descriptions

The Design view of a table, shown in Figure 3.2, includes a Description column. You should use that column to provide a short description of the intended use of each field.

As mentioned in Chapter 1, it's vitally important for you to make it easy for anyone to understand the structure of your application. This applies as much to the structure of your tables as it does to other aspects of applications.

At the time you design a table, the purpose of every field should be very clear to you. You might think that the names you've given to fields adequately describe the purpose of each field. Two years from now, though, when you have to modify the application, are you sure you'll completely understand the purpose of each field? What if someone else has to modify the application? Will that person understand the purpose of each field?

To be on the safe side, use the Description column to write a few words that clarify the purpose of each field, even if you feel those words are redundant. Chances are you or someone else will be glad you did that when the time comes to modify the application.

TIP

After you switch to Datasheet view of a table, you can click any field in the table to see the text in the Description column for that field in the status bar. After you bind a control on a form to a field in a table, the text in that field's Description column appears in the status bar at the bottom of the screen.

If the status bar isn't displayed on your screen, choose Tools, Options and, in the Show section of the View tab, check Status Bar.

Indexing Tables to Speed Up Your Application

Access applications are used to find information and often to sort information. These types of operations run much faster if the data in your tables is indexed. Normally you should index all fields that are frequently used as the basis for finding and sorting information.

> **NOTE**
>
> If you think about trying to find specific information in a book that isn't indexed, you'll have a rough understanding about why indexing speeds up finding information.

You probably won't notice any speed enhancement due to indexing if you have a small number of records in your tables. If you have a large number of records, you can expect to experience significantly improved speed after you appropriately set indexes for fields.

Although indexing fields is beneficial when you're finding and sorting information, it does slightly slow down data input. That's because whenever you add a new record, delete a record, or update a record, Access has to update the indexes. Bear in mind there's a separate index for each indexed field. For that reason, don't index fields unnecessarily.

> **NOTE**
>
> This section deals with indexing from the perspective of accessing records. Indexing is also important for managing relationships between tables, as explained in the subsequent section, "Managing Relationships Between Tables."

Indexing on Single Fields

As you've already seen, fields of all data types except Hyperlink, Memo, and OLE Object have an Indexed property. To create an index based on a specific field, set that field's Indexed property to Yes. When you do so, you can allow or disallow duplicate values in an indexed field. In most cases, you should allow duplicate values. Disallow duplicate values only if you're certain duplicate values can't exist.

You can quickly review your indexed fields by choosing View, Indexes to display the dialog box shown in Figure 3.4.

Each row of the Indexes dialog box represents a separate index. The first column shows the names of indexes, the second column shows the field on which each index is based, and the third column, by default, shows that the sort order is Ascending.

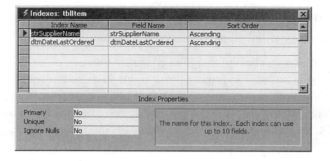

FIGURE 3.4

This dialog box displays a summary of the indexed fields in a table. In this case, two indexes are listed.

> **NOTE**
>
> You can change the sort order of any index to Descending. To do so, click in the Sort Order column for a specific index, click the button that appears at the right end of that column, and select Descending.

Indexing on Two or More Fields

By default, all indexes are based on a single field. However, you can create indexes based on up to ten fields. To index on more than one field:

1. This step is necessary only if the index to which you want to add a field is not the last one listed in the Indexes dialog box. Select the index below the one to which you want to add a field and press the Insert key. This creates an empty row.

2. In the empty row, click in the Field Name column, and then click the button at the right end of that column. Access displays a list of fields.

3. Select the field you want to add to the index. That field name appears in what was previously the empty row.

You can add more fields, up to a maximum of ten, in this way.

Access treats all the listed fields as a single index until it reaches a new index name. When indexing occurs, Access initially sorts by the first field. If this results in duplicate index entries, Access sorts those entries by the second field, and so on.

Changing Index Properties

Each index has three properties, all of which you can change.

One, and only one, index can be a primary index, the significance of which is explained in the next section. To change an index to primary, click in the Primary box, click the button that appears at the right end of that box, and select Yes. When you do so, a key symbol appears in the narrow column at the left end of list of indexes. If you subsequently make a different index the primary one, Access automatically changes the original primary index back to a normal index.

Click the Unique box, and then select Yes if you want to disallow duplicate values for the index, or select No if you want to allow duplicate values.

Click the Ignore Nulls box, and then select Yes if you want records containing Null values to be excluded from the index, or click No if you want records containing Null values to be included in the index.

Managing Relationships Between Tables

A fundamental problem with the table shown in Figure 3.2 is that all the information about each item is contained within a single record in one table. Suppose you purchase 100 items from a single supplier. In that case, you (or a person using your application) need to create 100 records, each record containing all the information about an item together with all the information about that item's supplier. That means you have to enter the supplier's address, phone number, Web address, and more in 100 different records. What a chore!

What's more, suppose the supplier moves to a different location or gets a different phone number. In that case, you have to edit the information in 100 records. Can you afford the time to do that? Can you be sure you changed the information correctly in all the records?

The solution to this problem is to create two tables. One table contains records that have information only about the item together with a single field that identifies the supplier. The second table contains information only about suppliers. By relating the field that identifies the supplier in the Items table to a specific record in the Suppliers table, you can greatly simplify your application as well as minimize your work. You can use the same technique to easily identify the items used in each of your products.

Splitting a Table into Two Related Tables

Suppose you have a table such as the one shown in Figure 3.2 and you realize you need to split that into two tables, one table containing only item-specific fields and the other containing only supplier-specific fields. One way to do that is to make two copies of the existing table and delete the appropriate fields from each table. To do that, perform the following steps:

1. Display the Access database window, choose Tables in the Objects bar, and select the original table.
2. Press Ctrl+C to copy that table into the Clipboard.
3. Press Ctrl+V. Access displays the dialog box shown in Figure 3.5.

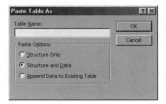

FIGURE 3.5
Use this dialog box to give the new table a name such as tblItemOnly. Also, select the appropriate paste option.

4. Choose OK to create the new table.

> **NOTE**
>
> In step 3 of the preceding procedure, the default paste option Structure and Data is usually appropriate.

Repeat the same four steps to create a second copy of the table, giving that table a name such as tblSupplier. Now you have two new tables.

Open the tblItemOnly table and delete all the supplier-specific fields from it. After you've done that, the Design view of the table looks like the one in Figure 3.6.

Open the tblSupplier table and delete all the item-specific fields from it. After you've done that, the Design view of the table looks like the one in Figure 3.7.

> **TIP**
>
> Instead of splitting a table manually, you can use the Database Splitter Wizard. To do so, display the table you want to split in Design view, choose Tools, move the pointer onto Database Utilities, and then choose Database Splitter to display the wizard's first window. Follow through the various wizard windows to split the table.

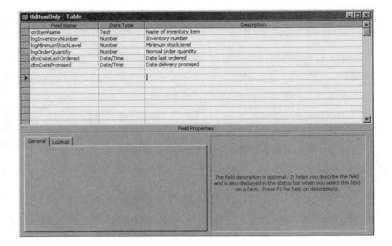

FIGURE 3.6

This is the Design view of a table that contains only information about inventory items.

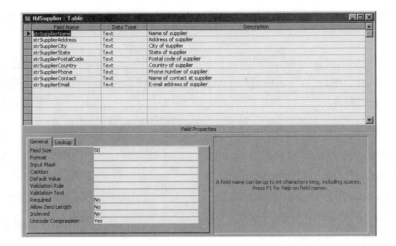

FIGURE 3.7

This is the Design view of a table that contains only information about suppliers.

Relating Two Tables

Now you have to relate the two tables by adding a field in each of them. You have to relate each record in the table that contains information about inventory items with a record in the table that contains information about suppliers. Note that each inventory item can be related to only one supplier, whereas one supplier can be related to many items. A relationship of this type is known as a *one-to-many* relationship.

Add the field name lngSupplierID to the supplier table and set that field's data type to AutoNumber. Accept the default Field Size property of Long Integer. While you have the pointer in the new field, choose Edit, Primary Key to make that field the primary key for the table. Although it's not necessary, most designers make the primary key field the first field in a table. When you designate a field as a primary key, Access automatically indexes that field and a key symbol appears in the narrow column at the left of the Field Name column. The primary key is a value that uniquely identifies a record in the table.

NOTE

The reason for choosing AutoNumber as the data type for the new field in the supplier table is to ensure each record in that table is identified by a unique number. If the suppliers table already has a field that contains a unique value for each record, it isn't necessary to add an AutoNumber field. Instead, use the existing unique field as the primary key.

Add a field named lngSupplierID to the tblItemOnly table and set that field's data type to Number. Accept the default Field Size property of Long Integer. Make sure this field is indexed with duplicates allowed. This field is known as a foreign key because it provides a link to another (foreign) table.

NOTE

If, instead of adding an AutoNumber field to the tblSupplier table, you used an existing field in that table, add a corresponding field to the tblItemOnly table. The data type and Field Size properties of the primary key and the foreign key must be the same. The two keys don't necessarily have the same name.

At this stage, you're ready to establish a relationship between the two tables, but that relationship doesn't yet exist. Make sure you've saved and closed both tables; then, to create the relationship, perform the following steps:

1. Choose Tools, Relationships to display a dialog box that graphically displays any relationships that already exist. Choose View, Show Table to display the dialog box shown in Figure 3.8.

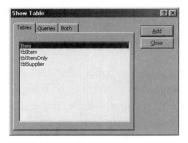

FIGURE 3.8

This dialog box lists the available tables.

2. Select the names of the two tables you want to relate and choose Add.

3. Choose Close to close the dialog box. Access displays the window shown in Figure 3.9.

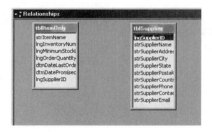

FIGURE 3.9

This window shows the fields in the two tables you selected.

4. Point to lngSupplierID in the tblItemOnly table, press the mouse button, and drag to lngSupplierID in the tblSupplier table. When you release the mouse button, Access displays the dialog box shown in Figure 3.10.

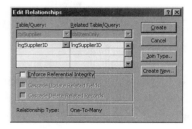

FIGURE 3.10

This dialog box shows the names of the tables you're relating at the top and also the names of the fields in those tables.

5. Assuming the correct tables and fields are shown in the dialog box, choose Create to create the relationship. Access displays the relationship graphically, as shown in Figure 3.11.

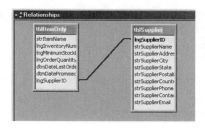

FIGURE 3.11
The line between the two tables shows the relationship you've just established.

In this example, the tblSupplier table is said to be on the *one* side of the relationship because each item has only one supplier. The tblItemOnly table is said to be on the *many* side of the relationship because each supplier can be the source of many items.

Establishing a Relationship Between Composite Keys

A *composite key* is a key that uses a combination of table fields as a single key. I usually advise people to stay away from composite keys; it's usually better to use a single field as a key. Can you really be sure that a combination of fields is always going to be unique so that you can safely use that combination as a primary key? That's up to you to judge in the case of the application you're creating. Likewise for a foreign key, make sure the combination of fields you use sufficiently identifies the records you want to use.

If you want to use composite keys in a relationship, display the Edit Relationships dialog box shown previously in Figure 3.10. In that dialog box, select the table or query for the tables on the one and many sides of the relationship, and then select the fields in each of those tables or queries that form the composite keys.

Removing a Relationship

To remove a relationship, right-click the line between the two tables shown in Figure 3.11 to display a context menu. Choose Delete in the context menu. The line that defines the relationship disappears indicating the relationship no longer exists.

Editing a Relationship

You can make changes to a relationship while you're creating it or subsequently by using the Edit Relationships dialog box similar to the one previously shown in Figure 3.10.

NOTE

After you've established a relationship, double-click the line between the two tables to redisplay the Edit Relationships dialog box. Alternatively, right-click the line to display a context menu and choose Edit Relationship.

Notice, at the bottom of the Edit Relationships dialog box, that the relationship is a One-To-Many type. Access automatically creates this type of relationship when one, but not both, of the tables has a primary key or unique index.

Changing the Related Fields

If you made a mistake in selecting the fields in either table, you can change the names in either column in the Edit Relationships dialog box. Just click the arrow button at the right of a field name to display a list of fields, and select the correct field.

Changing the Join Type

The word *join*, used on a button in the Edit Relationships dialog box, is a synonym for *relationship*. Choose Join Type to display the dialog box shown in Figure 3.12.

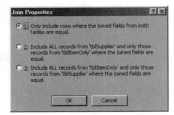

FIGURE 3.12

You can use this dialog box to control how Access establishes a relationship between tables.

For the present, notice only that three possibilities exist. Refer to Chapter 4 to see examples that show how these three possibilities affect what Access does when you choose one of these join properties.

Enforcing Referential Integrity

Before you consider whether, and how, to enforce referential integrity, you have to know what referential integrity is. To get your application to work properly, you have to get this issue right.

Referential integrity exists when the value of every record's foreign key corresponds to a primary key value. Because every item must have a supplier, to have referential integrity you must ensure that the value in each item's foreign key field corresponds to a primary key value in one of the suppliers table records.

TIP

Access has some built-in capabilities to enforce referential integrity, as described here. Use these if you're sure you understand them and they satisfy your needs. Otherwise, you'll have to create VBA code that maintains referential integrity according to your needs.

You can ensure referential integrity at the time a user enters data by allowing selection of an existing supplier only when a new item is added to the item table. One way of doing this is described in Chapter 6. However, if you allow users to remove suppliers from the database, you run the risk of removing a supplier for an existing item.

By default, the Enforce Referential Integrity check box in the Edit Relationships dialog box is unchecked, as shown in Figure 3.10. If you leave the check box unchecked, Access doesn't concern itself about maintaining referential integrity. If you check that box, the Cascade Update Related Fields and Cascade Delete Related Records check boxes become available. You can check either or both of these boxes.

NOTE

For Access to enforce referential integrity, the two related tables must be stored in the same Access database. That means you can't use the built-in ability to enforce referential integrity between tables that exist in separate linked databases.

After you check the Enforce Referential Integrity box and choose Create, Access displays the relationship with the one and many sides of the relationship clearly indicated, as shown in Figure 3.13. This occurs even if neither of the other two check boxes in the Edit Relationships dialog box is checked.

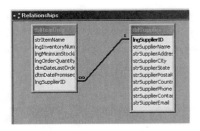

FIGURE 3.13

The many side of the relationship is indicated by the infinity symbol. The one side of the relationship is indicated by 1.

After you check Cascade Update Related Fields and subsequently change a value of a primary key in the table on the one side of the relationship, Access automatically makes the same change in all foreign key fields in related records on the many side of the relationship.

> **NOTE**
>
> If you use an AutoNumber field for the primary key in the table on the one side of the relationship, users can't change the value in that field. In this case, it's unnecessary to check the Cascade Update Related Fields box.

After you check Cascade Delete Related Records and subsequently delete a record on the one side of the relationship, Access warns you that it is about to delete records from the table on the many side of the relationship. You can choose No to avoid deleting records in both tables or Yes to allow Access to continue. If you choose Yes, Access automatically deletes the selected records in the one side of the relationship and all records in the table on the many side of the relationship in which the value of the foreign key is the same as the value of the primary key in the deleted records.

Creating a Many-to-Many Relationship

The preceding pages have described how you can create and modify a one-to-many relationship, the type of relationship you'll probably use most frequently to manage your data efficiently. There are times, though, when you need a many-to-many relationship. This is the case, for example, if you purchase one or more items from two or more suppliers.

Access doesn't provide a direct way to create many-to-many relationships. Instead, you can create such a relationship by using an additional table, known as a *junction table* or *linking table*. Then you create two one-to-many relationships, one between the junction table and each of the original tables.

Proceed as follows to create a many-to-many relationship between the tblItemOnly table and the tblSupplier table. After you've done that, you will be able to use the application in two ways:

- To find all the suppliers for specific items
- To find all the items you purchase from specific suppliers

    1. Make sure the tblItemOnly table and the tblSupplier table each have a primary key. This can be an AutoNumber field or any other field that's unique for every item and supplier.

    2. Create a new table and create two fields in that table. One field should have the same data type and size as the primary key of the tblItemOnly table. The other field should have the same data type and size as the primary key of the tblSupplier table. Both fields should have the Index property set to Yes (Duplicates OK). These fields are foreign keys.

    3. Save the new table with a name such as tblItemSupplier. Close the table.

    4. Choose Tools, Relationships to display the Relationships dialog box. If necessary, choose View, Show Table to display a list of available tables.

    5. Select the tblItemOnly table, the tblSupplier table, and the new junction table. Choose Add to display all three tables in the Relationships dialog box. Choose Close to close the Show Table dialog box.

    6. Move the tables so that the junction table is between the other two tables. You can move a table by pointing into its title bar and dragging.

    7. Drag from the primary key in the tblItemOnly table to the corresponding foreign key in the junction table. Drag from the primary key in the tblSupplier table to the corresponding foreign key in the junction table. When you've done that, the Relationships dialog box should be similar to the one in Figure 3.14.

3

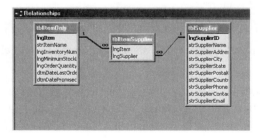

FIGURE 3.14

This is a diagram of a many-to-many relationship.

Creating a One-to-One Relationship

A one-to-one relationship establishes a connection between one table and one other table. Such a relationship is not often used because it's usually simpler to gather the fields from both tables into a single table.

One reason you might find it convenient to have a one-to-one relationship is if you have data that belongs on one table, but some of the fields are accessible to all users whereas other fields are accessible to only a restricted set of users. To satisfy this need, you can place the fields to which everyone has access in one table and the restricted fields in a second table. You can then choose Tools, Security to assign appropriate permissions to each table. Refer to Chapter 17, "Extending Access to the Web," for detailed information about assigning permissions.

To create a one-to-one relationship, link the primary key of one table to the primary key of the second table.

Creating a Self-Join Relationship

A self-join relationship is one that involves only one table and in which one field in that table is related to another field in the same table.

An example of where you might use a self-join is a table that contains information about personal friends, some of whom are married. Some of the fields in a table of this type might well be

    lngPerson—The primary key
    strFname
    strMname
    strLname
    lngSpouse

To create a self-join for this table:

1. Choose Tools, Relationships to display the Relationships dialog box.
2. Choose Relationships, Show Table to display the Show Table dialog box.
3. Select the table that contains the name of your friends and choose Add to add that table to the Relationships dialog box.
4. Select the same table again and choose Add to add a second copy of that table to the Relationships dialog box.
5. Drag from the lngPerson field (the primary key) in the first table to the lngSpouse key in the second table.
6. Choose Create to create the self-join, as shown in Figure 3.15.

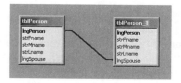

FIGURE 3.15
This is a self-join between two fields in the same table.

After you've created a self-join, you can create forms and reports that show information about your friends, together with the names of their spouses.

Creating Multiple Relationships

The preceding sections have described relationships between only two tables. As you create more sophisticated Access applications, you'll find you need more than two tables and need to relate some tables to more than one other table. The Northwind application supplied with Access provides an example of these types of relationships.

To see a typical set of relationships, open the Northwind application, and choose Tools, Relationships to display the dialog box shown in Figure 3.16.

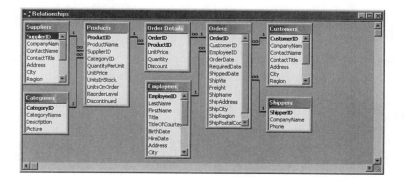

FIGURE 3.16
These are the relationships in the Northwind application.

All the relationships shown in Figure 3.16 are one-to-many. Notice, though, that the one-to-many relationship between the Products and Order Details tables, and between the Orders and Order Details tables provides a many-to-many relationship. That's because one product can be included in many orders and because one order can contain many products. Notice, also, that one table can be related to more than one other table.

Printing a Report of Relationships

Access 2000 has the ability to print a special kind of report that shows relationship diagrams, a facility that didn't exist in previous Access versions. To print this report

1. Choose Tools, Relationships to display the Relationships dialog box that shows the relationships you've created.

2. Choose File, Print Relationships to display a diagram of the relationships in a report, such as that shown in Figure 3.17.

3. Choose File, Print to print the report.

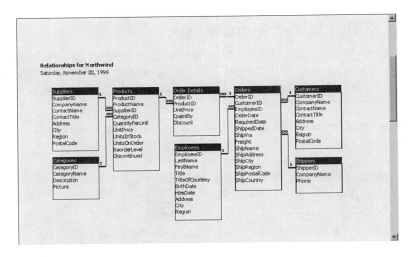

FIGURE 3.17
This is a typical report illustrating relationships.

Entering Data into Tables

As stated at the beginning of this chapter, you'll normally create forms to be used for entering data. Access enables you to enter data directly into tables. If you have a simple, single-table application, you might want to save yourself the effort of creating data-entry forms. However, if your application involves related forms, it's very difficult to keep the relationships correct if you enter data directly into tables.

You probably already know how to enter data into tables. After you've designed a table, open the table in Datasheet view. Access displays the table with field names displayed from left to right at the top, with one empty record displayed, and with the insertion point in the first field for the empty record.

Enter data into the first field, then press Tab to move to the second field. Proceed in this way until you've completed entering data for the first record. When you press Tab after entering all the data for the first record, Access displays a blank row for the next record. If you want to leave any field empty, just press Tab when the insertion point is in that field.

NOTE

The preceding paragraph is based on the assumption you haven't set the Required property of any field to Yes. If you've set one or more fields' Required properties to Yes and leave one or more of those fields empty, Access won't let you move to another record until you've entered data into all those fields.

Displaying Data in Datasheets and Subdatasheets

After you've entered data into a table, that data is displayed in a Datasheet view such as that shown in Figure 3.18. You can scroll down or across to see data that's not initially displayed.

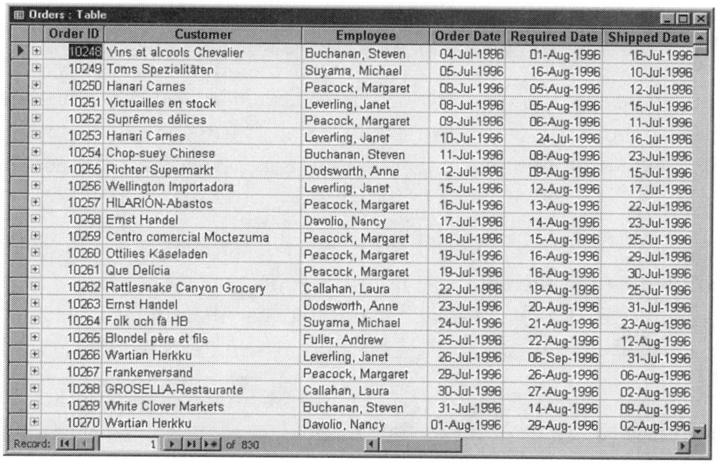

	Order ID	Customer	Employee	Order Date	Required Date	Shipped Date
+	10248	Vins et alcools Chevalier	Buchanan, Steven	04-Jul-1996	01-Aug-1996	16-Jul-1996
+	10249	Toms Spezialitäten	Suyama, Michael	05-Jul-1996	16-Aug-1996	10-Jul-1996
+	10250	Hanari Carnes	Peacock, Margaret	08-Jul-1996	05-Aug-1996	12-Jul-1996
+	10251	Victuailles en stock	Leverling, Janet	08-Jul-1996	05-Aug-1996	15-Jul-1996
+	10252	Suprêmes délices	Peacock, Margaret	09-Jul-1996	06-Aug-1996	11-Jul-1996
+	10253	Hanari Carnes	Leverling, Janet	10-Jul-1996	24-Jul-1996	16-Jul-1996
+	10254	Chop-suey Chinese	Buchanan, Steven	11-Jul-1996	08-Aug-1996	23-Jul-1996
+	10255	Richter Supermarkt	Dodsworth, Anne	12-Jul-1996	09-Aug-1996	15-Jul-1996
+	10256	Wellington Importadora	Leverling, Janet	15-Jul-1996	12-Aug-1996	17-Jul-1996
+	10257	HILARIÓN-Abastos	Peacock, Margaret	16-Jul-1996	13-Aug-1996	22-Jul-1996
+	10258	Ernst Handel	Davolio, Nancy	17-Jul-1996	14-Aug-1996	23-Jul-1996
+	10259	Centro comercial Moctezuma	Peacock, Margaret	18-Jul-1996	15-Aug-1996	25-Jul-1996
+	10260	Ottilies Käseladen	Peacock, Margaret	19-Jul-1996	16-Aug-1996	29-Jul-1996
+	10261	Que Delícia	Peacock, Margaret	19-Jul-1996	16-Aug-1996	30-Jul-1996
+	10262	Rattlesnake Canyon Grocery	Callahan, Laura	22-Jul-1996	19-Aug-1996	25-Jul-1996
+	10263	Ernst Handel	Dodsworth, Anne	23-Jul-1996	20-Aug-1996	31-Jul-1996
+	10264	Folk och fä HB	Suyama, Michael	24-Jul-1996	21-Aug-1996	23-Aug-1996
+	10265	Blondel père et fils	Fuller, Andrew	25-Jul-1996	22-Aug-1996	12-Aug-1996
+	10266	Wartian Herkku	Leverling, Janet	26-Jul-1996	06-Sep-1996	31-Jul-1996
+	10267	Frankenversand	Peacock, Margaret	29-Jul-1996	26-Aug-1996	06-Aug-1996
+	10268	GROSELLA-Restaurante	Callahan, Laura	30-Jul-1996	27-Aug-1996	02-Aug-1996
+	10269	White Clover Markets	Buchanan, Steven	31-Jul-1996	14-Aug-1996	09-Aug-1996
+	10270	Wartian Herkku	Davolio, Nancy	01-Aug-1996	29-Aug-1996	02-Aug-1996

Record: 1 of 830

FIGURE 3.18

This Datasheet view shows the data in the Orders table that's part of the Northwind database you can install as an example when you install Access.

Notice the + sign at the left end of each row in Figure 3.18. This indicates that another table is linked to the one whose Datasheet view is displayed. You can click a + sign to show data in the linked table, as shown in Figure 3.19.

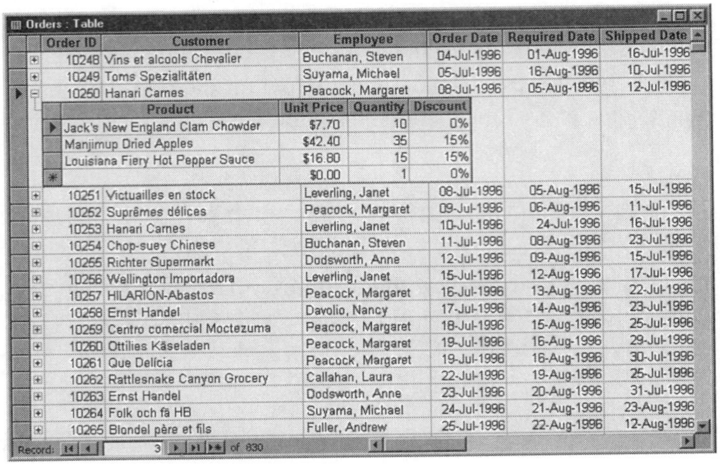

FIGURE 3.19
Data displayed in this manner is known as a Subdatasheet view.

You can enter new data into a subdatasheet as well as edit existing data.

Summary

An Access-based application converts raw data into meaningful information. Access saves your raw data in tables. In order for Access to easily translate raw data into meaningful information, you must pay detailed attention to the design of your data tables. This chapter showed you how to do that.

All but the simplest Access-based applications refer to data saved in several or many tables. It's your responsibility to design each of these tables with the appropriate fields of information. It's also your responsibility to design the relationships between these tables in such a manner that the information users of your application can readily extract the information they need.

When designing an Access-based application, or any other type of application, it's important that your application explains itself by such techniques as providing a description of each field of information in the tables.

Pay particular attention to indexing your tables. Although an Access-based application doesn't require that your tables be indexed, proper indexing ensures your application can rapidly find the data it needs.

Creating Information Out of Data

IN THIS CHAPTER

The principal purpose of an Access-based application is to provide information. Chapter 3, "Storing Your Data Efficiently," contains a lot of information about how Access stores raw data. The present chapter focuses on converting that data into useful information.

There are a few ways in which you can manipulate Access tables to organize data, as described in the first few pages of this chapter. However, queries are the key to getting useful information out of Access tables. You use queries, specifically Select queries, to ask questions to which Access provides answers.

In addition to using Select queries, you can use other types of queries to manipulate data in tables in various ways. Crosstab queries, for example, provide a particularly powerful way to analyze numeric data stored in tables. This chapter contains an example of creating a crosstab query and shows the type of information it produces.

Tables and queries based on those tables provide the foundation for Access applications.

Manipulating Data in Tables

Access stores your data in one or more files on your hard drive, one record after another in the order you enter that data. Initially, the Datasheet view of a table lists records in order of entry.

The next few sections describe various ways in which you can work with data in tables. If you want to experiment with these techniques, you can use one of your own tables or a table (such as the Products table) in the Northwind database supplied with Access.

Changing Record Order in the Datasheet View

You can change the order in which the Datasheet view displays records by sorting on fields of any data type except Hyperlink, Memo, and OLE Object. When you change the order in which records are displayed, Access doesn't change the order in which records are stored in the table; it merely changes the view of those records. In fact, you never need to be concerned about the order in which Access stores records in tables.

To change the order in which records are displayed

1. Select the column that contains the field on which you want to sort records by clicking the field name at the top of that column.

2. Choose Records, and then move the pointer onto Sort.

3. Choose Ascending or Descending.

You can choose to sort on more than one field. If you select more than one column in step 1, Access sorts first on the left-most selected field, and then on the next selected field to the right, and so on. To control the order in which Access uses fields for sorting records, change the order in which those fields appear in the Datasheet view. You can do so by moving the pointer onto the name of a field in the Datasheet view and then dragging to the right or left.

To restore the original order of records in the Datasheet view, choose Records, Remove Filter/Sort.

Finding Records in the Datasheet View

You can find individual records that contain specific values in a field.

To find records that contain specific values,

1. Select the column that contains the field in which you want to find values by clicking the field name at the top of that column.

2. Choose Edit, Find to display the dialog box shown in Figure 4.1.

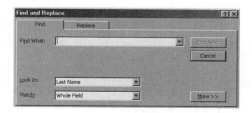

FIGURE 4.1

Use the Find tab in this dialog box if you want to find records that contain only certain values. Use the Replace tab if you want to automatically replace values in found records.

3. Enter the value you want to find in the Find What box.

4. By default, the Look In box contains the name of the field you selected in step 1. You can click the button at the right end of that box and then select the current table. That expands the search to include all fields in the table instead of just the selected one.

5. By default, the Match box contains Whole Field. If you accept that value, Access searches for records in which the entire contents of a field is what you entered in step 3. You can click the button at the right end of the Match box and then select either Any Part of Field or Start of Field.

6. If necessary, you can choose More to gain more control over the search, as shown in Figure 4.2.

7. When the Search box contains All (the default), Access searches the table from the first record to the last. You can click the button at the right end of the box and then select either Up or Down to search the table from the currently selected record to the top or to the bottom.

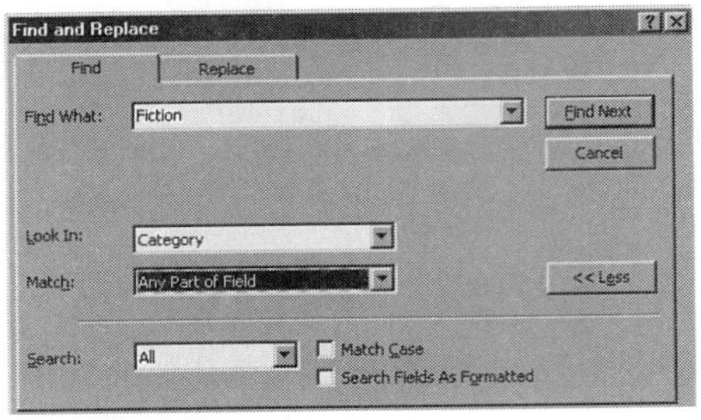

FIGURE 4.2

The three boxes at the bottom of this dialog box increase your control of the search.

8. By default, the search is not case-sensitive. Check the Match Case box if you want a case-sensitive search.

9. By default, Access searches for values as they are actually stored within the table, not as they are formatted for display. If you want to search for values as they are displayed, check the Search Fields As Formatted box.

NOTE

The section "Setting Text Field Properties" in Chapter 3 explained how the Format property controls how Access displays and prints data. If you have set this property for the field on which you are searching and want to search a table for text as Access displays or prints it, check the Search Fields as Formatted box. If you leave this box unchecked, Access searches for text as it's stored, not as it's displayed or printed.

10. Choose Find Next to start the search.

Replacing Values in the Datasheet View

If you want to find and replace values, choose the Replace tab, as shown in Figure 4.3.

You use the Replace tab in much the same manner as the Find tab. After you've specified a replacement value, choose Find Next to begin the search. When Access has found a record, you can choose Replace to make the replacement in that record, or choose Find Next to proceed without making the replacement. At any time, you can choose Replace All to make replacements in all matching records without first inspecting those records.

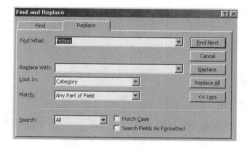

FIGURE 4.3
You can specify a replacement value in this dialog box.

CAUTION

Be careful about using the Replace All command. Doing that can easily lead to replacements being made where they're not appropriate.

Filtering Records in the Datasheet View

You can filter records in the Datasheet view of a table so that only records which satisfy certain criteria are displayed. Access provides four ways for you to filter records:

- Filter By Form
- Filter By Selection
- Filter Excluding Selection
- Advanced Filter/Sort

To begin setting up a filter, choose Records and move the pointer onto Filter. Select the type of filter you want from those listed. Each is explained in the following sections.

Filter By Form

When you choose Filter By Form, Access displays what looks like the top of a Datasheet view with one empty record, as shown in Figure 4.4.

The following steps are based on using the Northwind Customers table. These steps filter the table so that only customers in Germany and the USA are listed. Start by opening that table in Datasheet view.

1. Choose Records, move the pointer onto Filter, and select Filter By Form to display the form shown in Figure 4.4.

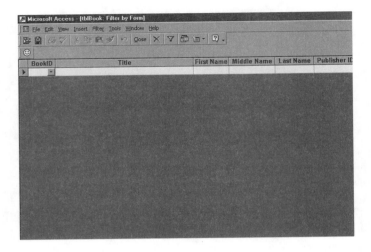

FIGURE 4.4

This is the form in which you specify the filter.

2. Scroll to the right until the Country field is visible, click in that field, and then click the button that appears at the right end of that field. Access displays a list of all the countries that exist in values in the table, as shown in Figure 4.5.

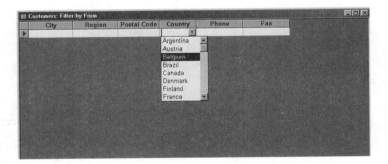

FIGURE 4.5

This is the beginning of a list of all the countries in which Northwind has customers.

3. Select the first country (such as Germany) for which you want to list customers. Access displays that company name, enclosed within quotation marks, in the form, as shown in Figure 4.6.

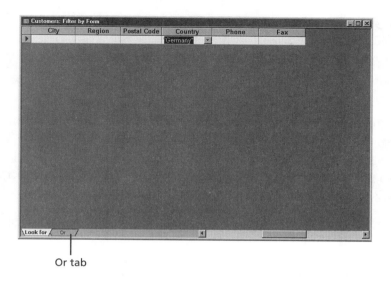

Or tab

FIGURE 4.6

At this stage, you have one country selected.

4. Click the Or tab at the bottom of the form shown in Figure 4.6. Then repeat steps 2 and 3, this time selecting another country, such as USA. If you want to add more countries, repeat steps 2 and 3 as many times as necessary.

5. When you've finished selecting countries, choose Filter, Apply Filter/Sort. Access returns to the Datasheet view, now displaying only records for customers in the countries you selected.

At this stage, you have information about customers in specific countries, but these records are listed in the original table order. If you want to list records sorted by country, you can use the method described in the previous section "Changing Record Order in the Datasheet View."

To clear the filter so that the complete table is displayed, choose Records, Remove Filter/Sort.

You can use Filter By Form to filter on more than one field. For example, you can filter the Customers table to show records only for owners of customers in Germany and the USA. To do so, follow steps 1 through 4, open the Contact Title list, and select Owner. When you apply this filter, Access displays a Datasheet view that contains the records you want.

NOTE

In addition to the methods described here to define a filter, you can also use expressions to create more elaborate filters. Refer to Chapter 15, "Calculating Values and Making Decisions," for information about expressions.

4

CREATING
INFORMATION
OUT OF DATA

Filter By Selection

Filter By Selection gives you a quick way to create a filter, but offers less flexibility than Filter By Form. You can use Filter By Selection to specify only one filtering criterion.

As an example, suppose you want to display records just for people for whom the Contact Title field in the Customers form contains Owner:

1. In the Datasheet view of the Customer table, find a record in which the Contact Title field contains Owner. Select the word Owner in that field.
2. Choose Records, move the pointer onto Filter, and select Filter By Selection. Access displays a filtered Datasheet view containing only those records for which the Contact Field contains Owner.

The way Filter By Selection works depends on exactly how you make a selection. You can select

- The entire content of a field. The filtered view contains records with fields that exactly match the selected value.
- A partial value at the beginning of a field. The filtered view contains records with fields that start with the selected value.
- A partial value at the end of a field. The filtered view contains records with fields that end with the selected value.
- A partial value within a field. The filtered view contains records with fields that include the selected value.

Filter Excluding Selection

This filtering mode operates in the reverse manner to Filter By Selection. Instead of displaying records that match the selection, all the records that don't match the selection are displayed.

Advanced Filter/Sort

The Advanced Filter/Sort capability in Access is based on queries so I'll postpone describing this until after covering queries. See the section "Using Advanced Filter/Sort" near the end of this chapter.

Using Select Queries to Organize Data

As the previous pages of this chapter show, you can use various tools to locate and organize data in your tables, but there are some serious limitations to what you can do. You can't, for example, use those tools to work with data in more than one table at a time. Queries overcome that and other limitations of the previously described tools.

> **NOTE**
>
> Access gives you the ability to employ several types of queries. This section is primarily about Select queries. Subsequent sections of this chapter contain information about using other types of queries.

A Select query creates a temporary table based on information in an Access table or in related Access tables. Alternatively, a query can establish table relationships that don't already exist. A temporary table created by a query is known as a recordset.

> **NOTE**
>
> In addition to creating a recordset based directly on tables, a query can create a recordset based on other recordsets, that is, on the results of other queries.

Some of the things you can do with queries are

- Create a recordset that contains selected fields from a single table or related tables
- Create temporary relationships between tables
- Control the order in which fields occur in a recordset
- Control the order of records in a recordset
- Specify criteria for records to be included in a recordset
- Display a Datasheet view of the contents of a recordset
- Create forms and reports that contain information in a recordset
- Display the SQL code that's the basis of a query
- Print the results of running a query

The Access tool used to create queries is known as Query by Example (QBE). The easiest way to become familiar with QBE is to start working with it. The next section provides a basic understanding by considering a query based on a single table.

Creating a Query Based on a Single Table

This example of creating a query is based on the Publisher table that's part of the Book application introduced in Chapter 2, "The Anatomy of an Access Application." You can find that application in the Chapter 2 section on the CD-ROM that accompanies this book.

> ## TIP
>
> You might prefer to follow what's suggested here, using one of your own tables instead of the Publisher table in the Book application.

To create a query containing selected fields from a table,

1. Open the Book application to display the Database window.

2. Choose Queries in the Objects bar and then choose New to display the New Query dialog box. Select Design View, as shown in Figure 4.7.

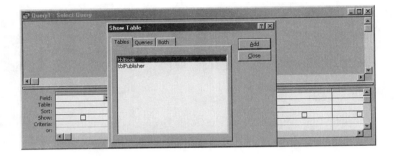

FIGURE 4.7

The Show Table dialog box opens superimposed on a Query window.

3. In the Show Table dialog box, select the table (tblPublisher in this case) on which you want to base a query, then choose Add to display a list of the selected table's fields in the Query window.

4. Choose Close to close the Show Table dialog box. Now only the Query window is visible, as shown in Figure 4.8.

5. At this stage, you can drag the lower border of the Query window down to increase the box's height. You can drag the border between the two panes down to allow more space for the representation of the table, and drag the bottom of the table representation down so that all the field names are visible. You can, of course, also drag the vertical borders to change the width of the dialog box.

6. Move the pointer onto the lngPubID field name in the list of fields, and drag it to the first position in the Field row in the QBE grid. The name of the field appears in the Field row and the name of the table it came from appears in the Table row.

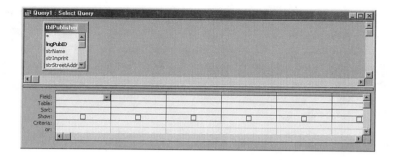

FIGURE 4.8
The Query window has two panes. The upper pane contains a representation of the table you selected with a partial list of its fields. The lower pane contains the Query By Example (QBE) grid in which you construct your query.

NOTE

Instead of dragging a field name, as described in step 6, you can double-click a field name in the list of fields. When you do that, Access places the field name in the first empty position in the QBE grid. Alternatively, you can enter a field name and a table name into the Field and Table rows of the QBE grid.

7. Individually, move the pointer onto other field names in the list of fields and drag them to successive columns in the QBE grid. After you've done that, the pane looks something like that shown in Figure 4.9.

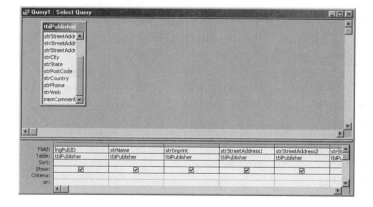

FIGURE 4.9
This is part of the QBE grid after you've dragged several fields into it.

Notice that each column in the QBE grid contains a field name and table name. The order of the columns in the grid depends on the order in which you dragged fields to the grid; it is independent of the order of the fields in the table. At this time, the Sort row in the grid is empty because you haven't specified a sort order for any field. In each column, the Show row contains a checked box to indicate that the recordset resulting from the query will contain all the fields. The Criteria row for each column is empty because you haven't specified any criteria for including records in the recordset.

To see the recordset resulting from the query, choose View, Datasheet View. Access displays the recordset, as shown in Figure 4.10.

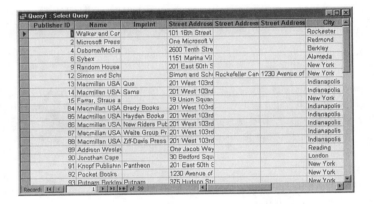

FIGURE 4.10

The Datasheet view displays the result of a query.

To return to the Query window that displays the QBE grid, choose View, Design View.

NOTE

If you want a recordset to contain all the fields in a table, drag the asterisk at the top of the list of fields into the leftmost position in the Field row of the QBE grid. If you want a recordset to contain several fields from a table in the same order that those fields occur in the table, select those fields and drag the fields as a group into the Field row.

Modifying a Recordset

You can modify your initial recordset in several ways, some of which are described in the following sections. These sections apply only if you dragged individual fields into the QBE grid, not if you dragged the asterisk to include all the table fields.

Adding a Field to a Recordset

To add a field to a recordset, drag a new field name from the list in the table to the Field row in the QBE grid. If you drag onto a column in the grid that already contains a field name, the new field is inserted into the grid and all previously existing fields in the grid move to the right.

Deleting a Field from a Recordset

To delete a field from a recordset, move the pointer onto the shallow, gray row at the top of that field in the QBE grid. The pointer changes to a black, down-pointing arrow when it's in the correct position. Click to select that column, and then press Delete. Access removes the selected column. All fields to the right of that column move one place to the left.

If you want to remove all fields from the grid, choose Edit, Clear Grid.

Changing Field Names in a Recordset

When you create a query based on a table, the field names shown in the list of table fields in the upper pane of the Query window are the same as the names shown in the Design view of the table. This is so even if you have set the Caption properties in the table's Design view to different names. However, the field names shown in the Datasheet view of a query reflect values you entered for the fields' Caption properties in the table Design view. (See the section "Setting Text Field Properties" in Chapter 3, for information about field properties.)

If you haven't set a Caption property for a field in the table Design view, you can change the name of a recordset field in the query Design view. The tblPublisher table has a field named strName. When you create a query based on tblPublisher, the QBE grid shows the field with the same name—strName. To make this name more meaningful to users, change it to Publisher Name. In the Field row, enter

```
Publisher Name: strName
```

The item Publisher Name is the new caption (name) for the field, and the colon indicates that it equals the old property, strName. In other words, the text to the left of the colon is what users see in the Datasheet view instead of the field's real name.

After you do this, the field name shown in the Datasheet view of the recordset is Publisher Name. Changing a field name in this way is known as *creating an alias*.

4

CREATING
INFORMATION
OUT OF DATA

However, if you create an alias for a field name in the original table (by setting its Caption property as explained in the section "Setting Text Field Properties" in Chapter 3), you can't create a different alias in the QBE grid. The QBE grid appears to enable you to do so, but when you display the Datasheet view, you'll see the alias you created in the table Design view, not the alias you tried to create in the QBE grid. Therefore, to be consistent, you should normally create aliases for field names in tables, rather than in queries.

Changing the Order of Fields in a Recordset

You can change the order in which fields appear in the Datasheet view of a recordset. To do so, move the pointer onto the shallow, gray row at the top of a field you want to move in the QBE grid and click. Then drag to the left or right to change the position of that column.

Changing the Order of Records in a Recordset

By default, the records displayed in the Datasheet view of a recordset appear in the order of those records in the underlying table. You can change that to display records in ascending or descending order of any fields. To change the order of records displayed in the Datasheet view of a recordset, click in the Sort row of the column of the field you want to use to control the sort order. Then click the button that appears at the right end of that column. You can choose Ascending, Descending, or Not Sorted.

If you choose to control the sort order by two or more fields, Access sorts on the left-most field first, and then the next right field for which you've specified a sort order, and so on. To change the priorities of sort orders, you have to change the order of fields in the QBE grid, as described in the preceding section.

You can sort records in a recordset based on fields that don't appear in the recordset. To do so, place the field on which you want to sort in the QBE grid and set Sort for that field to Ascending or Descending. Click the Show check box in that column to remove the check mark. When you display the recordset, the records are displayed in an order based on that field even though the recordset doesn't contain that field.

Setting Criteria for a Recordset

By default, a query creates a recordset that contains records based on each record in the table from which the query was created. You can use criteria to filter the table records so that only some of them appear in the recordset. In the current example of a query based on the tblPublisher table, you can set a criterion so that the recordset contains only publishers in a specific state. To do so, enter a state abbreviation enclosed within quotation marks in the Criteria row of the QBE grid, as shown in Figure 4.11.

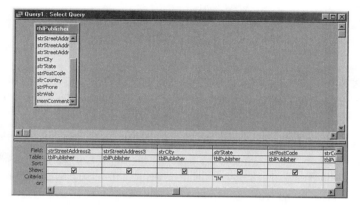

FIGURE 4.11

In this example, a criterion for selecting only publishers in Indiana is set.

TIP

Although it isn't always necessary to enclose criterion text within quotation marks, it's good practice to do so. If the text you enter happens to be a reserved word (a word that has a special meaning within Access), you'll see an error message if you don't use quotation marks. For example, if you enter IN (the abbreviation for Indiana) without using quotation marks, you'll get an error message. That's because IN is a reserved word—it's used within SQL statements, as you'll see later in this chapter.

Don't use quotation marks for numbers in Number fields. Do use quotation marks for numbers in Text fields. When setting criteria for Date/Time fields, enclose dates with number symbols (#), as in #5/25/2000#.

If you want the resulting recordset to contain records for publishers in two states, enter the abbreviation for the second state in the Or row of the QBE grid, immediately under the abbreviation for the first state. You can add criteria in as many Or rows as you like. If you enter "IN" in one row and "WA" in another row, the recordset will contain records for publishers in both states—where one criterion or the other is satisfied.

You can also create queries in which two or more criteria must be satisfied. For example, if you have a table that contains information about your contacts, that table might have a field named strCategory in which you can classify contacts as Family, Friend, Business, Politician, and so on. You can create a query based on that table in which you enter a state abbreviation as a criterion in the strState column of the QBE grid and "Family" as the strCategory criterion, both criteria being in the Criteria row. This query will create a recordset that contains information only about family members in a specific state.

More elaborate criteria can involve operators. In the case of publishers, for example, you can enter the criterion

```
Not "IN"
```

to create a recordset containing information about publishers in all states except Indiana. In this example, Not is an operator that reverses the criterion. (See Chapter 15 for more detailed information about operators.)

Eliminating a Field from a Recordset

By default, Access automatically checks the boxes in the Show row, as you've seen in the preceding examples. You can uncheck any of these boxes to eliminate corresponding fields from the recordset created by a query. Why would you want to include a field in QBE grid and not have that field in the resulting query? One reason, mentioned previously in the section "Changing the Order of Records in a Recordset," is that you might want to control the order of records in a recordset without having the field that controls the order in the recordset.

Suppose you create a query to create a recordset containing information about publishers in California. You don't need the recordset to contain a State field, because you know all the records in that recordset are for California. In that case you can, if you like, uncheck the box in the State field.

Setting a Query's Properties

Like other objects in an Access application, each query has many properties. Each property is automatically set to a default value, but you can change that value to suit your requirements. To see the properties of a query in a query's Design view, click any unoccupied space in the upper pane and then choose View, Properties. Access displays a list of properties, as shown in Figure 4.12.

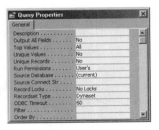

FIGURE 4.12

This is a list of properties for a query.

I'll leave you to look at the information in the Access online help to get information about each property. To get information about a property, place the insertion point within a property's value and press F1. When you place the insertion point within some property values, a button appears that you can click to see a list of available values from which you can select. In other cases, you have to enter a property value.

You should enter text to describe the purpose of each query in the Description property. If you create relatively straightforward applications, you probably won't need to be concerned with the other query properties. However, some of these properties are very useful in more complex applications.

Combining Table Fields into Recordset Fields

Instead of creating separate fields in a recordset that correspond to individual fields in a table, you can combine table fields into one recordset field. For example, in the case of a recordset based on the tblPublisher table, you might want to create a field that combines the publisher and imprint names, separated by a comma. Combining table fields involves the use of operators. Refer to Chapter 15 for detailed information about operators.

> **NOTE**
>
> An *imprint* is the name under which a publisher publishes a book. An imprint might be the actual name of a publisher, but is not necessarily so. Some publishers, usually very large ones, publish books under several imprints. Macmillan USA, for example, uses such imprints as Sams Publishing and Que.

To combine these two fields in a recordset field, place the insertion point into an empty position in the Field row of the QBE grid, and then enter

```
strNameImprint: [strName] & ", " & [strImprint]
```

Enter the name of the table that contains the two fields in the Table row.

The text at the left of the colon becomes the name of the field in the recordset. You can choose any name that isn't the same as a name of a field within the table. The names of the two fields to be combined are individually enclosed within brackets. The comma and the space that follows it are enclosed within quotation marks to indicate that those two characters are literal values. The two ampersand characters concatenate (string together) the three elements. You can see the result of combining fields in the Datasheet view, shown in Figure 4.13.

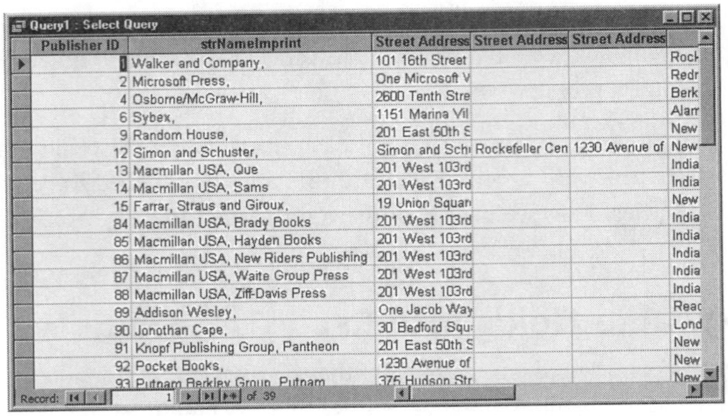

FIGURE 4.13

This is the result of combining two table fields into a single recordset field.

Although this works, it does present a problem in the case of a publisher that doesn't use a name (in addition to its corporate name) as an imprint, such as Microsoft Press in this example. An unwanted comma follows the publisher's name in the Datasheet view. You can solve this problem by using one of the built-in (intrinsic) VBA functions—IIf. (Refer to Appendix A, "Visual Basic for Applications Primer," for detailed information about VBA built-in functions.) Replace what you previously entered into the Field row with

```
strNameImprint: IIf(IsNull([strImprint]),[strName],
➥[strname] & ", " & [strImprint])
```

all in one line.

> **NOTE**
>
> The code continuation character, which appears as an arrow at the beginning of the second line of code, indicates that a single line of code has been broken to accommodate the margins in this book. You should, therefore, enter the code as a single line.

The IIf function has three parts separated by commas:

- The first part specifies a condition.
- The second part specifies what happens if the condition is true.
- The third part specifies what happens if the condition is false.

As explained in Chapter 3, if you leave a field empty in a table, Access automatically inserts a Null value in that field. The condition used in this statement is IsNull([strImprint]). This condition is true for table records that contain no entry for the Imprint field; consequently, the recordset field contains only the publisher's name. The condition is false for table records that contain an entry in the Imprint field; consequently, the recordset field contains the publisher's name and the imprint name, separated by a comma.

In addition to concatenating text fields, you can make calculations based on numeric fields. For example, you might have a table that contains two fields such as

- intQuantity—The number of items
- curCost—The cost of each item

You can combine these two fields in a recordset to create a field that contains the total cost of items by entering

```
curTotalCost: [intQuantity]*[curCost]
```

in the field row of the Query By Example pane. The asterisk in this statement represents mathematical multiplication.

By using this technique, the value in the cutTotalCost field in the recordset is always based on the current values in the intQuantity and curCost fields.

Working with the Datasheet View of a Query

As stated previously in this chapter, a Select query creates a temporary table known as a recordset. Access can create two kinds of recordsets. The default is a Dynaset that's dynamically linked to the underlying table, meaning that any changes you make to the Dynaset recordset automatically update the underlying tables. The alternative is a Snapshot that records the content of the underlying table at the time the recordset is created. A Snapshot isn't dynamically linked to the underlying table; it's read-only.

NOTE
By default, Access creates a Dynaset type of recordset. To create a Snapshot recordset, you have to change the Recordset Type property of the query from Dynaset to Snapshot.

Because a Dynaset is dynamically linked to the underlying table, you can

- Add records to the Dynaset
- Delete records from the Dynaset
- Edit values in fields of any record in the Dynaset

4

All changes you make to the Dynaset in this way cause the same changes to occur in the underlying table. You can't use a Snapshot to make changes in the underlying table.

Creating a Query Based on Several Tables

So far, you've learned about creating a query based on a single table. You can also create queries based on two or more tables. These can be tables for which you've already set up relationships, as described in Chapter 3, or they can be unrelated tables for which you set up relationships within the Query dialog box

Creating a Query Based on Related Tables

The Book application introduced in Chapter 2 contains the two related tables tblBook and tblPublisher. To create a query based on these tables,

1. In the Database window, choose Queries.

2. Choose New and, in the New Query dialog box, select Design View to display the Show Table dialog box, previously shown in Figure 4.7.

3. Select tblBook and tblPublisher, and then choose Add.

4. Choose Close to close the Show Table dialog box. Access displays the Select Query dialog box with the two tables related, as shown in Figure 4.14.

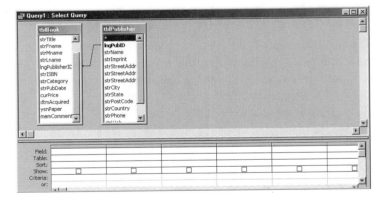

FIGURE 4.14

The link shown here indicates the relationship previously created between the two tables.

Creating a Query Based on Unrelated Tables

While you're creating a query, you can establish a relationship between previously unrelated tables. To do so, follow the four steps described in the preceding section. This time, the Select Query dialog box shows the two tables, in almost the same way as in Figure 4.14, but without any relationship between them.

If the two tables contain appropriate fields that can be related, move the pointer onto the field in one table and drag to the related field in the other table. After you've done that, the link is indicated as shown in Figure 4.14.

NOTE

The example shown here and in the preceding section shows only two related tables. You can create a query based on three or more related tables in the same way.

Adding Fields to a Recordset

You can drag fields from either of the two tables into the QBE grid, as explained previously in this chapter. Notice that the Table row in the QBE grid identifies which table each field comes from.

Modifying the Join Properties

In SQL terminology, the relationship between tables is known as a *join*. By default, the Datasheet view of a query that contains a one-to-many relationship between two tables shows only records based on table records in which the values in both linking fields are equal. (See Chapter 3 for information about one-to-many relationships.)

The tblPublisher table can contain publisher records for whom no books are listed in the tblBook table; a recordset created by the default one-to-many relationship won't contain any information about these publishers. Likewise, the tblBook table can contain information about books for which the publisher is unknown, although not if relational integrity is enforced. A recordset created by the default relationship won't contain these books.

To change how a one-to-many relationship relates tables, right-click the line between the two tables in the upper pane of the QBE dialog box, and then choose Join Properties. Access displays the dialog box shown in Figure 4.15.

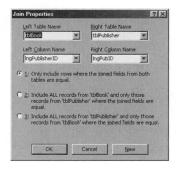

FIGURE 4.15

The lower part of this dialog box contains three properties from which you can choose one.

The upper part of this dialog box identifies the tables that are joined and the related fields (columns) in those tables.

The three properties in the lower part of the dialog box are described there. Choose

- The first (the default), if you want the recordset to contain only records for which there are matching values in the two linking fields. In this case, the Datasheet view shows only records about books for which a publisher is identified and only for publishers for whom one or more books are listed.

- The second, if you want the recordset to contain records for all books, including those for which no publisher is identified.

- The third, if you want the recordset to contain records for all publishers, including those for whom no books are listed.

Understanding the SQL View of a Query

With either a Design or Datasheet view of a query displayed, choose View, SQL View to display the SQL view, such as the one shown in Figure 4.16.

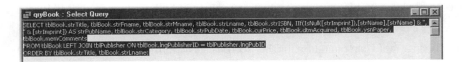

FIGURE 4.16

The SQL view of a query defines a query in terms of the SQL language.

> **NOTE**
>
> You can find a summary of the SQL language in Appendix B, "SQL Primer," and more detailed information in Chapter 23 of the book *Special Edition Using Microsoft Access 2000*, published by Que. For more information about SQL, see *Sams Teach Yourself SQL in 10 Minutes*, published by Sams.

An SQL statement starts with the keyword SELECT and ends with a semicolon. Linebreaks within the statement have no significance. SQL is not case sensitive, but it is usual to make keywords (words that are part of the SQL language) all uppercase. Other words in the statement refer to Access objects and are capitalized in the normal manner.

The SQL statement shown in Figure 4.16 consists of several clauses, each beginning with a keyword. To make the statement more understandable, here is a simpler SQL statement with each clause starting on a separate line

```
SELECT tbl.Book.strTitle, tblBook.strFname, tblBook.strLname,
tblPublisher.strName, tblPublisher.Imprint
FROM tblPublisher INNER JOIN tblBook
ON tblPublisher.lngPubID = tblBook.lngPublisherID;
```

Written like this, the structure of the statement will be reasonably clear.

- The SELECT clause lists the fields used in the query, a comma separating one field name from the next.
- The FROM clause lists the tables on which the query is based and defines how those tables are joined. Even though the SELECT clause identifies the table that contains each field, the FROM clause is required.
- The ON clause defines the join (relationship) between the two fields.

Access automatically creates SQL code from the query you create in the QBE grid. It is this code, not your grid, that directly controls how Access creates a recordset. In most cases, you don't have to work with SQL code, but there are times when you have to do so in order to achieve a specific objective.

TIP

When you get to developing applications that depend on VBA code, you'll frequently want to define queries within your code as SQL statements. One time-saving way to do this is to create a query in the QBE grid, display that query as a SQL statement, copy the SQL statement to the Clipboard, and then paste it into your code.

4

Creating a Join Not Directly Allowed by Access

You can use the Relationships dialog box and the QBE grid to create most of the joins you'll ever need. However, there might come a time when you need a relationship you can't create in that way. The SQL language is the answer to that problem.

One example of a query that's often useful, but that can't be created graphically in the QBE grid, is a union query. This type of query can only be created by writing an SQL statement. (See "Joining Tables and Queries," later in this chapter, for information about union queries.)

Suppose you need a non-equi join—that's a join in which the two relating fields are other than equal. You can't do that directly in Access. What you can do, though, is create an SQL statement, or edit an existing one. The ON clause in the SQL statement shown in the preceding section has = between the names of the relating fields to indicate that the values of those two fields must be equal. You can replace = with another operator such as:

- <>   Not equal
- >   Greater than
- <   Less than
- >=   Greater than or equal to
- <=   Less than or equal to

Access can't display a Design view of a query that's not directly supported. If you replace the = in the ON clause with one of the operators listed previously and then attempt to display the Design view, Access displays an error message saying "Microsoft Access can't represent the join expression…". You can switch to the Datasheet view to see the recordset created by the changed SQL statement.

Minimizing the Number of Queries

When you create a complex application based on Access, you might find it necessary to have many queries. Consider the example of an application that maintains financial records for many years. You might well decide to keep the records for each year in a separate table. Going one step further, if the application is to be used by a large organization, it might be appropriate to keep the records for each division in a separate table. If records are to be kept for 10 years for an organization that has six divisions, you would need 60 tables. Suppose you require four queries for each table; that would mean a total of 240 queries.

An application with that number of queries would be next to impossible to manage. One solution to this problem is to use SQL statements embedded within VBA code, rather than queries, to create relationships between tables. You might be thinking that would mean creating 240 SQL statements, but that's not necessarily so. You can replace the actual names of tables and fields with variables and then, in code, set the values of those variables according to the year and division you're currently working with. To do this, perform the following steps:

1. Use Access to create four prototype queries, using one year and one division.
2. Display the SQL view of one prototype query. Select the SQL statement and copy it to the Clipboard.
3. Open your VBA code and paste the prototype SQL code into it.
4. Replace all table and field names in the SQL code with variables.
5. Add whatever VBA statements are necessary to declare those variables and assign values to them.

Making Your Queries Run Faster

Many of the operations Access does depend on running queries or, as you've seen, on running SQL code. There are a number of things you can do to increase the speed of queries, some of which are

- Always index the fields on both sides of a join. Indexing increases the speed of accessing table records, although it somewhat decreases the speed of updating table records. On the whole, indexing is beneficial.
- Work with small tables as far as possible. In large applications, try to keep the data you're currently working with in a table that's separate from other data.
- Use the smallest possible data types for fields in your tables.
- Add only the fields you really need to the QBE grid. If you occasionally need other fields in a recordset, consider creating separate queries for those needs.
- Always index fields you use for criteria in the QBE grid.
- Uncheck the Show check box for fields used for criteria that aren't needed in the recordset.
- Compact the Access file that contains your tables frequently.
- Create separate queries for each recordset you need, instead of creating one recordset that serves several purposes.

Take the time to test your queries with realistic data in your tables. If you expect your application to be used with tables containing thousands of records, you can't gain any idea about the speed of your queries by testing with only a few records. You should run tests of this type on a single computer, rather than over a network so that network delays don't affect the validity of your results.

Using Parameter Queries

A Parameter query is a Select query (or another type of query) that relies on a criterion but in which the criterion isn't stated. When you run a Parameter query, Access displays a dialog box asking you to supply the missing criterion.

Suppose you want to modify the book application so that you can easily find a list of books written by a specific author. You can easily do that by creating a query and entering the author's name in the Criteria position under strLname. That's fine as far as it goes. The problem is that you would have to create a separate query for each author—hardly practical if you might want to search for books by many individual authors. The solution is to modify a Select query so that it becomes a Parameter query.

Instead of entering an author's name in the Criteria position under strLname, enter a phrase enclosed with brackets, as shown in Figure 4.17.

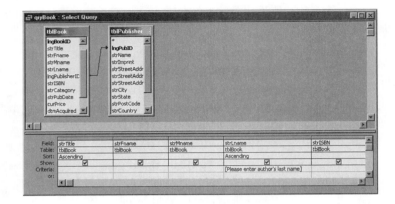

FIGURE 4.17

The brackets in which the criterion phrase is enclosed are required.

When you try to open the Datasheet view, Access displays the input box shown in Figure 4.18.

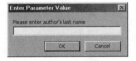

FIGURE 4.18

The input box contains the phrase you entered into the QBE grid.

Enter the last name of the author for whom you want to see a list of books. The Datasheet view contains a list of books by that author. If no books by the author are available, the Datasheet view is empty.

Analyzing Numeric Information

You can analyze data in one or more tables by using a Crosstab query. Crosstab queries are very useful for analyzing numeric data and for creating charts that illustrate that data.

If crosstabs are new to you, you'll probably find it takes a while to feel comfortable with them. Be assured, though, that the effort is worthwhile. The following sections show how to use Crosstab queries in specific cases. After you've followed these examples, you'll be well prepared to create your own Crosstab queries.

Analyzing Sales by Month

Because a lot of numeric information is required to effectively demonstrate the use of a Crosstab query, this section uses some tables in the Northwind application that's supplied with Access. Three related tables in that application—Order Details, Orders, and Products—provide information about orders received. There's no way to use these three tables to directly provide a month-by-month summary of the orders received for each product. As explained in this section, you can use a Crosstab query to analyze orders on a monthly basis. The steps described here create a Datasheet view that displays information in a spreadsheet-like format.

Creating a Crosstab query involves quite a lot of work. However, you'll probably think the result is worth the effort. Follow these steps to create a Crosstab query that provides a month-by-month analysis of orders received:

1. Open the Northwind application, choose Queries in the Database dialog box, and choose New. In the New Query dialog box, select Design View.

2. In the Show Table dialog box, select the Order Details, Orders, and Products tables and choose Add. Choose Close to close the dialog box.

3. Adjust the height of the Select Query dialog box and the height of the lists of table fields in the upper pane, so that you see the relationships between the three tables.

4. Drag the ProductID and ProductName fields from the Products table to the first two columns in the QBE grid. Drag the OrderDate field from the Orders table to the third column in the QBE grid.

5. Open the drop-down list in the Sort row for the ProductName field and select Ascending so that products are listed in alphabetical order.

6. Choose Query, Crosstab Query. The dialog box's title bar changes to contain the phrase "Crosstab Query". Also, Access adds a new row named "Crosstab" in the QBE grid, as shown in Figure 4.19.

7. Now choose row headings ProductID and ProductName as the row headings for the recordset. Open the drop-down list in the ProductID column's Crosstab row and select Row Heading. Open the drop-down list in the ProductName column's Crosstab row and select Row Heading.

8. Open the Total drop-down list in the OrderDate column's Total row and select Where.

9. In the Criteria row of the OrderDate column, enter

   `Like "*/*/97"`

   or

   `Like "*/*/1997"`

   to restrict the recordset to having records for only a specific year.

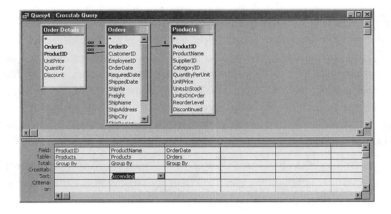

FIGURE 4.19

With this grid displayed, you're ready to start creating the Crosstab query.

NOTE

The format you use for specifying a date must match the Regional Settings Properties in your Windows control panel. If those settings specify a two-digit year, enter a two-digit year in the criterion. Otherwise, if those settings specify a four-digit year, enter a four-digit year in the criterion.

---

10. Now, create a recordset field that contains the result of a calculation. In the fourth column of the QBE grid, place the insertion point in the Field column and enter

    ```
    Sales: Sum([Order Details]![Quantity]*[Order Details]![UnitPrice])
    ```

    This creates a recordset field that contains the sum of the values of orders received for a specific item.

11. In the Total row for the Sales column, open the drop-down list and select Expression. In the Crosstab row, open the drop-down list and select Value.

12. Now, create a field that creates another column for your recordset. Place the insertion point in the Field row of the fifth column in the QBE grid and enter

    ```
    Format([OrderDate], "mmm")
    ```

    This formats dates to display months as a three-character abbreviation.

    When you move the insertion point to a different cell in the grid, Access automatically gives the new field the name Expr1.

13. Open the drop-down list in the Crosstab row and select Column Heading.

That completes creating the Crosstab query. Most of the final QBE grid is shown in Figure 4.20.

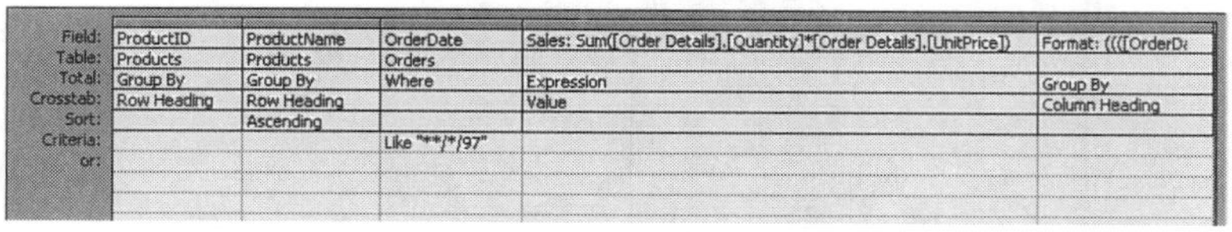

Field:	ProductID	ProductName	OrderDate	Sales: Sum([Order Details].[Quantity]*[Order Details].[UnitPrice])	Format: ((([OrderDa
Table:	Products	Products	Orders		
Total:	Group By	Group By	Where	Expression	Group By
Crosstab:	Row Heading	Row Heading		Value	Column Heading
Sort:		Ascending			
Criteria:			Like "**/*/97"		
or:					

FIGURE 4.20
The QBE grid shown here shows only part of the fifth column. On your screen, you can enlarge the width of that column to see it in its entirety.

After you've finished creating the Crosstab query, you can see the resulting recordset by choosing View in the toolbar, as shown in Figure 4.21.

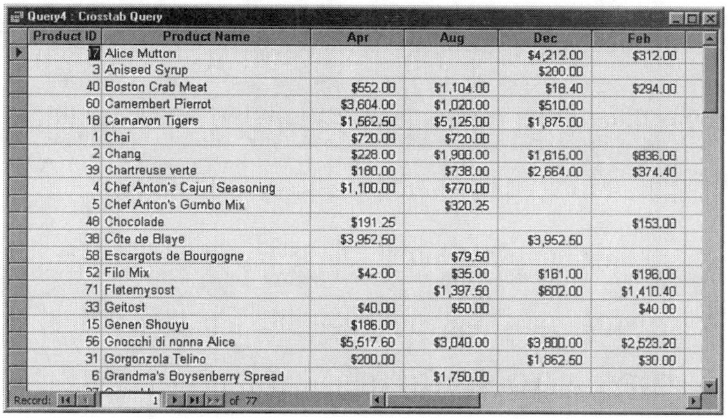

FIGURE 4.21
This is part of the recordset created by your Crosstab query.

You might be disappointed about the way the recordset displays monthly results. It displays months in alphabetic order across the width of your screen, rather than in the calendar order that you'd probably refer. The next section describes how you can solve this problem.

Controlling Column Order in a Crosstab Query

Follow these steps to set the column order:

1. Display the Design view of the Crosstab query you created in the previous section.

2. Make sure nothing is selected in the QBE grid, and then choose View, Properties to display the Property sheet shown in Figure 4.22. Compare this Property sheet with the one shown previously in Figure 4.12.

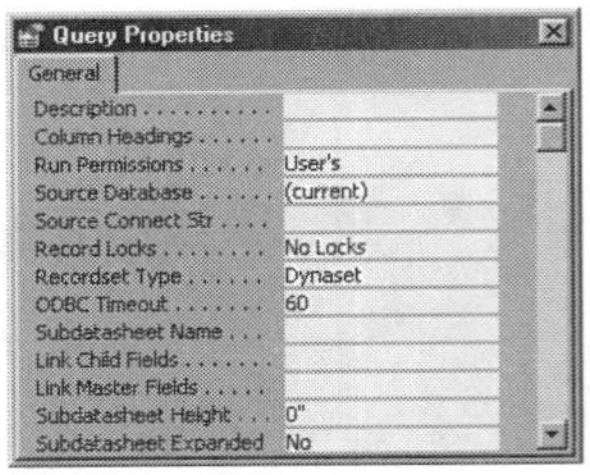

FIGURE 4.22

The Column Headings property is available only for Crosstab queries.

Enter three-character abbreviations for months in month order for the Column Headings property, separating one abbreviation from the next with a comma or semicolon as in

```
Jan,Feb,Mar,Apr,May,Jun,Jul,Aug,Sep,Oct,Nov,Dec
```

> **NOTE**
>
> After you've entered the last month, move the insertion point to a different property. When you do that, Access automatically encloses each month's abbreviation within quotation marks.

Now you can display the Datasheet view of the Crosstab query and see months displayed in the calendar order.

Joining Tables and Queries

Previously in this chapter, the section "Making Your Queries Run Faster" suggested minimizing the number of records in tables by keeping records pertaining to each year in separate tables. That's fine as long you only want to work with one year's data at a time. Sometimes, though, you might want to create a recordset that contains data from more than one year. You can do that by using a Union query.

You can't create a Union query in the QBE grid. Instead, you have to use a SQL statement.

Suppose you have two tables named tblReceipt1998 and tblReceipt1999. The two tables contain identical fields, including those named curAmount and dtmDateReceived.

To create a Union query that results in a recordset containing all the records from both tables, write this SQL statement:

```
SELECT [tblReceipt1998].[curAmount],[tblReceipt1998].[dtmDateReceived]
FROM [tblReceipt1998]
```

```
UNION ALL SELECT
➥[tblReceipt1999].[curAmount],[tblReceipt1999].[dtmDateReceived]
FROM [tblReceipt1999];
```

> **NOTE**
>
> This SQL statement shows all table and field names enclosed within brackets, something that's not strictly necessary because the names don't contain spaces or other nonalphanumeric characters. It's never wrong to enclose names within brackets. Rather than omitting brackets when they're required, I recommend that you always enclose table and field names within brackets.

Some points to notice about this SQL statement are

- You must have the same number of fields listed in the SELECT and UNION ALL SELECT clauses. The fields in the two clauses don't necessarily have the same names. If the names are different, the field names in the resulting recordset come from the SELECT clause.

- The order of fields in the SELECT and UNION ALL SELECT clauses must be the same.

- You can create a union between more than two tables by adding more UNION ALL SELECT clauses.

- By including UNION ALL SELECT clauses, the recordset contains all records from both tables, even if that results in duplicate records. To exclude duplicate records, replace UNION ALL SELECT with UNION SELECT.

> **NOTE**
>
> You can see a complete example of a Union query in the Northwind database. The query named Customers and Suppliers by City is a Union query.

Using Advanced Filter/Sort

As mentioned previously in this chapter, Advanced Filter/Sort is somewhat similar to a query. Now that you know a lot about queries, it's time to learn about Advanced Filter/Sort.

To see how Advanced Filter/Sort works, open the Book application and open the tblBook table. Choose Records, move the pointer onto Filter, and choose Advanced Filter/Sort to display the window shown in Figure 4.23. The grid in the bottom part of this window is known as the Design grid because that's where you design a filter.

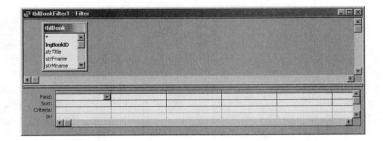

FIGURE 4.23

This window is quite similar to the Query window.

You can use the Design grid to specify a sort order for the table and to specify criteria for displaying records. Do this in the same way that you create a query in the QBE grid. You can drag any fields from the list in the upper part of the dialog box to columns in the Design grid. You can use one or more fields in the Design grid to control the sort order by Selecting Ascending or Descending. Specifying criteria is described in the previous part of this chapter "Setting Criteria for a Recordset."

After you've created a filter in this way, choose Filter, Apply Filter/Sort to display the table with the filter applied.

Summary

Everything you do in Access depends on data in tables. Sometimes, data in tables is all you need and all you have time to work with. In the ideal world, you don't always have the time and resources to create an application that takes full advantage of the Access capabilities. When that's not the case, there's a lot you can do just using tables.

Access stores data in tables in the order you enter that data. You don't have to display the data in the order it's entered. You can display the data in ascending or descending order based on any data field.

You can use queries to display data based on one or more tables. A query creates a temporary table, known as a recordset, that contains data from selected fields in tables. Queries are the basis of information you display in forms and print in reports.

Subsequent chapters of this book illustrate how you can build applications based on tables and queries.

Using Forms to Enter and Display Data

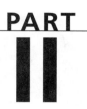

PART

II

IN THIS PART

Making Your Forms Smarter

IN THIS CHAPTER

You know how to create tables, how to enter data into those tables, and how to display existing data in tables. You probably know how to sort and, perhaps, filter data in tables. To be an access application developer, you have to create forms that become the interface users see. In fact, users should rarely see tables; they should use forms as a means of entering data into tables and as a means of displaying data stored in tables.

Regard tables as an application's skeleton. Just as an animal's skeleton holds that animal together but is never seen (at least while the animal is alive), so tables are the foundation of an Access application but are never seen by people who use the application.

This chapter shows how you can begin to take charge of Access by using macros and Visual Basic for Applications.

Displaying a Form Automatically

Many people display a form by going through several steps. They launch Access, select the application they want to run, and then, in the Database window, open the form. That's quite a lot of unnecessary work.

You can easily eliminate the need to display the Database window and then choose a form. Alternatively, you can run your application automatically with a startup form displayed when Access starts, as described in the following sections.

Displaying a Startup Form When an Application Starts

You can avoid displaying the Database window and, instead, display a startup form when your application starts. To do so, perform the following steps:

1. Start Access and start an application such as the Northwind application. Access displays the Database window.

2. Choose Tools, Startup to display the dialog box shown in Figure 5.1.

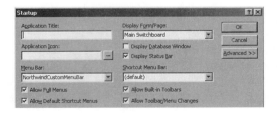

FIGURE 5.1

Use this dialog box to control what Access displays when your application starts.

3. Open the drop-down Display Form/Page list. The list contains the names of the forms available in your application.

4. Select the name of the form you want Access to display when your application starts. If you're working with the Northwind application, select the Main Switchboard form.

5. Make sure the Display Database Window box is unchecked.

NOTE

Before you close the Startup dialog box, examine the choices available. You can make choices here to affect what a user sees and can do. Be careful not to uncheck any of the items you want to be active.

The next time your application starts, it displays the form you selected without first displaying the Database window.

After you start an application in this way, the Database window is no longer available. You can verify that by opening the View menu in which you'll see the Datasheet View menu item is dimmed.

TIP

You can override hiding the Database window. To do so, hold down Shift while you start the application.

If you distribute your application in the runtime environment, users can't override hiding the Database window. See Chapter 20, "Sharing an Application with Other People," for information about distributing an Access application in the runtime environment.

Starting an Application Automatically

You can create a shortcut icon on your Windows desktop. When you double-click that icon, Access opens displaying the startup form in your application.

Follow these steps to create an icon on the Windows desktop that automatically starts a specific Access application:

1. Close Access if it's running, open Windows Explorer, and navigate to the folder that contains Msaccess.exe (probably C:\Program Files\Microsoft Office\Office).

2. If Windows Explorer is maximized, click the Restore button in the title bar so that some of the Windows desktop is visible.

3. Drag Msaccess.exe onto the Windows desktop to create an icon labeled Shortcut to Msaccess.exe.

4. Close Windows Explorer.

5. Right-click the new icon on the Windows desktop to display a context menu. Choose Properties in that menu to display the dialog box shown in Figure 5.2.

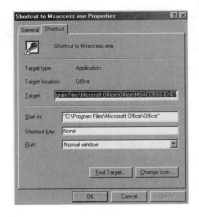

FIGURE 5.2
The Properties dialog box opens with the Shortcut tab selected.

6. Place the insertion point at the right end of the text in the Target box. Enter a space, a forward slash, and the full path name of the application you want to run. The path name must be enclosed within quotation marks. For example, if you have installed Access and the Northwind application in the default folders, the Target box would contain

```
"C:\Program Files\Microsoft Office\Office\Msaccess.exe"
➥"C:\Program Files\Microsoft Office\Office\Samples\Northwind.mdb"
```

NOTE

The sample text for the Target box is shown here in two lines to fit on this book's page. In the dialog box, the text is on a single line.

7. Choose OK to close the Properties dialog box.

8. In the Windows desktop, right-click the new icon to display its context menu. In the context menu, choose Rename. Change the name of the icon to an appropriate name such as Northwind.

9. Drag the icon to an approximate position on the desktop. Right-click an unoccupied space on the desktop to display a context menu. Choose Line Up Icons if you like to have your icons neatly arranged.

Now, you can double-click the icon on the desktop to open Access with a specific application running. If you have chosen to display a specific form on startup, that form is displayed without displaying the Database window.

TIP

You can create several shortcut icons on the Windows desktop to provide immediate access to various applications.

Creating a Switchboard Form

If you followed the steps in the previous section, you can double-click the new icon on the Windows desktop to display the Northwind Main Switchboard form shown in Figure 5.3.

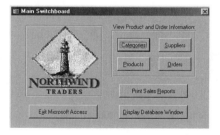

FIGURE 5.3

Northwind's Main Switchboard form contains buttons a user can click to gain access to various parts of the application.

The example in Figure 5.3 of a switchboard in the Northwind application is a good illustration of how you can make applications easier for people to use. You should consider incorporating a switchboard into applications you create.

If you've set up your application so that a user doesn't see the Database window, you can provide a switchboard to provide access to various other forms. In this section, you learn how to create a switchboard form for your own applications. As you do so, you'll find out a lot about creating forms.

> **TIP**
>
> You should strive to keep all forms, particularly switchboards, as simple and unclut-tered as possible. The purpose of a switchboard is to make it easy for people to get around in your application. Usually provide buttons that give access to only the major parts of your application.
>
> Use the position and grouping of buttons on your switchboards to give users help with the order in which they should use the various parts of your application.

This example creates a switchboard form from which a user can click buttons to access two other forms and also to exit from Access.

Having seen a switchboard form in action, you're ready to create one of your own, as described in the following sections.

Creating a New Form with a Displayed Title

Start Access and open an application for which you want to create a switchboard. The Book application is used here as an example. Proceed as follows:

1. In the Database window's Objects bar, choose Forms and then choose New in the tool-bar. Access displays a New Form dialog box in which you can select how you want to create a form. Select Design View. This form is not based on a table or query, so leave the box in which you can select a table or query empty. Click OK. Access displays an empty Design view of a form, as shown in Figure 5.4.

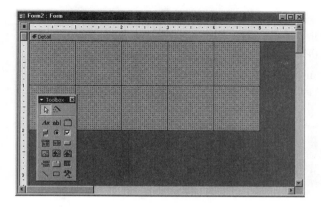

FIGURE 5.4
The Design view contains a grid that helps you place objects on the form.

2. If the Toolbox isn't displayed, choose View, Toolbox to display it.

NOTE

The toolbox contains icons representing objects, known as controls, you can place on a form. You can place as many copies of each object as necessary. Controls are represented by the 18 icons under the horizontal line. If you move the pointer onto one of these icons and pause for a moment, Access displays the name of the control. You can drag the toolbox to any position on your screen.

3. First, place a label control on the form. If the Control Wizards icon—the one in the center above the horizontal line in the toolbox—appears pressed, click it so that it isn't pressed. Click the Label icon—that's the one on the left immediately under the horizontal line.

4. Move the pointer onto the form's grid, press the mouse button, and drag to outline a rectangle. When you release the mouse button, the rectangle becomes white with an insertion point at the top-left corner.

5. Type the name you want to appear on the form, such as Book Application, and press Enter. The rectangle's background reverts to gray. The small, black squares (known as *handles*) at the corners and on the edges of the rectangle indicate it's selected.

At this point, you might like to see what the form looks like. To do so, choose View, Form View. Access displays the form as shown in Figure 5.5.

5

MAKING YOUR FORMS SMARTER

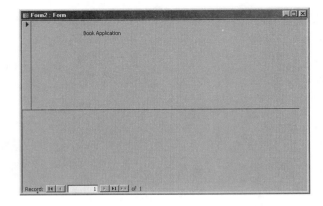

FIGURE 5.5

Form view shows a form as the application user will see it.

You'll probably want to change the size of the displayed form as well as the size and position of the label on that form. To do so, choose View, Design View.

Changing the Size of a Form

By default, Access creates a form that is five inches wide by two inches high. You can change the size of a form by changing its properties. To do so, choose View, Properties to display the Property sheet shown in Figure 5.6.

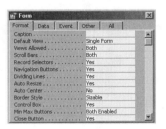

FIGURE 5.6

A Property sheet lists the properties of a form or a selected object on that form. In this case, the Property sheet displays some of the properties of the label you just created.

NOTE

The left end of a Property sheet's title bar names the object for which properties are displayed.

To change the width of a form or any other of its properties, make sure the Property sheet is displaying the form's properties. If the Property sheet's title bar doesn't contain the word "Form," click the small square at the left end of the horizontal ruler, just under the form's title bar.

NOTE

The Property sheet arranges properties in four tabs labeled Format, Data, Event, and Other. The All tab displays all properties. You can drag the Property sheet to any position on your screen.

To change the form's width, complete the following steps:

1. Make sure the Property sheet is displaying the form's properties and the Format tab is selected. Scroll down the Property sheet until you see Width.

2. Place the insertion point in the Width box and change the value of the property. Press Enter to move to the next property. The width of the form changes to the new value.

NOTE

By default, Access uses dimensions based on the settings in the Windows Control Panel's Regional Settings Properties dialog box. So, if your regional settings are for the United States, the default dimensions are inches. If you don't specify a dimension, Access assumes you're using inches. If you want Access to interpret your dimensions differently, such as centimeters, enter a space and then "cm" after the value of the width.

You won't find a Height property for a form. That's because a form can contain several sections, one of which is the Detail section. The Detail section is the part of a form in which you place controls.

To set the height of a form, click in an unoccupied part of the form. The name in the Property sheet's title bar changes to Section: Detail, and the Format tab includes a Height property. You can change the value of the Height property in the same way you changed the value of the form's Width property.

> **TIP**
>
> Instead of setting numerical values for a form's width and height in the Property sheet, you can change a form's size by dragging its borders. The advantage of setting the size numerically is that you can set exact values, something that is helpful when you're trying to design an attractive form with controls carefully arranged on it.

Changing the Form's Background Color

By default, the background color for a form is gray. You'll notice that the list of properties for the form doesn't include background color. That's because you can't set the background color for an entire form. You can, though, set the background color for a form's individual sections, such as the Detail section you normally use.

To change the color of a form's Detail section:

1. Click an unoccupied space within the Detail section.
2. If the Property sheet isn't already displayed, choose View, Properties.
3. Click in the Back Color box, and then click the button marked with ellipsis points (three dots) that appears at the right of that box. Access displays the dialog box shown in Figure 5.7.

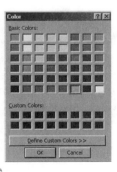

FIGURE 5.7
The Color dialog box displays an array of colors with the gray button in the bottom row selected.

4. Click any color in the array to select that as the background color, and then click OK to close the Color dialog box. Press Enter to select the next property. The section's background color changes to the color you selected.

Changing the Properties of a Label on the Form

You can change the appearance of the label on the form by setting its properties. To do so, perform the following steps:

1. Click the label. Small squares appear at the corners and on the edges of the box that contains the label to indicate the label control is selected. These small squares are known as handles.

2. Choose View, Properties to display the Property sheet similar to the one shown previously in Figure 5.6. Make sure the Format tab in the Property sheet is selected.

3. Scroll down the list of properties until the Font Size property is visible. Click near the right end of the Font Size box to display a list of font sizes. Select the size you want. The text in the label immediately changes to the new font size.

4. If the box containing the label isn't wide enough to display the entire label, change the Width property to a larger value. Similarly, if the box isn't high enough to display the entire label, change the Height property.

5. Change other properties, such as Font Weight, according to your preferences. You should also change the Text Align property to Center.

Positioning the Label

You're almost done optimizing the label. What remains to be done is to position it on the form. One way to position the form is to perform the following steps:

1. Click anywhere on an unoccupied part of the form to deselect the label.

2. Move the pointer onto the label, and then press the mouse button and hold it down. The pointer changes to the shape of a hand.

3. Drag the label to a new position. When the position is satisfactory, release the mouse button.

That method relies on your visual judgment. If you want to position the label exactly, click the label to select it and display its properties in a Property sheet. There, you can set the Top and Left properties to precisely position the top-left corner of the label. These properties define the position of the label as measured from the top-left corner of the form.

NOTE

Access helps you to position and size controls when you drag by snapping to grid points. You can turn snapping off or on by choosing Format, Snap to Grid. By default, there are 24 grid points per inch. You can change the spacing of grid points in a form's Property sheet. With the Format tab selected, change the value of the Grid X and Grid Y properties.

Setting Other Label Properties

There are many other properties you can set or change to affect how the label appears on the form. Some of these properties are

- Display When—Normally choose Always (the default). If you want the label to be visible only when the form is displayed on the screen, select Screen Only. If you want the label to be visible only when the form is printed, select Print Only.

- Back Style—If you want the label's background to be transparent so that the text in the label appears on the form's background color, select Transparent (the default). If you want the label box to have its own background color, select Normal.

- Back Color—If you've selected Normal as the Back Style and you want to select a background color for the label, click the button that appears at the right of the Back Color box. Select a background color for the label in the Color dialog box.

- Special Effect—Select Flat (the default) if you don't want the label to be emphasized on the form. You can emphasize the label by selecting Raised, Sunken, Etched, Shadowed, or Chiseled.

- Border Style—Select Transparent (the default) if you don't want the label's border to show. If you do want the border to show, select Solid, Dashes, Short Dashes, Dots, Sparse Dots, Dash Dot, or Dash Dot Dot.

- Border Color—If you select anything other than Transparent for Border Style, you can select a border color in the same way that you select a background color.

- Border Width—If you select anything other than Transparent for Border Style, you can select a width for the border. Select Hairline, 1 pt, 2 pt, 3 pt, 4 pt, 5 pt, or 6 pt. Hairline borders have a width of one pixel. Other widths are in points (1/72 of an inch).

- Fore Color—The color of the text in the label (the default is black). Select a different color in the same way you select a background color.

Adding Command Buttons to the Form

You need to place three command buttons on the switchboard form: one to access the Book form, one to access the Publisher form, and one to close Access. The three buttons should be the same size and use the same font for their captions. Instead of creating the three buttons separately, it's easier to create one button, adjust that button's properties, and then duplicate the button twice to create the other two buttons.

The steps that follow are based on the assumption that the Control Wizards button in the toolbox is turned off, as explained in the section "Creating a New Form with a Displayed Title" previously in this chapter. Place the first button on the form in the same way that you placed the label.

1. Click the command button in the toolbox. That's the third icon in the third row under the horizontal line in the toolbox.

2. Move the pointer onto the form and drag to create a rectangle the approximate size of the button you want. Access automatically creates the caption Command1 for the button.

NOTE

The caption is the text that appears on the face of the button. The button also has a name by which you can refer to it from VBA code. Initially, the caption and the name are the same.

3. If necessary, open the Property sheet. Because you've just created the button, it's selected and the Property sheet shows the button's properties. Select the Property sheet's Format tab.

4. Change the Caption property to the one with the maximum number of characters of any of the three buttons; Publishers, in this case. To do so, delete the existing characters in the Caption property box, enter the characters of the new caption, and then press Enter to move to the next property. Access replaces the previous characters in the button's face with the new ones.

5. If you want to change the caption's font, scroll down the Property sheet and change the Font size, as you previously did for the label.

6. At this time, the original button might not be large enough for the caption. If that's the case, either drag the handles on the edges of the button or change the Width and Height properties in the Property sheet.

7. Select the Property sheet's Other tab. The Name property at the top of the list of properties is Command1, the name Access initially supplied. Change this name to a more meaningful name, such as cmdPublisher.

NOTE

The suggested name follows the practice of using a naming convention, as described in Chapter 3, "Storing Your Data Efficiently." I strongly recommend you use a naming convention for all the controls you place on a form. The prefix cmd identifies a command button.

Apart from positioning the button on the form, this completes creating the first button.

Duplicating a Command Button

You can now duplicate the button twice to create the other two buttons by using the following steps:

1. If the button isn't already selected, click the button to select it.

2. Choose Edit, Duplicate twice to create two duplicate buttons. The duplicate buttons appear under the original button, as shown in Figure 5.8.

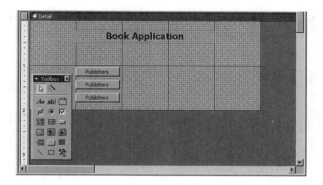

FIGURE 5.8

The form looks like this after you've duplicated the button twice.

Select one of the new buttons to display its properties in the Property sheet. Change the Caption and Name properties to something more appropriate, such as Books and cmdBook. Select the remaining button and change its Caption and Name properties to something more appropriate, such as Close and cmdClose.

Positioning the Buttons

You could carefully drag the three buttons into place. You could also set the Top and Left properties of the three buttons to position them. An easier way is described here:

1. Drag the Books button to the position where you want it. While you drag, you can use the horizontal and vertical rulers to verify the button's exact position.

2. Drag the Publishers button somewhere to the right of the Books button, without bothering to place it exactly.

3. Drag the Close button to the right of the Publishers button, making sure it's in the correct horizontal position.

4. At this time, the Close button is selected. Hold down Shift while you click first the Publishers button and then the Books button. Now all three buttons are selected.

> **TIP**
>
> Here's another way to select several controls at a time. Move the pointer into the vertical ruler. When you do so, the pointer changes to a black, down-pointing arrow. At this point, if you click, all the controls below the black arrow are selected. You can also click in the horizontal ruler to select all the controls to the right.

5. Choose Format, move the pointer onto Align, and choose Top. The Publishers and Close buttons move vertically so that their top edges are aligned with the Books button.

> **NOTE**
>
> When you select two or more controls and then align those controls, Access uses the last selected control as the basis of the alignment.

6. With the three buttons still selected, choose Format, move the pointer onto Horizontal Spacing, and choose Make Equal. Access adjusts the spacing between the controls so that they are equally spaced, as shown in Figure 5.9.

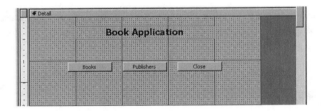

FIGURE 5.9
Now, the three buttons are properly positioned.

> **TIP**
>
> When you have two or more controls selected, Access handles them as a group. The Property sheet lists the properties the selected controls share but not those that are different. You can change a shared property in the Property sheet to change the property for all selected controls.
>
> Also, with two or more controls selected, you can move them as a group. To do so, move the pointer onto any one of the selected controls and drag.

Cleaning Up the Form

Choose View, Form View to see the form as users will see it. Notice the narrow bar at the left edge—that's the record selector. Also notice the buttons at the bottom—those are navigation buttons. The record selector and the navigation buttons are useful on forms that display records from a table or recordset, but they have no purpose on a switchboard form. You can easily remove these elements from the form by performing the following steps:

1. Return to Design view and, if necessary, display the Property sheet. Make sure the Property sheet is displaying the form's properties, not the properties of a control on the form.

2. Select the Property sheet's Format tab. The Record Selectors and Navigation Buttons properties are both set to Yes. In each of these property boxes, click near the right end to display a list box. Select No for both properties.

3. While you still have the Property sheet displayed, set the Auto Center property to Yes so that the form is automatically centered on users' screens.

When you return to the Form view, you'll see the record selector and navigation buttons are no longer present. It's necessary to close and reopen the form for auto centering to take effect.

Making the Buttons Work

With the form view displayed, you can click any of the three buttons and you see that the button appears to be pressed. At this stage, that's all a button does. To make a button do something useful, you have to create macros or write VBA code—this chapter illustrates the use of macros.

First create two other forms so that the buttons have forms to open. These forms don't need to have any controls on them, but they must each have a name.

1. Close the switchboard form if it's open.

2. In the Database window, choose Forms in the Objects bar, choose New, and select Design View.

3. Choose File, Save. In the Save As dialog box, enter a name for the form, such as frmBook. Close the form.

4. Repeat steps 2 and 3, this time naming the form frmPublisher.

Now you have two forms for the switchboard form to open.

To create a macro for the Books button, do the following:

1. Open the switchboard form in Design view and select the Books button.

2. If necessary, open the Property sheet and select the Event tab.

3. Click near the right end of the On Click property box. Two buttons appear: one containing a triangle at the right end of the box and another containing an ellipsis (three dots) at the right of the box. Click the box containing the ellipsis. Access displays the dialog box shown in Figure 5.10.

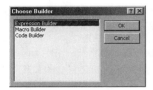

FIGURE 5.10

Select what you want to build in this dialog box.

4. Select Macro Builder. Access displays the Save As dialog box superimposed on the Macro dialog box. Enter a name for the macro, such as mcrBook. Now you're ready to build the macro.

> **NOTE**
>
> The top part of the Macro dialog box has two columns. The left column contains a list of macro actions. The right column contains any description of that action you choose to enter. The bottom part of the dialog box contains details of an action, known as *action arguments*.
>
> The top part of the macro dialog box may have additional columns with the titles Macro Names and Conditions. Choose View, Macro Names or View Conditions to display or hide those columns. You don't need those columns at present.

5. Click the button at the right end of the first row of the Action column. Access displays the beginning of a list of possible actions, as shown in Figure 5.11.

6. Scroll down the list of actions and select OpenForm. The word OpenForm appears as the first action, and the Action Arguments section contains six rows in which you can select or enter arguments, as shown in Figure 5.12.

7. Click at the right end of the Form Name argument box. Access displays a list of available forms. Select frmBook, the name of the form you want the button to open. You don't need to do anything about the remaining arguments in this case.

8. Choose File, Save to save the macro, and then File, Close to close the macro.

Repeat these steps, this time working with the Publishers button. In step 4, name the macro mcrPublisher. In step 7, select frmPublisher.

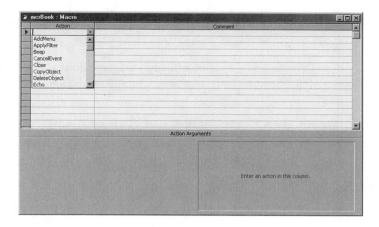

FIGURE 5.11
You can scroll down this list to show many more available actions.

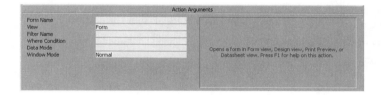

FIGURE 5.12
The action arguments are shown here after you've selected an action.

Switch to the Design view and click the Books button. The form you named frmBook immediately opens. Close that form by clicking the close button (marked with an X) at the right end of the title bar to return to the switchboard form. Click the Publishers button to open the form you named frmPublisher.

You can add a macro to the Close button so that Access closes when you click that button. To do so, follow the steps previously described for the Books button, with these exceptions:

- In step 4, name the macro mcrClose.
- In step 6, select the Quit action.
- Ignore step 7.

Return to the switchboard form in Form view. When you click the Close button, Access closes.

Reviewing What You've Learned About Macros

In the previous two sections, you've learned some of the basics about using macros:

- A macro consists of one or more actions. Although the three macros described each consist of only one action, a macro can consist of any number of actions that run one after the other.
- Most actions can have several arguments that control what the action does.
- Most macros run when an event, such as the user clicking a button, happens.

There's a lot more to learn about macros, much of which is described in the remaining chapters of this book.

The third point in the previous list referred to a macro running when an event happens. The three macros described run when a user clicks a command button—clicking a button is an event. In addition to events associated with a button, there are many other events. These include

- Opening or closing a form
- Inserting or changing data displayed in a control on a form
- The occurrence of an error
- The elapse of a certain period of time

While you work with more controls on a form, take the time to investigate the events associated with those controls. When you do that, you'll begin to appreciate the power of macros.

In addition to running when an event occurs on a form, you can also cause a macro to run by choosing a menu item. For example, with the switchboard form displayed in Form view:

1. Choose Tools, move the pointer onto Macro, and choose Run Macro. Access displays the Run Macro dialog box, in which you can open a list of macros in your application.
2. Select the name of a macro, and choose OK. The selected macro runs.

Displaying a Splash Screen While Access Starts

Whenever you start Windows, you see a splash screen that shows the Windows logo while Windows begins to load. Most professionally designed applications have a similar splash screen. You can provide a splash screen that announces your application while Access and your application are being prepared for use.

If you're using a fast computer and working with a fairly simple Access application, everything is set up very quickly—there's hardly time for a splash screen to be displayed. However, if the application is complex, and particularly if a user has a slow computer, there might be a significant delay between the time that user tries to initiate the application and the first screen appears. It's good practice to display a splash screen to assure a user that something is happening while the application gets started. One way to do it is with the AutoExec macro, as explained in the following sections.

Displaying a Splash Screen with AutoExec

To display a splash screen that gives your application a professional appearance, create a macro named AutoExec. This macro executes as soon as your application starts. Here's an example of how you can use an AutoExec macro to display a splash screen.

First, create the splash screen:

1. Create a new form and place on that form whatever objects you want on the splash screen. Give that form a name such as frmSplash.
2. Choose the Format tab of the form's Property sheet. Set the Scroll Bars property to Neither, the Record Selectors property to No, the Navigation Buttons property to No, the Auto Resize property to Yes, and the Auto Center property to Yes.
3. Choose the Other tab of the form's Property sheet and set the Popup property to Yes and the Modal property to Yes.
4. Save the form with the name frmSplash.

You need to write some VBA code to control the splash screen. There's no way in Access to immediately run VBA code while an application is being set up. What you can do, though, is to create a macro that does run automatically on startup, and use that macro to run VBA code.

To create an AutoExec macro, do the following:

1. In the Database window, choose Macros, and then choose New.
2. In the Macro dialog box, open the list of actions and select RunCode.
3. In the Action Arguments box, enter the name of the VBA function that will contain your code, such as AutoExec().
4. Save the macro with the name AutoExec. The macro runs automatically only if it has exactly that name.

NOTE

Access recognizes a macro to be run at startup by its name—AutoExec. Each Access application can contain only one AutoExec macro, although that macro can contain many actions. Naming a VBA function AutoExec has no significance other than to relate it in the human mind to the AutoExec macro.

Creating the AutoExec function remains to be done. You probably haven't written a VBA function before, so the following steps describe the process in detail.

To create the AutoExec function:

1. In the Database dialog box, choose Modules, and then choose New. Access displays a window similar to the one shown in Figure 5.13. This is the Visual Basic Editor (VBE) window. Don't be concerned if the window you see is somewhat different.

code window

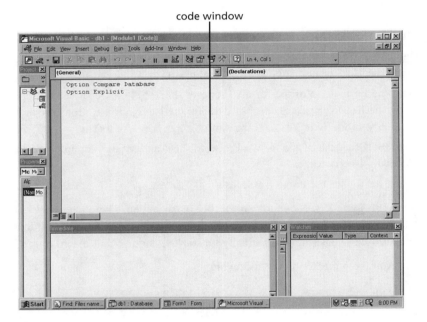

FIGURE 5.13

The large window shown here containing two statements is known as the code window.

2. If either or both of the statements shown in Figure 5.13 aren't present, enter those statements.

3. In the line below those statements, enter

```
Function AutoExec()
```

and press Enter. The window should now look like that in Figure 5.14.

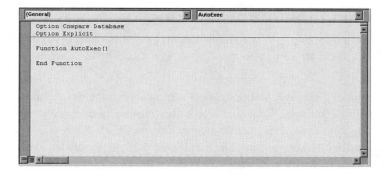

FIGURE 5.14
The Visual Basic Editor automatically marks the beginning of a new function with a horizontal line and also marks the end of the function with the statement "End Function."

4. Enter the nine statements shown in Figure 5.15. These statements are explained subsequently.

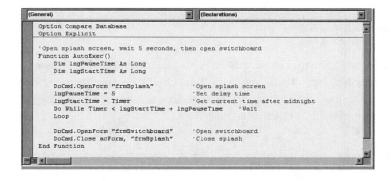

FIGURE 5.15
This is the complete function that displays the splash screen and subsequently displays the switchboard.

5. Choose Debug, Compile to check for errors in your code. Any errors found are highlighted. Correct any errors the VBE detects.

6. Choose File, Save to save your code. When you're asked for a module name, enter basGeneral.

7. Choose File, Close and Return to Microsoft Access.

Close your application, and then restart it. You should see the splash screen displayed for five seconds, and then the switchboard should appear.

Understanding the AutoExec Function

The function shown in Figure 5.16 is a simple example of VBA code. If you haven't previously worked with VBA, there are some important points to notice, one of which is the inclusion of comments.

All text to the right of a single quotation mark is comment text; that is, explanatory words that don't affect what the code does. Comments can be on lines by themselves, or can be at the right of VBA code. Use comments liberally so that anyone who looks at your code can easily understand its purpose. The comments shown in Figure 5.16 are somewhat excessive, but are included so that you can easily understand the code.

The function uses two variables (spaces in memory) to store values:

- lngPauseTime—Space for storing the number of seconds to delay
- lngStartTime—Space for storing the number of seconds after midnight when the function begins

The following two statements at the beginning of the function allocate memory for these variables:

```
Dim lngPauseTime As Long
Dim lngStartTime As Long
```

These statements are known as *declarations*. Each declaration provides a name for a variable and assigns it to a data type. The Long data type is chosen because the number of seconds after midnight can be too large for an Integer data type. The names used for variables follow the naming convention described in Chapter 3.

NOTE

See "Choosing Data Types" in Chapter 3 for information about data types. See "Using a Naming Convention for Field Names" in Chapter 3 for information about naming conventions.

The statement

```
DoCmd.OpenForm "frmSplash"
```

is self-explanatory. Just carefully notice its format.

The statement

```
lngPauseTime = 5
```

merely sets the value of the previously declared variable. If you want a delay of other than five seconds, change 5 to a different number.

The statement

```
lngStartTime = Timer
```

makes use of one of VBA's intrinsic (built-in) functions. The Timer function reads the current time from your computer's clock and calculates the number of seconds after midnight. The statement stores that value in the lngStartTime variable.

The next two statements cause the delay:

```
Do While Timer < lngStartTime + lngPauseTime
Loop
```

The two statements run repeatedly, each time comparing the current number of seconds after midnight with the sum of the two variables. When the current number of seconds becomes equal to or greater than the sum of the variables, the next statement is executed.

The next two statements are self-explanatory:

```
DoCmd.OpenForm "frmSwitchboard"
DoCmd.Close acForm, "frmSplash"
```

Be careful to notice the difference in format between the two statements.

Finally, think about the two statements at the top of the form. Notice that these two statements are placed outside the function. By being in that position, the statements affect the function and also all other functions you might subsequently create within the module.

The statement

```
Option Compare Database
```

controls how VBA compares strings. It's of no significance in this example.

The statement

```
Option Explicit
```

affects declaring variables. With that statement present, you must declare every variable used within all functions in the module. If you attempt to use a variable that's not declared, the VBE displays an error message.

If you omit the statement, it's not necessary to declare variables because VBA does so automatically. Although you might think that omission is convenient, in fact, it's dangerous. Suppose you omit the statement then, within your code you enter a variable name correctly in one place and incorrectly in another place. That's fine as far as VBA is concerned. The problem is that VBA generates two separate variables. When your code runs, it won't do what you expect.

Another disadvantage of allowing VBA to create variables automatically, instead of explicitly declaring them, is that automatically created variables all have Variant as their data types. Variant variables occupy more memory than is usually necessary.

TIP

I strongly recommend you include Option Explicit in all your code modules to avoid errors due to mistakes in entering variables. These errors are often difficult to find.

You can set a VBA option so that Option Explicit is automatically included in all your modules. To do so, perform the following steps:

1. With the Visual Basic Editor displayed, choose Tools, Options.
2. In the Editor tab, make sure Require Variable Declaration is checked.

NOTE

Setting this option affects all future modules you create. It doesn't affect existing modules.

Creating a Form Based on a Table or Query

The switchboard form and the form used as a splash screen (described in preceding sections) don't display information based on tables. Most forms, however, do display information that's contained in tables. The next few sections describe how you can create such a form, using the Publishers form as an example. Figure 5.16 shows the completed form.

Choosing What Information to Display on a Form

A form can display information for various purposes. The form shown here displays information that's based on a table. You can click the navigation buttons at the bottom of the form to display information about one publisher after another.

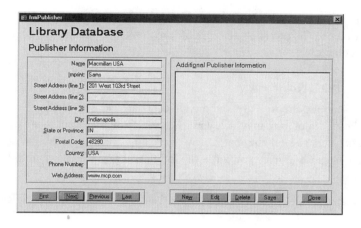

FIGURE 5.16

This is the completed Publishers form that displays information about individual publishers.

You could base this form directly on a table, in which case the order in which information about publishers is displayed by the form depends on how the table is indexed. If you want publishers to be displayed in alphabetical order, index the table on the field that contains publishers' names.

The problem with this approach is that you might want to have another form that displays information about publishers, but does so in a different order. The way around this problem is to create a query that creates a recordset listing information in the order you want it to appear on the form. Subsequently, you can create another query based on the same table if you want another form showing records in a different order. By basing what's displayed in a form on a query, you can also use a form to display information based on two or more tables.

TIP

To gain maximum flexibility, you should almost always base a form on a recordset, not directly on a table.

Creating a Query on Which to Base a Form

The first step in creating a form of this type is to create a query based on one or more tables. The Publishers form uses data from only one table, so create a query based on the tblPublisher table. Don't automatically include all the fields from the table in the query; include only those fields you intend to display in the form. Index the fields in the query according to the order in which the form should show records. Save the query with an appropriate name, such as qryPublisher. (Refer to Chapter 4, "Creating Information Out of Data," for detailed information about creating a query.)

Creating a Form

In the Database window, choose Forms in the Objects bar, and then choose New. Access displays the New Form dialog box in which you can select how you want to create the form. Although Access offers several automated way of creating forms, this section describes the manual approach because it gives you more flexibility and provides more understanding of forms.

Select Design View and then open the drop-down list of tables and queries. Select which table or query is to be used. In this case, select qryPublisher. When you choose OK, Access displays a prototype form in Design view with a list of fields in the table or query you previously selected, as shown in Figure 5.17.

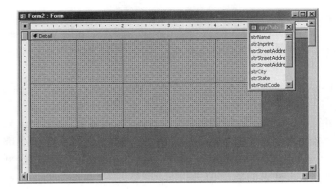

FIGURE 5.17
You can display information from any of the listed fields on the form.

If the field list isn't displayed, choose View, Field List to display it.

At this point, you should usually maximize the form's Design view to give yourself as much working space as possible. Also, drag the bottom border of the form down and drag the right border to the right to the approximate size that you expect the finished form to be.

Placing Fields on the Form

Before placing fields on the form, create a title at the top. Click the Label control in the toolbox, and then create the label as explained in the section "Creating a Switchboard Form," previously in this chapter.

Now place fields on the form. Drag fields from the Field List, one at a time, to the approximate position where each field should appear on the form. Figure 5.18 shows one field dragged onto it the form.

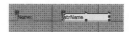

FIGURE 5.18
Each field you drag onto the form consists of a label and a text box.

The label is the name of the field in the underlying table unless you provide a Caption property in the table's Design view. If you entered text in the Caption property, that text is used as the label. Even if you have provided Caption properties for fields in the table, the original field name appears in the corresponding text box.

Continue to drag fields from the Field List onto the form, placing each field approximately where you want it to be. For the reason you'll soon see, place fields vertically and horizontally a little closer than you want them to be.

> **TIP**
>
> If you're reproducing the Publishers form shown previously in Figure 5.17, use that illustration for guidance. If you're creating a different form, make a rough sketch of the form before you start placing fields.

Figure 5.19 shows the form at this stage.

Finalizing the Form

You can do several things to improve the appearance of the form, mainly by setting properties of the controls on the form.

Once you have sized the controls on the form, you will need to add command buttons to the form for navigation. The typical command buttons for navigation are First, Previous, Next, and Last. Depending upon your application, you will want to add appropriate command buttons to guide the user. Just click the Command Button icon in the toolbox and click and drag on your form in an appropriate location.

5

MAKING YOUR
FORMS SMARTER

> ### TIP
>
> You don't have to change properties for individual controls. You can save yourself a lot of time by selecting controls as a group and then changing properties for the entire group.

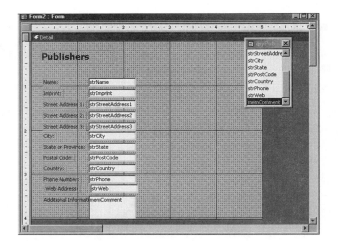

FIGURE 5.19

This is a typical rough layout of a form.

By default, text on a form is displayed using the Tahoma font at eight-point size. If the application is to be used by various people, don't be tempted to change the font to one of your favorites unless you're certain that font is available on all the other users' computers. If you use a font that isn't available on someone else's computer, Windows automatically makes a font substitution, resulting in your form having an appearance that you didn't intend. Remember, some fonts occupy more space than others, even though they have the same Font Size property.

The default font size is quite small, so you might want to select a larger size. You can do so by selecting all the controls to which you want to make a change, and then making a font-size change in the Property sheet. One property change affects all the selected controls.

Use one of the following methods to select multiple controls:

- Select one control. Then, while holding down Shift, select other controls.
- With the Select Objects icon in the toolbar selected, move the pointer onto the form, press the mouse button, and drag to create a rectangle (sometimes known as a *marquee*)

in such a way that at least part of every control you want to select is included within the rectangle.

After using either of these methods, set one or more properties in the Property sheet. If you've selected all label and text box controls and changed the Font Size property to 10, all those controls display text in that size.

If you enlarge fonts, you'll find the height and width of the label and text box controls are no longer sufficient. You need to select all these controls and in the Property sheet replace the original Height and Width properties with larger values. After doing that, you'll find the label controls overlap the text box controls. Group the label controls and change the Left property to something smaller.

When you originally placed controls on the form, you were probably able to align a vertical or horizontal group of controls by taking advantage of Snap to Grid. If you need to correct any misalignment, you can select a group of controls, choose Format, move the pointer onto Align, and choose how you want to align those controls. Remember, Access aligns controls with respect to the last selected control.

The vertical set of controls shown in Figure 5.20 probably isn't evenly spaced. To correct this problem, do the following:

1. Select the lowest pair of label and text box controls, and drag them to the correct vertical position.

2. Select all the controls in the vertical columns.

3. Choose Format, move the pointer onto Vertical Spacing, and choose Make Equal.

It would take many pages, pages that would be boring to read, to describe all the ways you can improve the appearance of a form without having to set individual control properties. The examples described here are intended to introduce you to the facilities Access offers. Take the time to experiment.

Setting the Form's Properties

After setting properties of controls on a form and positioning those controls, you need to set the form's properties. You can finalize the width and height of the form by dragging its bottom and right borders in Design view. Alternatively, you can set the width of the form by clicking the small box at the left of the horizontal ruler to display the form's properties, and then setting the Width property to an appropriate value. You can set the height of the form by clicking in an unoccupied place on the form to display the Section properties, and then setting the Height property.

With the Form properties displayed, set the Auto Resize and the Auto Center properties to Yes. Also, set the Record Selectors property to No. Then, save the form with a name such as frmPublisher and close the form.

Using the Form You've Created

After you've created a form as described, you can use that form to display information in the underlying table. In the Database window, choose Forms in the Objects bar, select the name of the form, and choose Open. Access displays the form as shown previously in Figure 5.17.

You can use the navigation buttons at the bottom of the form to move forward and backward through the publisher records.

You can also enter new records into the underlying table. To do so

1. Click the navigation button containing a triangle and an asterisk (the rightmost navigation button) to display a form in which all fields, other than those for which you set a default property in the table, are empty.

2. Enter text into any or all the fields.

3. Click one of the other navigation buttons to save the new information in the underlying table.

When you're entering new information into a form, press Tab to move from one field to another. By default, pressing Tab moves the insertion point according to the order in which you created fields in the form. After you've initially created a form, you might want to insert an additional field. In that case, pressing Tab won't access fields in the order they appear on the form.

The order in which fields are accessed in a form is known as the *tab order*. You can display the tab order in Design view by choosing View, Tab Order to display a dialog box such as that shown in Figure 5.20.

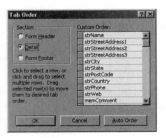

FIGURE 5.20

This dialog box displays the names of fields on a form in the order they're accessed on a form.

You can change the order in which fields are accessed by completing these steps:

1. Click the narrow column at the left of the list of fields to select a field.
2. Drag the selected field up or down in the list to change its tabbing order position.

You can also control the order in which fields in a form are accessed by changing those fields' properties. With a field selected, look in the Other tab of that field's Property sheet. In most cases, the Tab Stop property is set to Yes, meaning that tabbing allows that field to be accessed by pressing Tab. If you don't want the field to be accessed by tabbing, set the property to No. The Tab Index property sets the order in which the field is accessed by tabbing. You can change the number of that property. When you do so, Access automatically renumbers the Tab Index properties of other fields.

Summary

In almost all cases, you don't want a user to have to make choices in the Database window in order to start working with your application. Instead, you can create a switchboard form that opens automatically when a user starts your application. A switchboard form contains buttons that user can click to immediately move to different areas of your application.

If your application is complex, and specifically if users have slow computers, there might be a considerable delay between the time Access opens and the time your application displays its first form. You can take this as an opportunity to display a splash screen, just as Microsoft and other professional developers do. Splash screens usually contain a logo, the identity of the organization that developed the application, and, perhaps, some copyright information.

Access makes it easy for you to create forms to display data stored in tables or information derived from that data. You can make those forms inviting to use by taking advantage of the many tools in Access for labeling and positioning items on forms.

There's much more to Access than making choices from menus. By taking advantage of macros, you can easily customize what Access does. Going one step further, you can employ Visual Basic for Applications code to further optimize an application.

These topics are all described in more detail in subsequent chapters of this book.

Making Data Input Fast and Accurate

IN THIS CHAPTER

The purpose of an Access application is to provide useful information. For that to be possible, the application needs to have access to accurate data. Someone has to enter that data into the application's tables. There's a lot you can do in the design of the application to speed the process of entering data and to help ensure the data entered is accurate.

This chapter describes how you can create forms in which users can automatically enter values into a new record in a table, choose from several available values for fields in lieu of entering values, provide automatic validation of input, and obtain help to provide correctly formatted data. The chapter also contains many suggestions for keeping your users informed while waiting for Access to complete an operation.

Making Automatic Entries in Tables

One way to speed data entry is to take advantage of default values in tables, as explained in Chapter 3, "Storing Your Data Efficiently," in the section "Setting Text Field Properties." The same property exists for most other types of fields.

If a field in a table has the same value for most records, enter that value at the time you design the table. For example, if the table contains addresses including a Country field, it's likely that most records you enter will contain the name of your own country in the Country field. If you set the Default Value property of a Country field to a specific country name, Access automatically places that value in the Country field for all new records.

The default values in tables appear on forms based on those tables. In the few cases in which the required value is other than the default, the person entering data can replace the default value.

Making Choices on a Form

Forms often contain controls to which only a limited set of responses is possible. Rather than have the person entering data respond by entering text, it's preferable for that person to select from a list of possible responses. Not only does this speed data input, it also helps to ensure accuracy by making spelling mistakes impossible and by avoiding responses that can be abbreviated in various ways.

NOTE

If a control on a form asks for a country name and a particular record is for an address in England, the person entering data might type "England," "United Kingdom," or "UK." By providing a choice of countries, the risk of this confusion is eliminated.

Choosing Between Two Values

In many cases, the response to a control on a form can be only one of two values. In a book database, for example, there might be a control to enter if you own each book; the response can only be Yes or No. A database containing records about people might have a control that asks if a person is employed; again, the answer is usually Yes or No.

For controls of this type, use a check box on a form. If the form is bound to a table that has a Yes/No field and you drag that field from the Field list, Access creates a check box on the form together with a label, as shown in Figure 6.1.

FIGURE 6.1
The label adjacent to the check box contains the name of the field in the table to which the form is bound.

NOTE

A form is said to be *bound* to a table when individual controls on a form display data stored in fields within the table, and when data entered into controls on a form is automatically entered into the corresponding data fields.

Although the check box is always shown checked in Design view, in Form view the check box is checked or unchecked according to the field's value in the table.

A check box isn't necessarily bound to a field in a table, even though the form is bound to a table. To create an unbound check box, click the Check Box icon in the toolbox, and then click on the form where you want the check box to be placed. In this case, you have to write Visual Basic for Applications (VBA) code in order to control what happens as a result of checking or unchecking the box. (See Chapter 13, "Taking More Control of Access," for information about using VBA code to control what happens as a result of checking or unchecking a check box.)

Choosing Between More Than Two Values

Sometimes you need to be able to select one of several possibilities. For example, a form used to display information about people might provide the choice of Employed, Self-employed, or Unemployed. You can't use a check box to do that. Instead, use three option buttons (sometimes known as radio buttons). Each option button can be on or off. An option button that's on has a black center, whereas an option button that's off has a white center. Click an option button to change it from on to off, or vice versa.

Option buttons have no direct equivalent table fields, although you can manually bind an option button to a Yes/No field in a table. The usual way to create option buttons on a form is by using the toolbox.

Option buttons are almost always grouped within an option group control. By doing that, you ensure only one of the group of option buttons can be on at any time. When you click an option button that's off to turn it on, Access automatically turns off the button that was previously on.

Creating a Group of Option Buttons

If the Control Wizards button in the toolbox is disabled, follow these steps to create three option buttons on a form:

1. Click the Option Group icon in the toolbox, and then move the pointer onto the form and drag to create a rectangle large enough to contain the three option buttons and their labels.
2. Double-click the Option Button icon in the toolbox.
3. Click the three places on the form where you want to have option buttons. Each option button is displayed with a label at its right, as shown in Figure 6.2.

FIGURE 6.2
Because the option buttons are not bound to a field, Access automatically provides consecutively numbered labels.

4. Click the Select Objects icon in the toolbox.
5. With the Property sheet displayed, select the three option button labels one at a time. Each time you select a label, the Property sheet lists that label's properties. Enter the text for each label in the Caption property. You can also set the Caption property for the label within the top edge of the option group.
6. Notice that each option button has an Option Value property (displayed in the Property sheet's Data tab). Access automatically assigns an option value of 1 to the first option button placed within an option group, a value of 2 to the second option button, and so on. You can change these values, but each option button within a single option group must have a different value; only integer values can be used.

Making Data Input Fast and Accurate

CHAPTER 6

155

6

MAKING DATA
INPUT FAST AND
ACCURATE

7. Select the option group. In the Property sheet's Data tab, set the Default Value property to the value corresponding to the Option Value of the option button that should be on when the form is first displayed.

TIP

You learned a time-saving trick in steps 2, 3, and 4. If you want to add several controls of the same type from the toolbox, double-click the icon that represents the control in the toolbox. Then you can add as many controls of the same type as necessary onto the form. This is in contrast to the normal procedure in which you click once in the toolbox for each control to be placed on the form.

After you've made a tool available for multiple placement, you have to click the Select Objects icon in the toolbox before you can select another tool.

As mentioned previously, these steps assume the Control Wizards button in the toolbox is not enabled. If the Control Wizards button is enabled, a wizard leads you through the process of creating option buttons.

After creating a group of option buttons in this manner, if you switch to Form view, you might be surprised to see that all the option buttons have a gray center. To solve that problem, save the form, close it, and then reopen it in Form view. Now you will see the correct option button on and the other option buttons off.

Saving the Result of Clicking Option Buttons

As previously mentioned, option buttons aren't normally bound to a table. However, you can bind an option group to a table.

When you use a form that has a group of option buttons within an option group, the action of clicking an option button to turn it on sets the option group's value to correspond to that button's value.

To bind an option group to a field in a table,

1. In the table to which the form is bound, create a text or number field.

2. Open the form in Design view, select the option group (not an option button within the group), and choose the Property sheet's Data tab.

3. Click the right end of the Control Source property box to display a list of fields in the table to which the form is bound.

4. Select the field to which you want to bind the option group.

Now, the action of clicking an option button places that button's value into the table field.

As an alternative to directly binding an option group to a field in a table, you can write VBA code that performs certain actions when an option group's value changes. For example, instead of placing a number in the table field, you can place text in that field according to which option button is on. (For information about writing VBA code, see Chapter 12, "Accessing Data.")

Choosing from a List

Option buttons are useful when you want to provide a choice among only a few possibilities, usually four at the most. Suppose you want to provide a choice among many possibilities, such as choosing one of the 50 states in the USA. You wouldn't want to have 50 option buttons on a form. Instead, you can use a list box, such as the one shown in Figure 6.3.

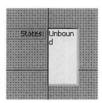

FIGURE 6.3

A list box such as this can provide a choice among any number of items, without taking up too much space on a form.

Creating a List Box

Follow these steps to create a list box on a form:

1. With a form displayed in Design view, click the List Box icon in the toolbox.

2. Move the pointer onto the form and drag to create a rectangle to define the size of the list box.

3. You can specify the items in the list in several ways. One of these is to enter the items in a Property sheet. To do this, choose the Property sheet's Data tab, point near the right end of the Row Source Type property, and select Value List.

4. In the Row Source property box, enter the items you want the list to contain, separating each item from the next with a semicolon.

5. Switch to Form view to see the items in the list, as shown in Figure 6.4.

Instead of entering the list of items in the Property sheet, you can use a table or query as the source of data to display in a list box. To do so, instead of selecting Value List in step 3 of the preceding procedure, select Table/Query. Then, in step 4, click near the right end of the Row Source property box to display a list of tables and queries. Select the table or query from which you want the list box to obtain its values.

Making Data Input Fast and Accurate

CHAPTER 6

157

6

MAKING DATA
INPUT FAST AND
ACCURATE

FIGURE 6.4
Access automatically inserts a vertical scroll bar at the right edge of the list if more items exist than can be shown at one time.

NOTE

One of the advantages of using a table as the row source is that the list becomes dynamic. In the Book application on the CD-ROM with this book, the Book form allows a user to select a publisher from a list that's created from the Publishers table. Whenever a user adds a publisher to the Publishers table, that publisher becomes available to be selected in the Book form.

By default, a list box that obtains values from a table or query displays only the first field in that table or query. If you want to display more than the first field, choose the Property sheet's Format tab and change the Column Count property to the number of fields you want the list box to display.

When a list box displays several fields from a table or query, you can control the width of each column in the list box. To do so, enter widths consecutively in the Column Widths property box, separating each width from the next with a semicolon.

TIP

Set the width of any column you don't want to be displayed as 0 (zero). For example, if you want to display only the second column from a table, set the Column Count property to 2 and set the Column Width property to 0;1. The actual value you set for the second column doesn't matter as long as it's not zero. The last visible column in a list box occupies as much width as is available.

By default, a list box lists values without showing a header for each column. To display header values for list boxes that show data from a table or query, click near the right end of the Column Heads property in the Property sheet's Format tab and select Yes.

When you use a form that contains a list box, click the value in the list to select that value. The selected value becomes the value of the list box. If the list box is bound to a field in a table or query, the selected value is inserted into the underlying table field.

Things are a little more complicated if the list box uses a table or query as a source of items it lists, and two or more columns are listed. By default, the first listed column is the source of the list box's value. That's true, even if the width of the first column is set to zero so that you can't see the values in that column. If you want the value of the list box to be other than the value in the first column, set the Bound Column property in the Property sheet's Data tab to the number of the required column.

Creating a Drop-Down List Box

The list box described in the preceding section shows several or many items in a list. That's convenient if you have sufficient space on your form for such a list. If space is limited, a drop-down list box is a better choice. This is a list box (actually a combo box) that initially displays only its current value.

To place a drop-down list box on a form,

1. Click the Combo Box icon in the toolbox, and then click on the form where you want the drop-down list box to be placed. Access creates the drop-down list box with a label at its left, as shown in Figure 6.5.

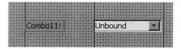

FIGURE 6.5
The drop-down list box initially appears like this.

2. In the Property sheet's Data tab, set the Limit To List property to Yes.

NOTE

By setting the Limit To List property to Yes, you're saying that a user can only choose from a displayed list of values. This differentiates a drop-down list box from a true combo box. See the next section for information about combo boxes.

---

3. Set other properties for the drop-down list box in the manner described in the preceding section.

In most respects, a drop-down list box works the same as the list box described in the previous section. The only significant difference a user sees is the need to open the list before a selection can be made.

Instead of opening the list and selecting a value in that list, a user can enter a value directly into the drop-down list box control. As characters are entered, Access attempts to match those characters to items in the list; if a match is found, the list opens with the matching item highlighted. The user presses Enter to accept the highlighted item. If a user enters characters for which no match is found in the list, Access displays an error message saying "The text you entered isn't an item in the list," and rejects the entry.

Creating a Combo Box

A list box and a drop-down list box allow a user to select from a predefined set of values. There are times, though, when a user needs to select from a list of values and also to be able to enter a value that's not in the list. This might be the case, for example, if you provide a list of countries from which a user can select. Although the list could contain the names of most countries, there might well be the need to enter the name of a country that's not in the list. A combo box provides this functionality.

Create a combo box in the manner described previously for generating a drop-down list box. The difference is, in step 2 of the procedure, leave the Limit To List property at its default value of No.

On the Form view of a form, a combo box looks the same as a drop-down list box. The only difference is that Access allows a user to enter a value that's not in the list.

Validating Input Data

As often as possible, you should provide choices from which a user of your application can select, rather than requiring that user to enter data by typing. In many cases, though, that's not possible. If a user is entering information about a person, you can make it possible to select from a list of names if the database is concerned only with a certain population, such as company employees. However, if the user is entering information about customers, there's no way to provide a list from which to choose.

In many cases, you can provide ways of at least partially validating input data before committing that data to your tables. Here are some examples:

- For a field that's used to record the date an order is received, you can check that the entered date isn't later than today.
- For text in a memo field, you can check for possible spelling errors.
- For text that must always have a certain number of characters, such as a Social Security number in the United States, you can verify the number of characters.

- For numeric identifiers, such as a book's ISBN number, in which one number is a check digit, you can verify the validity of the number.

- For number fields for which only a certain range of values is expected, you can verify that an entered value falls within those limits.

Employing validation checks of this type can help prevent data entry errors. You should be careful about how you use them. Anticipate the fact that a value outside the expected limits might be valid in some cases. Give users the ability to override Access's validation checks where this might be necessary.

The remaining pages of this chapter contain some examples of how you can validate entered data.

Validating a Table Field

When you're creating tables, you can specify validation for most types of fields. For example, if you have a table that contains a numeric field, the default value of that field is 0 (zero), unless you've specified a different default value. In many cases, 0 is not an acceptable value. When you create the table, you can specify a Validation Rule property such as >0 (greater than zero), so that Access will only accept a value that's greater than zero for that field. You can also specify a Validation Text property for the field. The text you enter for this property is displayed if the condition specified in the Validation Rule property isn't satisfied.

Likewise, you can validate data entered into Date/Time fields, by stating that only dates within a certain range are acceptable. The following sections provide specific examples of validating data.

NOTE

The values you enter into Validation Rule properties can be either explicit values or calculated values.

Validating Numeric Fields

To create a validation rule for a number field in a table, open the table in Design view, select the field, and enter an expression in the Validation Rule property box. Some examples of rules are

- >0—Only values greater than zero are acceptable.

- <>0—All values except zero are acceptable.

- >0 AND <100—Only values greater than zero and less than 100 are acceptable.

Usually, simple expressions like these are sufficient. However, Access accepts much more complex expressions containing up to 2,048 characters. (Refer to Chapter 15, "Calculating Values and Making Decisions," for additional information about using expressions to create validation rules.)

In addition to the validation rule, enter text in the Validation Text property box for Access to display if a user attempts to enter a noncompliant value. Validation text must not exceed 255 characters.

A validation rule created in this manner operates when data is directly entered into a table, when data is entered into the table from a form bound to the table, and when data is entered as a result of a calculation. Whichever way you use to enter data into a table, the validation text appears in a message box if the entered value doesn't comply with the validation rule.

Validating Text Fields

You can validate text fields in a similar manner to number fields by entering a validation rule expression and validation text.

Suppose you have a field for entering a part number and all part numbers have a certain number of characters. If all part numbers have 12 characters, the validation rule will be

```
Like ????????????
```

In this expression, each question mark represents any single character.

If all part numbers start with the letters PN followed by 10 characters, the validation rule will be

```
Like PN??????????
```

In addition to using a question mark to represent one character, you can use an asterisk to represent any number of characters. If part numbers start with the letters PN and can have any number of subsequent characters, the validation rule will be

```
Like PN*
```

Unlike how you might have used an asterisk as a wild card in the past, you can have characters after the asterisk. For example, if all part numbers start with PN and end with X, Y, or Z, with any number of characters between the first two characters and the final character, the validation rule will be

```
Like PN*X OR LIKE PN*Y OR LIKE PN*Z
```

Validating Date/Time Fields

You can enter a validation rule for a Date/Time field in two ways. Suppose you want to enable the entry of dates only for April of the year 2000. You can enter the validation rule as

```
BETWEEN #4/1/2000# AND #4/30/2000#
```

or

```
>= #4/1/2000# AND <= #4/30/2000#
```

Notice that in both formats, dates must enclosed within # characters. In both cases, the limiting dates are inclusive, although the word "BETWEEN" seems to imply the opposite.

> **TIP**
>
> Even though you must enclose dates in a validation rule within # characters, this isn't required for dates you enter into a table or form.

Validating an Identification Code

Many of the identification codes we use on a daily basis are validated by means of a *check digit*. A check digit is a digit that really isn't part of an identification code; it's calculated from the other digits within the identification code. You can look at an identification code and recalculate the check digit. If the calculated check digit is the same as the check digit in the code, there's a good chance the code is valid.

> **NOTE**
>
> One of the simplest check digits is calculated by counting the number of odd digits in an identification code. Although better than nothing, this does not provide effective validation.

Social Security numbers and credit card numbers are examples of identification codes that make use of check digits. When the user of an Access application has to enter a code of this type, it's good practice to have the application verify the code's authenticity by calculating the check digit and comparing that result with the check digit the user entered.

Making Data Input Fast and Accurate

CHAPTER 6

163

6

MAKING DATA
INPUT FAST AND
ACCURATE

This section explains how to authenticate an identification code, using an International Standard Book Number (ISBN) as an example. As you probably know, an ISBN uniquely identifies every book published since the late 1960s. Every ISBN number consists of ten characters, the first nine of which are always digits, and the last of which (the check digit) is a digit or the letter X. The ISBN number for this book, for example, is 0-672-31894-6.

ISBN numbers are normally printed with the ten characters in four groups, which are separated by hyphens, as shown in the previous paragraph. However, the grouping isn't always the same. Neither is it required to include hyphens. The ISBN number for this book can be printed as 0672318946.

One way to authenticate an ISBN number is to remove any hyphens and then check that the number contains exactly ten characters. Another is to make sure the check digit is correct. I won't go into how a check digit is initially calculated here, but I will explain how you can verify that it is correct. Here's the process:

1. Multiply the first digit of the ISBN number by 10 and save the result.

2. Multiply the second digit of the ISBN number by 9 and save the result.

3. Multiply the third digit of the ISBN number by 8 and save the result.

4. Continue in this manner, multiplying each digit by successively decreasing numbers, until you come to the tenth character. Multiply that digit by 1 and save the result—an X in that position represents the value 10.

5. Add the results of the ten multiplications.

6. Divide the result by 11. If there's no remainder from the division, the check digit is valid.

The next section explains in detail how you can write a VBA procedure that verifies an ISBN. Although what's required might initially seem quite complex, only a few lines of code are required. You can create a similar procedure to verify other types of identification numbers.

Creating a Procedure to Verify an Identification Code

You can prepare to write VBA code that verifies an ISBN number as follows:

1. Create a text box control on a form. Give the control a name such as txtISBN.

2. Select that control and then choose the Event tab in the Property sheet.

3. Click in the AfterUpdate Property box and then click the button containing an ellipsis at the right of that box to display the Choose Builder dialog box.

4. Select Code Builder and choose OK. The Visual Basic Editor (VBE) window appears, as shown in Figure 6.6.

NOTE

AfterUpdate is an event that occurs when you change what's in a control—the txtISBN control in this example—and then move to another control.

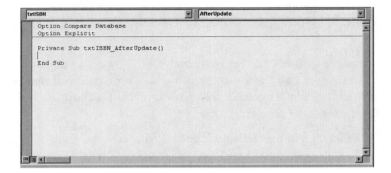

FIGURE 6.6

The Visual Basic Editor window contains the first and last statements of a procedure that runs when a user updates the txtISBN control.

NOTE

The first and last statements of a procedure are known as a *stub*. A procedure of this type is known as an *event procedure* because it runs when an event occurs. In this case, the event occurs when the control is active and the user presses Enter or Tab to move to another control.

Add the comment before the first statement in the stub and add the remaining code between the first and last statements in the stub, as shown in Listing 6.1.

LISTING 6.1 Checking ISBN Validity

```
'Check ISBN validity
Private Sub txtISBN_AfterUpdate()
    Dim strISBN As String          'Temporary copy of ISBN
    Dim intPosition As Integer     'Position of hyphen in ISBN
    Dim intTotal As Integer        'Summation of calculated values
```

Making Data Input Fast and Accurate

165

CHAPTER 6

6

MAKING DATA
INPUT FAST AND
ACCURATE

```
        Dim intPosInISBN As Integer      'Position in ISBN
        Dim intMultiplier As Integer     'ISBN multiplier
        Dim intRemainder As Integer      'Remainder after division

        'Create temporary copy of ISBN
        strISBN = txtISBN
        strISBN = RTrim(strISBN)

        'Remove all hyphens from temporary ISBN
        Do
            intPosition = InStr(strISBN, "-")
            If intPosition <> 0 Then
                strISBN = Left(strISBN, intPosition - 1)
                strISBN = strISBN & Right(strISBN, Len(strISBN - intPosition)
            End If
        Loop Until intPosition = 0

        'Check for correct number of characters
        If Len(strISBN) <> 10 Then
            MsgBox "Incorrect number of characters in ISBN."
            Exit Sub
        End If

        'Calculate validity summation for first 9 digits of ISBN
        intTotal = 0
        intPosInISBN = 1
        intMultiplier = 10
        Do While intMultiplier <> 1
            intTotal = intTotal + Mid(strISBN, intPosInISBN, 1) * intMultiplier
            intPosInISBN = intPosInISBN + 1
            intMultiplier = intMultiplier - 1
        Loop

        'Accommodate condition that 10th character can be "X"
        If Mid(strISBN, 10, 1) = "X" Then
            intTotal = intTotal + 10
        Else
            intTotal = intTotal + Mid(strISBN, 10, 1)
        End If

        'Check validity
        intRemainder = intTotal Mod 11

        If intRemainder <> 0 Then
            MsgBox "Invalid ISBN."
        End If
End Sub
```

> **Note**
>
> If you need to learn, or refresh your memory, about VBA code, refer to Appendix A, "Visual Basic for Applications Primer."

Understanding the Procedure for Checking a Code

You can learn a lot about using VBA to manipulate strings (text) by studying the code explained here. Although Listing 6.1. refers to the specific case of checking the validity of an ISBN, you can use the same technique to check the validity of other identification codes.

The VBA code for checking the validity of an ISBN number starts with a comment that explains the purpose of the procedure. Always include a comment such as this so that anyone looking at your code knows what the procedure is supposed to do.

After the statement that declares the procedure, there's a list of variables used within the procedure. Note these points:

- Each variable is declared on a separate line. This isn't required, but it's good practice.
- Each variable name has a prefix that identifies its data type.
- Each variable is declared with a specific data type. If you don't declare a data type, Access uses the default Variant data type which doesn't use your system resources efficiently.
- Each variable declaration has a comment that explains the variable's use.

It's good practice to declare variables in this manner.

Each section of the code starts with a comment that explains the purpose of that section.

The first section of the code, after the variable declarations, assigns the value of the ISBN code entered on the form to a variable that's subsequently manipulated without affecting the entered value. The statement

```
strISBN = RTrim(strISBN)
```

removes any space characters a user might have entered after the ISBN number. RTrim is an intrinsic (built-in) function in VBA.

The next section of the code

```
Do
    intPosition = InStr(strISBN, "-")
    If intPosition <> 0 Then
        strISBN = Left(strISBN, intPosition - 1)
```

Making Data Input Fast and Accurate

CHAPTER 6

167

6

MAKING DATA
INPUT FAST AND
ACCURATE

```
      strISBN = strISBN & Right(strISBN, Len(strISBN - intPosition)
End If
Loop Until intPosition = 0
```

removes all hyphens from the ISBN the user entered. This is necessary in order to subse-quently verify the number of characters in the ISBN and to process those characters.

The code uses the InStr, Len, Left, and Right intrinsic functions. It also illustrates the use of a Do loop.

The first statement within the Do loop uses the InStr function to locate the first occurrence of a hyphen within the ISBN number. This statement returns the position of the first hyphen as the value of intPosition or, if no hyphen is found, returns 0 (zero).

If a hyphen is found—in which case the value of intPosition is other than zero—the third state-ment reconstructs the ISBN with the first hyphen omitted.

The Do loop is repeated until no hyphens remain in the temporary ISBN.

The next section of the procedure measures the length of the ISBN with the hyphens removed:

```
If Len(strISBN) <> 10 Then
   MsgBox "Incorrect number of characters in ISBN."
   Exit Sub
End If
```

The Len function simply returns the number of characters in a string. If the number of charac-ters is other than ten, a message is displayed and, when the user acknowledges that message, the procedure terminates. There's no point in continuing if an ISBN doesn't have the required ten characters, not counting hyphens.

If the ISBN does have ten characters, the procedure goes on to run an algorithm (mathematical process) that evaluates the validity of the ISBN. The code

```
intTotal = 0
IntPosInISBN = 1
IntMultiplier = 10
Do While IntMultiplier <> 1
   intTotal = intTotal + Mid(strISBN, intPosInISBN, 1) * intMultiplier
   intPosInISBN = intPosInISBN + 1
   intintMultiplier = intMultiplier - 1
Loop
```

runs the algorithm for the first nine characters of an ISBN, multiplying each digit by succes-sively decreasing values, starting with 10, and adding the result of each multiplication to the results of the previous multiplications. The tenth character has to be handled separately because it might be a digit or the character X (representing 10).

The next section of the code takes into account the fact that an X in the tenth position represents 10:

```
If Mid(strISBN, 10, 1) = "X" Then
    intTotal = intTotal + 10
Else
    intTotal = intTotal + Mid(strISBN, 10, 1)
End If
```

If the character in the tenth position isn't X, the character is recognized as a digit.

Finally the procedure uses the MOD operator to divide the value of the intTotal by 11. Then, it examines the result of the MOD operation to see if the remainder of the division is other than zero. If the remainder is other than zero, an error message is displayed.

Although this procedure is fairly complete, it omits error checking. For example, there's no check to verify a user enters only digits in the first nine characters of an ISBN, or digits or X for the tenth character. This subject is covered in Chapter 13.

Formatting Your Data in Forms and Reports

By setting Format properties for controls on forms and reports, you can ensure that data is displayed and printed in a consistent manner, even if users don't enter data consistently. Properly formatted forms and reports are easier for users to work with than forms and reports that aren't properly formatted.

Formatting determines how data is displayed in tables and on forms, and how it's printed in reports; formatting doesn't affect how data is stored in tables. For example, a number field in a table can contain a value such as 2. By setting the Format property, you can control if the value is displayed and printed as 2, 2.0, 2.00, and so on.

Because you normally display data in forms, you should set the Format property within those forms, as described in the following sections. You can set formats in reports in the same manner. An advantage of setting formats in forms and reports, instead of in tables, is that you can display data in specific formats appropriate for those forms, instead of relying on the format in the underlying tables.

You can select from built-in formats and, for most data types, define custom formats.

NOTE

This chapter contains information only about Format properties. Access also has a Format function you can use within VBA code. The Format function enables more flexibility in formatting than is possible with Format properties. Refer to Appendix A for information about the Format function.

Formatting Number Controls on a Form

With a form displayed in Design view, select a number control, and choose the Format tab in the Property sheet. Click near the right end of the Format property box to display the list of built-in formats shown in Figure 6.7 and then select the format you want to use.

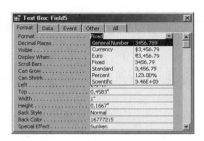

FIGURE 6.7
General Number, the default format, displays a number as entered.

> **NOTE**
>
> The Currency, Fixed, Standard, and Percent formats use the setting selected in the Windows Control Panel for negative amounts and decimal symbols.
>
> The Currency and Fixed formats use the setting selected in the Windows Control Panel for currency symbols.
>
> The Euro format uses the euro symbol for currency, regardless of the setting in the Windows Control Panel.

Instead of using one of the built-in formats, you can construct a custom format. A custom format has one, two, three, or four sections with semicolons separating one section from the next. Each section applies to a specific type of value in the control, as listed in Table 6.1.

TABLE 6.1   Sections in a Custom Number Format

Section	Description
First	Format for positive numbers
Second	Format for negative numbers
Third	Format for zero values
Fourth	Format for Null values

You can use various symbols in each section to create a format definition. These symbols are listed in Table 6.2.

TABLE 6.2 Symbols Used in a Number Format Definition

Symbol	Purpose
. (period)	Decimal separator
, (comma)	Thousands separator
0 (zero)	Digit placeholder (displays a digit or 0)
#	Digit placeholder (displays a digit or nothing)
$	Displays the literal character $
%	Value is multiplied by 100 with a percent sign appended
E- or e-	Scientific notation with minus sign next to negative exponents and nothing next to positive exponents
E+ or e+	Scientific notation with minus sign next to negative exponents and plus sign next to positive exponents

In addition,

- Any characters enclosed within quotation marks are displayed literally.
- Any spaces are displayed literally.
- A character preceded by a backslash is displayed literally.
- You can define a color in any section by including the name of a color enclosed within brackets.

The following is an example of a custom format:

```
$#,##0.00[Green];$#,##0.00[Red];"Zero";"Null"
```

This format displays positive values in green and negative values in red, in each case with two decimal places. Zero values are represented by the word "Zero" and Null values are represented by the word "Null."

TIP

If you're new to formatting controls on a form, the displayed formats might not always appear as you intend. After you've constructed a Format property, experiment with values to make sure they are correctly displayed.

Formatting Text and Memo Controls on a Form

Access offers no built-in formats for text and memo controls. It does provide some capabilities to create custom formats. These can have one, two, or three sections, as listed in Table 6.3.

TABLE 6.3 Sections in a Custom Text or Memo Format

Section	Description
First	Controls containing text
Second	Controls containing zero-length strings
Third	Controls containing Null values

You can use various symbols in each section to create a format definition. These symbols are listed in Table 6.4.

TABLE 6.4 Symbols Used in a Text or Memo Format Definition

Symbol	Purpose
@	Required text character
&	Optional text character
<	All characters in control lowercase
>	All characters in control uppercase

Formatting Date/Time Controls on a Form

With a form displayed in Design view, select a Date/Time control, and choose the Format tab in the Property sheet. Click near the right end of the Format property box to display the list of built-in formats shown in Figure 6.8, and then select the format you want to use.

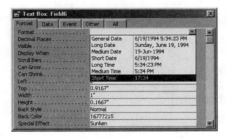

FIGURE 6.8
These seven built-in Date/Time formats are available.

Instead of using a built-in format, you can construct a custom format. A custom format for a Date/Time control always has one section. You can use various symbols to define the format, as listed in Table 6.5.

TABLE 6.5   Symbols Used in a Date/Time Format Definition

Symbol	Purpose
: (colon)	Time separator
/	Date separator
c	Same as General Date built-in format
d	Day of month (one or two digits)
dd	Day of month (always two digits)
ddd	Three-letter abbreviation of day name
dddd	Day name in full
ddddd	Same as Short Date built-in format
dddddd	Same as Long Date built-in format
w	Day of week (1–7)
ww	Week of year (1–52)
m	Month of year (one or two digits)
mm	Month of year (always two digits)
mmm	Three-letter abbreviation of month name
mmmm	Month name in full
q	Quarter of year (one digit)
y	Day of year (1–366)
yy	Last two digits of year
yyyy	Year in full (four digits)
h	Hour of 24-hour day (one or two digits)
hh	Hour of 24-hour day (always two digits)
n	Minute of hour (one or two digits)
nn	Minute of hour (always two digits)
s	Second of hour (one or two digits)
ss	Second of hour (always two digits)
ttttt	Same as Long Time built-in format
AM/PM	Time in 12-hour format with AM or PM appended
am/pm	Time in 12-hour format with am or pm appended
A/P	Time in 12-hour format with A or P appended

Making Data Input Fast and Accurate

CHAPTER 6

173

6

MAKING DATA
INPUT FAST AND
ACCURATE

Symbol	Purpose
a/p	Time in 12-hour format with a or p appended
AMPM	Time in 12-hour format with morning or afternoon characters as defined in the Windows Control Panel

Text within quotation marks is displayed literally. Spaces are also displayed literally.

If today is Friday, April 21, 2000, the format

```
"Today is "dddd
```

displays "Today is Friday".

The format

```
mmmm dd", "yyyy
```

displays "April 21, 2000".

Setting Input Mask Properties for Controls on a Form

The primary purpose of the Input Mask property is to simplify data entry and to control what data can be entered.

TIP

Although the Input Mask property can simplify data input, it might make data input impossible. This property enforces a data format that can be what you want almost all the time, but can prohibit the occasional input of data that doesn't conform to the norm. Before you set an input mask, be sure that mask is appropriate for all data to be entered.

The Input Mask property has some built-in masks for Text and Date/Time controls from which you can choose. It doesn't have built-in masks for other types of controls. You can create custom input masks for most other types of controls.

> **TIP**
>
> If you intend to set an Input Mask property for a control, don't also set a Format property. That's because a Format property always takes precedence over an Input Mask property.

Creating an Input Mask Using the Input Mask Wizard

Here's how to use the Input Mask Wizard:

1. With a form displayed in Design view, select a Text control and choose the Property sheet's Data tab.

2. Click in the Input Mask property box, and then choose the button marked with an ellipsis at its right. Access displays the first Input Mask Wizard window, shown in Figure 6.9.

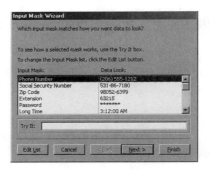

FIGURE 6.9

The Input Mask Wizard offers several input masks and shows examples of their effects.

3. Select one of the available masks, and then click in the Try It box. That box displays the mask as a user will see it in a control on a form. Notice that the positions where characters are to be entered are shown by an underscore as a placeholder character. Enter representative data into the Try It box to see how the mask works.

4. Choose Next > to display the second wizard window, shown in Figure 6.10.

5. If you want to modify the mask, you can do so in the Input Mask box.

6. If you want to change the default placeholder character from an underscore to something else, open the drop-down Placeholder Character list and select one of the available characters.

7. Choose Next to display the final wizard window. Choose Finish to close the wizard and return to the Property sheet that now contains the Input Mask definition.

Making Data Input Fast and Accurate

CHAPTER 6

175

6

MAKING DATA
INPUT FAST AND
ACCURATE

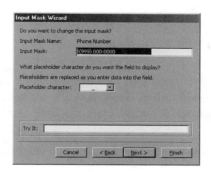

FIGURE 6.10
This window displays the mask as it will appear in the control's Property sheet.

You can add input masks to the wizard. To do so, with the first wizard window, shown in Figure 6.9, displayed, choose Edit List to display the dialog box shown in Figure 6.11.

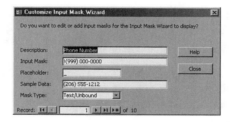

FIGURE 6.11
You can use this dialog box to edit input masks already available in the wizard and to add new masks.

Creating a Custom Input Mask

You can enter a custom input mask definition in the Input Mask box on the Data tab of the Property sheet.

An input mask definition can have one, two, or three sections, as listed in Table 6.6. Semicolons separate one section from the next.

TABLE 6.6   Sections in a Custom Text or Memo Format

Section	Description
First	The body of the input box definition.
Second	Enter 0 if you want literal characters to be saved with entered characters. Enter 1 if you want only entered characters to be saved.

continues

TABLE 6.6 Continued

Section	Description
Third	Enter a placeholder character to be used when the input mask is displayed on a form. You can use any character as a placeholder character. If you want to have a space as a placeholder, enter a space enclosed in quotation marks.

You can construct the input mask within the first section by using the characters listed in Table 6.7.

TABLE 6.7 Characters Used in an Input Mask

Character	Purpose
0	Required digit
9	Optional digit or space
#	Optional digit, space, +, or -
L	Required alphabetic character
?	Optional alphabetic character
A or a	Required alphabetic or numeric character
&	Required character of any type
C	Optional character of any type
. , : ; - /	Decimal placeholder and thousands, date, and time separators
<	All characters lowercase
>	All characters uppercase
!	Display mask from right to left
\	Display next character literally

You can also set the Input Mask property to Password, in which case characters entered into the control are saved literally, but displayed as asterisks.

Characters that don't have a specific meaning, as listed in Table 6.7, are displayed literally.

After you've created an input mask for a control on a form, that mask appears in Form view. A user can enter data by typing over the mask.

You can use the Input Mask Wizard to see examples of what an input mask looks like. Table 6.8 contains some examples of custom input masks.

Making Data Input Fast and Accurate

CHAPTER 6

177

6

MAKING DATA
INPUT FAST AND
ACCURATE

TABLE 6.8 Examples of Input Masks

Input Mask	Description
>L<???????????????????	The first character, which must be alphabetic, is uppercase. The remaining characters (up to 20) are lowercase.
0-&&&&&&&&&-&	This input mask can be used for a book's ISBN number. The first character, which is required and must be numeric, is followed by a hyphen and then nine other characters. The & is used because one of these characters is a hyphen. These characters are followed by a hyphen and then &. The final character in an ISBN code can be a digit or the letter X; that's why it's necessary to use & rather than 0.

Formatting Your Data Programmatically

An input mask is useful if you know, with 100 percent certainty, that for the life of your application specific fields of information will always have certain patterns. Initially, you might think that Social Security numbers in the United States fall into this category, but do they really? Isn't it likely that, within a few years, the population will have grown to the extent that more than nine digits are required for a Social Security number?

Using an input mask can constrict your application so that it can't accept some future requirements. If you're intent on creating a professional application, you should consider writing VBA code that tests input data, rather than relying on Access's input masks.

The details of writing VBA code to test input data is beyond the scope of this book. All I can do here is to draw your attention to the fact that input masks, although initially useful, can lead to problems in the future.

Automatically Updating Data

The preceding pages of this chapter are concerned with adding new data into your application. That's only part of your task. The other part is to maintain already-existing data. By using the information here, you can make your application easier to use.

Data changes! For example, the publisher of this book used to be called "Macmillan Computer Publishing." Now, it's called "Macmillan USA." If you have an application that contains a table listing contacts in that company, you can open each record and manually change the Company field. A better approach is to update records automatically by using an Access Update query.

Here's another example of automating the process of maintaining data. Suppose you have an application that contains information about your clients. One of those clients goes out of business (presumably not because of your efforts). Instead of manually deleting records pertaining to that client, you can use a Delete query to automatically delete those records.

Chapter 4, "Creating Information Out of Data," introduced you to queries in Outlook. That chapter referred only to Select queries that create a recordset based on information in one or more tables. Here, we turn to the subject of Action queries that create new tables and modify the data in existing tables. Access provides the action queries listed in Table 6.9.

TABLE 6.9 Action Queries in Access

Query	Purpose
Append	Adds new records to tables
Delete	Deletes records from tables
Make-table	Creates a new table by using fields in existing tables
Update	Changes values of fields in existing tables

All these action queries are great time savers. After taking only a few seconds to create one of these queries, Access can perform operations that would take a long time if you attempted to perform the same operations manually.

You should already be familiar with working interactively with Action queries. If not, refer to a book such as *Sams Teach Yourself Microsoft Access 2000 in 21 Days*, published by Sams Publishing.

Most of the more advanced material about queries covered in Chapter 4 applies to Action queries as well as to Select queries. In particular, remember that working with the SQL view of a query allows you more flexibility than working only in the QBE grid.

Keeping Users Informed

While you're developing an application, you'll probably be working with relatively small amounts of data. For that reason, almost everything the application does is likely to be very fast. When the application is finished and put to work, it's likely that users will be handling large, perhaps very large, amounts of data. Operations that seemed almost instantaneous in the development stage might incur considerable delays in the real world.

Another probable difference between your development environment and users' environments concerns location of data. In the development environment, you'll likely have the application and all files it uses on your own computer. In contrast, people using your application might be accessing files external to their own computers by way of a network. This can be another reason why users experience delays that you don't see.

Although you'll endeavor to make your application run as fast as possible, the fact is that some operations take a noticeable amount of time. When this is the case, don't leave users in the dark, possibly thinking their computers have hung up. One of the simplest solutions is to display the hourglass pointer on the screen while the application is doing something that might not otherwise be obvious. Another is to display a message in the status bar at the bottom of a window.

Displaying the Hourglass Pointer

You can use a macro or VBA procedure to display the hourglass pointer and subsequently restore the normal pointer.

To create a macro that displays the hourglass pointer,

1. Choose Macros in the Objects bar of the Database window, and then choose New.
2. Select the Hourglass action.
3. In the Action Arguments pane, accept the default Hourglass On argument of Yes.

Add subsequent actions within the same macro to control the operations that are likely to take some time. Then create an action to restore the normal pointer. This is the same as the first action, with the exception of choosing No as the argument in step 3.

To display the hourglass pointer using VBA code, include this statement in a procedure:

```
DoCmd.Hourglass True
```

A similar statement

```
DoCmd.Hourglass False
```

restores the normal pointer.

Code between these two statements controls whatever operations are likely to take some amount of time, during which you want the hourglass to be displayed.

Displaying a Message in the Status Bar

You can use the status bar to display various messages to users. The problem with doing this is that the status bar doesn't grab users' attention. Users have to know to keep an eye on the status bar.

You probably already know you can use the status bar to display information about a control that's active on a form or report. Do that by entering the text to be displayed in the control's Status Bar Text property. By writing VBA code, you can display a message in the status bar while an operation is occurring.

Use the SysCmd function to set and clear text within the status bar. Because this is a function, it returns a value. Even though you probably won't use that value, you have to declare a variable into which the function returns a value. In the declarations section of the procedure in which you want to use the SysCmd function, write a declaration statement such as

```
Dim varReturn As Variant
```

Then, at the place within the procedure where you want the message to appear in the status bar, write a statement such as

```
varReturn = SysCmd(SYSCMD_SETSTATUS, "Sorting - please wait")
```

When you run the procedure, the text within the quotation marks appears in the status bar.

After statements that initiate the time-consuming operations, use the SysCmd function again to clear the text in the status bar by writing

```
varReturn = SysCmd(SYSCMD_SETSTATUS, " ")
```

NOTE

VBA doesn't allow a zero-length string as a SysCmd argument. You must enclose at least one space character between the quotation marks.

Displaying a Progress Meter in the Status Bar

Displaying an hourglass or a message in the status bar is better than doing nothing and possibly leading users to believe their computers are hung up. But the problem still remains that users don't really know if anything is happening. A better solution is to display a progress meter in the status bar, something you've probably seen in applications you've used. A progress meter displays a series of dots growing from the left to the right to indicate the progress of an operation.

TIP

By including progress meters in your application, you provide useful feedback to users and give your application a professional appearance.

This section describes how to include a progress meter in an application. The Book application on the CD-ROM that accompanies this book contains a working example.

Suppose you're writing a procedure that performs some operations on all the records in a recordset and you know there are, say, 10,000 records in the recordset.

At the place in the procedure just before the statements that perform operations on records, write the statement

```
varReturn = SysCmd(SYSCMD_INITMETER, "Starting sort", 10000)
```

to display the initial progress meter.

Now, write a control structure that progresses through the records. Each iteration through the control structure contains a statement that updates the progress meter. A typical control structure of this type is

```
For intRecNum = 1 to 10000
   varReturn = SysCmd(SYSCMD_UPDATEMETER, intRecNum)
   'statements here do something to the current record
   'move to next record
Next intRecNum
```

After the operation is complete, use the statement

```
varReturn = SysCmd(SYSCMD_SETSTATUS, " ")
```

to clear the status bar.

Displaying Messages to Users

You can use macros or VBA statements to display messages to users. The purpose of these messages is to let users know what is going on and to give those users some choices. Access displays these messages in response to some event happening within your application.

For example, you might have a button on a form that, when clicked, does something a user might not really want to do, such as deleting some records. If you provide a button like this, the event procedure that runs when the button is clicked can display a message box that describes the consequences and asks whether the user really wants to do that. The user can choose Yes to continue or No to not proceed with the deletion.

Using Macros to Display Messages

To display a message box within a series of actions in a macro, select the MsgBox action. The Action Arguments section of the Macro window contains the four arguments shown in Figure 6.12.

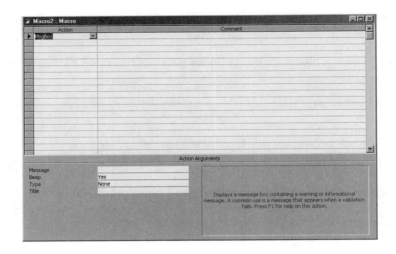

FIGURE 6.12

A MsgBox action has four arguments.

Enter arguments as follows:

- For the Message argument, enter the text to be displayed in the message box.
- For the Beep box, accept the default No if you don't want a beep to sound when the message is displayed. Click near the right end of the Beep box and choose Yes if you do want a beep to sound.
- Click the right end of the Type box to display a list of icons that can be displayed in a message box. Select the icon you want.
- Enter the text you want to display in the message box's title bar in the Title box.

Using VBA Code to Display Messages

To use VBA code to display a message box, include a MsgBox statement or function within a procedure. Use a MsgBox statement if you want to display information only; use a MsgBox function if you want a user to make a choice that affects something your application does.

Here's an example of a simple MsgBox statement:

```
MsgBox "Your disk is nearly full"
```

When your application executes that statement, Access displays a message box containing the words in that statement, with a single OK button. Program execution pauses until the user clicks the button.

Making Data Input Fast and Accurate

CHAPTER 6

183

6
MAKING DATA
INPUT FAST AND
ACCURATE

To use a MsgBox function, you must declare a variable into which the function can return a value, such as

```
Dim intMsgBox As Integer
```

The variable is declared as an integer because that's the data type a MsgBox function returns.

Here's an example, of a simple MsgBox function:

```
intMsgBox = MsgBox("Your disk is nearly full")
```

A user sees no difference whether a MsgBox statement or a MsgBox function executes. The significant difference is how an executing procedure responds. In the case of a statement, execution merely continues. In the case of a function, VBA assigns a value to the intMsgBox variable and then execution continues.

To see the value of the function form, look more closely at its options.

This is an example of a more useful MsgBox function:

```
intMsgBox = msgBox("Do you want to continue?", vbYesNo + vbQuestion, _
"Library Application")
```

NOTE

You'll often find that VBA statements contain more characters than can be displayed in the width of your screen. VBA doesn't have any problem with that, but you'd probably prefer to be able to see complete statements without having to scroll horizontally.

You can format a VBA statement so that it's displayed or printed in any number of lines by using a continuation character sequence—a space followed by an underscore—within the statement, as illustrated in the preceding statement. You can use this character sequence wherever a space occurs within a VBA statement, other than within a string.

When this function executes, VBA displays a message box such as the one shown in Figure 6.13.

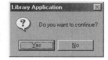

FIGURE 6.13

This message box gives the user a choice.

The preceding example of a message box function has three arguments:

- The message to be displayed within the box
- The buttons to be displayed at the bottom of the box and the icon to be displayed at the left
- The words to be displayed in the box's title bar

The first argument is required. Subsequent arguments are optional.

NOTE

MsgBox functions can have two additional arguments that identify a help file and a context within that file. These arguments aren't covered in this book.

A MsgBox function's second argument can contain the various intrinsic (built-in) constants listed in Tables 6.10–6.15.

TABLE 6.10   Button Constants for Use in a MsgBox Function

Constant	Description
vbOKOnly	Display OK button only
vbOKCancel	Display OK and Cancel buttons
vbAbortRetryIgnore	Display Abort, Retry, and Ignore buttons
vbYesNoCancel	Display Yes, No, and Cancel buttons
vbYesNo	Display Yes and No buttons
vbRetryCancel	Display Retry and Cancel buttons

TABLE 6.11   Icon Constants for Use in a MsgBox Function

Constant	Description
vbCritical	Display Critical Message icon
vbQuestion	Display Query icon
vbExclamation	Display Warning icon
vbInformation	Display Information icon

TABLE 6.12   Button Default Constants for Use in a MsgBox Function

Constant	Description
vbDefaultButton1	First button is default
vbDefaultButton2	Second button is default
vbDefaultButton3	Third button is default
vbDefaultButton4	Fourth button is default

TABLE 6.13   Modal Constants for Use in a MsgBox Function

Constant	Description
vbApplicationModal	User must click a button in the message box before continuing work in the current application
vbSystemModal	User must click a button in the message box before continuing work in any application

TABLE 6.14   Help Constants for Use in a MsgBox Function

Constant	Description
vbMsgBoxHelpButton	Display Help button
vbMsgBoxSetForeground	Set message box as the foreground window

TABLE 6.15   Direction Constant for Use in a MsgBox Function

Constant	Description
vbMsgBoxRtlReading	Text displayed from right to left (used for Arabic and Hebrew languages)

You can include only one constant from each of the six tables. Separate one constant from the next with a plus symbol (+).

Returning a Value from the MsgBox Function

The value returned by the function is determined by which button a user clicks. Table 6.16 lists all possible values.

TABLE 6.16   Values Returned by the MsgBox Function

Button	Value
OK	1
Cancel	2
Abort	3
Retry	4
Ignore	5
Yes	6
No	7

Subsequent statements in your code can use the returned value to control what happens next.

Controlling Text in a Message Box

VBA enables you to have as many as 1,024 characters displayed in a message box, more than you're likely to need. If you want to display more than five or six words, you'll probably want to control where line breaks occur. You can do that by dividing the message in separate parts for each line and inserting a line-break constant (vbCrLf) between the parts. For example,

```
"This will permanently delete data." & vbCrLf & "Proceed anyway?"
```

> **NOTE**
>
> Notice that the first line to be displayed is enclosed within quotation marks, as is the second line. The & operator is necessary to concatenate the first line with the line-break constant and to concatenate that constant with the second line. See Chapter 14, "Making Access Applications Easy to Use," for more information about operators.

You can divide the message to be displayed in as many lines as necessary in this manner.

Making Your VBA Code Readable

When you're writing VBA code in the Visual Basic Editor (VBE), there's no limit to the length of lines. However, your screen limits the number of characters you can see at one time. Subsequently, when you print your code, your printer wraps lines within the available margins, making the code difficult to read. For these reasons, it's good practice to limit the length of lines to what can be seen on your screen and to what can be printed in one line.

Making Data Input Fast and Accurate

CHAPTER 6

187

6

MAKING DATA
INPUT FAST AND
ACCURATE

MsgBox functions often require more characters than can be displayed on the screen or printed in one line. One way to overcome this problem is to declare variables for each of the arguments, assign values to those variables, and then use the variables within the MsgBox statement, as the example, in Listing 6.2 shows.

LISTING 6.2   Displaying a Message Box

```
Dim strMessage As String
Dim intSetting As Integer
Dim strTitle As String
...
strMessage = "Do you want to continue?"
intSetting = vbYesNo + vbQuestion
strTitle = "Library Application"

intMsgBox = msgBox(strMessage, intSetting, strTitle)
```

This technique almost always solves the problem as far as the setting and title arguments are concerned. The message argument, though, might still be too long. You can divide a message into as many lines in your VBA code as necessary, as shown in this example:

```
strMessage = "If you choose to continue, this application" & vbCrLf
strMessage = strMessage & "will permanently delete records" & vbCrLf
strMessage = strMessage & "from your disk." & vbCrLf & vbCrLf
strMessage = strMessage & "Do you want to continue?"
```

You can build long messages in this manner without having excessive line lengths.

Using Variables Within a Message

You can mix text and variables within the message argument and within the title argument. Suppose code elsewhere sets the variable strUser to the current user's name. Then, the message argument might contain

```
"Current user is: " & strUser
```

Or, perhaps previous code has set a variable such as intRecord to the number of records in a table. Then the message argument could contain

```
"Number of records is: " & intRecord
```

Notice that the last example mixes data types within a statement. The part enclosed within quotation marks is a string, what the MsgBox function expects for the first argument. However, the intRecord variable is a number. You might expect Access to display an error message when you mix data types in this manner. However, Access is smart enough to automatically convert the data type of the variable to string, so the function runs without a problem.

> **TIP**
>
> By no means can you rely on Access to automatically convert data types in all situations. In general, you should be careful not to mix data types. VBA contains functions that convert one data type to another. For example, to explicitly convert the intRecord to the string data type, use the CStr function, as in CStr(intRecord).

Using Temporary Message Boxes As a Debugging Aid

One of the techniques you can use to debug VBA code is to insert temporary MsgBox statements that display the values of one or more variables. After you've debugged the code, remove these temporary statements.

Summary

You can, in many cases, avoid the necessity for entering data by providing default values for table fields. As a result, users have to enter data only when a value is other than the default.

As far as possible, let users make selections instead of having them enter values. You can use check boxes for fields that can accept only one of two different values. Try groups of option buttons when there is a small number of possibilities from which to choose. For fields that can have one of many values, show those options in a list box or drop-down list box.

Where it's not possible to allow users to choose entry values, you can use validation rules to compare entered values with specific requirements. Using a book's ISBN number as an example, you can use VBA code to verify identification numbers that contain a check digit.

You can include format prototypes in forms and reports so that data is displayed and printed in a standard format, even if that data is stored in a different format. You can also provide input masks that force users to enter data in specific formats.

A valuable mechanism you can build into your applications is a means of informing people about the progress of various processes, especially when those people must wait for Access to complete an operation. Although this is not a matter of data entry, an hourglass icon or status bar message can positively affect data entry by preventing people from thinking the program has frozen, thereby causing them to either repeat actions or close and restart the program. In fact, a good rule of thumb is to give people as much positive feedback as possible so that they never wonder whether a button was clicked or a menu item was chosen, or become otherwise frustrated.

Enhancing Your Application with Pictures and Other Graphics

CHAPTER

7

IN THIS CHAPTER

You can use graphics to enhance your Access-based applications by using graphics objects. Make sure, though, that these objects really enhance the application, not just decorate it. The principal uses of graphics on forms and reports are to increase legibility, establish a corporate or organizational identity, visually provide extra information, and simplify the presentation of information.

This chapter deals principally with the first three points because they apply equally to forms and reports. Charts and graphs are principally used in reports, so that subject is covered in Chapter 8, "Creating Informative Reports."

Using Lines and Boxes as Design Elements

The printed forms you see every day use lines and boxes to focus your attention. Lines separate one part of a form from another; boxes enclose related items on forms.

The forms you create in Access can do the same. You can use the Line control to draw straight lines that horizontally, vertically, or even diagonally divide forms into separate parts. You can also use the Rectangle control to group related controls on a form.

NOTE

This section talks specifically about forms. The techniques described here apply also to reports.

Figure 7.1 shows an example of a form that makes use of lines and boxes as design elements. The form also includes a logo, but we'll ignore the logo for now.

The form in Figure 7.1 has a line under the form's title to provide emphasis. Various controls on the form are enclosed within boxes to give visual clues that they're related. After you've created controls on a form, you can draw lines and rectangles to enhance the appearance of that form.

TIP

Lines are almost always horizontal or vertical. You can, though, draw lines with any orientation.

You can create rectangles only with horizontal and vertical borders. You can create shapes bordered by lines in any orientation simply by creating multiple adjoining lines.

Access provides no direct way to create other shapes such as circles and ellipses. You can create these shapes using application such as PhotoDraw, and import them into Access forms and reports. However, you shouldn't do that unless you have a compelling reason to include special shapes because the use of imported shapes slows down your application.

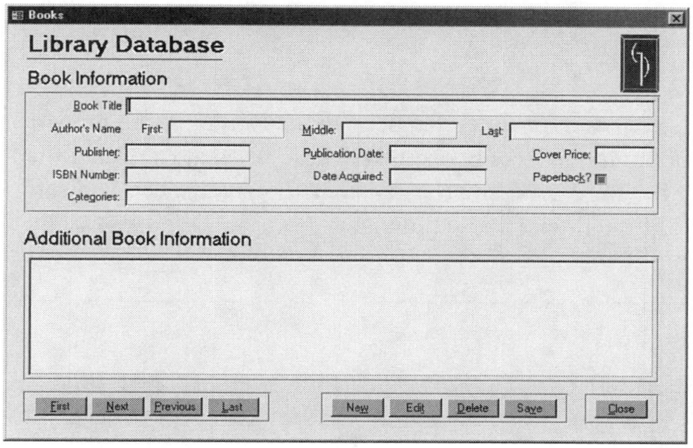

FIGURE 7.1

This screen illustrates the use of one line, several boxes, and a logo.

To add lines and rectangles to a form, display the form in Design view. If necessary, choose View, Toolbox to display the toolbox. Proceed as follows:

1. Click the Line icon (the left icon in the bottom row of the toolbox) or the Rectangle icon (the center icon in the bottom row of the toolbox).

NOTE

The icons might be in different positions if you have resized your toolbox.

2. Move the pointer onto the position on the form where you want the line to begin or where you want the top-left corner of the rectangle to be.

3. Press the mouse button and drag to where you want the line to end or to where you want the bottom-right corner of the rectangle to be. Release the mouse button.

After you've done that, if the line or rectangle isn't exactly in the right place, you can drag the handles to adjust the control's position. Alternatively, with the Property sheet's Format tab displayed, you can change values for the Left, Top, Width, and Height properties.

TIP

For a horizontal line, the Height property should be 0 (zero). For a vertical line, the Width property should be 0 (zero).

By default, Access creates a line or rectangle with the Border Width property of Hairline. A hairline is a line or border that's only one pixel wide. To create a thicker line, you can select a different value for the Border Width property in the Property sheet. You can't specify a width other than the widths the Property sheet offers.

TIP

The Hairline width for lines and rectangles in a form displayed on your screen is always visible. However, if you're creating a form or report to be printed, you might find that some printers can't print such a thin line. It's usually best to change the Border Width property to a value greater than Hairline for forms and reports to be printed.

Incorporating a Logo To Give Forms and Reports an Identity

Including a small logo, such as that shown in Figure 7.1, in forms and reports helps to give them an identity and gives them a more professional appearance. Notice the adjective "small" in the preceding sentence; make a logo large enough to be noticed, but not so large that it is distracting.

Preparing to Insert Graphics Files

A logo or other graphic image has to exist as a separate file before you can place it in a form or report. Access can insert files in the formats listed in Table 7.1.

TABLE 7.1   Graphic Files Access Can Import

Graphic File Type	Filename Extension
Enhanced Metafile	.emf
Icon	.ico
Windows Bitmap	.bmp, .rle, or .dib
Windows Metafile	.wmf

If the file you want to insert is in one of these formats, there's no preparation you need to do.

By installing filters that work with Office 2000 applications, you can give Access the ability to insert graphics files in the formats listed in Table 7.2.

> **NOTE**
>
> Microsoft supplies the filters for the graphics formats listed in Table 7.2 with the Professional and Premier editions of Office 2000. These filters are not supplied with other editions of Office 2000, nor are they supplied with the standalone version of Access 2000.

TABLE 7.2   Graphics Files That Can Be Imported with the Help of Filters

Graphic File Type	Filename Extension
Computer Graphics Metafile	.cgm
CorelDRAW	.cdr
Encapsulated PostScript	.eps
Flashpix	.fpx
Graphic Interchange Format	.gif
Hanako	.jsh, .jah, .jbh
JPEG File Interchange Format	.jpg
Kodak Photo CD	.pcd
Macintosh PICT	.pct
PC Paintbrush	.pcx
Portable Network Graphics	.png
Tagged Image File Format	.tif
WordPerfect Graphics	.wpg
X-Bitmap	.xbm

If the file you want to insert is in one of the formats listed in Table 7.2, and you already have the appropriate filter installed, again no preparation is required. To install a filter, run the Office 2000 setup program.

> **TIP**
>
> Online Help for Access doesn't provide information about individual graphics file formats. You can find detailed information about graphics file types in the online Help for Word 2000. Open the "Working with Graphics and Drawing Objects" book and then open the topic "Graphics File Types Word Can Use" to see a list of graphics file types. Double-click any file type to get detailed information about it.

Despite the long list of graphics file formats supported by Access and other Office 2000 applications, you might want to import a graphics file that isn't in the list. You can do that by converting the format of your file from its native format to a format supported by Office. You can perform the conversion:

- By importing the file into a graphics application and then exporting from that application
- By using a graphics conversion utility

Many graphics applications (some free, others very inexpensive) are available on the Web from such sites as http://www.tucows.com and http://home.cnet.com. Both sites have graphics utilities you can download.

> **TIP**
>
> Although the concept of graphics file conversion is simple, the process of creating a conversion utility can be quite complex. Each conversion utility has its own characteristics. You might have to try several utilities to find one that satisfies your needs.

Inserting a Graphics File

A form's toolbox contains icons for three controls you can use as containers for graphics objects. These three controls are in the third row from the bottom of the toolbox. Of these, the Image control is the one to use to place a logo or similar graphic on a form.

To place a graphic on a form:

1. Click the Image icon in the toolbox, point on the form, and drag to create a rectangle on the form in the approximate position and of the approximate size that you want the graphic to be.

> **NOTE**
>
> A rectangle on a form that is a container for a graphics object is known as a *bounding box*.

2. When you release the mouse button, Access displays the Insert Picture dialog box. Navigate to the folder that contains the graphic you want to insert, and then choose OK. At this stage, most likely only a small part of the graphic image is displayed in the bounding box.

3. In the Property sheet, open the Format tab and click at the right end of the Size Mode property box to display a list of three values, as shown in Figure 7.2.

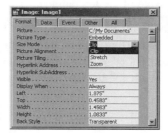

FIGURE 7.2
Table 7.3 explains the three available Size Mode property values.

4. Select Zoom as the Size Mode property value. Access displays the whole of the graphic within the bounding box.

5. Adjust the position and size of the graphic in the normal way.

TABLE 7.3   The Image Control's Size Mode Property Values

Property Value	Explanation
Clip	Access displays the graphic at its original size. If the graphic is larger than the bounding box, only the part of the graphic that fits within the bounding box is visible.
Stretch	Access adjusts the size of the graphic to exactly fill the bounding box. Unless the aspect ratio of the bounding box happens to be exactly the same as the aspect ratio of the original graphic, the graphic is distorted.
Zoom	Access adjusts the size of the graphic without changing its aspect ratio so that the entire graphic fits within the bounding box. This is the property value you'll almost always use.

Step 5 of the preceding procedure is okay as far as it goes, but there's more you need to know. Suppose you want to have a logo at the top-right of your form, as shown in Figure 7.1. Suppose, also, that the bounding box you create on the form is wider than required. In that case, with the Size Mode property set to Zoom, the imported image is horizontally centered in the bounding box. Having gone so far, you want to horizontally align the logo so that its right edge is vertically above the right edge of the Rectangle control just below it.

If you select the Image control and (with Shift pressed) select the Rectangle control, and then choose Format, move the pointer onto Align, and choose Right, the right edge of the bounding box that contains the logo (not the right edge of the logo itself) is aligned with the right edge of the Rectangle control. That's not what you want.

To correct this problem

1. Select the Image control.
2. In the Property sheet, set the Picture Alignment property to Top Right or Bottom Right. In this example, the assumption is that the graphic image is within a wider-than-necessary Image control, so that graphic image fills the height of the Image control.

The result of setting the Picture Alignment property in this way is that the graphic image moves to the right side of the Image control. Now, you can align the Image control with the Rectangle control below it to align the graphics image with the Rectangle control.

> **TIP**
>
> The preceding paragraphs describe a specific case of aligning a graphic image within an Image control with other controls on a form. You can use the same ideas to align images that are vertically centered within an Image control, and to align images horizontally with other controls on a form.

Using a Form or Report to Display Pictures from Records

The previous section described how you can include an identifying logo or graphic that always appears on a form or report. You can also have a form display, or a report print, a graphic that's a different illustration for each record in a table. The following items are examples:

- A form that displays information about people can include a photograph of each person. The Northwind database that Microsoft supplies with Access contains examples of this.

- A form that displays information about items in a catalog can include photographs or line drawings of each item in the catalog.

- A form that displays information about books can include a reproduction of each book's cover. Go to a Web site such as http://www.amazon.com to see examples of this.

Deciding When to Use Graphics

Like much in our lives, if you can have it and it's free with no penalties, go for it! In reality, much of what's attractive isn't free and does impose penalties, so think carefully before you go for it.

A form that displays a graphic image of the information displayed is certainly attractive. It enhances users' interest in the form and gives your form a professional appearance. These advantages are not free and do impose penalties:

- Each graphic image occupies file space. The larger and more complex the image is, the more file space it occupies.

- Because graphic images tend to consist of many bytes of information, displaying them slows your application. Users might be annoyed by having to wait for graphic images to be displayed.

- Before a graphic image can be incorporated in your application, it must first be created. The process of creating graphic images requires considerable time and effort.

Having considered these points, if you decide graphic images are worthwhile, plan to create those images so that they are saved in the smallest possible files. There's no point, for example, in saving a graphic in a multi-megabyte TIFF file if the graphic is to be displayed in your application as a small image.

Saving Graphics Objects in Access Tables

To save a graphics object in a table, that table must have a field with OLE Object as its data type. This field can used to save any other type of binary file in addition to a graphics object. Create a field of this type in a table to which a form is bound.

Creating a Control to Display a Graphics Object on a Form

In the form on which you want to show the graphics object displayed in Design view

1. Click the Bound Object Frame icon in the toolbox, and then drag to create a bounding box (a Bound Object Frame control) for the graphics object.

2. With the Bound Object Frame control selected, choose the Property sheet's Data tab, open the list of possible values for the Control Source property, and select the field that contains the graphics object.

3. By default, the Size Mode property of the Bound Object Frame is set to Clip. You should usually change that property to Zoom so that the displayed object's size is automatically adjusted to fill either the width or the height of the control. See Table 7.3 earlier in this chapter for an explanation of the Size Mode property.

Now, you can use that form to display graphics objects already in the underlying table, and also to enter new graphics objects into the table.

To display existing graphics objects, simply choose the Form view of the form. The graphics objects in each record of the underlying table appear with the other data.

Inserting a New Graphics Object

To use a form to insert a new graphics object into a table:

1. In the form's Form view, select the Bound Object Frame control, and then choose Insert, Object to display the dialog box shown in Figure 7.3.

2. Assuming you want to insert an already-existing object, choose Create From File to modify the previously displayed dialog box, as shown in Figure 7.4.

3. If you know the full path name of the file to be inserted, enter that name in the Create From File box. Otherwise, choose Browse to locate the file.

4. Choose OK to insert the file. The graphic appears within the Bound Object Frame control and is saved in the underlying table.

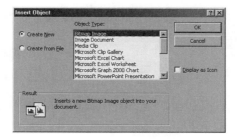

FIGURE 7.3

You can choose to select an already-existing object or to create a new object.

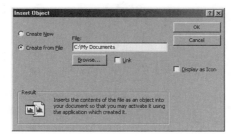

FIGURE 7.4

Use this dialog box to locate the file to be inserted.

If, in step 2, you choose Create New, you can select an application that's available on your computer to create and subsequently save a new graphics object.

Summary

You can enhance your applications by displaying graphics in forms and printing graphics in reports. The line and rectangle icons available in the toolbox can be used to create design elements on forms and reports to help present information in a way that's easy to understand. You can also use a graphics object created in another application, such as a logo, in forms and reports.

Access tables can include graphics objects, such as photographs of people and drawings of items in a price list. These graphics objects can be displayed in forms and printed in reports.

Finding and Printing Information

IN THIS PART

Creating Informative Reports

IN THIS CHAPTER

Reports are what Access uses to provide information based on the data stored in your tables. Unlike forms, which are intended to be viewed on users' screens, reports are principally intended to be printed, although they can be viewed on screens.

Even though there's been a lot of talk about the paperless office during the last few years, the fact is that many people like to have printed information. For that reason, few if any of the applications you create will be complete without the ability to print information. You'll usually provide buttons on forms that people using your applications can click to choose the report they want to print.

Most reports consist of many pages, sometimes hundreds of pages. You can design reports that provide detailed information based on the data in tables, together with summaries of various sections. Reports can include charts and graphs based on the data.

You can, of course, create any number of reports based on the same data. For example, you can use the data in the Book database that accompanies this book to print separate reports listing books by title, author, publisher, order of acquisition date, and so on. This chapter shows you how to create reports and how to enhance their appearance and performance.

Understanding Access Reporting

Access offers three principal means of creating reports:

- AutoReport—This provides a quick way to create a report based on a single table or query.
- Report Wizard—This wizard steps you through the process of generating custom reports, although with some limitations.
- Manually Designing a Report—This method gives you the flexibility to design highly customized reports in which you can take advantage of VBA programming techniques.

This chapter assumes you are familiar with using AutoReport and the Report Wizard to create reports and concentrates almost entirely on manual methods.

TIP

A useful time-saver is to use the Report Wizard to design a preliminary report and subsequently enhance that report using manual methods.

In addition to the three methods of generating reports listed previously, you can also use a third-party report writing utility, such as Crystal Reports from Seagate Software, to gain even more flexibility in report generation than is available in Access. (For detailed information about Crystal Reports, go to the Web site `http://www.seagatesoftware.com`.)

Creating a Report

The initial steps involved in creating a report manually are similar to those you use to create a form. The steps that follow refer specifically to creating a report that lists books by category and alphabetically by title within each category.

Basing a Report on a Query

Start by creating a query on which to base the report. The query should contain those fields, and only those fields, that will appear in the report. There's no need to set any fields to be sorted because you set the sort order later when you use the query to create a report.

Instead of always creating individual fields, create combination fields in the query where those are required in the report. For example, you probably want the report to show authors' names in the format *Brown, John* (*last name, first name*) in a single field, rather than have authors' first, middle, and last names in separate fields. To do this, create a combination field in the QBE grid, such as

```
strAuthor: [tblBook].[strLname] & ", " & [tblBook].[strFname]
```

Refer to the section "Creating a Query Based on a Single Table" in Chapter 4, "Creating Information Out of Data," if you need to be reminded about the QBE grid. If you plan your report to have other combination fields, create those fields in the query. In the example used here, the publisher and imprint fields are combined using the IIf function, as explained in the section "Combining Table Fields into Recordset Fields" in Chapter 4.

After you've created a query that contains all the fields needed in the report, you're ready to start work on the report.

8

CREATING
INFORMATIVE
REPORTS

TIP

To create a report containing only certain records in your tables, set appropriate criteria in your query.

Designing the Report

Follow these steps to create the report design:

1. With the Database window displayed, choose Reports in the Objects bar, select Create Report in Design View, and choose New to display the New Report dialog box.

2. In the New Report dialog box, select the query on which the report is to be based. Access displays a blank report in Design view, as shown in Figure 8.1.

> **NOTE**
>
> Previous advice about using a naming convention to name tables and queries meaningfully makes selecting the correct query easy.

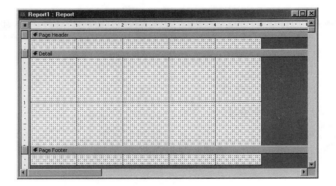

FIGURE 8.1

Unlike the initial Design view of a form, the initial Design view of a report includes a page header and a page footer section.

The Detail section in the Design view of a report is where the information from your tables appears.

The Page Header and Page Footer sections shown in Figure 8.1 appear at the top and bottom, respectively, of every page of the report. You can use these sections to display such information as the name of the report and page numbers. If you don't want these sections to appear, choose View, Page Header/Footer. Choose the same command to subsequently restore the page header and footer.

A report can also have a Report Header and Report Footer section. The Report Header section appears at the top of the first page of the report; the Report Footer section appears at the end of the last page of the report. Display or hide these sections by choosing View, Report Header/Footer. Figure 8.2 shows a report in Design view with these sections displayed.

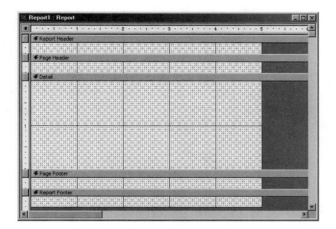

FIGURE 8.2
You can use the Report Header and Report Footer sections for information to be printed at the beginning and end of a report.

Within the Detail section of a report, you can group information based on fields in the query on which the report is based. In this example, recall the objective is to list books grouped by category. To group books by category, choose View, Sorting and Grouping to display the dialog box shown in Figure 8.3.

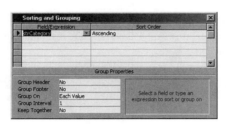

FIGURE 8.3
The dialog box is shown here with grouping on the strCategory field enabled.

When the Sorting and Grouping dialog box first appears, nothing is selected in the Field/Expression column. Open the drop-down list in that column and select the field on which you want to group the report. You can change the default Ascending sort order to Descending.

After you've selected the first grouping field, you can select others in sequence. For example, if within each category group you want to sort by book title, you can select strTitle (the book title field) in the second row of the Sorting and Grouping dialog box.

> **TIP**
>
> Instead of grouping on specific fields in the query to which the report is bound, you can enter an expression as a basis for grouping. An expression can group on the basis of a combination of fields.

Having fields or expressions in the Field/Expression column of the Sorting and Grouping dialog box controls the order in which the report lists data from your query. The order defined here overrides any order that's defined for the same fields in the QBE grid.

If, in addition to controlling data order, you want to group that data, you can create group headers and group footers. Unlike report and page headers and footers, group headers and footers can be enabled independently. Most often, you'll probably want group headers but not group footers. To enable a group header, select the appropriate field in the Field/Expression column in the Sorting and Grouping dialog box, and then, in the Group Properties section of the dialog box, change Group Header from No to Yes. After you do that, the Design view of the report is similar to that shown in Figure 8.4. In that figure, the name in the group header is the name of the field you selected as the basis for grouping in the Sorting and Grouping dialog box.

This example shows only one group header. You can create as many group headers as are needed for the design of a specific report.

After creating the appropriate sections for the report, you place controls in those sections in much the same way as you place controls on a form. The following sections summarize how this is done.

Adjusting the Size of the Report

By default, Access proposes to create a report suitable for printing in portrait orientation on paper that's 8-1/2 inches wide by 11 inches high, and with top, bottom, left, and right margins of one inch. Before placing fields on the report in Design view, you should set up the page you intend to use.

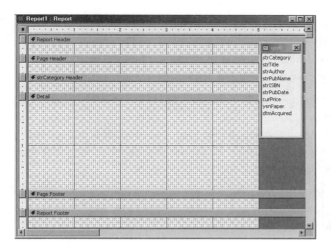

FIGURE 8.4
This is a Design view of a report with a group header (strCategory Header) *displayed.*

To do so, choose File, Page Setup to display the Page Setup dialog box. Use the Margins tab to set the margins, the Page tab to set the orientation and paper size, and, if your report has columns, the Columns tab to set column dimensions.

After completing the page setup, adjust the width of the report in Design view. For example, if the paper is 8-1/2 inches wide and you're using one-inch margins, set the width of the report to no more than 6-1/2 inches.

TIP

If the width of a report is larger than the space between the margins on the printed page, Access prints each intended page on two or more sheets of paper. Avoid this problem by taking care not to make the report wider than the width of the page, minus the width of the left and right margins.

Set the width of the report in the report's Property sheet. Make sure the report's Property sheet, not a Property sheet for a section or control, is displayed. Choose the Format tab, and set the Width property to the appropriate value. The width you set for the report determines the width of all the sections of the report.

Placing Fields in the Detail Section

Drag fields from the Field List, shown at the right in Figure 8.4, onto the Details section of the report. Include all the fields you want to be printed in the report with the exception of any fields that should appear in Group Header sections.

Assuming you want all the labels in the report to be printed in the same font, select all the labels and then set their font properties in the Property sheet. Likewise, select all the controls in which field values will appear, and set their font properties in the Property sheet. If you want to change the text in any of the labels, do so now. Make sure that all the controls are properly named according to your naming convention.

Now, adjust the size of the controls and drag those controls to position them on the report. Minimize the height of controls and the vertical space between them so that your printed report doesn't occupy more pages than necessary.

TIP

You can use the same shortcut methods to align controls on a report as you do on a form. Refer to "Positioning the Buttons" in Chapter 5, "Making Your Forms Smarter."

If you move a control so that any part of it extends beyond the right edge of the report, Access automatically moves the right edge farther to the right, resulting in a report that might be too wide to print on a single sheet. Watch for this possible problem and be prepared to reset the report width to its intended value.

If you think any graphics elements such as lines and boxes will add to the appearance of your report without cluttering it, you can add them as described in "Using Lines and Boxes as Design Elements" in Chapter 7, "Enhancing Your Application with Pictures and Other Graphics." Inserting a horizontal line immediately under the lowest controls in the Design view often helps to separate information about one item from the next. Make the border width of all lines and boxes at least one point to make sure they will be printed properly.

Finally, adjust the height of the Detail section so that there's just enough space for the controls.

Placing Fields in the Group Header Section

If you have a Group Header section, drag the appropriate field from the Field List into that section. You'll probably want to make the font in this section a little larger and, perhaps, bold to make it stand out. Adjust the positions of the two controls. Make sure the height of these controls is sufficient to display the descenders of all characters in those controls (the tails of such characters as g, j, p, q, and y).

Depending on your preference, you might insert a horizontal line under the text in the Group header. If you used one point for the border size in the Detail section, use two points for the border size here. Make sure the vertical position of the horizontal line doesn't cut off the descenders in characters in the group header.

Adjust the height of the Group Header section so that it's only just enough for the text and line. Drag other fields from the Field List into the Detail section of the report and adjust the position of those fields.

At this stage, the Design view of your report will look something like the one shown in Figure 8.5.

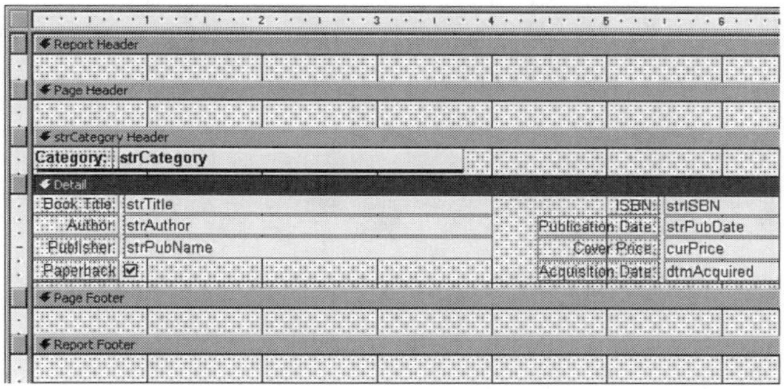

FIGURE 8.5
This is the Design view of a typical report with the Detail and Group Header sections complete.

Checking the Design

Before going any further, check your design by using it to display real data. Choose View, Layout Preview to display the report as it will appear when printed, as shown in Figure 8.6.

> **TIP**
>
> Layout Preview provides an accurate display of a report's layout. It doesn't necessarily display data from your tables and queries accurately. If you want to verify how a report prints your data, use Print Preview instead of Layout Preview.
>
> You can magnify the Layout Preview display by choosing View, moving the pointer onto Zoom, and selecting a percentage magnification.

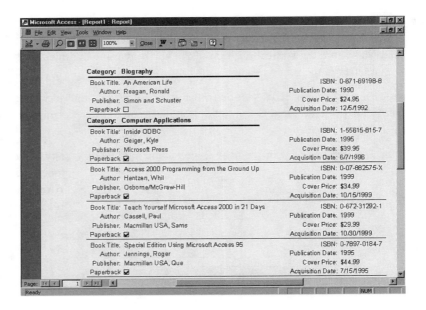

FIGURE 8.6

This is a typical Layout Preview.

Some of the things to look for in the Layout Preview are

- Are there any spelling mistakes in your labels? It's much easier to see spelling mistakes in the Layout Preview than in the Design view. Correct any spelling mistakes.

- Have you allowed enough horizontal space for the text that's to be displayed from your tables? Some fields in your tables always require almost exactly the same space—this is easy to check. Other fields, such as a field that contains a book's title, might require a different amount of space for each record. The next section contains some suggestions about dealing with this problem.

- Have you allowed enough vertical space for text? Look for text that contains lowercase characters with descenders (g, j, p, q, and y in most fonts). Make sure the descenders aren't cut off. If they are cut off, you'll have to return to the Design view and increase the height of the controls.

- Are there any alignment problems? If so, go back to the Design view and correct them.

Accommodating Long Fields

As mentioned in the preceding section, sometimes you face the problem that there isn't enough horizontal space in a report to display all the text in some fields. If you do nothing about that, Access simply truncates the text, giving distinctly unprofessional results.

If the problem is consistent for all records, the solution is to redesign the layout to allow more horizontal space for the troublesome field. This could happen, for example, if the space you've allowed for a date is insufficient. A minor layout change can solve the problem.

However, if the problem is with a control that contains characters from a field that can have any number of characters, it usually doesn't make sense to make this control wide enough for the longest field you have now. The problem with that approach is that you might need an even longer field tomorrow.

Access provides a very neat solution to this problem—the Can Grow property, which is most often used for Text Box controls on reports. By default, the value of this property is No, in which case it has no effect. If, in the Property sheet, you set this property to Yes, the height of the control automatically grows to provide as much space as is necessary to contain the text in the control.

You should make it a habit to set the Can Grow property to Yes for all controls on a report that might contain more text than there is space for in the normal control width. In the case of a report that contains information about books, for example, you should set the Can Grow property to Yes for the controls that contain such information as a book title, author's name, and publisher's name.

When one or more controls on a report have the Can Grow property set to Yes and, in the case of a specific record, those controls do increase in height to accommodate text, Access increases the vertical space available for the information about that record.

Placing Fields in the Report and Page Headers and Footers

You can use the Report Headers and Footers sections for information you want to have printed at the beginning and end of a report. Similarly, you can use the Page Headers and Footers sections for information you want to have printed at the top and bottom of each page of a report. In each of these sections, you can include various controls.

The Report Header section typical contains a Label control, in which you set the Caption property to provide a title for the report. In this section, you can also include a Text Box control, in which you can set the Control Source property to call the Date function. This will display the date the report is printed. Enter the Date function in the format

```
=Date()
```

to return the system date. After you do that, each report shows the date the report was printed in the report header.

If appropriate, you can place similar controls in the Report Footer section.

You might want the Report Header and Report Footer sections to be printed on separate pages of the report. You can do so by setting the Force New Page property in the Property sheet. By default, this property is set to None. To print the Report Header section on a page by itself, set this property to After Section. To print the Report Footer section on a separate page, set this property to Before Section.

The Page Header and Page Footer sections are used for information you want to appear at the top and bottom of every page of the report. Either of these sections typically contains the name of the report and the page number. To display the name of the report, place a Label control in the section and set the control's Caption property to the name of the report. To display the page number, place a Text Box control in the section and set the control's Control Source property to display the report's Page and Pages properties

```
="Page " & [Page] & " of " & [Pages]
```

so that the current page number and the total number of pages in the report is printed on every page.

NOTE

The Page property contains the current page number while the report is being printed. The Pages property contains the total number of pages in the report.

The final Design view of the report described in the preceding pages is illustrated in Figure 8.7.

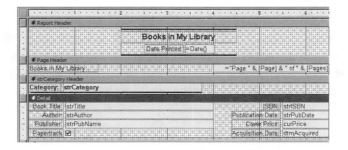

FIGURE 8.7

This Design view shows a report with the Report Header, Page Header, Group Header, and Detail sections complete.

Keeping a Group Together

By default, Access creates page breaks whenever printing reaches the bottom of a page of paper. This can result, for example, in a Group Header appearing at the bottom of one page and the detailed information about that group starting at the top of the next page. You can set the Keep Together property to control this behavior.

The Keep Together property for a group can have these values:

- No—The default. Page breaks occur at the bottom of each printed page of paper.
- Whole Group—Prints the Group Header and as much as possible of the Detail section on the same page of paper.
- With First Detail—Prints the Group Header on a page only if there is room on that page of paper for the first Detail record.

Keeping a Record Together

By default, Access doesn't attempt to keep information about a record together on a page. You can use the Keep Together property in the Detail section to control this behavior.

The Keep Together property for a Detail section can have these values:

- No—The default. Page breaks can occur within a record.
- Yes—If there's not enough space for a complete record on the current page of paper, Access starts the record on the next page.

Printing Column Headings

Reports can be used for many different purposes in addition to those illustrated so far in this chapter. You can see examples of various types of reports in the Northwind database that Microsoft supplies with Access.

Unlike the Books report, several of the Northwind reports, such as the Sales By Year report, present numerical information in columns. For this type of report, it's useful to have headings printed above the columns. You can do this by placing Label controls in the Group Header section above the Detail section, as shown in Figure 8.8.

Counting Records in a Report

A report can show the number of records in the entire report and also the number of records within each group.

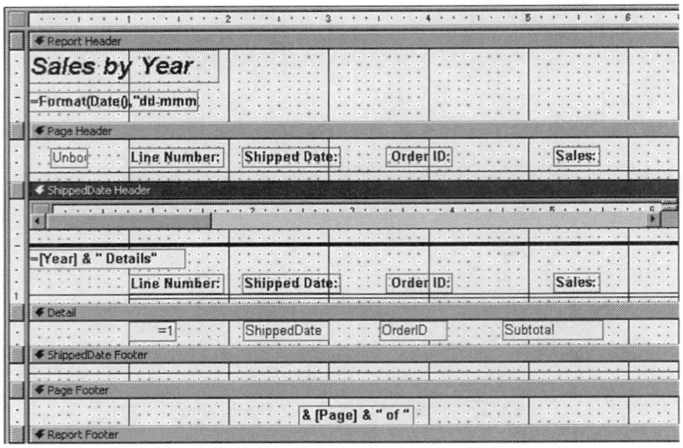

Figure 8.8

This Northwind report illustrates the use of labels for column headings in a Group Header (ShippedDate Header) section.

To print the number of records in an entire report based on the Book database

1. In the Report Header or Report Footer section, place a Text Box control.

2. Change the Label's Caption property to display text such as Total Number of Books in This Report.

3. In the Text Box control's Control Source property, set the value to =Count(*).

Note

The Text Box control uses the Count function to count the number of records in the report.

Display the report in Layout Preview to see the effect of the Count function.

Printing the number of records in each group is less straightforward. It involves creating an invisible control within the Detail section. Follow these steps:

1. Place a Text Box control anywhere within the Detail section of the report. It doesn't matter where you place the control because you'll subsequently hide it.

2. Set the Name property of the Text Box control to a unique name such as txtRecordCount.

3. Set the Control Source property of the Text Box control to =1

4. Set the Running Sum property of the Text Box control to Over Group.

5. Set the Visible property of the Text Box control to No. Although you set the Visible property to No, the control is still visible in Design view—it's not visible in Layout Preview or when the form is printed.

6. Choose View, Sorting and Grouping to display the Sorting and Grouping dialog box. Select the name of the group (such as strCategory) and set that group's Group Footer property to Yes to display the group footer.

7. Place a Text Box control in the Group Footer section.

8. Set the Control Source property of the Text Box control in the Group Footer section to =txtRecordCount (referring to the name of the Text Box control in the Detail section that you set in Step 2).

Display the report in Layout Preview to see the effect of counting records in each group.

Summing Values in a Report

You can sum values within an entire report and also within individual groups. The following procedure shows how to calculate the total cover price of books listed in a report and to print that total in the Report Footer section:

1. Place a Text Box control in the Report Footer section and provide a suitable caption for the associated Label control.

2. Set the Control Source property of the Text Box control to =Sum([curPrice]). This assumes individual records have a control named curPrice that contains the cover price of each book.

3. Set the Format property of the Text Box control to Currency.

When you display the report in Layout Preview, you'll see the total of the cover prices in the Report Footer section.

You can use the same technique to display the total cover price within each group. The only difference is that you place the Text Box control in which the total is displayed in the Group Footer section.

After you made these additions, the Design view of the report will be similar to the one shown in Figure 8.9.

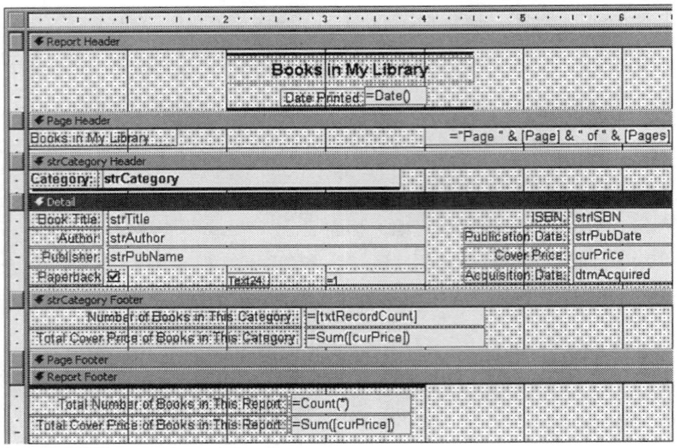

Figure 8.9
This is the final Design view of the report described in the previous sections.

Enhancing Reports with Graphics

The preceding sections of this chapter contain several suggestions for using horizontal lines in reports to enhance their legibility. You can also outline specific parts of a report by using the Rectangle control and by inserting other graphic elements. As always, be careful to use graphic elements only to enhance a report; make sure your graphic elements don't create clutter that makes a report confusing. The information about adding graphics elements to forms in Chapter 7 applies equally to reports.

Reports that deal with financial and other numeric data usually show that data in tabular form. Although they provide the information people need to know, tables don't do a very good job of conveying the meaning of that data. To solve that problem, Access makes it relatively easy to supplement those tables with graphs and charts. You should take advantage of this to help the people who receive your reports to understand the significance of the information your reports provide.

Like other graphics elements, graphs and charts can be unbound or bound to records. An unbound graph or chart usually appears just once on a single-page report. A bound graph or chart illustrates data separately for individual records. The following sections deal first with an example of an unbound chart and then with an example of a bound chart.

Because a lot of numerical data is required to illustrate creation of graphs and charts, the following sections make use of some of the data in the Northwind application supplied with Access.

Like other reports, a report that contains charts is based on a query, so the first thing to do is to create a query.

Creating a Query on Which to Base an Unbound Chart

Start by displaying the Database window for the Northwind application. Proceed as follows:

1. In the Database window, choose Queries in the Objects bar, and then choose New to create a new query.
2. Add the Categories, Order Details, Orders, and Products tables to the query.
3. Drag the CategoryName field from the Categories table into the first column of the QBE grid.
4. Insert the following text into the second column of the QBE grid:

```
Amount: CCur([Order Details].[UnitPrice]*[Order Details].[Quantity]*
➡(1 - [Order Details].[Discount]))
```

NOTE

The second column of the QBE grid now represents the total value of items in a category. Notice the use of the CCur function to change the data type to Currency.

5. Drag the ShippedDate field from the Orders table to the third column of the QBE grid and select Ascending in the Sort row.
6. Add the criterion

```
Between #1/1/1997# And #12/31/1997#
```

to the ShippedDate column.
7. Save the query with a name such as qryChart.

The final QBE grid is shown in Figure 8.10.

8

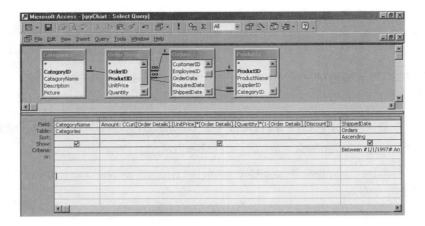

FIGURE 8.10

This is the QBE grid that forms the basis of a chart.

Creating the Chart

The Chart Wizard in Access makes it easy to create a variety of different charts. The following steps illustrate the use of the Chart Wizard to create a line chart:

1. In the Database window's Objects bar, select Reports and then choose New. In the New Report dialog box, select Chart Wizard. Open the drop-down list of tables and queries and select the query you created in the preceding section. Choose OK. Access displays the Chart Wizard's first window.

2. Click the >> button to copy the three available fields into the Fields for Chart list.

3. Choose Next > to display the second wizard window, as shown in Figure 8.11.

4. This example creates a line chart, so select the third icon in the third row, and then choose Next > to display the third wizard window.

NOTE

The right part of the third wizard window lists the fields to be used to create the charts. The wizard initially proposes to use one of these fields for the vertical axis, one for the horizontal axis, and the other for the chart legend, as shown in the left part of the window. The wizard's proposal is probably not what you want. The following steps show how to change the wizard's proposal.

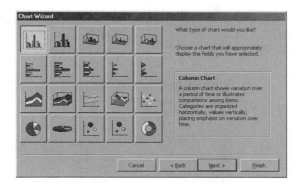

FIGURE 8.11
Select the type of chart you want to create in this window.

5. Drag CategoryName from the right part of the window to the legend position in the left part of the window.

6. Drag ShippedDate from the right part of the window to the horizontal axis position in the left part of the window.

TIP

At any time while you're working in this window, you can click Preview Chart at the top left to check your work.

---

7. Double-click ShippedDate in the horizontal axis position to open the Group dialog box, in which you can select the interval for the horizontal axis. You can select various intervals ranging from Year to Minute. In this case, select Month.

NOTE

In the Group dialog box, you can also define a range of dates. By default, the range corresponds to the range of values in the query. You can select a smaller range within the range of values in the query.

---

8. Choose Next > to display the fourth wizard window. In this window enter a title for your chart, and then choose Finish. Access displays a preliminary version of the chart, as shown in Figure 8.12.

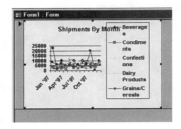

FIGURE 8.12
Access initially displays a small version of the graph in Form view.

9. Switch to the Design view of the graph and select the graph. The Property sheet's title bar shows that the graph is in an Unbound Object Frame control.

10. In the Property sheet's Format tab, increase the width of the Unbound Object Frame control to six inches and increase the height to four inches so that you can subsequently enlarge the chart. Set the Border Width property to four points.

11. In the Property sheet's Data tab, make sure the Enabled property is set to Yes and the Locked property is set to No.

12. Display the Form's Property sheet. Set the Scroll Bars property to Neither; set the Record Selectors property to No; set the Navigation Buttons property to No.

13. Save the form with a name such as frmMonthlySales.

Although you now have a chart based on data in your tables, that chart probably isn't displayed in the way you want. You can't enhance the chart directly within Access. However, you can use Graph 2000, an application supplied with Office, to manipulate the chart.

Enhancing the Chart

The chart is embedded in an Unbound Object Frame control, as you saw in the preceding section. You can use in-place editing to edit the chart using Graph 2000.

NOTE

If you installed Office in the default locations, Graph 2000 should be in your C:\Program Files\Microsoft Office\Office folder.

To edit the chart,

1. Open the form you created in the preceding section using Form view.
2. Double-click the chart to activate Graph 2000 as shown in Figure 8.13.

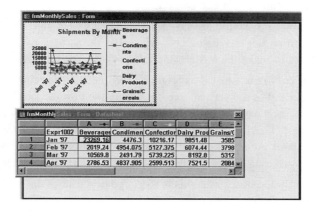

FIGURE 8.13

The diagonally hashed border around the chart indicates it's open for in-place editing. The datasheet displays the values on which the chart is based.

NOTE

When the chart is open for in-place editing, the menu bar and the menus it contains change to those applicable to Graph 2000. Similarly, the toolbars displayed provide access to Graph 2000 functionality.

3. Close the datasheet so that you have more working space.
4. Drag the handle in the middle of the chart's right border to the right to almost fill the width of the Unbound Object Frame control. Drag the handle in the middle of the chart's bottom border down to almost fill the height of the control.

TIP

The next four steps deal with changing the formatting of the chart. The choices available are very similar to those in Excel, with which you're probably already familiar.

5. If you want to change the format of the chart title, double-click the title to display the Format Chart Title dialog box, which has three tabs. Use the Patterns tab to do such things as creating a border for the title and choosing a background color for it. Use the Font tab to change the title's font, font style, font size, and color. Use the Alignment tab to change the title's alignment and orientation.

6. You probably want to make the legend somewhat smaller. Double-click within the legend to display the Format Legend dialog box, which has the same three tabs as the Format Chart dialog box. To make the legend smaller, choose a smaller font in the Font tab.

7. The values adjacent to the vertical axis will be formatted as currency. Double-click one of the values adjacent to the vertical axis to display the Format Axis dialog box, which contains five tabs. You can use the Patterns, Font, and Alignment tabs in the manner described in Step 5. Use the Number tab to display a list of number formats and select Currency. By default, Access proposes to show two decimal places; change this to display no decimal places. You can use the Scale tab to modify the vertical axis scale.

8. The text adjacent to the horizontal axis is too large of a font to display all the month names. Double-click any of the text to display the Format Axis dialog box, which has the tabs described in Step 7. Use the Font tab to select a smaller font size.

9. Click anywhere in the form region outside the hashed chart border to deactivate Graph 2000.

After making changes such as those described in the preceding steps, the chart looks like the one in Figure 8.14.

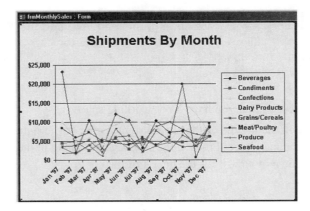

FIGURE 8.14

The legend at the right identifies each line in the chart by color.

> **TIP**
>
> Access automatically assigns different colors to each of the lines in the chart. You can use Graph 2000 to change the colors of those lines. With Graph 2000 activated, double-click a line in the chart to display the Format Data Series dialog box. Use the Patterns tab in that dialog box to select a color for the line. Repeat this for each line in the chart.
>
> Having different colored lines is fine if the chart is to be printed on a color printer. If some people won't be using a color printer, use the Format Data Series dialog box to select a different style (solid, dashed, dotted, and so on) for each line.

Changing the Chart Type

After you've gone through all the work of creating a chart, you might decide a different type of chart would display the data more meaningfully. You can use Graph 2000 to change from one type of chart to another. Here's how:

1. With the chart displayed in Form view, double-click the chart to activate Graph 2000.
2. Choose Chart, Chart Type to display the dialog box shown in Figure 8.15.

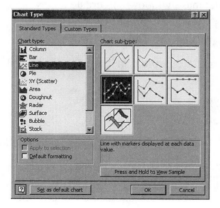

FIGURE 8.15
You can use this dialog box to select among many chart types.

3. Select a primary type of chart in the Chart Type list at the left. Access displays several chart sub-types at the right.

4. Select the chart sub-type icon from the Chart Sub-Type section in the right side of the dialog box.

5. Choose OK to see the data displayed by the new chart type.

Creating a Crosstab Query for a Chart

The Chart Wizard generates a behind-the-scenes Crosstab query in order to create a chart. As you saw in the preceding sections, you don't necessarily need to know about that Crosstab query. However, in some circumstances you need to take charge by creating your own Crosstab query. This is the case, for example, if you want to create a bound chart, as described subsequently in this chapter.

> **Note**
>
> See "Summarizing Data with Crosstab Queries" in Chapter 4, if you need detailed information about Crosstab queries.

The following steps show how you can base an unbound chart on your own Crosstab query:

1. Open the Northwind database window and create a new query based on the query qryChart you previously created.

2. Choose Query, Crosstab Query.

3. Drag the CategoryName field into the first column of the QBE grid. In the Field row, change the name to

   `Categories:CategoryName`

   In the Crosstab row, select Row Heading.

4. Drag the ShippedDate field to the second column in the QBE grid. Replace the name in the title row with

   `ShipDate:Format([ShippedDate], "mmm")`

   so that three-character month abbreviations are used. In the Crosstab row, select Column Heading.

5. Drag the Amount field to the third column of the QBE grid. Change the Total row to Sum. Change the Crosstab cell to Value.

6. Click an unoccupied place in the upper part of the Query window, then open the Query Property sheet. In the Property sheet, enter three-character month abbreviations in month order into the Column Headings property as

   `Jan,Feb,Mar,Apr,May,Jun,Jul,Aug,Sep,Oct,Nov,Dec`

> **NOTE**
>
> Refer to "Summarizing Data with Crosstab Queries" in Chapter 4 for information about using this technique to display months in calendar order. If you don't enter month abbreviations into the Column Headings property in this way, the query displays months in alphabetic order.

7. Save the query as qrySalesByCategory.

8. Display the Datasheet view of the query. You will see tabular results as shown in Figure 8.16.

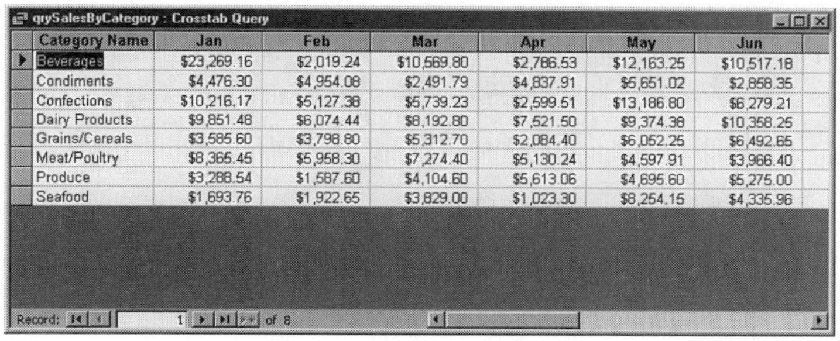

FIGURE 8.16
This is part of the Datasheet view of the Crosstab query.

Having constructed your own Crosstab query, you can now apply that query to the chart you previously created.

1. Open the form frmMonthlySales that contains the chart you previously created. The form will be open in Form view. Select the chart.

2. In the Data tab of the Property sheet, open the Row Source drop-down list and select qrySalesByCategory, the Crosstab query you just created. At this point, the chart lists months in the legend and shows category names for the horizontal axis.

3. Double-click the chart to activate Graph 2000. Choose Data, Series in Rows. Now, the chart shows months on the horizontal axis, as shown previously in Figure 8.16.

Creating Bound Charts

You can bind a chart to a query so that the chart represents data in only one record in a recordset at a time. The example in this section bases a chart on the recordset created by the Crosstab query described in the preceding section.

1. Open the form that contains the unbound chart you previously created. Select Design view and open the form's Property sheet.

2. In the Data tab, open the Record Source drop-down list and select the Crosstab query you created in the previous section. Now, the form is bound to the Crosstab query.

3. In the Property sheet's Format tab, set the Navigation Buttons property to Yes.

4. Click an unoccupied place on the chart to display the Unbound Object Frame's Property sheet. Select the Data tab.

5. Make sure the Row Source property is set to the Crosstab query (qrySalesByCategory).

6. Enter the value Categories for the Link Child Fields and Link Master Fields properties. This links the current record to the appropriate row of the Crosstab query.

7. Choose View, Form View to redisplay the form. The form now contains the chart with a single line, as shown in Figure 8.17.

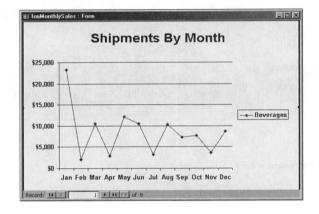

FIGURE 8.17
This chart shows monthly sales for a single category.

You can click the navigation buttons below the chart to show a line chart for each category separately.

A line chart such as this one with only a single line doesn't need a legend but can benefit by having a subtitle to name each category. You can easily modify the chart to accomplish this, as follows:

1. With the chart displayed in Form view, double-click the chart to activate Graph 2000.

2. Drag the legend from its position at the right of the chart to just below the chart's title.

3. With the legend selected, choose Format, Selected Legend to display the Format Legend dialog box. In the Border section of the dialog box, choose None to remove the border.

Combining Reports

You can combine two or more reports so that they appear as a single report. When you do this, one report is the master report; the other reports are *subreports*, sometimes known as *child reports*. You can link a subreport to a master report so that the information displayed in the subreport depends on what's displayed in the master report. As an alternative, you can create a master report that contains two or more unrelated subreports.

You can see how subreports work by following this straightforward example that's based on the Book application on the CD-ROM that accompanies this book. The example uses two reports:

- A report that prints information about books, without any information about publishers. This is the main report.
- A report that prints information about publishers, without any information about books. This is the subreport.

The subreport is placed within the Detail section of the main report and is linked to the main report. The printed report contains all the information about each book that's in the main report together with all the information about the book's publisher that's in the linked subreport.

Follow these steps to create the linked report and subreport:

1. Create a query that contains whichever fields in the book table you want to have in the main report. The query must contain the lngPublisherID field that refers to a publisher record, even though this field isn't printed in the report. Give the query a name such as qryBookOnly.

2. Create a query that contains whichever fields in the publisher table you want to have in the subreport. The query must contain the lngPubID field that indexes publisher records. Give the query a name such as qryPublisherOnly.

3. Create a report based on the qryBookOnly query, placing whichever fields you want to have printed in that report. You don't need to include the lngPublisherID field. Give the report a name such as rptBookOnly. This will be the main report.

4. Create a report based on the qryPublisherOnly query, placing whichever fields you want to have printed in that report. You don't need to include the lngPubID field. Give the report a name such as rptPublisherOnly. This will be the subreport.

5. Display the rptBookOnly report in Design view. Press F11 to display the database window. Select Reports in the Objects bar.

6. Drag the rptPublisherOnly report from the database window onto the main report. The rprPublisherOnly report becomes the subreport.

7. With the subreport selected, open the Property sheet and select the Data tab. The Property sheet's title bar tells you you're looking at the properties of a subform or subreport.

8

CREATING
INFORMATIVE
REPORTS

8. Click near the right end of the Link Child Field property box, and then click the button that appears at the right of that box to display the dialog box shown in Figure 8.18.

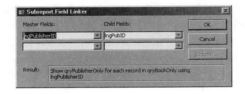

Figure 8.18

This dialog box is shown after you've selected linking fields.

9. Open the top drop-down list under Master Fields to display a list of fields in the query on which the main report is based. Select lngPublisherID, the field that references a publisher.

10. Open the top drop-down list under Child Fields to display a list of fields in the query on which the subreport is based. Select lngPubID, the field that indexes publishers.

11. Choose OK to close the dialog box, and then display the combined main report and subreport in Form view.

You will see information from the first book record and also information about the publisher of that book. You can click the navigation buttons to move to information about other books, each time seeing information about that book's publisher.

After following through this description of creating a subreport, you might find it beneficial to look at some examples of the same technique in the Northwind database.

Improving Report Performance

The performance of a report is a measure of how well it provides the information that people need, and how quickly it provides that information. Here are some suggestions you can use to improve the performance of your reports:

- Make sure that your reports provide exactly the information people need. Avoid creating reports that simply dump all the data in your tables. Instead, design individual reports, each of which provides exactly the information that specific people need.

- Base reports on queries, rather than directly on tables. Make sure those queries contain only the fields required by a report, and make sure those queries are optimized. (Refer to the section "Making Your Queries Run Faster" in Chapter 4 for additional suggestions for optimizing queries.)

- Minimize the number of controls on a report.
- Don't use OLE controls unless you really have to.
- Replaced all unbound object frames that contain graphics with image controls.
- Don't overlap controls on a report.
- Use graphics elements in reports only when they those elements provide useful information. Make graphics objects as small as reasonable. Unless you plan to print reports in color, use only black-and-white graphics.
- Index all fields used for sorting and grouping.
- Use only essential sorting and grouping expressions and make those that are essential as simple as possible.
- Don't use expressions as the basis for sorting and grouping, unless it's essential to do so.
- Index all fields in a subreport that are linked to the main report. Also, index all subreport fields used for establishing criteria.
- Regularly compact your database and defragment the disk that contains your database.

Evaluate the performance of reports using tables that contain realistic data. Reports that seem to have high performance when evaluated with a small set of data have reduced performance when working with the large number of records that users might have. Also, evaluate the performance on a computer that is typical of the computers your users have. The instantaneous performance you see on your high-powered development computer might be reduced to a crawl on the previous-generation computers users might have.

Summary

Before you start designing an Access application, be sure that you thoroughly understand what information people who will use that application need it to provide, particularly the reports they need to print.

Designing a report to be printed has much in common with designing a form to be displayed. You design a report by placing controls on the report's Design view and either directly binding those controls to data in tables or, preferably, indirectly binding those controls to tables by way of queries. As you'll see later in this book, Access enables you to use VBA code to gain comprehensive control over what's printed in your reports.

Pay particular attention to the size of paper on which your reports will be printed. Make sure that each report fits within the margins of that paper.

Reports don't have to contain just text. You can make your reports more meaningful by including charts that illustrate what the information means. The Chart Wizard in Access makes it easy to create many different kinds of charts based on data in your tables, and to include those charts in reports.

Always remember, the purpose of a database application is not to store data; it's to convert raw data into useful information. If your Access application saves data in a way you can easily use to create useful reports, you've achieved your purpose. If, on the other hand, you have difficulty in creating useful reports, you need to rethink the way you're saving data. That's what the rest of this book is about.

Finding Records in a Database

IN THIS CHAPTER

Chapter 8, "Creating Informative Reports," showed how you can use Access to print various kinds of reports that provide a lot of organized information. You'll also want to be able to provide a means whereby people who use your application can find specific information quickly and easily. That's what this chapter is about.

The section "Finding Records in the Datasheet View" in Chapter 4, "Creating Information Out of Data," showed how you can find a specific record in a table or in a recordset created by a query. This chapter shows how to add command buttons on a form to navigate from one record to another, and create combo boxes that make it easy to find records that contain specific information.

This chapter also takes the opportunity to show how Access creates Visual Basic for Applications (VBA) code automatically. The chapter explains that code so that you can modify it where necessary and begin to be prepared to write your own VBA code from scratch.

Displaying Records Consecutively on a Form

You're probably already familiar with using navigation buttons at the bottom of a form to select the first and last records in a recordset and to move to the next or previous record. If you're creating an application for widespread use, you should consider replacing the navigation buttons with buttons on the form itself. This is because many users aren't familiar with navigation buttons and find them somewhat confusing.

As you'll see in the next few sections, creating your own buttons to move among records is quite easy to do because Access does most of the work for you.

Creating Navigation Buttons on a Form

Start by creating a sample form that contains a few fields from a query. The example here assumes you have created a query based on the tblBook table, such as the form shown in Figure 9.1.

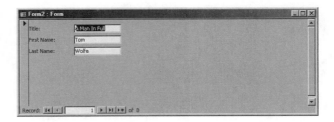

FIGURE 9.1

This sample form contains only three fields that display data.

Proceed as follows:

1. In the Format tab of the form's Property sheet, set the Record Selectors and Navigation Buttons properties to No. After you've created your own buttons, you don't need record selectors or navigation buttons.

2. In the toolbox, click the Control Wizards icon so that it appears to be pressed.

3. Click the Command Button icon and then click the approximate position on the form where you want to place a command button. Access displays the first Command Button Wizard window, shown in Figure 9.2.

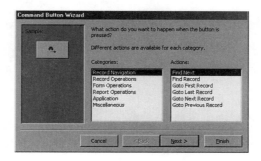

FIGURE 9.2
Use this wizard window to select what you want the command button to do.

4. Accept the default selection of Record Navigation in the Categories list on the left and select Goto First Record in the Actions list on the right. Choose Next > to display the second wizard window.

5. Use this window to define what's to be shown on the button's face. Select the Text option button and accept the default text First Record as the button's caption. Choose Next > to display the third wizard window.

6. Enter a name, such as cmdFirst, by which VBA can refer to your button. This name is consistent with the naming convention introduced in Chapter 3, "Storing Your Data Efficiently." Choose Finish to close the wizard.

After completing these steps, you have one command button on the form. Repeat steps 2 through 6 three times to create three more buttons. In steps 4, 5, and 6, choose or enter the following values:

Button	Action	Caption	Name
1	Goto First Record	First Record	cmdFirst
2	Goto Next Record	Next Record	cmdNext

continues

Button	Action	Caption	Name
3	Goto Previous	Previous Record	cmdPrevious Record
4	Goto Last Record	Last Record	cmdLast

After you've done that, the form should be similar to the one shown in Figure 9.3.

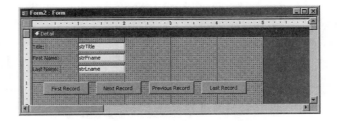

FIGURE 9.3

This is the form with four command buttons.

NOTE

If necessary, use the techniques described in the section "Positioning the Buttons" in Chapter 5, "Making Your Forms Smarter," to adjust the positions of the buttons.

Using the Command Buttons

To see the command buttons in action, switch to Form view. The form should open displaying the first record in the recordset. Click the Next Record button; the form should display the next record. Try the other buttons; you should be able to navigate among the records by clicking the various buttons.

Understanding How the Buttons Work

When you used the Command Button Wizard to create the buttons, Access created VBA code within the form. Actually, Access created four VBA event procedures, each of which runs when you click one of the buttons.

To see the VBA code Access created, switch back to Design view, right-click one of the buttons to display its context menu, and choose Build Event. Access opens the Visual Basic Editor (VBE) and displays four event procedures.

NOTE

Refer to "Creating a Procedure to Verify an Identification Code" in Chapter 6, "Making Data Input Fast and Accurate," for information about the VBE.

The four event procedures are very similar. The first procedure consists of the statements in Listing 9.1.

LISTING 9.1   Procedure to Display the First Record

```
Private Sub cmdFirst_Click()
On Error GoTo Err_cmdFirst_Click
    DoCmd.GoToRecord , , acFirst
Exit_cmdFirst_Click:
    Exit Sub
Err_cmdFirst_Click:
    MsgBox Err.Description
    Resume Exit_cmdFirst_Click
End Sub
```

If this procedure has you scratching your head, that's because the Command Button Wizard is smart enough to include standard error trapping within the code it generates. Here's the same code with the error trapping removed:

```
Private Sub cmdFirst_Click()
    DoCmd.GoToRecord , , acFirst
End Sub
```

You'll surely agree that it looks much simpler. Ignoring error trapping for the time being, each of the event procedures consists of only three statements.

NOTE

Don't interpret the absence of error trapping in the following explanation as a suggestion that you should ignore error trapping. If the application you create doesn't contain provisions to respond in a friendly manner to errors, people who use your application will inevitably see error messages they don't understand.

Anticipating errors in something you need to pay much attention to when creating applications. This subject is covered in Chapter 13, "Taking More Control of Access."

The first statement

```
Private Sub cmdFirst_Click()
```

declares the procedure and gives it a name. The keyword Private makes the procedure accessible only within the form that contains the procedure.

The last statement

```
End Sub
```

simply marks the end of the procedure.

The statement

```
DoCmd.GoToRecord , , acFirst
```

is what does the work.

> **NOTE**
>
> DoCmd is one of Access's objects. Like other objects, it has methods. These methods correspond to the actions available for macros. In this specific case, the DoCmd object runs the GoToRecord method.

The GoToRecord method of the DoCmd object carries out the GoToRecord action. The full syntax of the GoToRecord method is

```
DoCmd.GoToRecord [objecttype, objectname][,record][,offset]
```

in which the brackets enclose optional items. Optional items may be omitted (in which case a default value is assumed), although the omission must be marked with a comma.

> **NOTE**
>
> If the *objecttype, objectname* argument is omitted, the default object is the active object.
>
> If the *record* argument is omitted, the default constant is acNext.
>
> If the *offset* argument is omitted, the default is 1 (one). This argument is used only when the second argument is acNext or acPrevious.

The four event procedures each contain this statement, the difference between them being the value of the record argument. The record argument can have one of these six values, each of which is an Access intrinsic (built-in) constant that represents a numeric value:

```
acFirst

acGoTo

acLast

acNewRec

acNext

acPrevious
```

The event procedures associated with the buttons you created use four of these six arguments.

TIP

For more detailed information about the GoToRecord method, consult the Access online help.

NOTE

For information about the error-trapping code included in the event procedures Access creates, refer to Chapter 13.

Displaying a Record That Contains Specific Information

If your tables contain only a few records, it's not too much of a chore to step through records using the buttons described in the first section of this chapter. But what if your tables contain thousands of records? You need a better way.

Finding a Record

You need a way to find records that contain a certain word or phrase. Here's one way you can do that.

1. With the form you created previously in this chapter displayed in Design view, and with the Control Wizards icon selected in the toolbox, click the Combo Box icon in the toolbox.

2. Click where you want to place a combo box on your form. Access displays the first Combo Box Wizard window shown in Figure 9.4.

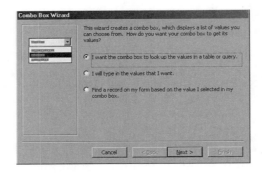

FIGURE 9.4

The Combo Box Wizard offers you a choice of how you want it to work.

3. Select the third option button because you want to find a record. Choose Next >.

4. The second wizard window invites you to select the field, or fields, you want to use to find a record. Select the fields you want to use and click > to move those fields to the Selected Fields list. If you want to find book titles, you would choose strTitle. Choose Next >.

5. The third wizard window lists the contents of the first few fields you selected in Step 4. Drag to change the width of the column or columns used to display those fields. Choose Next >.

6. Access asks you to supply a label for the combo box that will be displayed on your form. Assuming you want to find book titles, enter Select Book Title. Choose Finish.

Now you can see how the combo box works. Switch to Form view to see the form, as shown in Figure 9.5.

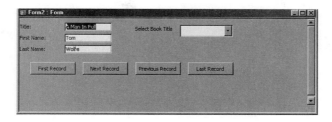

FIGURE 9.5

The form now contains a combo box you can use to select a book by title.

In Form view, click the arrow at the right end of the Select Book Title combo box to display a list of book titles. Scroll down the list of book and select the book you want to see to display information about that book in the form.

If you have a long list of books, it isn't necessary to scroll down the list. Instead, in the combo box, enter the first few characters of the book's title. The combo box automatically finds book titles corresponding to the characters you enter.

What's Behind the Combo Box?

Like the command buttons described previously in the chapter, the combo box uses VBA code created by the Combo Box Wizard. To see this code

1. Display the form in Design view and select the combo box.

2. In the Property sheet, select the Event tab.

3. Click the button marked with an ellipsis at the right of the After Update property to display the VBA code.

The VBA code you'll see is something like that shown in Listing 9.2.

LISTING 9.2   VBA Code to Find Text Selected in a Combo Box

```
Private Sub Combo10_AfterUpdate()
   'Find record that matches the control
   Dim rs As Object
   Set rs = Me.Recordset.Clone
   rs.FindFirst "[strTitle] = '" & Me![Combo10} & "'"
   Me.Bookmark = rs.Bookmark
End Sub
```

Although this VBA code is quite short, it needs some explanation so that you can understand what's happening.

Unlike the Command Button Wizard described previously in this chapter, the Combo Box Wizard doesn't give you the opportunity to provide a name for the combo box control. Consequently, the combo box has a name automatically assigned by Access—Combo10 in this example.

The event procedure is declared by the statement

```
Private Sub Combo10_AfterUpdate()
```

in which Private says that the procedure is only available in the current form. Combo10_AfterUpdate is the name of the procedure. AfterUpdate says that the procedure runs when the content of the combo box is updated—that's when you select one of the values in the combo box list.

The next statement

```
'Find record that matches the control
```

is a comment that describes the purpose of the procedure. All text to the right of a single quotation mark doesn't affect what happens, it merely provides information to anyone who reads the code.

The next statement

```
Dim rs As Object
```

declares rs as a variable of data type Object and reserves memory space for that variable.

The next statement

```
Set rs = Me.Recordset.Clone
```

specifies exactly what that variable is. Me is one of VBA's keywords that refers to the current form or report. This statement sets the variable rs (an object variable) to reserve memory for a clone (copy) of the current recordset. By creating clone of a recordset, you can manipulate the clone without affecting the original recordset.

The next statement

```
rs.FindFirst "[strTitle] = '" & Me![Combo10} & "'"
```

might look somewhat intimidating, but it isn't if you take it part by part.

FindFirst is one of the methods of a recordset. The method locates the first record in a recordset that satisfies a certain criterion. In this case, the criterion is that the value of the strTitle field is equal to the value you selected in the combo box. The criterion is similar to the WHERE clause in a SQL statement.

The next statement

```
Me.Bookmark = rs.Bookmark
```

is an assignment statement that makes use of the Bookmark property of a recordset. The previous statement located a record in the clone of the recordset the form uses to display information. After that statement executes, the expression rs.Bookmark has a value that identifies the found record. The assignment statement makes the same record the current record in the recordset the form uses to display information. Consequently, the form displays the values of the fields in the found record.

TIP

When you develop your own applications, you'll frequently find the need to use VBA code to go somewhat beyond what Access can do automatically. You'll find it a great time saver to use the VBA code Access generates as the basis for code you write.

Summary

You can use wizards to help you automate your forms by providing navigation buttons to display data from specific records and by providing a combo box that makes it easy to locate specific records. Wizards are available to do much more than is described in this chapter.

VBA code is the power behind Access. You don't necessarily have to understand VBA code in order to take advantage of it. Just let a wizard generate the code for you. However, if you want Access to do things wizards can't do automatically, you must be prepared to create some of your own VBA code. Instead of creating that code from scratch, it's often much easier to use a wizard to generate code that's similar to what you need, and then modify that code.

As you read the remaining chapters of this book, you'll come across much information about using VBA code.

Accessing External Data and Applications

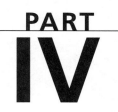

PART

IV

IN THIS PART

Using External Data in an Access Application

IN THIS CHAPTER

The primary purpose of an Access-based application is to convert raw data into useful information. The raw data can exist in many formats. Microsoft's choice of the name "Access" hints that the application is more than a self-contained database—it's a way of accessing data.

If you're creating an Access-based application from scratch and the amount of data to be handled is not enormous, you'll probably save the data in Access tables. However, if you expect to be dealing with large amounts of data, you should consider using Access as a front end for a database server, such as SQL Server.

It's possible that the Access-based application you want to create deals with data already existing in another format. The data you want to access might exist in other Office applications, such as Excel workbooks, Outlook folders or Word documents. Alternatively, the data might already exist in a back-end database server. This chapter shows how to import data from various sources into an Access application or, alternatively, to create links to data in external sources. You will also learn to export data from Access tables in formats that can be used by other applications.

Choosing a Database Configuration

Before starting serious development of an Access application, you should give some thought to how much data the application will eventually need to access, the number of people who will use the application, and how those people will share data.

TIP

The topics "Microsoft Access specifications" and "Microsoft Access database table specifications" in the online help contain detailed information you need to know.

The maximum size of an Access file is two gigabytes; the maximum size of a single Access table is one gigabyte; the maximum number of concurrent users of an Access application is 225. From these three specifications you can conclude

- Access, by itself, is suitable for use in fairly large applications.
- If you anticipate having several tables that are quite large, you should create each table in its own Access file and link those files to the file that contains the interface.
- If any table is likely to be larger than one gigabyte, you'll need to use a back-end database server, such as SQL Server, as a data store. With this type of configuration, you can still use Access as the front end that gives users access to the data.

> **NOTE**
>
> The maximum file size for SQL Server is one terabyte (one trillion bytes).

Linking and Importing Data

Most Access users, even many experienced users, create an Access-based application all in one file. That file contains the entire application—its tables, queries, forms, reports, macros, and modules. This single-file approach is fine for small applications running on a single computer, but it's not the best approach for applications that handle a lot of data or for applications to be used by more than one person.

Consider this scenario. A few months ago, you finished developing the first version of an application and gave copies of it to other people. Those people began to use the application, creating their own data. In the meantime, you've added more functionality to the application and made some improvements to the its interface. You want to share the improved application.

If the entire application is in one file, people can't just replace the old application with the new one on their computers because, if they do, they'll lose all their data. Instead, they'll have to export their original data to a temporary file, replace the old application with the improved one, and then import the tables they saved into the improved application. Although that's not an enormous task, chances are that some people will make mistakes resulting in lost data.

The solution to this problem is to create the original application in two or more Access files. One file contains the front-end components—queries, forms, reports, macros, and modules—and the other files contain the tables. The file that contains the front-end components has links to the tables in the other files. The advantage of this configuration is that you can replace the file that contains the interface components without causing any changes to the linked tables.

Linking Tables

To link tables to an Access application,

1. Open the Access file to which you want to link tables.
2. With the Database window displayed, choose File, Get External Data.
3. Select Link Tables to display the Link dialog box.
4. Navigate to the folder that contains the file that contains the table to be linked.
5. Select the file that contains the table or tables to be linked and choose Link. Access displays the Link Table dialog box, which lists the tables in the selected file.
6. Select the table or tables to be linked and choose OK. Access displays the linked tables in the Database window, as shown in Figure 10.1.

10

USING EXTERNAL DATA IN AN APPLICATION

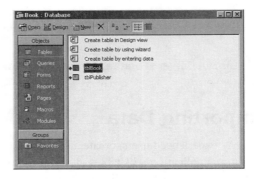

FIGURE 10.1
The arrows at the left of the table icons indicate the tables are linked.

NOTE

By default, Access assumes you want to link Access tables. However, in step 5 you can open the Files of Type drop-down list and select files that contain these other data sources:

Microsoft Excel	HTML documents
Text files	dBASE III
Exchange	dBASE IV
Outlook	dBASE 5
Paradox	ODBC databases

The topic "Data sources Microsoft Access can import or link" in online Help provides information about specific version numbers for data sources.

After you've created a link to an Access table, you can, with one exception, work with that table as if it were included rather than linked. The exception is you can't open the linked file in Design view to modify its properties. If you try to open a linked table in Design view, Access displays a message stating that the table "is a linked table with some properties that can't be modified." To modify the properties of a linked table, you have to open the Access file in which the table exists.

Importing Data

Instead of linking an existing table, you can import that table. Use the same steps as those in the preceding section. The only difference is in step 3; instead of selecting Link Tables, select Import.

After you import a table, that table is shown in the Database window without an arrow at its left.

Importing Data from a Spreadsheet

You can link and import data from a Microsoft Excel or Lotus 1-2-3 spreadsheet into an Access table.

> **TIP**
>
> If you want to import a spreadsheet created in an application other than Excel or Lotus 1-2-3, first import that spreadsheet into Excel. You can import spreadsheets from Quattro Pro, SYLK, and Data Interchange Format into Excel.

In most cases, you'll want to import only some of the information in a spreadsheet into an Access table. To make this possible, you must first identify the data in the spreadsheet as a named range.

The example that follows uses the States.xls Excel workbook (on the CD-ROM that accompanies this book) as a data source. The data to be imported is in the worksheet named State Information and in the range named StateInfo.

> **TIP**
>
> To name a range in Excel, select all the cells in the range, and then choose Insert. Move the pointer onto Name, and choose Define to display the Define Name dialog box. The range you select should preferably include column titles in the first row, although that's not essential. Enter the name you want to use for the selected range of cells.

To import from Excel,

1. Open the Access database into which you want to import tables from Excel.
2. Choose File, move the pointer onto Get External Data, and choose Import. Access displays the Import dialog box.
3. Navigate to the folder that contains the Excel workbook from which you want to import data.

10

4. Open the drop-down Files of Type list and select Microsoft Excel (*.xls).

5. Select the Excel file that contains the workbook from which you want to import a named range (States.xls in this example) and choose Import. Access displays the first Import Spreadsheet Wizard window, as shown in Figure 10.2.

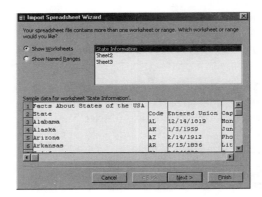

FIGURE 10.2
Use this window to define what you want to import.

6. To import a named range, as you'll normally want to do, choose Show Named Ranges. The window displays a list of named ranges in the workbook file. Select the named range you want to import. Choose Next > to continue. At this point, you might see a message stating that "The first row contains some data that can't be used for valid Access field names. In these cases, the wizard will automatically assign valid field names." Choose OK to display the second wizard window.

7. The second window contains a check box labeled First Row Contains Column Headings. By default, this box is checked. If the first row of the Excel range doesn't contain column headings, uncheck this box. Choose Next > to display the third wizard window.

8. The third window contains two option buttons. By default, the option button labeled In a New Table is selected. You will normally accept this. However, if you already have a table that contains fields into which you want to import data from the spreadsheet, you can choose In an Existing Table and then open a drop-down list to select the table into which you want to import the spreadsheet data. Choose Next > to display the fourth wizard window, as shown in Figure 10.3.

9. For each field to be imported, this window gives you the opportunity to specify a field name in the Access table, in some cases, to specify a data type, and to specify whether the field should be indexed. You can also choose not to import the field. Select fields one at a time in the lower part of the window. After you've made your choices in this window, choose Next > to display the fifth wizard window.

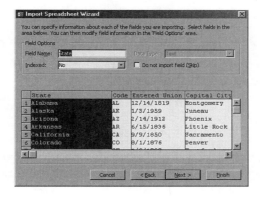

FIGURE 10.3
You can use this window to customize the fields imported from the Excel named range.

10. This window encourages you to allow Access to add an automatic primary key to the new table. You can choose to let Access add an automatic primary key, choose your own primary key, or not create a primary key. If you're following this example, it would be good to choose your own primary key, open the drop-down list, and select Code as the primary key because each state code is unique. Choose Next > to display the final wizard window.

11. In the final wizard window you can, if you like, change the name of the imported table. You can also ask the wizard to analyze your table, which is something you shouldn't normally do. Choose Finish to import the data and close the wizard.

NOTE

In step 11, I suggested you shouldn't ask the wizard to analyze your table. I made this recommendation because I've found the Table Analyzer doesn't always work reliably.

After you've imported the table, you can open it and examine its contents and design.

> **NOTE**
>
> You can use the same steps to import data from a Lotus 1-2-3 spreadsheet. The only difference is that, in step 4, you select Lotus 1-2-3 (*.wk*).

If you open the new table in Design view, you'll see that

- All the field names from the Excel worksheet are correctly imported into the Access table. If you're using a naming convention, it's a good idea to change these field names to conform to your convention.

- Text fields in the Excel worksheet appear as text fields in the Access table. All text fields in the Access table have a Field Size property of 255. You should change this property to a suitable value for all text fields. You might also want to change some of the other property values.

- The Entered Union field in the Excel worksheet contains dates. However after importing into Access, the field data type is Text. You should change the data type to Date/Time and select an appropriate value for the Format property, such as Short Date. This change is necessary if you subsequently want Access to handle dates properly.

- All the numeric fields in the Excel worksheet have a data type of Number with a Field Size property of Double in the Access table. A Field Size property of Double is unnecessarily large for the example used here and is likely to be too large for most data you import from Excel. For this example, change the Field Size property of all the numeric fields except the last to Long Integer; change the Field Size property of the last numeric field (Population Per Square Mile) to Single. To improve the way numbers are displayed in the table, set the Format property of all number fields to standard, set the Decimal Places property for all except the last numeric field to 0 (zero), and set the Decimal Places property for the last numeric field to 1 (one).

Importing Data into Access from Outlook or Exchange Client

You can use Access to import data from Outlook and you can also export data from Outlook into an Access table. This section first describes how to use Access to import data from Outlook and then how to gain more control over the process by exporting from Outlook. One benefit of importing data from Outlook into Access is to be able to use the more versatile report-writing capabilities in Access. (The information in this section is based on the assumption that Outlook is your default email client.)

Outlook Versus Exchange

Many people are confused by references to Exchange. Let me try to clarify this matter. Windows 95 included an application named Exchange that provided capabilities to send and receive email. In the same year that Microsoft introduced Windows 95, the company also introduced Office for Windows 95, a package of applications that included Schedule+. Schedule+ provided the ability to manage a personal calendar.

A couple of years later, Microsoft introduced Office 97. Outlook, a new application in this package, combined the functionality of Exchange in Windows 95 and Schedule+ in Office 95, and offered more. Users who chose to move to Outlook didn't need Exchange or Schedule+ any more.

Soon after Windows 95 became available, Microsoft introduced Exchange Server, a server-based application that runs under Windows NT Server to provide a complete communications and collaboration environment. Initially, people could use the original Exchange component of Windows 95 on their personal computers to communicate with Exchange Server on their servers. After the introduction of Office 97, users could choose to retain using Exchange (a component of Windows 95) and Schedule+ (a component of Office 95), or they could switch to Outlook 97.

In an attempt to clarify the difference between the original Exchange (a component of Windows 95) and Exchange Server (a separate application that runs under Windows NT Server), Microsoft renamed the original Exchange and now calls it Windows Messaging. Unfortunately, though, this renaming is not consistent throughout Microsoft's printed and online documentation.

The Import Exchange/Outlook Wizard is a case in point. In the name of this wizard, "Exchange" refers to the original Exchange in Windows 95, now known as Windows Messaging.

Office 2000 users should not be using Exchange (Windows Messaging) as their messaging client. Instead, they should be using Outlook 2000.

As you probably know, Outlook saves items of information either in a Personal Folders file or in an Exchange Server store. In either case, Outlook uses separate containers for each type of information item, one container for information about your contacts, one for information about appointments, one for messages you've received, one for messages you've sent, and so on.

> **NOTE**
>
> I've deliberately used the word *container* in the preceding paragraph. In fact, Outlook calls these containers *folders*, but they're not folders in the sense you usually use that word—that is, they're not folders you can see in Windows Explorer. Instead, Outlook's folders are information containers within a single file.

You can import the contents of a single Outlook folder into an Access table. The following steps show how to import the contents of the Outlook Contacts folder:

1. Open the Access database into which you want to import the contents of an Outlook folder.

2. Choose File, move the pointer onto Get External Data, and choose Import. Access displays the Import dialog box.

3. Open the drop-down Files of Type list and select Outlook(). Access displays the first Import Exchange/Outlook Wizard window, as shown in Figure 10.4.

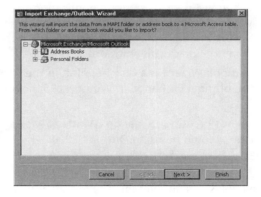

FIGURE 10.4

The wizard automatically finds your Personal Folders file and wants to know what you want to import.

4. The first wizard window lists two categories of folders that you can import. Office 2000 makes address books redundant, so the assumption here is that you want to import from one of the folders in your Personal Folders file. Click the plus sign (+) at the left of Personal Folders to display a list of individual folders, as shown in Figure 10.5.

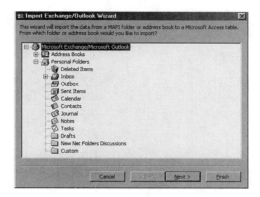

FIGURE 10.5
The list of folders in your Personal Folders file looks something like this.

5. To import the contents of your Contacts folder into an Access table, select Contacts in this list. Choose Next > to display the next wizard window.

6. This wizard window wants to know whether you want to store your data in a new table or in an existing table. You probably want to store the data in a new table, so select In a New Table. Choose Next > to display the next wizard window.

7. For each field to be imported, this window gives you the opportunity to specify a field name in the Access table, in some cases to specify a data type, and to specify whether the field should be indexed. You can also choose not to import the field. Select fields one at a time in the lower part of the window. After you've made your choices in this window, choose Next > to display the fourth wizard window.

8. This window encourages you to allow Access to add an automatic primary key to the new table. You can let Access add an automatic primary key, choose your own primary key, or not create a primary key. You're importing from an Outlook Contacts folder, so there is probably no field you can guarantee to be unique. Accept the default Let Access Add Primary Key. Choose Next > to display the final wizard window.

9. In the final wizard window, you can replace the table name the wizard suggests with a different name. Choose Finish to create the Access table.

The wizard provides no opportunity for you to select which fields from the Outlook folder are copied into the Access table. Only 44 of the 123 fields in an Outlook Contacts folder are copied. (If you want to copy other fields, you have to use VBA to create your own copying procedure):

10

USING EXTERNAL
DATA IN AN
APPLICATION

First	Email Type
Last	Email Address
Title	Account
Company	Assistant
Department	Send Rich Text
Office	Primary
Post Office Box	File As
Address	Home Address
City	Business Address
State	Other Address
Zip/Postal Code	Journal
Country	Web Page
Phone	Business Address Street
Mobile Phone	Business Address City
Pager Phone	Business Address State
Home2 Phone	Business Address Postal Code
Assistant Phone Number	Business Address Country
Business Fax	Business Address PO Box
Home Fax	User Field 1
Other Fax	User Field 2
Telex Number	User Field 3
Display Name	User Field 4

Exporting Data from Outlook into Access

Instead of using Access to import information from Outlook, you can use Outlook to export Contact information into Access. This method has the advantage that you have control over which Outlook fields are exported.

1. Open Outlook 2000 and, with an Information viewer (the window in which Outlook displays information about items) displayed, choose File, Import and Export to display the first Import and Export Wizard window, as shown in Figure 10.6.

2. In the first wizard window, select Export to a File, and then choose Next > to display the second wizard window, which contains a list of targets to which you can export.

3. In the second wizard window, select Microsoft Access, and then choose Next > to display the third wizard window, which contains a list of your Outlook folders.

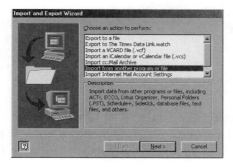

FIGURE 10.6

Use this wizard window to begin the process of exporting from Outlook.

4. In the third wizard window, select your Contacts folder, and then choose Next > to display the fourth wizard window.

5. In the fourth wizard window, enter the full pathname of the file you want to create, and then choose Next > to display the fifth wizard window, as shown in Figure 10.7.

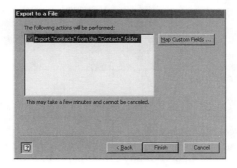

FIGURE 10.7

The wizard window summarizes the action that's about to be performed and also gives you an opportunity to select which fields to export.

6. For the present, ignore the Map Custom Fields button. Choose Finish to start exporting.

After the export is complete, open Access and look at the table Outlook created. You'll see the table contains only these nine fields:

FirstName

MiddleName

LastName

Company

BusinessStreet

BusinessCity

BusinessState

BusinessPostalCode

BusinessCountry

Instead of accepting Outlook's entire default list of fields, you can completely control which fields Outlook exports by choosing the Map Custom Fields button in the wizard window shown in Figure 10.7. When you click this button, Outlook displays the dialog box shown in Figure 10.8.

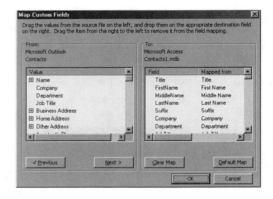

FIGURE 10.8

The list on the right contains the names of the default fields Outlook proposes to export. The list on the left contains all the fields in your Outlook Contacts folder in groups.

Click the plus sign (+) button at the left of any group name to show all the fields within that group. You can use this dialog box to customize the list of fields to be exported. Some of the things you can do are

- Remove a field name from the list of fields to be exported by dragging that name from the right list into the left list.

- Add a field name to the list of fields to be exported by dragging a name from the left list to the right list.

- Remove all field names from the right list by choosing Clear Map.

- Restore the default list of field to be exported by choosing Default Map.

- Change the name of a field as it will appear in the Access table by double-clicking a field name in the right list and then editing the name.

After you've constructed the list of fields you want to export, choose OK to return to the wizard window and choose Finish to export the selected fields.

Importing Text Files

You can import text files in several formats into an Access table. When you choose File, move the pointer onto Get External Data, and choose Import, the Files of Type drop-down list at the bottom of the Import dialog box contains Text Files (*.txt, *.csv, *.tab, *.asc). After you choose one of these four filename extensions, the dialog box displays the names of all files that have that extension.

Just because a file has one of these filename extensions is no guarantee that Access can import what's in the file. For Access to be able to import data from a text file, the text file must be in one of the formats listed in Table 10.1.

TABLE 10.1 Text File Formats Access Can Import

Format	Explanation
Comma-Delimited	Each field is separated from the next by a comma. Each record is on a separate line.
Tab-Delimited	Each field is separated from the next by a tab. Each record is on a separate line.
Space-Delimited	Each field is separated from the next by a space. Each record is on a separate line.
Fixed-Width	Each field contains a fixed number of characters. Each record is on a separate line.

NOTE

The four formats listed in Table 10.1 are the most common ones you'll encounter. The Import Text Wizard allows you to designate any character as a delimiting character.

After you've chosen a text file to import, proceed as follows. The steps shown here are specifically for importing a delimited file. The steps are slightly different for a fixed width file.

1. Choose Import. Access attempts to recognize the format of the selected file and then displays the first Import Text Wizard window in which either the Delimited or the Fixed Width option button is selected. In the unlikely event that Access incorrectly identifies the type of file, you can choose a different option button. The window also displays a

10

USING EXTERNAL DATA IN AN APPLICATION

small sample of the data to be imported. Choose Next > to display the second wizard window.

2. The second wizard window confirms the delimiting character Access has detected and gives you the opportunity to designate a different character. If Access detected that the first row of data in the file contains field names, the First Row Contains Field Names box is checked. You can check or uncheck this box. Choose Next > to display the third wizard window.

3. You can use the third wizard window to specify whether the data should be imported into a new table or added to an existing table. Choose Next > to display the fourth wizard window.

4. The fourth wizard window lets you provide a name and specify a data type for each field. You can also choose whether each field should be indexed. You can mark a field not to be imported. Choose Next > to display the fifth wizard window.

5. The fifth wizard window lets you choose whether to let Access add a primary key, to choose a specific field as a primary key, or to have no primary key. Choose Next > to display the final wizard window.

6. Use the final wizard window to provide a name for the table. Choose Finish to import the file.

Each of the Import Text Wizard windows contains an Advanced button you can choose to display the Input Specification dialog box, shown in Figure 10.9.

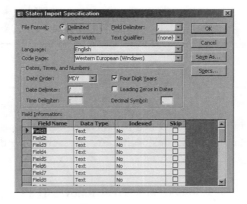

FIGURE 10.9

You can use this dialog box to save an input specification for reuse.

The Input Specification dialog box summarizes the current import settings. You can change any of the settings and then choose Save As to save those settings. Access saves the current specification within the database into which you are importing the data. After you've saved a specification, you can subsequently reuse that specification by displaying the Import Specification dialog box and choosing Specs. That causes Access to display a list of the specifications you have previously saved. You can select one of those previously saved specifications and choose Open to display the Import Specifications dialog box. Choose OK to return to the Import Text Wizard, then choose Finish to import data using all the conditions in the specification you selected.

Exporting Data from an Access Application

The purpose of this book is to encourage you to develop applications based on Access. For that reason, the primary focus of this chapter is to show how you can use data that already exists in various formats in your applications. However, you should also recognize that you, and people who use the applications you develop, can use data maintained by Access in other applications.

Exporting Directly from Access

You can export data directly from Access tables in a format other applications can use. Basically, Access can export data in most of the formats from which Access can import data.

To export data from Access, follow these steps:

1. Open the Access database from which you want to export data.
2. In the Database window, select Tables in the Objects bar.
3. Select the table you want to export.
4. Choose File, Export to display the Export Table dialog box.
5. Open the Save as Type drop-down list and select the format in which want to save your data. The available formats are listed in Table 10.2.
6. Enter a filename in the File Name box, and then choose Save.

TABLE 10.2   Access Export Formats

Format	Notes
Microsoft Access database	Versions 2.0, 7.0/95, 8.0/97, and 9.0/2000
Microsoft Access project	Version 2000
Microsoft Visual FoxPro	Versions 3.0, 5.0, and 6.x
dBASE	Versions III, III+, IV, 5, and 7. Version 7 requires Borland Database Engine 4.x or later

continues

10

TABLE 10.2 Continued

Format	Notes
Paradox and Paradox for Windows	Versions 3.x, 4.x, 5.0, and 8.0. Version 8.0 requires Borland Database Engine 4.x or later
HTML documents	
Microsoft Excel	Versions 3.0, 4.0, 5.0, 7.0/95, 8.0/97, and 9.0/2000
Rich Text Format (RTF)	Can be used to export data to Microsoft Word
Lotus 1-2-3	.wk1 and .wk3 formats
Text Files	Delimited and fixed-width formats
HTML and IDC/HTX	Version 1.0 (list only). Versions 2.0, 3.x, and 4.x (if a table or list)
Microsoft Active Server Pages	
ODBC Databases	ODBC drivers required

Depending on the export format you choose, several additional steps might be required. If you choose to export to Excel, no additional steps are required. However, if you choose to export the data as a text file, the Export Text Wizard presents several windows in which you choose delimited or fixed-width format and such additional factors as a delimiting character (for delimited formats) and field width (for fixed-width formats).

TIP

The drop-down list of file types in the Export Table dialog box contains frequently used file types. If this list doesn't contain a file type you need to use, you can use an intermediate file type such as Rich Text Format, a delimited text file, or a fixed-width text file. It's likely that the application you want to use can import data in at least one of these formats.

Exporting to Outlook

Access doesn't provide a means to export data to an Outlook folder. However, Outlook is able to import from Access.

If you want to import data into a new Outlook folder, create that folder before starting the steps listed here. To import data from an Access table into an Outlook folder,

1. Open Outlook and, with an Information viewer displayed, choose File, Import and Export to display the first Import and Export Wizard window.

2. Select Import from Another Program or File and choose Next > to open the second wizard window.

3. Select Microsoft Access and choose Next > to open the third wizard window.

4. Navigate to the Access file from which you want to import data. This window provides a choice among three options: Replace duplications with items imported, Allow duplicates to be created, and Do not import duplicate items. The second option is selected by default—that's usually the option to use. Choose Next > to open the fourth wizard window.

5. The fourth wizard window displays a list of your Outlook folders. Select the folder into which you want to import data from the Access table. If you're importing from a table that contains information about people and organizations, select your Contacts folder or, if you've created a new folder, select that folder. Choose Next > to open the final wizard window.

6. In the window, you can choose Map Custom Fields if you want to choose which fields to import (as described in the section "Importing Data into Access from Outlook or Exchange Client," previously in this chapter). Alternatively, you can accept the default fields. Choose Finish to begin importing data.

Summary

If you're developing an Access-based application for your personal use, you'll probably have a single file that contains the application's front end and its data tables. However, if you're developing an application for other people to use, you should have one file for the front end and one or more separate files for the data tables. Access is suitable for small- to medium-sized applications. If your application is likely to be used by many people simultaneously, or a large amount of data is involved, you can use Access as the front end, and employ a server such as SQL Server to store and manage the data.

Access can use data in the native Access format and also in many other formats. You can create links to data tables in other formats so that, in many ways, these data tables appear to be the same as native Access tables. You can also import data from many other formats into Access tables. It's particularly easy to import data into Access from other Office applications such as Excel and Outlook. One advantage of importing from Outlook is to be able to create reports that take advantage of Access's versatile capabilities.

You can also export data from Access tables in many formats. Although Access doesn't have a way of exporting directly to Outlook, Outlook does have the built-in capability of importing from Access.

Using Object Models Within the Office Environment

IN THIS CHAPTER

You might be tempted to skip this chapter, but you should resist that temptation. Some understanding of objects and object models is key to being able to make Access do what you want it to do.

You might find you could get Access to do all you need without ever having to become involved with objects and the relationships between objects. However, the fact that you're reading this book suggests you want to be able to do more with Access than is available on the surface. By understanding Access objects, and learning to control those objects with VBA code, you can tailor Access to satisfy your extended needs.

The concept of objects and object models gives you the ability to have Access interact with other Office and Office-compatible applications. After you understand objects and object models, you can integrate the functionality of other applications into your Access-based application. Chapter 8, "Creating Informative Reports," provided an example of this. In that chapter, you learned how to create charts by integrating the power of Graph 2000 (an application supplied with Office 2000) into Access. There, you didn't have to think about objects because Access handled the details for you.

In this chapter, you'll gain an insight into what is going on behind the scenes so that you're no longer limited to what Access does automatically. You'll be able to incorporate whatever objects you need into your applications.

Although this chapter is primarily about Access objects, much of the material here applies equally to other office applications. After introducing you to Access objects, this chapter uses the Excel object model to illustrate the similarities between various applications' object models. In this chapter, you'll learn about the Access object model and the collections and objects it contains; about the properties, methods, and events associated with collections and objects, and how to obtain information about them; how to use VBA to work with objects; and how to work with objects that belong to one application from within another application.

Understanding Objects and Object Models

To gain an understanding of objects, it's helpful to think about a more concrete environment than Access. Take a car, for example. A car is something you can experience as an entity. In the sense of the word "object" used here, a car is an object:

- Like other objects, a car has characteristics you can describe, such as its color, weight, and current odometer reading. In object terminology, these characteristics are known as *properties*.

- A car can do certain things in response to stimuli. For example, when you press the brake pedal, the car slows down. The things a car can do are known, in object terminology, as its *methods*.

- A car can respond to things that happen. For example, a car can incorporate an automatic system that turns on the lights at nightfall. The outside light falling below a certain level is an *event* to which the car responds.

This example of a car illustrates one important point about objects: Objects can have properties, methods, and events associated with them.

Although you can think of a car as one object, it has components, each of which is also an object. A car usually has four wheels, each wheel being an object. In object terminology the four wheels as a group are known as a collection—the collection itself is an object. The wheels collection can have its own properties, methods, and events. Each wheel within that collection has its own properties, methods, and events.

There are many more collections within the car object, such as seats, switches, windows, brakes, and so on. Each collection contains separate objects. Do you begin to get the idea? The concept of objects and collections is used in the same way to define Access and other Office applications.

NOTE

All objects and collections have names. In general, Access and other Office applications use singular names for objects and plural names for collections. Not all names adhere to this rule.

Having some general ideas about objects, consider how these ideas apply to Access.

Displaying the Access Object Model

An *object model* is a definition of objects within an environment and of the relationships between those objects. The Object Browser described subsequently in this section presents an object model as an interactive table. Access online Help also presents the object model graphically, as shown in Figure 11.1.

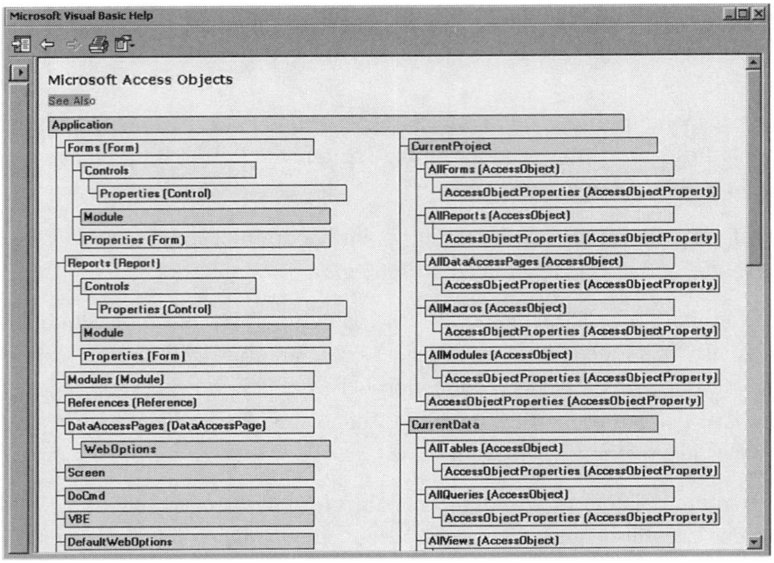

FIGURE 11.1

This is part of the graphical representation of the Access object model.

TIP

To display the Access object model, open an Access form in Design view and choose View, Code to display the Visual Basic Editor window. In that window, choose Help, Microsoft Visual Basic Help. With the Index tab selected, enter Object in the Type Keywords box and choose Search. Select the topic Microsoft Access Objects.

You'll find it useful to refer to this graphical object model frequently while you work with the objects within Access.

In the object model, the blocks with a yellow background (shown as light gray in Figure 11.1) represent a collection that contains individual objects; blocks with a blue background (shown as dark gray in Figure 11.1) represent individual objects. Unfortunately, the background colors are not totally consistent.

Table 11.1 lists the collections and objects in the Access object model. You can click a collection or object in the graphical object model to find more information.

Using Object Models Within the Office Environment

CHAPTER 11

271

11

USING OBJECT
MODELS WITHIN
OFFICE

> **TIP**
>
> Don't regard the information in Table 11.1 as something you should immediately understand and memorize. Instead, regard the table as something you can refer to as necessary while you're developing Access-based applications.

TABLE 11.1 Collections and Objects in the Access Object Model

Collection or Object	Description
Application Object	The top-level object through which you can gain access to all other collections and objects.
Forms Collection	Contains all the open forms in an Access database.
Form Object	Represents a specific form.
Controls Collection	Contains all controls on a form, report or section, within another control, or attached to another control.
Control Object	Represents a specific control.
Module Object	Represents a standard or class module.
Properties Collection	Contains all the built-in properties in an instance of an open form, report, or control object.
Property Object	Represents an individual property.
Reports Collection	Contains all the open reports in an Access database.
Report Object	Represents a specific report.
Modules Collection	Contains all the open standard and class modules in a database.
Module Object	Represents a specific standard or class module.
References Collection	Contains all the available references to object libraries.
Reference Object	Represents a specific available object library.
DataAccessPages Collection	Contains all currently open Data Access Pages in a database or project.
Data Access Page Object	Represents a specific Data Access Page.
WebOptions Object	Represents a specific Data Access Page's properties.
Screen Object	Represents a specific form, report, or control that currently has the focus.
DoCmd Object	Contains methods you can use to run most Access actions from VBA code.

continues

TABLE 11.1 Continued

Collection or Object	Description
VBE Object	Contains all other collections and objects represented in VBA.
DefaultWebOptions Object	Contains global application-level attributes used by Access when you save a Data Access Page as a Web page or open a Web page.
Assistant Object	Represents the Office Assistant.
CommandBars Collection	Contains CommandBar objects in the container application.
CommandBarControls Collection	Contains the CommandBarControl objects on a command bar.
CommandBarButton Object	Represents a Command Button control on a command bar.
CommandBarComboBox Object	Represents a ComboBox control on a command bar.
CommandBarPopup Object	Represents a Popup control on a command bar.
DBEngine Object	Represents the top-level object in the DAO object model.
FileSearch Object	Represents the functionality of the Open dialog box.
COMAddIns Collection	Contains the available COMAddIn objects.
COMAddIn Object	Represents a registered COM Addin.
AnswerWizard Object	Represents the Answer Wizard in an Office application.
LanguageSettings Object	Returns information about the current language settings.
CurrentProject Object	Represents the current Access database or project.
AllForms Collection	Contains an AccessObject object for each form in the CurrentProject or CodeProject object.
AccessObject Object	Refers to a specific Access object within the AllDataAccessPages, AllDatabaseDiagrams, AllForms, AllMacros, AllModules, AllQueries, AllReports, AllStoredProcedures, AllTables, and AllViews collections.
AllReports Collection	Contains an AccessObject object for each report in the CurrentProject or CodeProject object.
AllDataAccessPages Collection	Contains an AccessObject object for each DataAccess Page in the CurrentProject or CodeProject object.

Collection or Object	Description
AllMacros Collection	Contains an AccessObject object for each macro in the CurrentProject or CodeProject object.
AllModules Collection	Contains an AccessObject object for each module in the CurrentProject or CodeProject object.
AccessObjectProperties Collection	Contains all the custom AccessObjectProperty objects (properties) that uniquely characterize an instance of an object.
CurrentData Object	Represents the objects stored in the current database by the source application.
AllTables Collection	Contains an AccessObject object for each table in the CurrentData or CodeData object.
AllQueries Collection	Contains an AccessObject object for each query in the CurrentData or CodeData object.
AllViews Collection	Contains an AccessObject object for each view in the CurrentData or CodeData object.
AllStoredProcedures Collection	Contains an AccessObject object for each stored procedure in the CurrentData or CodeData object.
AllDatabaseDiagrams Collection	Contains an AccessObject object for each database diagram in the CurrentData or CodeData object.
CodeProject Object	Refers to the project for the code database of a project or database.
CodeData Object	Refers to objects stored within the code database by the source application.

Working with Object Libraries

The objects you have at your disposal while you're working with Access are grouped in a set of *object libraries*. You choose which object libraries are available according to the needs of your application.

To see which object libraries are available

1. Open Access and, in the Microsoft Access dialog box, choose Blank Access database. Accept the default filename, and choose Create.

2. In the Database window's Objects bar, select Modules and then choose New. This displays the Visual Basic Editor (VBE) window.

3. Choose Tools, References to display the dialog box shown in Figure 11.2.

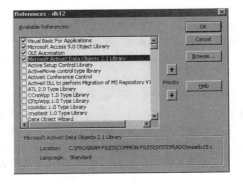

FIGURE 11.2
The References dialog box contains a list of object libraries such as those shown here.

> **NOTE**
>
> The preceding procedure displayed the object libraries Access makes available by default. At any time while you're developing an application, you can return to the References dialog box to see which libraries are currently available.

The object libraries listed in the References dialog box vary according to what you have installed on your computer. Some of these libraries are installed (and registered in the registry) when you install Office. Other libraries are registered when you install other applications and programming environments.

The object libraries available to Access appear at the top of the list of libraries with checked boxes at the left of the library names. All other registered libraries are listed alphabetically below the available libraries, but are not checked. By default, the available libraries are

- Visual Basic for Applications—Objects that belong to VBA
- Microsoft Access 9.0 Object Library—Objects that are specific to Access 2000
- OLE Automation—Objects that provide OLE Automation functionality
- Microsoft ActiveX Data Objects 2.1 Library—Objects that provide the core functionality for manipulating data

You can make other object libraries available by scrolling down the list of object libraries and checking those you want. You can make an object library unavailable by unchecking it in the list.

Each object library contains many objects. In some cases, two or more libraries contain objects with the same name. When you use such an object, Access assumes you want the object in the library that is highest in the list. You can adjust this priority by selecting an available object library and clicking one of the two Priority buttons.

> **TIP**
>
> Don't make any object libraries available unless you're sure you need them. If, after you've begun developing your application, you find you need another object library, you can return to the References dialog box to make another library available.

Displaying Information About Objects

The Object Browser displays detailed information about the objects in your available object libraries. From the VBE window, choose View, Object Browser to display the Object Browser shown in Figure 11.3.

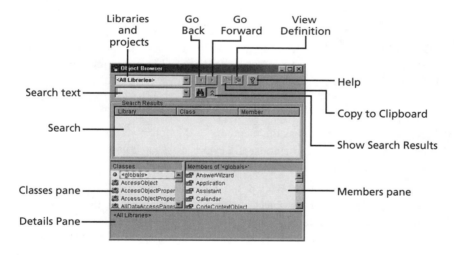

FIGURE 11.3

The Object Browser window is your source of information about currently available objects.

Here's a brief description of what's in the Object Browser window.

- Libraries and Projects—When the Object Browser is first displayed, the box at the top-left contains "<All Libraries>," meaning that the browser is displaying information about objects in all the available libraries. If you've opened Access and created a new database, the list includes the libraries listed in the preceding section. You can open the drop-down list of libraries and select one of those libraries to limit the Object Browser to displaying only the objects in the selected library.

  In addition to the libraries made available in the References dialog box, the list of libraries includes the name of your current database project. If you choose that, the Object Browser shows objects defined within the project.

- Classes Pane—This pane lists the object classes and constant enumerations in the selected library or project. You can select any object listed in this pane. The symbol at the left of each name in this list signifies an object or enumerated list. With only a few exceptions, a singular name for an object usually represents an individual object whereas a plural name usually represents a collection.

Note

An English dictionary defines "enumerate" as "to count or name one by one." Items in the Classes pane that are *constant enumerations* contain members that are individual constants.

- Members Pane—This pane lists the members of the object selected in the Classes pane. Members are the properties, methods, and events associated with the selected object, or the individual constants in an enumerated list.

- Details Pane—With an object selected in the Classes pane, the Details pane identifies the type of object selected and the object of which it is a member. With an object selected in the Members pane, the Details pane provides information about the selected the member; the information provided varies according to whether the member is a property, method, or event.

- Go Back and Go Forward Buttons—After you've selected various objects in the Classes pane and various members in the Members pane, you can use the Go Back and Go Forward Buttons to retrace your previous selections.

- Search Text Box and Search Button—You can use this box and button to find text in the Class and Member lists. Enter the text you want to find in the Search Text box, and then click the Search button. The Object Browser displays the Search Results pane, as shown in Figure 11.4.

Using Object Models Within the Office Environment

CHAPTER 11

277

11

USING OBJECT
MODELS WITHIN
OFFICE

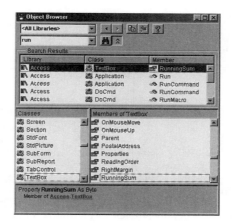

FIGURE 11.4

The Search Results pane shown here displays the results of searching for the word "Run."

The Search Results pane lists every occurrence of the search text in the Class and Members panes.

Each time you make a search, the Object Browser saves the search text. You can open the drop-down Search Text list to select any previously used search text.

- Search Results/Hide Search Results Button—Click this button to display or hide the Search Results pane.

- Copy To Clipboard—Use this button to copy the syntax for a property or method into the Clipboard. With the property or method selected in the Members pane, select the syntax in the Details pane and then click Copy to Clipboard. You can subsequently paste the syntax from the Clipboard into your VBA code. You can also select a constant name in the Members pane, choose Copy to Clipboard, and subsequently paste the constant name into your VBA code.

- Help Button—Many objects and members of objects have help topics associated them. With an object or member selected, you can choose the Help button to display the associated help topic.

You can gain more control over the Object Browser by right-clicking an unoccupied place within the window to display the context menu shown in Figure 11.5.

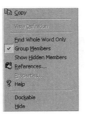

FIGURE 11.5
This is the Object Browser's context menu.

Some of the more useful items in the context menu are

- Find Whole Word Only—By default, the Object Browser's Search Results pane lists every instance of the search text whether the text occurs as a whole word or within a word. After choosing this menu item, the Search Results pane shows only objects and members in which the search text is a whole word.

- Group Members—By default, the Object Browser's Classes pane lists objects in one alphabetically ordered list and the Members pane lists properties, methods, and events in one alphabetically ordered list. After choosing this menu item, the Classes pane groups objects and enumerations of constants in separate alphabetically ordered lists; the Members pane groups properties, methods, and events in separate alphabetically ordered lists.

- Show Hidden Members—By default, the Object Browser's Classes pane hides system objects. After choosing this menu item, the pane displays the names of system objects.

- References—Choose this menu item to display the References dialog box, shown previously in Figure 11.2. You can use this dialog box to add or remove referenced libraries, without having to leave the Object Browser.

Getting Information About Collections and Objects

If you haven't used the Object Browser before, this example will help you get the hang of it.

1. Start Access and open a new database to ensure you have the default libraries available.

2. With the Database window displayed, select Modules in the Objects bar, and then choose New to display the VBE window.

3. Choose View, Object Browser to display the Object Browser.

4. Open the drop-down list of libraries and projects and select Access so that the Object Browser displays only objects within the Access library.

5. In the Classes pane, select Controls, a collection object. The Members pane displays the members of the Controls object class, as shown in Figure 11.6.

Using Object Models Within the Office Environment

CHAPTER 11

279

11

USING OBJECT
MODELS WITHIN
OFFICE

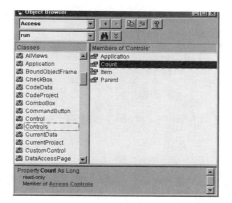

FIGURE 11.6
The only members of the Controls collection are four properties. The Object Browser is shown here with one member selected.

6. Select the Count property in the Members pane. The Count property is the number of objects in the collection. The Details pane displays information about the selected property, as shown in Figure 11.6. Notice that the Details pane

- Confirms the member you've selected is a property and tells you its data type—Long in this example

- Tells you that the property is read-only

- Shows how the selected property fits into the object model hierarchy—Member of Access.Controls

---

NOTE

Notice the small blue circle above Item in the Members pane. This signifies that Item is the default property of the Controls collection. The significance of this is explained in the section "Referring to Properties" subsequently in this chapter.

---

7. With the Count property still selected in the Members pane, select Help. Access displays the help topic that explains the Count property.

Now, take a look at an individual object:

1. Select Control (an individual object, not a collection) in the Classes pane. The Members pane displays a long list of members.

2. Select various members of the Control object, examine the information in the Details pane, and open the help topic for some members.

> **NOTE**
>
> Most of the members of the Control object are properties. Five of them, marked with a green icon, are methods—things a control can do.

Take a look at one more object in the Classes pane, CommandButton. The Members pane contains many properties, most of which you'll recognize as properties you can set in a command button's Property sheet when you're working in a form. As you scroll down the list of members, you'll find three methods (marked with a green icon) and 12 events (marked with a yellow icon).

Getting Information About Constants

Each object library contains many built-in (intrinsic) constants you'll frequently want to use in your code. It's usually much faster to find these constants in the Object Browser than it is to refer to reference books.

As an example, suppose you want to look up the various constants available for use with messages boxes. Because messages boxes are available in VBA, you'll find these constants listed in the VBA library.

The Object Browser's Classes pane lists groups of constants (known as enumerations). Each group of constants in the VBA library has a name that starts with Vb. When you select a group name in the Classes pane, the Object browser displays the individual constants within that group in the Members pane. Each individual constant in the VBA library has a name that starts with vb.

To find information about message box constants,

1. With the Object Browser displayed, open the drop-down list of libraries and projects and select VBA.

2. Scroll down the Classes pane and select VbMsgBoxResult. The Object Browser Members pane lists the seven available constants, as shown in Figure 11.7.

3. Select one of the available constants. Notice that the Details pane tells you the numerical value of the selected constant.

4. In the Classes pane, select VbMsgBoxStyle. Now the Members pane displays a list of 20 constants you can use to define the appearance of a message box.

Using Object Models Within the Office Environment

CHAPTER 11

281

11

USING OBJECT
MODELS WITHIN
OFFICE

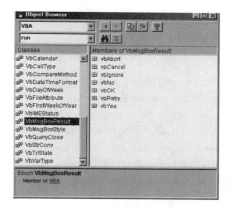

FIGURE 11.7
These seven constants are the possible values that can be returned from the MsgBox function.

If, after selecting one of the VbMsgBoxResult or VbMsgBoxStyle constants, you click the Help button, Access displays a help topic that lists that constant, its equivalent numerical value, and a brief description.

> **TIP**
>
> When you're writing or debugging VBA code and need information about intrinsic constants, it's usually much faster to find that information by using the Object Browser than by searching through reference books.

Displaying the Excel Object Model

The purpose of this section is to draw your attention to the fact that there's a lot of similarity between the Access object model and the Excel object model. This similarity extends to other components of Office and also to Office-compatible applications.

To display a graphical representation of the Excel object model,

1. Open Excel.

2. Choose Tools, move the pointer onto Macro, and choose Visual Basic Editor to display the VBE window.

3. In the VBE window, choose Help, Microsoft Visual Basic Help.

4. In the Microsoft Visual Basic Help window, select the Index tab and, in the Type Keywords box, enter Object.

5. Choose Search to display a diagram of the Excel object model.

You can explore the Excel object model in the same way you explore the Access object model(as described previously in this chapter). One important thing to notice is that the top-most object in the model is Application, an object that provides access to all the collections and objects within the Excel object model. You'll see that some of the collections and objects in the object model are the same as, or similar to, the objects in the Access object model. Other collections and objects are different because the structure of Excel is different from that of Access.

Here's the big deal. From within Access you can use VBA code to refer to the Excel Application object and, by way of that, gain access to any of the collections and objects within Excel. Similarly, from within Excel, you can use VBA code to refer to the Access Application object and, by way of that, gain access to any of the collections and objects within Access. Those previous two statements assume you have Access and Excel installed on your computer.

It gets better than that. All the major components of Office have similar object structures. The same goes for other Office-compatible applications available from Microsoft and other suppliers. From one application, such as Access, you can gain access to the capabilities of another application by way of that application's Application object.

Each Office application focuses on helping you accomplish specific goals. Access focuses on data management; Excel provides tools for analyzing data; PowerPoint is for creating presentations; Word principally lets you create text. Office-compatible applications have other goals: Visio, for example, is a powerful tool for creating diagrams.

In the real world, it's often the case that each of these applications doesn't totally satisfy your needs. You need some of what one application can do and some of what some other applications can do. That's where the power of the object model concept comes to your rescue. Working principally in one application, you can call up other applications by way of their Application objects.

In the remaining sections of this chapter, you'll discover how you can use the Access object model to begin to take control of Access objects, and then how, from within Access, you can use the Excel object model to use Excel capabilities from within Access.

Working Within a Single Access Application

When you're creating an Access application, you frequently need to refer to objects within forms and reports. Remember that the Forms collection contains all open forms and the

Reports collection contains all open reports. You can refer to a specific open form using the syntax:

`Forms![FormName]`

or to a specific open report using the syntax:

`Reports![ReportName]`

> **NOTE**
>
> The remaining pages of this section refer only to forms, but the information applies equally to reports.

For example, if an open form is named frmBook, you can refer to that form as

`Forms![frmBook]`

In effect, this says look in the collection of open forms and refer to the specific form named frmBook. Notice the use of the exclamation point operator after the name of the collection. This operator is often referred to as a *bang*.

The brackets enclosing the form name are necessary only if the form name contains characters (such as a space) that aren't allowed in VBA statements. However, because using brackets is never wrong in this context, it's good practice to enclose all form names within brackets.

> **TIP**
>
> The syntax `Forms![frmBook]` referred to previously is only one of three possible formats you can use for referring to an open form. Another syntax is `Forms("frmBook")`. Yet another syntax is `Forms(0)` in which the number within parentheses represents the position of the form within the Forms collection.
>
> The position of an object within a collection is known as its index. The index of the first object in the Forms collection is 0 (zero). In some other collections, the index of the first object is 1 (one).

You often refer to an object because you want to ascertain or set some of its properties, as explained in the next few sections.

Referring to Properties

You might want to ascertain the value of one of the properties of a form, or to set the value of that property. You can display the Object Browser and select Form in the Classes pane to see a list of available properties in the Members pane. To refer to a specific property such as the Width property, write

```
Forms![frmBook].Width
```

Notice the *dot* operator (.) precedes the property name.

To discover the width of a form, use the assignment statement

```
intFormWidth = Forms![frmBook].Width
```

in which the variable `intFormWidth` has been previously declared with a data type of `Integer`.

> **NOTE**
>
> Access internally uses *twips* as the unit of measurement to maintain widths and heights, as you'll see in the next code example. Twips are derived from the typographical measurement *point*. A point is 1/72 of an inch, and twip stands for *twentieth of a point*, resulting in 1440 twips to an inch. Therefore, using an Integer data type (which can contain positive values up to 32,7670) allows for screen widths up to 22.75 inches.
>
> When you start to work programmatically with Access, be on the lookout for surprises, such as finding twips being used for certain measurements.

To set the width of the form to five inches, use the assignment statement

```
Forms![frmBook].Width = 5 * 1440
```

in which multiplication by 1440 is used to convert inches to twips.

The statements shown so far can be used within any module in an application because they completely define the form as a member of the Forms collection. For example, you can create a command button on one form and create a click event procedure for that button to call a procedure in a standard module that displays the width of another form. The following is an example of such a procedure:

Using Object Models Within the Office Environment

CHAPTER 11

285

11

USING OBJECT
MODELS WITHIN
OFFICE

```
Public Sub FormWidth()
   Dim intFormWidth As Integer

   intFormWidth = Forms![frmBook].Width
   MsgBox "The form width is " & intFormWidth / 1440 & " inches."
End Sub
```

If you want to display a property, such as the width, of the currently active form, you can simplify the code by using the Me keyword.

> **NOTE**
>
> The Me keyword is available in a class module, such as the module behind a form that contains the code for that form. Used in this way, Me refers to the currently active form.

The following is a sample of a click event procedure for a command button that displays the width of the form containing the command button.

```
Private Sub cmdFormWidth_Click()
   Dim intFormWidth As Integer

   intFormWidth = Me.Width
   MsgBox "The width of this form is " & intFormWidth / 1440 & " inches."
End Sub
```

Some objects designate one property as a default property. For example, the Forms object (available in the Access object library) designates Item as the default property. The small, blue circle above the icon at the left of Item in the Members pane indicates the default property.

If you want to refer to the first item in the Forms collection, you can use

```
Forms.Item(0)
```

or, taking advantage of the fact that Item is the default property of the Forms collection, refer to it as

```
Forms(0)
```

Referring to Controls

When working with forms and reports, you'll often want to refer to controls on specific forms and reports. The full syntax for referring to a control on a form is

```
Forms![FormName].Controls![ControlName]
```

Thus, to refer to the control named `strTitle` on the form named `frmBook`, write

```
Forms![frmBook].Controls![strTitle]
```

This syntax refers to the Controls property of a form which is the collection of controls on a form. As before, use the bang operator (!) between the collection and name of the specific control.

In fact, the Controls property is the default property of a form. That means you can omit an explicit reference to that property, writing instead

```
Forms![frmBook]![strTitle]
```

Although, for clarity's sake, I suggest you don't omit explicit references.

One of the many properties of a `TextBox` control is Text, the text displayed in the text box. You can use the following assignment statements to retrieve and set the text displayed in a `TextBox` control

```
strTextBox = Forms![frmBook].Controls![strTitle]Forms![frmBook].Controls!
➥[strTitle] = strTextBox
```

In both cases, the variable `strTextBox` is previously declared with data type of String. The second statement assumes a string has been previously assigned to the variable.

Counting the Number of Objects in a Collection

All collections have a Count property you can use to find out how many items there are in a collection. For example, to find out how many controls exist on the `frmBook` form, you can use the Count property, as in

```
intControls = Forms![frmBook].Controls.Count
```

or, to find out how many controls exist on the currently active form,

```
intControls = Me.Controls.Count
```

Both these examples assume, of course, that the variable `intControls` is previously declared.

Discovering More About Access

There's no practical way for me to cover more than a few examples of how you navigate your way through the entire Access object model. What you learned so far in this chapter is intended to make you familiar with

- A graphical view of the Access object model that helps you see how all the objects are interrelated

- The Object Browser that provides a detailed insight into Access objects together with their properties, methods, and events
- The basics of using VBA to refer programmatically to objects

I encourage you to explore the Access object model using the techniques explained so far in this chapter. By doing so, you'll develop a fundamental understanding of how Access works and you'll prepare yourself for developing sophisticated and useful applications based on Access.

You've also seen in the preceding pages of this chapter that other Office applications each have an object model that's similar in concept to, though different in detail from, the Access object model. The remaining pages of this chapter introduce you to the concept of accessing one application's objects from within another application.

Extending the Scope of Access

Each of the major applications within Office focuses on a related set of tasks. Access, for example, focuses on data management. Excel primarily provides techniques for mathematically manipulating and analyzing numerical data. Outlook's strengths are sharing information and maintaining personal information.

In the real world, some of the things you want to do don't neatly fit into the primary focus of a single application. For example, your primary requirement might be data management—that's why you're using Access. But, perhaps some of your requirements include extensive mathematical manipulation of data. The Office environment offers two ways for you to solve this problem:

- You can construct the mathematical functionality you require by using VBA code within Access
- From within Access, you can call on the functionality that's already available within Excel

Following the long established philosophy of not re-inventing the wheel, you should consider using the functionality of another Office application, rather than taking the time to re-create that functionality within Access. The same principle applies when you're using an application other than Access; if you need something that Access does, call on Access to do it, rather than re-creating that capability within the other application.

Office includes a technology known as Automation (previously referred to as OLE Automation) that provides communication between applications. The next few sections provide an introduction to Automation.

Understanding Automation Basics

One key to understanding how to integrate one Office, or Office-compatible, application with another is the Application object (or its equivalent) that provides access to an application's complete object structure.

Something else you need to understand is the concept of Automation (Microsoft used to call it OLE Automation). *Automation* is the name Microsoft gives to the capability of one application to expose its object library to VBA and the capability of applications to use other applications' exposed object libraries. Applications that expose their object libraries are known as Automation servers; applications that can Access object libraries are known as Automation controllers. In Office 2000, Access, Excel, Outlook, PowerPoint, and Word can all act as Automation servers and as Automation controllers. Some applications—FrontPage, for example—can only act as Automation servers.

To use objects in another application's object library from within Access, you use Access as an Automation controller—you use Access to control objects served from an Automation server. To enable Access to work with an Automation server's objects, set up a reference to that server's objects, as explained in the section "Working with Object Libraries," previously in this chapter. For example, if you want to be able to work with Excel's object library, make the Microsoft Excel 9.0 Object Library available. After you've done that, the Object Browser's drop-down Project/Library list contains Excel. If you select the Excel library, the Object Browser's Classes pane lists all the objects available in the Excel library.

> **NOTE**
>
> Some objects appear in more than one library. For example, the Access and Excel object libraries each contain an Application object. Although these objects have the same name, the two objects are different. If you refer to the Application object, VBA assumes you mean the Application object in the first object library it encounters as it scans down the list of available libraries. If the Access library is listed above the Excel library, VBA uses the Application object in the Access library. As described later in this chapter, you can specify which object library VBA will use.

Using Access to Create an Excel Worksheet

This section illustrates an Access procedure that creates an Excel worksheet. An explanation of the each statement in the procedure follows the complete procedure. As explained previously in this chapter, you must create a reference to the Microsoft Excel 9.0 Object Library before creating the procedure.

Listing 11.1 is a simple version of the procedure.

LISTING 11.1   Creating an Excel Worksheet

```
'Create Excel worksheet
Public Sub CreateExcelWorksheet()
   Dim xlsApp as Excel.Application

   Set xlsApp = CreateObject("Excel.Application")

   With xlsApp
      .Workbooks.Add
      .ActiveCell.Value = 12345
      .ActiveWorkbook.SaveAs "C:\My Documents\ExcelTest.xls"
      .Quit
   End With

   Set xlsApp = Nothing
End Sub
```

As with all procedures, the code starts with a comment that explains the procedure's purpose. That's followed by a statement that declares the procedure.

The first statement in the procedure declares the variable xlsApp as an application object defined in the Excel object library. Define the variable's data type as Excel.Application instead of just Application. By doing so, you ensure that the correct application object is used, regardless of the order of object library available references in the References dialog box.

The second statement

```
Set xlsApp = CreateObject("Excel.Application")
```

creates a new instance of the Excel.Application Automation object and assigns the variable to that instance.

The next six statements

```
With xlsApp
   .Workbooks.Add
   .ActiveCell.Value = 12345
   .ActiveWorkbook.SaveAs "C:\My Documents\ExcelTest.xls"
   .Quit
End With
```

are equivalent to

```
xlsApp.Workbooks.Add
xlsApp.ActiveCell.Value = 12345
xlsApp.ActiveWorkbook.SaveAs "C:\My Documents\ExcelTest.xls"
xlsApp.Quit
```

The first of these four statements adds a new workbook to the Workbooks collection.

The second statement isn't really necessary. It's included here to give you a means to verify subsequently that a new workbook has been added. The statement simply sets the value of the top-left cell in the new workbook.

The third statement uses the SaveAs method of the ActiveWorkbook object to save the workbook in a specific folder.

The fourth statement simply quits the application.

The statement

```
Set xlsApp = Nothing
```

recovers the memory space previously reserved for the xlsApp variable.

The final line indicates the end of the procedure.

You can easily create this procedure in an Access standard module. One way to run the procedure is to create a Command button on a form and create a simple event procedure that responds to the button's Click event

```
Private Sub cmdRunCreateWorksheet_Click
    CreateExcelWorksheet
End Sub
```

After you've done that, click the button to run the CreateExcelWorksheet procedure. The procedure runs behind the scenes. The only clues you have that something is happening is that the mouse pointer changes momentarily to an hourglass and there's some hard disk activity. To verify the procedure has worked, use Windows Explorer to locate and then open the file ExcelTest.xls and then run that file. You will see a new worksheet with the value of cell A1 set to 12345.

Writing Data into an Excel Worksheet

Having established the basic principles of communicating with Excel from within Access, let's try something more ambitious. Listing 11.2 extends the preceding listing by writing data into a range of cells in an Excel worksheet.

Using Object Models Within the Office Environment

CHAPTER 11

291

11

USING OBJECT
MODELS WITHIN
OFFICE

LISTING 11.2   Writing Data into a Range of Excel Worksheet Cells

```
'Populate new Excel worksheet
'Public Sub PopulateExcelWorksheet()
   Dim xlsApp As Excel.Application
   Dim rngCell As Excel.Range
   Dim intCol As Integer
   Dim intRow As Integer
   Dim intValue As Integer

   Set xlsApp = CreateObject("Excel.Application")

   With xlsApp
      .Workbooks.Add
      For intCol = 1 To 5
         For intRow = 1 To 10
            .Worksheets("Sheet1").Cells.Item(intRow, intCol) = intValue
            intValue = intValue + 1
         Next intRow
      Next intCol
      .ActiveWorkbook.SaveAs "C:\My Documents\ExcelTest1.xls"
      .Quit
   End With
End Sub
```

The only significant difference between this procedure and the preceding one is the code within the `With...End With` section. This code uses two `For` control structures to generate cell addresses from A1 to E10. Notice that the VBA code requires addressing cells numerically; for example, cell A1 is addressed as `1, 1` (which is explained in the following paragraphs). For each cell, the `Worksheets` property is used to write a value into that cell. (For more information about using loops, refer to Appendix A, "Visual Basic for Applications Primer.")

The five statements after the procedure declaration declare variables used within the procedure. The statement

```
Set xlsApp = CreateObject("Excel.Application")
```

creates a new Excel Application object and declares the variable `xlsApp` to represent that object.

Some of the statements between

```
With xlsApp
```

and

```
End With
```

take advantage of the `With...End With` control structure. For example, the statement

```
.Workbooks.Add
```

is within the control structure, and is equivalent to

```
xlsAdd.Workbooks.Add
```

The statement

```
.Workbooks.Add
```

adds a new workbook to the Excel application.

The sequence of statements

```
For intCol = 1 To 5
   For IntRow = 1 To 10
      .Worksheets("Sheet1").Cells.Item(intRow, intCol) = intValue
      intValue = intValue + 1
   Next intRow
Next intCol
```

contains two nested `For...Next` control structures. These structures work as follows:

1. The variable `intCol` is initially set to 1.
2. The variable `intRow` is initially set to 1.
3. Cell (1, 1) in the worksheet named Sheet1 is set to 0 (zero)—the initial value of `intValue`.
4. 1 (one) is added to the previous value of `intValue`.
5. The variable `intRow` is set to the next value (2).
6. Cell (2, 1) in the worksheet is set to the value of `intValue`.
7. 1 (one) is added to the previous value of `intValue`.
8. The variable `intRow` is set to the next value (3).
9. This process continues so that cells (1, 1), (2, 1), (3, 1), (4, 1), (5, 1), (6, 1), (7, 1), (8, 1), (9, 1), and (10, 1) are set to values 0, 1, 2, 3, 4, 5, 6, 7, 8, and 9, respectively.
10. The variable `intCol` is set to the second value (2).
11. The inner `For...Next` structure runs as before to set cells (1, 2) through (10, 2) to the values 10 through 19, respectively.
12. The variable `intCol` is successively set to values 3 through 5 and, for each value, the inner `For...Next` structure sets the 10 cells in each column to the values 20 through 29, 30 through 39, and 40 through 49.

Using Object Models Within the Office Environment

CHAPTER 11

293

11

USING OBJECT
MODELS WITHIN
OFFICE

The statement

```
.ActiveWorkbook.SaveAs "C"\My Documents\ExcelTest1.xls"
```

saves the Excel workbook in the defined location on your disk.

The statement

```
.Quit
```

closes Excel.

As before, you can create a command button on a form to run the procedure. Then you can use Windows Explorer to find and open the worksheet so that you can confirm the procedure has correctly written values into the range of cells.

Copying Data Between Access and Other Applications

Although the example in the previous section illustrates the principles of using Automation to write data into an Excel worksheet, it doesn't do anything you're likely to need in the real world. This section covers a practical need that you're likely to have—copying data from an Access table into an Excel workbook.

Access provides an easy way for you copy data from a table into an Excel workbook:

1. Open an Access application and display the Database window.
2. Select the table that you want to copy, or select a query that creates a recordset containing the data you want to copy.
3. Choose Tools, Analyze It with MS Excel. Excel opens displaying a worksheet containing the data in the table you selected, or the data in the recordset created by the query.
4. Choose File, Save to save the Excel workbook.

By defining criteria in a query, you can usually transfer whatever data you want from Access tables to an Excel worksheet.

The section "Importing Data from a Spreadsheet" in Chapter 10, "Using External Data in an Access Application," explains how you can copy data from an Excel workbook into an Access table.

There might be times, though, when you need more control than is possible by using the interactive capabilities built in to Office applications. In that case, you can use VBA code to take complete control of what information is copied from Access into another application and copied from another application into Access. Before you can do that, you need to have some understanding of data access models, a subject that's covered in Chapter 12, "Accessing Data."

Summary

Access, as well as the other Office applications, is built on the concept of objects—software entities that have properties and methods and respond to events. The Access user interface hides this fundamental structure from people who use the application interactively. However, to create applications based on Access, you need an understanding of the object structure of Access.

The Microsoft Access Objects topic in Microsoft Visual Basic Help displays a diagram of Access objects that shows the relationship between objects. You can click any object within the diagram to see detailed information about that object. You can also use the built-in Object Browser to find information about objects. The VBA programming language gives you access to the objects within Access, as well as to objects in other Office applications.

From within Access, you can provide communication with objects in other Office and Office-compatible applications. That enables you to incorporate the functionality of Excel, for example, in your Access-based application.

Accessing Data

IN THIS CHAPTER

The primary purpose of an Access application is, of course, to provide access to data. Although that might seem like a very simplistic statement, it has deep implications because the data to be accessed may be stored in many different places and in many different formats.

If you're using a database application such as Access for personal purposes, you probably don't need to care very much about where the data is stored other than to be aware of the folder on your hard disk that holds the data. Likewise, you don't need to be concerned about the data format. Your application can save data in, and retrieve data from, its native format without you having to know much about that format.

Although you can use Access for small, personal databases, it's intended to cope with much more complex situations. You can use Access to work with data that's stored on your local hard disk or data that's available on a server. The data you work with can be in the native Access format, in other Office formats such as those that are native to Excel or Outlook, and in many other formats, such as SQL Server and Oracle.

To support this variety of data locations and formats, Access needs a mechanism that sits between the user interface and the actual data. This mechanism is called a *data access model*. Data access models are the subject of this chapter. This chapter provides an introduction to using ActiveX Data Objects (ADO) and Data Access Objects (DAO) for managing data in the native Access format.

Putting Data Access into Perspective

The purpose of this chapter is to introduce you to the basic information you need to know about data access models, not to provide comprehensive information about the subject.

> **TIP**
>
> After reading this chapter, if you need more detailed information about data access models, refer to such books as *Special Edition Using Microsoft Access 2000*, published by Que, or *Microsoft Access 2000 Unleashed*, published by Sams Publishing.

Versions of Access prior to Access 2000 included Data Access Objects (DAO) as a means of accessing data. DAO went through several upgrades up to version 3.5 in Access 97. Access 2000 is supplied with DAO version 3.6, a maintenance upgrade of DAO version 3.5. In DAO, you have access to workspaces that enable you to use the Jet database engine and also, in DAO versions 3.5 and 3.6, to use ODBCDirect to access data in any format that's ODBC-compliant.

NOTE

ODBC is an abbreviation for Open Database Connectivity, an interface that allows a database client, such as Access, to interact with data stored on a server.

The Jet database engine basically provides access to data in the default Access format. You can also use it to connect to databases in other common formats, but with some limitations. ODBCDirect provides more efficient connection to databases that conform to the ODBC standard than is possible by way of the Jet database engine.

Access 2000 introduced ActiveX Data Objects (ADO), a new, more efficient, and simpler way of accessing data that exists in many formats, including some formats DAO can't access.

If you're just beginning to think seriously about accessing data, you should probably concentrate your efforts on ADO because that's the way Microsoft plans to proceed. However, if you support existing database applications that include VBA code written for DAO, you can choose between

- Learning how to use VBA code to support DAO so that you can continue to use DAO
- Changing to ADO and modifying the existing VBA code to work with ADO

CAUTION

Microsoft apparently intends ADO to supercede DAO. Although ADO is, in some ways, more powerful than DAO, some capabilities of DAO are missing in the current version of ADO. It's important to bear in mind that some capabilities of ADO depend on functionality in the target database. For example, some things you can do with ADO when it's connected to the Jet database engine, you can't do when it's connected to SQL Server. Likewise, some things you can do with ADO when it's connected to SQL Server, you can't do when it's connected to the Jet database engine.

The description of ADO in this chapter is limited to working with the Jet database engine.

Understanding ActiveX Data Objects

ActiveX Data Objects provide a means for you to use Access to interact with data stored in many locations and in many formats. The objects available to you while you're working with Access depend on the currently available object libraries. When you open a new Access application, references are automatically made available to these object libraries:

- Visual Basic for Applications (VBA)
- Microsoft Access 9.0 Object Library (Access)
- OLE Automation (stdole)
- Microsoft ActiveX Data Objects 2.1 Library (ADODB)

> **NOTE**
>
> In this list, the names at the left are those that appear in the References dialog box. The abbreviations within parentheses are those listed in the Object Browser's drop-down Project/Library list.

The Microsoft ActiveX Data Objects 2.1 Library (ADODB) contains the ADO objects required for making connections to data sources, issuing commands, and working with record-sets. Several other ADO libraries are available, but the use of these is beyond the scope of this chapter.

> **NOTE**
>
> For detailed information about ADO, refer to the help file Ado210.chm. If you created a default installation of Office 2000, this file is in your C:\Program Files\Common Files\SYSTEM\ADO folder. You can find a wealth of additional information about ADO on the Web site http://www.microsoft.com/data/ado.

Accessing Data in the Native Access Format

This chapter focuses on working with data in the native Access format. Access and other Office applications use a software component known as the *Jet database engine* to work with data in this format. The first step in preparing to work programmatically with data is to establish a connection to that data.

Connecting to a Data Source Using ADO

To establish a connection to a database, you have to create a variable and then assign to that variable a value that specifies a provider, the type of access required, and the data source. The provider identifies the type of database you want to access; the data source specifies the location of the data. Listing 12.1 is a procedure that identifies the Jet database engine as the data provider, read/write as the type of access, and the Publisher table in the Book database as the data source.

> **NOTE**
>
> In order to make it as easy as possible for you to understand how to use VBA code to work with ActiveX Data Objects, the code examples in this chapter omit error checking. Refer to Chapter 13, "Taking More Control of Access," for information about error checking.

LISTING 12.1   Code to Identify the Jet Database Engine as the Data Provider

```
Sub ADOOpenPublisher()
    Dim cnnBook As New ADODB.Connection
    Dim strProvider As String
    Dim strDataSource As String

    'Create a connection
    strProvider = "Microsoft.Jet.OLEDB.4.0"
    strDataSource = "C:\My Documents\AccessNew\Book.mdb"

    cnnBook.mode = adModeReadWrite
    cnnBook.Open "Provider = " & strProvider & "; Data Source = " &
➥strDataSource
    ....            'Now do something with the data
    cnnBook.Close
End Sub
```

The procedure is declared by the statement

```
Sub ADOOpenPublisher()
```

that provides a name for the procedure. As always, the name should indicate the purpose of the procedure. The empty parentheses after the name show that the procedure has no arguments.

The first three statements in the procedure are declarations, the most significant of which is the first. That statement creates a variable that represents a new ADO connection.

> **TIP**
>
> The first declaration could be written
>
> ```
> Dim cnnBook As New Connection
> ```
>
> but that presents a potential problem in that it doesn't specify the Connection object in the ADODB object library. By writing the declaration as shown in the ADOOpenPublisher procedure, you can be sure the Connection object used is the one in the ADODB object library, even if another available object library contains a Connection object.

The next two declarations declare string variables to be used for the name of the data provider and the name of data source. Values are assigned to these string variables in the next two statements:

```
strProvider = "Microsoft.Jet.OLEDB.4.0"
strDataSource = "C:\My Documents\AccessNew\Book.mdb"
```

The first of these specifies the Jet database engine (version 4.0). The second assignment statement specifies the file that contains the data.

The next statement

```
cnnBook.mode = adModeReadWrite
```

defines a property for the cnnBook variable. adModeReadWrite is an ADO intrinsic constant that defines the mode of the opened data source to be read/write—you can read data from the data source, you can edit existing data, and you can add new data to the data source.

The constants listed in Table 12.1 can be used to specify the connection mode permissions.

TABLE 12.1   Connection Mode Constants

Constant	Description
adModeUnknown	Default; permissions haven't been set or cannot be determined
adModeRead	Read-only permission
adModeWrite	Write-only permission
adModeReadWrite	Read and write permissions
adModeShareDenyRead	Other users can't open connection with read permission
adModeShareDenyWrite	Other users can't open connection with write permission
adModeShareExclusive	Other users can't open connection
adModeShareDenyNone	Other users can't open connection with any permissions

The statement

```
cnnBook.Open "Provider = " & strProvider & "; Data Source = " & strDataSource
```

calls the Open method to use a specific provider to open a specific data source. The provider is defined by the variable `strProvider` which, in this case, was previously assigned the value Microsoft.Jet.OLEDB.4.0. This provider, which is installed with Office 2000, provides a connection to the Jet database engine (version 4.0).

The data source is defined by the variable strDataSource that identifies the database file. In the example used here, the database file is the Book database.

After making a connection to a data source, you want to do something with that data, such as creating a recordset and working with the data in that recordset, as described in the next section. The final statement in the procedure

```
cnnBook.Close
```

closes the connection and makes the memory used by it available for other purposes.

Creating a Recordset Using ADO

Recall from Chapter 4, "Creating Information Out of Data," that a recordset is a temporary table that exists in memory. To create a recordset based on data in the data source, first declare a recordset variable with a statement such as

```
Dim rstPub As Recordset
```

Then insert the following statements before the cnnBook.Close statement in the procedure described in the preceding section:

```
Set rstPub = New ADODB.Recordset
rstPub.Open "tblPublisher", cnnBook, adOpenDynamic, adLockOptimistic,
➥adCmdTable
rstPub.Close
```

The first of these three statements is an assignment that sets the rstPub variable to a new ADO recordset. The second statement uses the Open method to create a recordset that contains data from the Publisher table in the Book database. You'll find more information about this statement in the section "Digging Deeper into the Open Method" subsequently in this chapter. The third statement closes the recordset and recovers the space in memory occupied by the recordset.

Verifying Your Code Works

There's one significant problem here. When you run the procedure, you've no immediate way of knowing that it's working correctly. You can solve that problem by inserting this statement before the rstPub.Close statement

```
Debug.Print rstPub.Fields(0).Value, rstPub.Fields(1).Value
```

The preceding statement accesses the Fields collection within a record. Fields(0) accesses the first field in a record; Fields(1) accesses the second field in a record.

The Debug.Print statement is an extremely useful technique you can use to examine what your code does. It displays the results of running code in the Visual Basic Editor (VBE) Immediate window. Here's how it works.

Open the VBE window to display your ADOOpenPublisher procedure. The window should look like the one shown in Figure 12.1.

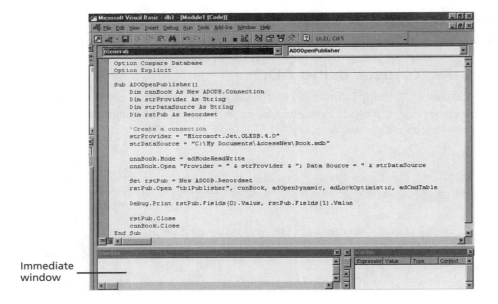

Immediate window

FIGURE 12.1

The large pane in the VBE window displays your code.

Make sure the Immediate window is displayed, although it might not be in the same position as the one shown in Figure 12.1. If the Immediate window isn't displayed, choose View, Immediate Window to display it.

Place the insertion point anywhere within your code, and then choose Run, Run Sub/UserForm. (Alternatively, press F5 or choose the Run Sub/UserForm button in the toolbar.) The Immediate window now shows the result of the Debug.Print statement. In this case, the Immediate window shows the values of the first two fields in the first record of the recordset. That confirms your code is running as expected.

Digging Deeper into the Open Method

The example you've just seen makes use of a recordset's Open method. That example probably leaves many questions to be answered before you can feel confident about using the Open method for your own purposes.

The general syntax of the Open method is

```
recordset.Open Source, ActiveConnection, CursorType, LockType, Options
```

As this syntax statement shows, the Open method can have the following five parameters:

- *Source*—The source of the recordset's data. This is usually the name of a table (such as Customers) or a SQL statement.

- *ActiveConnection*—The active connection to use. This is usually the name of a Connection object (such as cnnNorthwind).

- *CursorType*—The type of access to the recordset. The four available cursor types are defined by the constants listed in Table 12.2.

TABLE 12.2   *CursorType* Constants

Constant	Description
adOpenDynamic	Dynamic cursor. Used to find data and to update data. Forward and backward scrolling is possible. Additions, changes, and deletions made by other users are visible.
adOpenStatic	Static cursor. Provides a static copy of a set of records. Used to find data or generate reports. Forward and backward scrolling is possible. Additions, changes, and deletions made by other users are not visible.
adOpenForwardOnly	Forward-only cursor (default). Similar to a static cursor, except only forward scrolling is possible.
adOpenKeyset	Keyset cursor. Similar to a dynamic cursor, except records added by other users are not visible.

- *LockType*—The type of locking the provider uses when opening the recordset. The four available lock types are defined by the constants listed in Table 12.3.

Table 12.3 *LockType* Constants

Constant	Description
adLockReadOnly	Provides read-only access to the data (default).
adLockPessimistic	Pessimistic locking, record by record. The provider has the responsibility to ensure successful editing of records.
adLockOptimistic	Optimistic locking, record by record. The provider locks records on when the Update method is called.
adLockBatchOptimistic	Optimistic batch updates. Required for batch update mode but not for immediate update mode.

- *Options*—Various options that determine how a recordset is identified. The nine options available are listed in Table 12.4.

Table 12.4 *Options* Constants

Constant	Description
adCmdText	Provider evaluates *Source* as a text definition of a command (default).
adCmdTable	ADO generates a SQL query to return all rows from the table named in *Source*.
adCmdTableDirect	Provider returns all rows from the table named in *Source*.
adCmdStoredProc	Provider evaluates *Source* as a stored procedure.
adCmdUnknown	The type of command in *Source* is not known.
adCmdFile	The saved recordset should be restored from the file named in *Source*.
adAsyncExecute	Source should be executed asynchronously.
adAsyncFetch	After the initial quantity specified in the Initial Fetch Size property has been fetched, any remaining rows should be fetched asynchronously. If the required row has not been fetched, the main thread is blocked until the requested row becomes available.
adAsyncFetchNonBlocking	Similar to adAsyncFetch with the exception that the main thread is never blocked. If the requested row has not been fetched, the current row automatically moves to the end of the file.

Having a fairly complete picture of how the Open method can be used to open a recordset, take another look at the statement

```
rstPub.Open "tblPublisher", cnnPub, adOpenDynamic, adLockOptimistic, adCmdTable
```

One important thing to notice is that all five parameters of the Open method are explicitly stated. If you want to use the default value for any parameter, you can omit that parameter. When you do that, you must leave the commas in place, as in

```
rstPub.Open "tblPublisher", cnnPub, , , adCmdTable
```

As you can see in the preceding tables, the default for the *CursorType* parameter is adOpenForwardOnly and the default for the LockType parameter is adLockReadOnly.

In the statement, the Options parameter is adCmdTable, which is required for the Source parameter to be understood as the name of a table.

Putting this all together, the statement opens a recordset based on the Publisher table in the Book database, using a dynamic cursor, and allowing read/write access.

Using a SQL Statement in the Open Method

As the previous section described, an Open method's Source parameter can be the name of a table or query as used in the preceding example, or it can be a SQL statement. You could replace the name of a table with something like

```
"SELECT * FROM tblPublisher WHERE State = 'CA'"
```

in which case the complete statement becomes

```
rstCustomers.Open "SELECT * FROM tblPublisher _
WHERE State = 'CA'", cnnBook, , , adCmdTable
```

Using a SQL statement in this manner gives you the opportunity to use all the power of SQL to select which records from a table or recordset you want to include in the new recordset. In this case, the new recordset includes only publishers in the state of California.

Navigating Within a Recordset Using ADO

So far, you've seen how to connect to a data source using the Jet database engine, and how to create a recordset that contains records from the data source. Consider, now, how to access various records within the recordset.

Whenever a recordset is open, one of the records within the recordset is the current record. At the time a recordset is first opened, the first record in that recordset is the current record. That's why, previously in this chapter, when you used Debug.Print to verify the procedure was working, the VBE Immediate window showed the values of some fields in the first record.

When you retrieve a value from a field in a recordset, you always get the value of a field in the current record.

You can use the five methods listed in Table 12.5 to control which record is the current record.

TABLE 12.5   Methods That Change the Current Record in a Recordset

Method	Definition
Move	Move to a record some number of records before or after the current record or another specific record.
MoveFirst	Move to the first record in the recordset.
MoveLast	Move to the last record in the recordset.
MoveNext	Move to the next record in the recordset.
MovePrevious	Move to the previous record in the recordset.

You can use these methods to make any record within a recordset the current record. There are, however, two special cases you should know about. If the current record is the first record, the MovePrevious method makes a field known as BOF (Beginning Of File) the current record. Likewise, if the current record is the last record, the MoveNext method makes a field known as EOF (End Of File) the current record. BOF and EOF are not real records; they are dummy records you can use to test whether you have reached a record before the first record or beyond the last record.

TIP

If the current record is BOF, subsequent use of the MovePrevious method results in a runtime error. Likewise, if the current record is EOF, subsequent use of the MoveNext method results in a runtime error. To avoid these runtime errors, your VBA code should not allow use of MovePrevious if the current record is BOF. Neither should your code allow use of MoveNext if the current record is EOF.

NOTE

It's possible to have an empty recordset—a recordset that contains no records. In that case, the current record is simultaneously BOF and EOF. You can use this to test whether a recordset contains any records.

To illustrate how to move from one record to another within a recordset, let's see how you can open a recordset and display values in the last record. Listing 12.2 is the VBA code you can use.

LISTING 12.2   VBA Code to Display Last Record

```
Sub ADOOpenPublisher()
    Dim cnnPub As New ADODB.Connection
    Dim strProvider As String
    Dim strDataSource As String
    Dim rstPub As ADODB.Recordset

    'Create a connection
    strProvider = "Microsoft.Jet.OLEDB.4.0"
    strDataSource = "C:\My Documents\AccessNew\Book.mdb"

    cnnPub.mode = adModeRead
    cnnPub.Open "Provider = " & strProvider & "; Data Source = " & strDataSource

    'Create reference to recordset
    Set rstPub = New ADODB.Recordset
    rstPub.Open "tblPublisher", cnnBook, adOpenStatic, , adCmdTable

    'Move to last record
    rstPub.MoveLast

    'Display fields in Immediate window
    Debug.Print rstPub.Fields(0).Value, rstPub.Fields(1).Value

    'Close variables
    rstPub.Close
    cnnPub.Close
End Sub
```

Notice two things here:

- The CursorType parameter in the rstPub.Open statement must have a value that allows backward scrolling. In the example shown here, the CursorType parameter is set to adOpenStatic. Although it might not be obvious at first, moving to the last record of a recordset implies that you're subsequently going to want to scroll backward through the recordset.
- The statement rstPub.MoveLast sets the last record as the current record.

After creating this code, you can place the insertion point within the procedure and press F5 to run it. You'll see values from the last record in the Immediate window.

To further demonstrate how you can move from one record in a recordset to another, you can add statements in the procedure such as those shown in Listing 12.3.

LISTING 12.3   VBA Code to Display Various Records

```
Sub ADOOpenPublisher()
    Dim cnnPub As New ADODB.Connection
    Dim strProvider As String
    Dim strDataSource As String
    Dim rstPub As ADODB.Recordset

    'Create a connection
    strProvider = "Microsoft.Jet.OLEDB.4.0"
    strDataSource = "C:\My Documents\AccessNew\Book.mdb"
    cnnPub.mode = adModeRead
    cnnPub.Open "Provider = " & strProvider & "; Data Source = " & strDataSource

    'Create reference to recordset
    Set rstPub = New ADODB.Recordset
    rstPub.Open "tblPublisher", cnnBook, adOpenStatic, , adCmdTable

    'Move to last record
    rstPub.MoveLast

    'Display fields in Immediate window
    Debug.Print rstPub.Fields(0).Value, rstPub.Fields(1).Value

    'Display previous record
    rstPub.MovePrevious
    Debug.Print rstPub.Fields(0).Value, rstPub.Fields(1).Value

    'Display next record
    rstPub.MoveNext
    Debug.Print rstPub.Fields(0).Value, rstPub.Fields(1).Value

    'Display first record
    rstPub.MoveFirst
    Debug.Print rstPub.Fields(0).Value, rstPub.Fields(1).Value

    'Close variables
    rstPub.Close
    cnnPub.Close
End Sub
```

If you run this procedure as previously explained, you'll see in the Immediate window

- The values of the first two fields of the last record in the recordset
- The values of the first two fields of the penultimate record in the recordset
- The values of the first two fields of the last record in the recordset
- The values of the first two fields of the first record in the recordset

Although this demonstration illustrates how you can use the MoveFirst, MoveLast, MoveNext, and MovePrevious methods to navigate within a recordset, it doesn't provide detailed information about how you can use these methods in a practical application. In order to do that, we need to take a diversion to some important facts about variables. That's because a practical use of the MoveFirst, MoveLast, MoveNext, and MovePrevious methods relies on using a variable that's available in several procedures.

What You Need to Know About Variables

Within VBA, a *variable* is a named space in memory that's reserved for specific data. Some types of variables are quite easy to understand: For example, a variable of type Integer sets aside two bytes of memory that can contain values ranging from –32,768 through +32,767. Other variables, such as those of type Recordset, refer to the beginning of an area of memory that contains data of a specific kind.

When a variable is declared, such as in a Dim statement, some memory is reserved for that variable. When a value is assigned to a variable, the amount of memory reserved for it may be unchanged, as in the case of an Integer variable, or may be changed to accommodate the information the variable represents, as in the case of a Recordset variable.

After memory is reserved for a variable, that memory is off-limits for anything else until, one way or another, the memory is released.

If a variable is declared within a procedure, the memory it uses is normally reserved while the procedure is active. When the procedure terminates, all memory reserved for variables within that procedure is released for other uses. An exception to this is for Static variables. Memory reserved for Static variables within a procedure stays reserved for possible use the next time the same variable is used.

Variables can be declared in the following three places:

- Class modules—The class modules we're considering here contain the event procedures that respond to events that occur in forms and reports.
- Standard modules—Standard modules contain sub procedures and functions that may be called by event procedures in class modules and also by other sub procedures and function in standard modules.
- Property modules—Property modules are beyond the scope of this book.

A variable declared within a procedure is available only within that procedure—the scope of the variable is said to be *local*. You can't declare a variable within a procedure and make that variable available in other procedures.

A variable declared within a module, but not within a procedure, is available to all the procedures within that module if the variable is declared as Private, or is available to procedures in other modules if the variable is declared as Public.

If you want to use a variable in various procedures, you can

- Declare the variable as Private outside a procedure within a module and subsequently use it in any procedure within that module
- Declare the variable as Public outside a procedure within a module and subsequently use it in any procedure within any module

TIP

You should make your variables as private as possible in order to avoid unintended conflicts.

Displaying Information from a Recordset

This section uses the Publisher Information form, shown in Figure 12.2, in the Book database to show you how to put together what you've learned so far in this chapter.

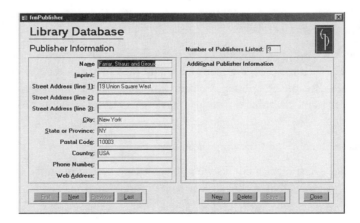

FIGURE 12.2

The Publisher Information form, shown here in Form view, displays information about publishers and contains command buttons you can use to move from one publisher to another.

NOTE

You can copy the Book application that contains the Publisher Information form from the CD-ROM that accompanies this book.

The left part of the form displays the principal information about a publisher; the right part displays any additional information from a memo field. You can click the four buttons at the bottom-left of the form to move from one publisher to another.

The functionality of the form is controlled by procedures in a class module behind the form. Five of these procedures are event procedures:

- Form_Open—This procedure, which runs when the form opens, establishes a connection to the Book database using the Microsoft Jet database engine as a provider. The event procedure also opens a recordset that contains data from a query based on the Publisher table, and controls which command buttons are initially enabled.

- cmdFirst_Click—This procedure, which runs when you click the First button, makes the first record in the recordset the current record.

- cmdNext_Click—This procedure, which runs when you click the Next button, makes the next record in the recordset the current record.

- cmdPrevious_Click—This procedure, which runs when you click the Previous button, makes the previous record in the recordset the current record.

- cmdLast_Click—This procedure, which runs when you click the Last button, makes the last record in the recordset the current record.

Although the four buttons change the current record from one record in the recordset to another, that change doesn't display data from the new current record in the form; the procedure DisplayPub does that.

The following sections explain how you can display information from one record at a time on a form.

Referencing Object Libraries

The form, as presented in Figure 12.2, makes use of the Microsoft ActiveX Data Objects 2.1 Library. Before you go any further, open the Visual Basic Editor and choose Tools, References. You should see these object libraries checked to indicate they are available:

- Visual Basic for Applications
- Microsoft Access 9.0 Object Library

- OLE Automation
- Microsoft ActiveX Data Objects 2.1 Library

These are the object libraries that are available by default when you start a new Access project. If any of these object libraries isn't available, use the method described in the section "Working with Object Libraries" in Chapter 11, "Using Object Models Within the Office Environment" to make these object libraries available.

Understanding the Form's Class Module

All the declarations and procedures used by the form are in the form's class module, as described in detail in this section and the next few sections.

All the procedures use, in one way or another, a variable that represents the recordset that the form deals with. If that variable were to be declared separately in each procedure, it would also be necessary to assign a value to it in this procedure. A much better way is to declare the variable at the module level so that it's available in all procedures within the module, as described in the section "What You Need to Know About Variables" previously in this chapter.

When you open the form, the Form_Open event occurs first. This event triggers the Form_Open event procedure that, among other things, assigns a value to the variable that represents the recordset. Because the variable is declared at the module level, the value assigned to it is available to all procedures within the module.

The variable that represents the recordset is declared by the statement

```
Dim mrstPub As Recordset
```

Notice that the prefix for the variable name is *mrst* instead of just *rst*. When you inspect the code and see this variable used within a procedure, the *mrst* prefix reminds you that the variable is declared at the module level.

Understanding the Form_Open Event Procedure

The Form_Open event procedure contains the code shown in Listing 12.4.

LISTING 12.4   Form_Open Event Procedure

```
'Open Publisher form
Private Sub Form_Open(Cancel As Integer)
    Dim cnnBook As New ADODB.Connection
    Dim strProvider As String
    Dim strDataSource As String
```

```
'Create a connection
strProvider = "Microsoft.Jet.OLEDB.4.0"
strDataSource = "C:\My Documents\AccessNew\Book.mdb"

cnnBook.Mode = adModeReadWrite
cnnBook.Open "Provider = " & strProvider & "; Data Source = " _
& strDataSource

'Open recordset
mrstPub.Open "qryPublisher", cnnBook, adOpenDynamic, _
adLockOptimistic, adCmdTable

'Enable and disable command buttons
cmdFirst.Enabled = False
cmdNext.Enabled = True
cmdPrevious.Enabled = False
cmdLast.Enabled = True
cmdNew.Enabled = True
cmdDelete.Enabled = True
cmdSave.Enabled = False
cmdClose.Enabled = True

'Display number of records in the recordset
CountRecord
'Display values of fields
DisplayPub
End Sub
```

To create this procedure, display the forms Property sheet and, in the Event tab, click the ellipsis at the right of the On Open event to display the VBE window. That window contains the first and last statements for the new event procedure

```
Private Sub Form_Open(Cancel As Integer)

End Sub
```

Unlike the event procedures described previously in this chapter, the Form_Open procedure has a single argument—Cancel As Integer—the purpose of which is described in the section "Canceling an Event" in Chapter 13.

The first few lines of code in this procedure create a connection to the Book database using the Jet database engine as a provider. This code is almost the same as that described in the sections "Connecting to a Data Source Using ADO" and "Creating a Recordset Using ADO" previously in this chapter. Notice, though, that the code assigns a value to the variable mrstPub that can be used in other procedures within the module.

After creating a connection to the Book database and declaring and assigning a value to the variable mrstPub, the procedure makes sure the correct command buttons are enabled and disabled. When the recordset is initially created, its first record is the current record. It makes no sense at that time to invite a user to click the First button (the button that makes the first record the current record). For that reason, the statement

```
cmdFirst.Enabled = False
```

disables (makes dim) the button labeled First.

Also, as described in the section "Navigating Within a Recordset Using ADO" previously in this chapter, you don't want a user to click the Previous button while the first record is selected. For that reason, the statement

```
cmdPrevious,Enabled = False
```

disables the button labeled Previous.

The statements

```
cmdNext.Enabled = True
cmdLast.Enabled = True
```

are not necessary because the Enabled property of each command button is normally set to True at design time, but the statements are included so that someone who reads the code completely understands your intentions.

The two statements

```
CountRecord
DisplayPub
```

call on other procedures that are described in detail subsequently in this chapter. The CountRecord procedure counts the number of records in the recordset. The DisplayPub procedure displays the values of fields in the current record on the form.

Moving from One Record to Another

The form has four buttons you can click to move from one record to another. Each button has a caption, a name, and a purpose, as shown in Table 12.5.

TABLE 12.5   Move Buttons

Caption	Name	Purpose
First	cmdFirst	Makes the first record the current record
Next	cmdNext	Makes the next record the current record
Previous	cmdPrevious	Makes the previous record the current record
Last	cmdLast	Makes the last record the current record

Each of these buttons triggers an event procedure when the button is clicked. The event procedure that runs when a user clicks the cmdFirst button is shown in Listing 12.5.

LISTING 12.5 VBA Code to Enable and Disable Command Buttons When First Record Is Selected

```
'Display first record
Private Sub cmdFirst_Click()
   mrstPub.MoveFirst
   txtName.SetFocus

   cmdFirst.Enabled = False
   cmdNext.Enabled = True
   cmdPrevious.Enabled = False
   cmdLast.Enabled = True
   DisplayPub
End Sub
```

The first statement in this procedure simply sets the current record to the first record in the mrstPub recordset.

When a user clicks the First button on the form, that button has, and retains, the focus. The properties of an object, such as a button, can't be changed while the object has the focus. Because a subsequent statement attempts to change one of the properties of the First button, it's necessary to move the focus from the First button to some other object on the form. The statement

```
txtName.SetFocus
```

moves the focus from the First button to the text box named txtName.

The next four statements in the procedure make the First, Next, Previous, and Last buttons enabled as appropriate. The First button is disabled because it makes no sense to use that button when the first record in the recordset is already the current record. The Previous button is disabled to prevent a user from attempting to move to a record before the first record. The Next and Last buttons are enabled to allow other records in the recordset to become the current record.

The final statement in the procedure calls the DisplayPub procedure to display the values of the first record in the recordset on the form. This procedure is necessary because the action of making a record the current record doesn't automatically display the values of fields in that record on the form. The DisplayPub procedure is described later in this chapter.

The Last button on the form works in much the same way as the First button. The essential difference is that statements in the cmdLast procedure enable the First and Previous buttons, and disable the Next and Last buttons.

The event procedures called by the Next and Previous buttons have a little more to take care of. Consider the Next button, for example. If the current record within the recordset is not the last record, it's okay to click the Next button to make the next record the current record. However, if the last record in the recordset is the current record, you need a protection mechanism to prevent attempting to make a record after the last record the current record.

The code for the cmdNext_Click event procedure is shown in Listing 12.6.

LISTING 12.6   Code to Enable and Disable Command Buttons When Next Record Is Selected

```
'Display next record
Private Sub cmdNext_Click()
    mrstPub.MoveNext
    txtName.SetFocus

    'Test for last record
    mrstPub.MoveNext
    If mrstPub.EOF Then
        cmdNext.Enabled = False
        cmdLast.Enabled = False
    Else
        cmdNext.Enabled = True
        cmdLast.Enabled = True
    End If
    cmdFirst.Enabled = True
    cmdPrevious.Enabled = True
    mrstPub.MovePrevious

    DisplayPub
End Sub
```

The first two statements in this code are similar to the first two statements in the cmdFirst_Click event procedure.

The next section of code tests to see whether the new current record is the last record in the recordset. It does this by using the MoveNext method to move to the next record and then testing to see whether the new current record is EOF. If that's the case, the Next and Last buttons are disabled; otherwise, these buttons are enabled. After making the test, the MovePrevious method restores the current record to what it was before the test.

The cmdPrevious_Click event procedure is similar to the cmdNext_Click procedure. The significant difference is that a test is made to see whether the new current record is the first record in the recordset.

Displaying Values of the Current Recordset's Fields

Each of the four event procedures—cmdFirst_Click, cmdNext_Click, cmdPrevious_Click, and cmdLast_Click—calls the DisplayPub procedure to update what's displayed on the form with the values of the fields in the new current record. The VBA code for this procedure is shown in Listing 12.7.

LISTING 12.7   Code to Update What's Displayed on the Form When a New Record Is Selected

```
'Display updated Publisher record
Private Sub DisplayPub()
   txtName = mrstPub!strName
   txtImprint = mrstPub!strImprint
   txtStreetAddress1 = mrstPub!strStreetAddress1
   txtStreetAddress2 = mrstPub!strStreetAddress2
   txtStreetAddress3 = mrstPub!strStreetAddress3
   txtCity = mrstPub!strCity
   txtState = mrstPub!strState
   txtPostCode = mrstPub!strPostCode
   txtCountry = mrstPub!strCountry
   txtPhone = mrstPub!strPhone
   txtWeb = mrstPub!strWeb
   memComment = mrstPub!memComment
End Sub
```

This procedure consists of several assignment statements, each of which makes the value of a control on the form equal to the value of a field in the current record.

Counting the Number of Records in a Recordset

The Form_Open event procedure, described previously in this chapter in the section "Understanding the Form_Open Event Procedure," calls the procedure CountRecord to count the number of records in the recordset and displays that number on the form.

ADO defines the property RecordCount for recordsets. The intention is that this property contains the number of records in a recordset. The RecordCount property requires support from the specific type of recordset being used, support that isn't available in recordsets provided by the Jet database engine. That means you can't make use of the RecordCount property in the example we're working with here.

> **NOTE**
>
> If you attempt to use the RecordCount property with the Jet database engine, you'll find it returns the value of 0 (zero) if the recordset contains no records, or –1 if the recordset contains one or more records.

Because you can't use the RecordCount property to find the number of records in the recordset, you have to create a short procedure to count records. The code for the CountRecord procedure is shown in Listing 12.8.

LISTING 12.8   VBA Code to Count the Number of Records in a Recordset

```
'Count number of records in recordset
Private Sub CountRecord()
   Dim intRecord as Integer

   mrstPub.MoveFirst
   Do Until mrstPub.EOF
      mrstPub.MoveNext
      intRecord = intRecord + 1
   Loop

   txtNumber = intRecord

   mrstPub.MoveFirst
End Sub
```

The first statement in this procedure declares an Integer variable to use for counting records. The use of the Integer data type is based on the assumption that there are no more than 32,767 records in the recordset. In the case of a recordset that contains information about publishers, that's probably a reasonable assumption. If you were dealing with a recordset that contained a different type of information for which there could be a large number of records, you would use a variable of type Long instead of Integer.

An Integer or Long variable is automatically assigned the value of zero when it's declared.

The next statement

```
mrstPub.MoveFirst
```

makes sure record counting always starts at the first record.

The short loop

```
Do Until mrstPub.EOF
   mrstPub.MoveNext
   intRecord = intRecord + 1
Loop
```

steps through the records in the recordset, adding one to the value of intRecord for each record. This continues until the current record becomes EOF—that is, until all the records have been counted.

The next statement

```
txtNumber = intRecord
```

assigns the final value of intRecord to the txtNumber control on the form.

Finally, the statement

```
mrstPub.MoveFirst
```

makes the first record the current record.

12

TIP

The method of counting records suggested here is fine for a recordset that contains a relatively small number of records. However, if you're working with a recordset that contains many millions of records, this technique can cause a significant deterioration in the performance of the application due to the time taken to scan through all the records. Before using this technique in a large application, particularly an application that shares data among many users, consider whether you really need to display the total number of records.

Learning More About ActiveX Data Objects

The preceding sections of this chapter have introduced you to some of the fundamentals of ActiveX Data Objects. The most important of these are

- Making a connection to a data source
- Creating a recordset object
- Manipulating the recordset object so that you can select a record and work with the fields within that record

continues

- Adding a new record to a recordset
- Deleting a record from a recordset

This should be enough to get you started with using ActiveX Data Objects. You can find more comprehensive and detailed information in Microsoft Visual Basic Help, on the Web site at http://www.microsoft.com/data/ado, and in books such as *Special Edition Using Microsoft Access 2000*, published by Que, and *Microsoft Access 2000 Unleashed*, published by Sams Publishing.

Using Data Access Objects Instead of ActiveX Data Objects

As mentioned at the beginning of this chapter, in Access 2000, you have the choice of using either ActiveX Data Objects (ADO) or Data Access Objects (DAO) to work programmatically with data. In most cases, you should choose one or the other. However, you can work with both within a single application.

You choose the type of objects you want to work with by establishing references to object libraries. To do that, open an Access application, open a module, and choose Tools, References to display a list of object libraries in the References dialog box. Those libraries that are currently referenced are named at the top of the list of references and are checked. All other object libraries are listed in alphabetical order and are unchecked. When you create a new Access application, the currently referenced object libraries are

- Visual Basic for Applications
- Microsoft Access 9.0 Object Library
- OLE Automation
- Microsoft ActiveX Data Objects 2.1 Library

With these references available, you can use ActiveX Data Objects.

If you open an Access application that was created with a version of Access prior to Access 2000, you won't see the Microsoft ActiveX Data Objects 2.1 Library in the list of available object libraries. Instead, you'll see Microsoft DAO 3.6 Object Library checked to indicate it's available.

The DAO object library provides much of the same functionality as the ADO object library but, as you'll see later in this chapter, some of this functionality requires the use of a distinctly different syntax.

TIP

In general, if you're creating a new Access application, I suggest you use ADO. On the other hand, if you're updating an application that already uses DAO, it's usually better to continue to use DAO.

Working with ADO and DAO

You don't necessarily have to choose between ADO and DAO; you can use both in one application. To do so, in the References dialog box make sure that the two object libraries

- Microsoft ActiveX Data Objects 2.1 Library
- Microsoft DAO Object Library

are both checked in the list of references.

With both object libraries available, you have to be very careful to designate explicitly which library you intend to use whenever you refer to an object. Suppose, for example, you want to use a recordset object. Write

```
ADODB.recordset
```

if you want to refer to the object in the ADO library. Write

```
DAO.recordset
```

if you want to refer to the object in the DAO library.

CAUTION

If you simply write

```
recordset
```

VBA uses the object in the ADO library if that library is ahead of the DAO library in the list of references, or it uses the object in the DAO library if that library is ahead of the ADO library in the list of references.

This can cause a problem because you or someone else might change the order of references during the life of the application.

The following sections contain some examples of the differences between using the ADO and the DAO object libraries. These examples refer only to using the Jet database engine as a data source.

Opening a Database Using DAO

The section "Connecting to a Data Source Using ADO" previously in this chapter shows how to use ADO to connect to a data source with the Jet database engine as a provider. You can achieve the same objective using DAO, although the syntax is quite different. Listing 12.9 is an example of using DAO.

LISTING 12.9   VBA Code to Connect to a Data Source with DAO

```
Sub DAOOpenPublisher()
    Dim dbBook As DAO.Database
    Dim strDataSource As String

    'Create a connection
    strDataSource = "C:\My Documents\AccessNew\Book.mdb"

    Set dbBook = DBEngine.OpenDatabase(strDataSource)
    ....              'Now do something with the data
    dbBook.Close
End Sub
```

The first statement declares the dbBook variable as a Database object. The second statement merely declares a string variable that's subsequently assigned to a string that contains the full path name of the data source.

The statement

```
Set dbBook = DBEngine.OpenDatabase(strDataSource)
```

assigns a value to the dbBook variable and uses the OpenDatabase method of the DBEngine object to open a specific data source. The DBEngine object represents the Jet database engine as a whole.

The OpenDatabase method is used in this example with only one parameter—the path name of the data source. The complete syntax of this method is

```
Set database = workspace.OpenDatabase(dbname, options, read-only, connect)
```

the parts of which are defined in Table 12.6.

TABLE 12.6   Parts of the OpenDatabase Method

Part	Definition
database	Object variable representing the database object to be opened.
workspace	Optional. Object variable representing an existing workspace object that will contain the database. If this parameter is omitted, the default workspace is used.
dbname	A string that contains the path name of the existing Jet database file or the Data Source Name (DSN) of an ODBC data source.
options	Optional. Either True or False (default). True opens the database in exclusive mode; False opens the database in shared mode.
read-only	Optional. Either True or False (default). True opens the database with read-only access; False opens the database with Read/Write access.
connect	Optional. Not used when the Jet database engine is the provider. For other data providers, *connect* can be used for connection information required by those providers.

Creating a Recordset Using DAO

The section "Creating a Recordset Using ADO" previously in this chapter showed how to create a recordset using ADO with the Jet database engine as a provider. You can achieve the same objective using DAO, as shown in this example.

First, add this declaration at the beginning of the procedure shown in the preceding section

```
Dim rstPub As DAO.Recordset
```

Then insert the following statements before the dbBook.Close statement in the procedure described in the preceding section.

```
Set rstPub = dbBook.OpenRecordSet("tblPublisher")
rstPub.Close
```

The first statement assigns a value to the rstPub variable and uses the OpenRecordset method to open a recordset based on a specific table.

The OpenRecordset method is used here with only one parameter. The full syntax of the OpenRecordset method is

```
Set recordset = object.OpenRecordset(source, type, options, lockedits)
```

the parts of which are defined in Table 12.7.

TABLE 12.7   Parts of the OpenRecordset Method

Part	Definition
recordset	Object variable representing the recordset object to be opened.
object	Object variable representing an existing object from which to create the new recordset.
source	String representing the source of the records for the new recordset. Can be a table or query name, or a SQL statement that returns records.
type	Optional. One of these constants:
	• dbOpenTable—Opens table-type recordset (Jet workspaces only).
	• dbOpenDynamic—Opens a dynamic-type recordset (ODBCDirect workspaces only).
	• dbOpenDynaset—Opens a dynaset-type recordset.
	• dbOpenSnapshot—Opens a snapshot-type recordset.
	• dnOpenForwardOnly—Opens a forward-only–type recordset.
options	Optional. One or more of these constants:
	• dbAppendOnly—Enables users to append new records but not to edit or delete existing records.
	• dbSQLPassThrough—Passes SQL statement to Jet-connected ODBC data source (snapshot-type recordset only).
	• dbSeeChanges—Generates runtime error if a user attempts to change data that another user is already editing.
	• dbDenyWrite—Prevents other users from adding records or modifying existing records.
	• dbDenyRead—Prevents other users from reading data from a table (Jet table-type recordset only).
	• dbForwardOnly—Creates forward-only recordset (Jet snapshot-type recordsets only). Obsolete. Instead, use dbOpenForwardOnly for the Type parameter.
	• dbReadOnly—Prevents users from making changes to the recordset (Jet only). Obsolete. Instead, use dbReadOnly for the Lockedits parameter.
	• dbRunAsync—Runs an asynchronous query (ODBCDirect workspaces only).
	• dbExecDirect—Runs a query by skipping SQLPrepare and directly calling SQLExecDirect (ODBCDirect workspaces only).
	• dbInconsistent—Allows inconsistent updates (Jet dynaset- and snapshot-type recordsets only).
	• dbConsistent—Allows only consistent updates (Jet dynaset- and snapshot-type recordsets only).

Part	Definition
lockedits	Optional. Constant that specifies locking. One of these constants:
	• dbReadOnly—Prevents users from making changes to the recordset. Default for ODBCDirect workspaces.
	• dbPessimistic—Entire page containing a record is locked as soon as a record is opened for editing. Default for Jet workspaces.
	• dbOptimistic—Page containing a record is locked only while the Update method executes.
	• dbOptimisticValue—Uses optimistic concurrency based on row values (ODBCDirect workspaces only).
	• dbOptimisticBatch—Uses batch optimistic updating (ODBCDirect workspaces only).

Navigating Within a Recordset Using DAO

DAO uses the same methods as ADO—MoveFirst, MoveLast, MoveNext, and MovePrevious—for making a specific record within a recordset the current record. These methods are used in DAO in the same way they are used in ADO. Refer to the section "Navigating Within a Recordset Using ADO" previously in this chapter for information.

Summary

The two mechanisms in Access 2000 for taking control over accessing data are Data Access Objects (DAO) and ActiveX Data Objects (ADO). Each has advantages and disadvantages, the significance of which depends on your requirements and previous experience.

If you have little or no previous experience in working with data objects, your best bet is to rely on ADO because that's Microsoft's vision of the future. The information in this chapter is intended to be enough to get you started with ADO, but there's a lot more you need to know if you want to become an expert. The chapter contains references to several useful sources of information about ADO.

If you have to support existing Access applications that already use DAO, your choice is less clear. If you expect those applications to have a long life and to require ongoing changes, you should consider changing them to use ADO. However, if you expect the life of those applications to be short and changes to be few, it's unlikely to be worth investing the time and effort required to switch to ADO. In that case, you need to develop an adequate knowledge of DAO. Sections toward the end of this chapter should be enough to get you started using DAO.

This chapter, and several preceding chapters, contain examples of using Visual Basic for Applications (VBA) code. Some of these examples might not have contained enough information for you to feel comfortable about what's going on. Chapter 13, "Taking More Control of Access," guides you into a more detailed understanding of VBA, not with the intention of making you a programmer, but with the purpose of empowering you to take control of Access.

Getting More Out of Access

IN THIS PART

Taking More Control of Access

IN THIS CHAPTER

By "Taking More Control of Access," I'm referring to the ability to do much more with Access than you can by such techniques as choosing from menus, responding to dialog boxes, and dragging objects from one place to another (such as dragging an icon from the toolbox onto a form or report). Access provides two ways for you to take more control: by using macros and by creating Visual Basic for Applications (VBA) code.

Some of the preceding chapters in this book contain examples of using macros and VBA code to achieve certain objectives. In Chapter 6, "Making Data Input Fast and Accurate," for example, the sections "Displaying the Hourglass Pointer" and "Using Macros to Display Messages" contain examples of using macros. Chapter 12, "Accessing Data," contains several examples of using VBA code.

After taking a quick look at some of the limitations of using macros, this chapter shows how VBA code can overcome those limitations and illustrates some of the useful things you can do with VBA code.

> **NOTE**
>
> This book doesn't attempt to teach you how to become a versatile VBA programmer. Instead, the book focuses on showing you how you can begin to use VBA to extend what you can do with Access.

In the first section of this chapter, you'll learn some of the advantages and disadvantages of using Access macros and how to convert macros into VBA code. The bulk of this chapter, however, teaches you how to create VBA code that responds to form and command button events and how to create bulletproof and efficient Access applications.

Understanding Macros in Access

If you've used macros in another Office application such as Excel or Word, you probably think of a macro as a way of automatically repeating keystrokes and selections. In Excel and Word, you can turn on the macro recorder and then perform a task that can involve choosing menu items, responding to dialog boxes, and the like. After you've completed the task, you turn off the macro recorder. At that time, all your actions are automatically saved as a sequence of VBA statements. Subsequently, you can replay what the macro recorder saved to repeat the recorded actions. You can also edit the recorded VBA statements to modify the actions performed by the macro.

Macros in Access are quite different from those in Excel and Word. Access doesn't have a macro recorder; you can't record a sequence of actions as you can in Excel and Word. Instead, follow these steps to create an Access macro:

1. In the Database window, select Macros in the Objects bar, and then choose New to display the Macro window.

2. Open the drop-down list of Actions and select which action you want to perform. In most cases, the Action Arguments pane at the bottom displays a list of arguments.

TIP	
	While you have the drop-down list of Actions open, take a few minutes to glance through the list. By doing so, you'll gain an understanding of the actions that can be incorporated in macros.

3. Either select from a drop-down list of values for each argument or enter a value for each argument.

4. Choose File, Save to save the macro with a specific name.

Access doesn't save a macro as VBA code in the way that Excel and Word do. The only way to edit an existing macro is to reopen it and change the selections you previously made or the values you entered.

After you've created an Access macro, you can run it in the same way you run an Excel or Word macro. Choose Tools, move the pointer onto Macro, and choose Run Macro.

Perhaps the most significant problem with macros in Access is that they have no way of trapping errors. If something goes wrong, all you see is an error message—there's no way to correct the problem other than to cancel, make whatever changes you think are necessary, and try running the macro again. Another problem with Access macros is they don't always let you do what you want to do. You can overcome both these possible problems by using VBA code. One more disadvantage of macros is that they run more slowly than the equivalent VBA code.

Some writers advise avoiding the use of Access macros because of their limitations and also because of the possibility that future versions of Access might not support macros. My take on this is that you should not use macros in major applications you expect to have in use when a new version of Access becomes available. Nonetheless, Access macros are useful in at least two ways.

If you need to develop an Access-based application fast and don't have the time to create optimized VBA code, you might find that a few well-chosen macros can come to your rescue. Granted, an application that uses macros may sometimes crash because it lacks error trapping, but, in the real world, it's sometimes better to have an application today that isn't bulletproof, than not to have the application when it's needed.

Another great use for Access macros is to develop prototype VBA code. Didn't you just read that Access doesn't save macros as VBA code? It's true that Access doesn't save macros as VBA code. However, something first introduced in Access 97 is the built-in capability to convert a macro to VBA code. After you've done that, you have a VBA procedure, not a macro. You can edit the VBA procedure created from the macro to tailor it for your needs. Let's see how this works.

1. Create a simple macro, such as one that displays the hourglass pointer.

2. Save the macro.

3. In the Database window, select the macro.

4. Choose Tools, move the pointer onto Macro, and choose Convert Macros to Visual Basic. Access displays the dialog box shown in Figure 13.1.

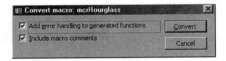

FIGURE 13.1
The Convert Macro dialog box offers two choices.

5. You probably want to leave the two check boxes checked, so choose Convert. After a brief delay, a message box appears declaring Conversion Finished. Choose OK.

6. In the Database window's Objects bar, select Modules. The list of modules includes one named Converted Macro.

7. Select the Converted Macro module and choose Design. The Visual Basic Editor (VBE) window opens displaying the VBA function that the conversion process has created, as shown in Figure 13.2.

TIP
To quickly gain an understanding of VBA code, create several macros, convert them to VBA code, and examine the code.

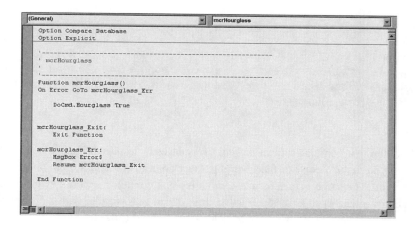

FIGURE 13.2
The conversion process creates a VBA function that includes error trapping.

You can edit the VBA code created by converting macros to tailor that code to suit your specific needs.

Responding to Form and Report Events

Access is an event-driven application. In Access, the occurrence of events triggers some action to occur. Events may be external or internal. *External events* are such things as a key being pressed or the mouse being moved. *Internal events* are such things as a form opening or closing, or an error occurring. You take control of Access by providing responses to events. These responses can be running a macro or a VBA event procedure.

> **NOTE**
>
> For a complete list of events, see the online help topic "Events and Event Properties Reference."

VBA event procedures (also known as *event handlers*) are sub procedures contained in class modules. Access automatically creates a class module when you write an event procedure to respond to an event related to a form or a report. Each form or report can have only one class module that contains all its event procedures.

> **NOTE**
>
> Previous versions of Access used the phrase *code behind forms* to refer to event procedures that respond to a form's or a report's events. This term is no longer used in Access 97 or Access 2000.

The class module that contains a form's event procedures is an integral part of that form. For that reason, if you make a copy of the form, the copy contains the class module with all its event procedures. The same is true for class modules that contain a report's event procedures. You can take advantage of this to save a lot of time if you have similar forms or reports within a single application, or if you have similar forms or reports in different applications.

The next few sections refer specifically to forms. Much of the information in those sections applies also to reports.

Creating Event Procedures for a Form's Events

You can create event procedures that run at the time a form opens or closes.

When you open a form, a sequence of events occurs in the order listed in Table 13.1.

TABLE 13.1 Events That Occur When a Form Opens

Event	Occurs
Open	After a form opens but before it displays values in its controls
Load	After values are displayed in the form's controls
Resize	Immediately after the Load event and also after the size of a form changes
Activate	When the form becomes active
GotFocus	Only if the form contains no visible controls or if all visible controls are disabled
Current	When a form is opened and also when the focus changes from one record to another

When you close a form, a sequence of events occurs in the order listed in Table 13.2.

TABLE 13.2   Events That Occur When a Form Closes

Event	Occurs
Unload	After a form is closed but before it's removed from the screen
LostFocus	Only if the form contains no visible controls or if all visible controls are disabled
Deactivate	When a form loses the focus to another form or to a Table, Query, Report, Macro, Module, or Database window
Close	After a form is closed and removed from the screen

When you switch between two open forms, the Deactivate event occurs for the currently active form and then the Activate event occurs for the newly active form.

It's very important to pay attention to when specific events occur and to the order in which they occur. For example, if you need an event procedure that runs when a form opens and also runs when you switch from one open form to another, you must create an event procedure that runs when the Activate event occurs. In contrast, if you want an event procedure to run when a form opens but not when you switch from one open form to another, you should create an event procedure that responds to the Open or Load event.

13

TAKING MORE
CONTROL OF
ACCESS

TIP

After you've created an event procedure that responds to a form event, test that procedure carefully to make sure that it runs when you want it to and doesn't run when you don't want it to.

Creating an Event Procedure That Responds to a Form Event

A form has many events to which it can respond, as shown in Figure 13.3.

To gain a detailed understanding of how forms work, I urge you to become familiar with each of the events a form can respond to. It's not necessary to understand each event in detail; just become familiar with the nature of each event. When you want to use a specific event, you can access Help to get all the information you need.

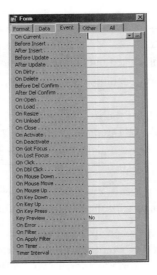

FIGURE 13.3

The Event tab in a form's Property sheet shows all the events to which a form can respond.

TIP

You can find detailed information about each of the events listed in Figure 13.3 by opening the "Events and Event Properties Reference" topic in Help. That topic contains an alphabetical listing of events. Click any event name to see information about that event.

To create an event procedure that responds to one of a form's events, follow these steps.

1. Display the form in Design view. If necessary, choose View, Properties to display the Property sheet.

2. Verify that the Property sheet's title bar contains the word Form. If not, click the button at the left end of the form's horizontal ruler.

3. Display the Property sheet's Event tab, as previously shown in Figure 13.3.

4. Click the name of the event for which you want to create an event procedure, such as On Load. A Builder button containing three dots appears at the right of the property box.

5. Click the Builder button to display the Choose Builder dialog box.

6. Select Code Builder and choose OK. Access displays the Visual Basic Editor (VBE) window shown in Figure 13.4.

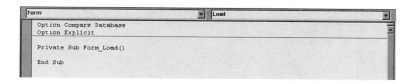

FIGURE 13.4
The VBE window opens with the first and last statements of the new procedure displayed.

The first and last statements of the new procedure are known as a *stub*. It's up to you to place statements within the stub that control what happens when the event occurs. For example, if the form contains certain command buttons, you might want to enable and disable specific buttons so that only those that are useful immediately after the Load event occurs are enabled. Assuming you have command buttons named cmdNew, cmdSave, cmdDelete, and cmdClose, you would enter code so that the command procedure consists of these statements:

```
Private Sub Form_Load()
    cmdNew.Enabled = True
    cmdSave.Enabled = False
    cmdDelete.Enabled = True
    cmdClose.Enabled = True
End Sub
```

13

TAKING MORE
CONTROL OF
ACCESS

NOTE

The section "Understanding the Form_Open Event Procedure" in Chapter 12, "Accessing Data," explains the statements in this example.

Canceling an Event

Some, but by no means all, event procedures allow you to cancel the associated event. For example, you can include code in a Form_Open event procedure to cancel the Open event; however, you can't include code in a Form_Load event procedure to cancel the Load event.

Figure 13.5 shows the stub for a Form_Open event procedure.

An *argument* is a value that's passed to a procedure. Arguments are listed in the first statement of a procedure after the procedure's name and enclosed within a pair of parentheses. Each argument is a variable that has a name (Cancel in this case) and a data type (Integer in this case). Only one argument is shown in Figure 13.5. Procedures can have more than one argument, in which case, each argument is separated from the next by a comma.

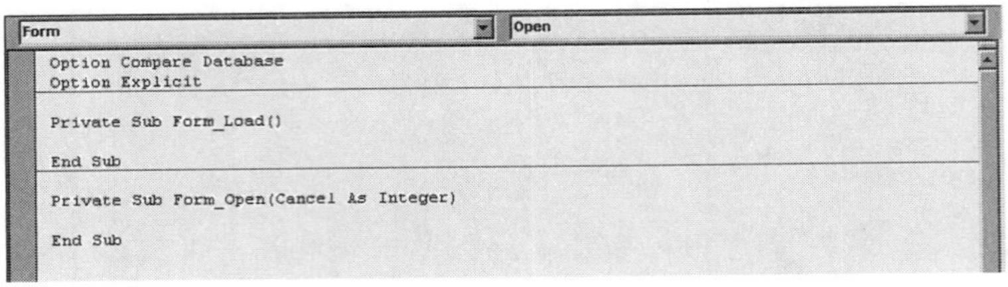

FIGURE 13.5

The first statement in a Form_Open *event procedure includes the argument* Cancel As Integer.

NOTE

Arguments are sometimes referred to as *parameters*. Because the word "parameter" has a special meaning in the context of queries within Access, I prefer to use "argument" for a value passed to a procedure.

When you create a stub for an event procedure such as Form_Open, the value of the Cancel argument is 0 (zero), which is the numerical equivalent of False. The argument's value remains unchanged unless you include code within the procedure to change it to True (or a numerical value other than 0). With the Cancel argument set to False, the argument has no effect—the Open event occurs and whatever statements are in the Open event procedure are executed.

Within the Open event procedure, you can include the statement

```
Cancel = True
```

which has the effect of canceling the Open event. If this code is executed within the event procedure, the form doesn't open.

There's no point in writing a Form_Open event procedure in which the Cancel variable is always set to true—that would mean the form never opens. Instead, the Cancel variable is set to True within an If control structure, or some other control structure that tests for a certain condition or conditions. If that condition occurs, or those conditions occur, your code should display a message to the user and then set the Cancel variable to True. For example, if you didn't want anyone to be able to open a form on a Sunday, you could write a Form_Open event procedure such as that in Listing 13.1.

LISTING 13.1 VBA Code to Demonstrate the Use of the Cancel Argument

```
Private Sub Form_Open(Cancel As Integer)
   If Weekday(Date) = vbSunday Then
      MsgBox "You can't open this form on a Sunday!"
      Cancel = True
   End If
      'Insert code here to control what happens when the
      'form opens on any day other than Sunday
End Sub
```

The first statement in the If control structure makes use of two Access functions. The Date function returns the current system date. The Weekday function returns the number of the day of the week. If the current date corresponds to a Sunday, Weekday(Date) returns a value of 1 (one) that corresponds to the Visual Basic intrinsic constant vbSunday. Consequently the condition is true, so the two statements within the If control structure execute. For any other day, the condition is not true, so the two statements within the If control structure don't execute, the value of the Cancel variable remains False, and the form opens.

Responding to Control Events

Controls, as you know, are objects you place on forms and reports. These objects include labels, text boxes, option buttons, check boxes, command buttons, list boxes, combo boxes, and more. Each of these controls can respond to various events. For example, the events to which command buttons can respond are listed in Figure 13.6.

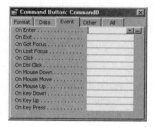

FIGURE 13.6

These are the events to which a command button can respond.

Although the On Click event for a command button is the event you'll use most frequently, take some time to understand the other events you can use.

You can create event procedures for controls in the same way that you create event procedures for forms and reports, as described in the section "Creating Event Procedures for a Form's Events" previously in this chapter.

13

TAKING MORE CONTROL OF ACCESS

Writing VBA Code Within Event Procedures

An event procedure can contain any VBA statements, some examples of which are included in this section. These examples show statements that change the values of properties, run DoCmd methods, and use the Access built-in functions.

Assigning Object Property Values

As you've learned, objects on a form or report have many properties, most of which you define in a Property sheet when you design a form or report. Most properties defined at design time (when the form is displayed in Design view) can be changed by VBA code that runs while a form is being used. Some properties can't be defined at design time, but are only accessible at runtime (when the form is displayed in Form view).

You can set or change the value of an object's properties by writing assignment statements within event procedures. For example, you can use the assignment statements

```
cmdSave.Enabled = True
```

```
cmdSave.Enabled = False
```

to enable or disable a command button named cmdSave.

Executing DoCmd Methods

Access contains a set of methods known as DoCmd methods, many of which have similar functionality to macro actions, but with the advantage of giving you the opportunity to have more control over what happens. The syntax for using one of these methods is

```
DoCmd.methodname(arguments)
```

The following is an example of how you can use one of the DoCmd methods. This event procedure uses the DoCmd.TransferSpreadsheet method to transfer the contents of the tblPublisher table in the Book database to an Excel worksheet. A button named cmdSpreadsheet in the frmPublisher form has the following event procedure for its Click event:

```
Private Sub cmdSpreadsheet_Click()
    DoCmd.TransferSpreadsheet acExport, acSpreadsheetTypeExcel9, _
    "tblPublisher", "C:\My Documents\Publisher.xls"
End Sub
```

After you add the cmdSpreadsheet button to the frmPublisher form and create the event procedure, clicking the button results in the contents of the tblPublisher table being copied into an Excel 2000 worksheet.

This example should help you understand the power that exists in some of the DoCmd methods.

Table 13.2 lists the DoCmd methods that Microsoft recommends for use in Access 2000 applications. Refer to the Help topic for each method for detailed information about its use, including the arguments required by some methods.

TABLE 13.2 DoCmd Methods

Method	Purpose
AddMenu	Replaces built-in menu bar for a form or report with a custom menu bar. Replaces built-in shortcut menu for a form, report, or control on a form with a custom shortcut menu.
ApplyFilter	Filters data available to a form or report.
Beep	Sounds a beep through the computer's speaker.
CancelEvent	Cancels the normal response to an event.
Close	Closes the active window or a specified window.
CopyObject	Copies a database object within the current database or to another database.
DeleteObject	Deletes a specified object.
FindNext	Finds the next record according to the criterion set in the most recent FindRecord or Find method.
FindRecord	Finds the first record in a table, recordset, or form object that satisfies specified criteria.
GoToControl	Moves the focus to a specified field or control in the current record of the open form, form datasheet, table datasheet, or query datasheet.
GoToRecord	Makes the specified record the current record in a table, recordset, or form.
Hourglass	Changes the mouse pointer from the normal icon to an hourglass icon, or restores the mouse pointer to the normal icon.
Maximize	Enlarges the active window to fill the Access window.
Minimize	Reduces the active window to a title bar in the Windows taskbar.
MoveSize	Moves or resizes the active window.
OpenDataAccessPage	Opens a data access page in Page or Design view.
OpenDiagram	Opens a database diagram in Design view.
OpenForm	Opens a form in Form view, Design view, Print Preview, or Datasheet view.
OpenModule	Opens a specified Visual Basic module at a specified procedure.

continues

13

TAKING MORE CONTROL OF ACCESS

TABLE 13.2   Continued

Method	Purpose
OpenQuery	Opens a select or crosstab query in Datasheet view, Design view, or Print Preview.
OpenReport	Opens a report in Design view or Print Preview, or prints a report.
OpenStoredProcedure	Opens a stored procedure in Datasheet view, Design view, or Print Preview.
OpenTable	Opens a table in Datasheet view, Design view, or Print Preview.
OpenView	Opens a view in Datasheet view, Design view, or Print Preview.
OutputTo	Outputs data from a datasheet, form, report, module, or data access page to a file in Excel, text, rich text format, HTML, or Internet Information Server formats.
PrintOut	Prints datasheets, forms, reports, data access pages, and modules in the open database.
Rename	Renames a specified database object.
RepaintObject	Completes any pending screen updates for a specified database object.
Requery	Updates data in a specified control from the data source.
Restore	Restores a maximized or minimized window to its original size.
RunCommand	Runs a command in a built-in menu or toolbar (not in a custom menu or toolbar).
Save	Saves a specified Access object.
SelectObject	Selects a specified database object.
SendObject	Includes a datasheet, form, report, module, or data access page in an email message.
SetMenuItem	Sets the state of menu items on the custom or global menu bar for the active window.
SetWarnings	Turns system messages on or off.
ShowAllRecords	Removes any applied filter from the active table, recordset, or form.
ShowToolbar	Displays or hides a built-in or custom toolbar.
TransferDatabase	Imports or exports data between the current Access database or Access project and another database.
TransferSpreadsheet	Imports or exports data between the current Access database or Access project and an Excel file.
TransferText	Imports or exports text between the current Access database or Access project and a text file and also a table or list in an HTML file.

Using Built-in Functions

VBA contains a large number of built-in functions you can use in any of your procedures. Because all the functions are conveniently listed and explained in Help, there's no point in explaining them all in this book.

> **NOTE**
>
> VBA Help contains an alphabetical list of all functions. To see this list, display the Visual Basic Editor window, and then choose Help, Microsoft Visual Basic Help. Display the Contents tab, open the Visual Basic Language Reference book, and then expand Functions.

Table 13.3 lists some of the most useful functions in several categories. In most cases, function names give you a strong clue about what functions do.

TABLE 13.3   Examples of VBA Functions;functions:VBA

Category	*Examples of Functions*
Calculation	Abs, Cos, Sin, Exp
Data	Array, Format, IIf
Data Types	CCur, CDate, CInt, CStr
Dates and Times	Date, DateAdd, Day, Hour, Month, Now, Timer
Errors	Error
Financial	DDB, FV, IRR, PV
Folders and Files	CurDir, Dir, EOF, FileLen, Input
Messages	InputBox, MsgBox
Object	CreateObject, GetObject
Program Flow	DoEvents, Shell
String	Asc, InStr, Left, Len, LTrim, Right, RTrim
Testing	IsDate, IsEmpty, IsNull, IsNumeric

Using Custom Procedures

You can create procedures and save those procedures in a standard module. Those procedures can be either sub procedures or functions. Sub procedures and functions are quite similar—the essential difference is that sub procedures don't return a value, whereas functions do return a value.

A custom procedure differs from an event procedure in two principal ways:

- A custom procedure can be saved in a standard module or a form's class module. The procedure must be saved in a standard module if it's called from procedures in several forms' class modules. The procedure can be saved in a form's class module if it's called only from procedures within that class module. An event procedure is always saved in a class (behind a form) module.

- A custom procedure doesn't directly respond to an event, as does an event procedure. A custom procedure is called from an event procedure or from another custom procedure.

The main reason for using custom procedures is to avoid unnecessary duplication of code and to save you a lot of work. Here's an example to show you what I mean.

Suppose you have several command buttons on a form and you need to write event procedures for all of them. Each of these event procedures contains some code that determines what makes each command button different. Quite likely, each event procedure contains some code that's the same for several buttons. Instead of repeating that code in all the event procedures, you can write that code in a separate sub procedure and call that sub procedure from each event procedure. Simply include the name of the sub procedure within the event procedure to call the sub procedure.

In outline form, here's an example of a sub procedure that can be called from an event procedure:

```
Public Sub EnableButtons()
    Place the shared statements here
End Sub
```

Also, in outline form, here's an example of an event procedure that calls the sub procedure:

```
Private Sub cmdSave_Click()
    Some statements
    EnableButtons
    Some more statements
End Sub
```

Notice that the sub procedure in this example is named EnableButtons and is declared as a public procedure so that it's available in modules other than the standard module in which it is saved.

The event procedure contains a statement that consists of the name of the sub procedure. When this statement executes, the sub procedure runs.

NOTE

Another benefit of creating custom procedures for code that's used in several places is that it simplifies program maintenance. If it becomes necessary to modify the code, you have to do so only in one place instead of separately in every place that code is repeated.

Responding to Runtime Errors

Whether you're creating an Access application to use yourself, for a few colleagues to use, or for a much wider audience, your objective should be to do all in your power to make sure errors can't occur when your application runs. Unfortunately, in all but the simplest applications, that ideal is not possible because you're not completely in control of what a user does.

Three categories of errors are possible in an application:

- Syntax Errors—These are errors in the use of the Visual Basic language. The Visual Basic Editor detects these types of errors automatically so that you can correct them.
- Logic Errors—Even though your VBA code has no syntax errors and it runs without indicating the presence of errors, it might not produce the results you intend due to the presence of logic errors. You can find errors of this type only by extensively testing your application using a wide range of conditions and circumstances.
- Runtime Errors—These are errors that occur due to some unanticipated problems while your program is running.

This section shows you how to deal with runtime errors.

A few of the things that can happen while your application is being used are

- Enough disk space might not be available for an operation
- A file that's needed might not be present or might not be accessible
- An attempt might be made to divide by 0 (zero)
- A printer might not be available, not be turned on, have jammed, or run out of paper
- An attempt to make a dial-up connection might fail because the phone line is busy

These are just some specific examples that are quite easy to think of. For each of these examples, you could probably write code that checks for that specific error condition before allowing code that might encounter that error to run. For example, you could write code that compares the disk space required by some data with the available disk space before the code that attempts to write data to disk runs. That might be okay if you're concerned only with a disk on the user's local computer to which only that user has access. What, though, if data can be written to a shared disk? In that case, it's possible that in the interval between testing the disk space and attempting to write to the disk, someone else writes a file to the same disk.

The point is that, however hard you might try to anticipate possible errors, you're unlikely to be completely successful. For that reason, VBA makes it possible for you to detect almost any error that occurs while an application is running and to write code that allows a user to deal with that error. The errors you can detect and deal with in this way are known as *trappable errors*. The methods of dealing with these errors are known as *error trapping*. By incorporating error trapping in your VBA code, you ensure that your application isn't likely to crash when the unexpected occurs

> **NOTE**
>
> If you don't provide for trapping errors within your code, VBA generates its own error messages. These error messages mostly don't convey meaningful information to a user. They don't provide any way for a user to recover from the error.

The Help topic "Trappable Errors" contains a complete list of trappable errors. Each trappable error has an error number and an error message.

The general method for trapping errors hasfour parts:

- Setting the trap
- Creating an error handler
- Resuming program execution
- Clearing the trap

These four parts are described in the next sections.

Setting the Error Trap

Each procedure should normally have a statement that sets an error trap before the first executable statement. Most people place this statement immediately after any declaration statements at the beginning of a procedure. The syntax of an error trapping statement is

```
On Error GoTo linelabel
```

in which *linelabel* marks the place in the procedure where error handling statements begin. A line label is text followed by a colon. No spaces or punctuation characters are allowed in a line label.

Listing 13.2 is a skeleton of a procedure with error trapping included.

Listing 13.2 Typical VBA Code to Set and Error Trap

```
Sub SubName()
   On Error GoTo ErrorHandler
   normal procedure statements
   Exit Sub
ErrorHandler:
   error handler statements
End Sub
```

When this procedure executes, the first statement sets up error trapping for all the subsequent statements in the procedure. Two possibilities exist:

- All the subsequent statements execute without detecting a trappable error. In this case, the statements proceed as far as the Exit Sub statement, at which time the procedure terminates and error trapping is turned off.

- A trappable error occurs when one of the statements in the procedure executes. At the first trappable error, execution switches to the first statement after the ErrorHandler line label and proceeds from there.

Now, let's turn to a practical example. Previously in this chapter, the section "Executing DoCmd Methods" showed this example of an event procedure:

```
Private Sub cmdSpreadsheet_Click()
   DoCmd.TransferSpreadsheet acExport, acSpreadsheetTypeExcel9, _
   "tblPublisher", "C:\My Documents\Publisher.xls"
End Sub
```

As explained in that section, this event procedure attempts to copy the content of an Access table to an Excel workbook. The statement creates the file C:\My Documents\Publisher.xls if that file doesn't already exist. If the file does already exist, the statement alerts you to that fact and asks whether you want to replace the existing file.

It's quite possible that this event could cause an error for several reasons, one of the most obvious of which is that there isn't enough space on the disk for the new Excel workbook. To control what happens when an error occurs, you need to create an error handler—VBA code that executes when an error occurs.

After you've set an error trap, that trap remains in effect until one of the following statements executes:

```
Err.Clear
```

```
Exit Function
```

```
Exit Property

Exit Sub

On Error GoTo 0

On Error GoTo line

On Error Resume Next

Resume

Resume line

Resume Next
```

Instead of trying to remember that list, think of the lifetime of an error trap in this way. An error trap remains in effect until

- You explicitly clear it with an `Err.Clear` or `On Error GoTo 0` statement
- The end of the procedure in which the trap is set
- An error is trapped and then code execution resumes

As mentioned in the section "Using Custom Procedures" previously in this chapter, you can call a procedure from within another procedure. If you set an error trap in one procedure and, while that error trap is in effect, call another procedure, the error trap remains in effect while the called procedure runs.

Creating an Error Handler

You can incorporate error trapping into the procedure described in the previous section by modifying it as shown in Listing 13.3.

LISTING 13.3   Error Handler with Message to the User

```
Private Sub cmdSpreadsheet_Click()
   On Error GoTo ErrorHandler
   DoCmd.TransferSpreadsheet acExport, acSpreadsheetTypeExcel9, _
   "tblPublisher", "C:\My Documents\Publisher.xls"
   Exit Sub
ErrorHandler:
   MsgBox "Can't copy the data to a spreadsheet."
   Resume Next
End Sub
```

With this improvement to the code, the data is successfully copied to the workbook if no error occurs. The code executes as far as the Exit Sub statement, at which point the procedure terminates. If you were to omit the Exit Sub statement, the subsequent error handler code executes, even if no error occurred.

If an error, such as insufficient space on the disk, does occur, the error handler section of the code displays a message saying that the data can't be copied. The Resume Next statement causes the execution of the next statement after the one that caused the error. The overall result is that the data isn't copied to the workbook, but the user can continue with other operations.

The error handler section of the code can do much more than is shown in this simple example. For example, the error handler section could make it possible for a user to save the workbook on another disk. But that assumes the reason for the user being unable to save the workbook is that insufficient disk space is available. Perhaps there are other reasons for being unable to save the worksheet.

Analyzing Errors

When an error occurs, VBA creates an error object, Err, that has several properties, the most useful of which are

- Number—Error number
- Description—Text that describes the error
- Source—Name of the project in which the error occurred

You can use these properties in an error handler as shown in Listing 13.4.

LISTING 13.4   Error Handler with Number, Description, and Source Properties

```
Private Sub cmdSpreadsheet_Click()
    Dim errNumber As Integer
    Dim errDescription As String
    Dim errSource As String
    Dim strMsg As String

    On Error GoTo ErrorHandler
    DoCmd.TransferSpreadsheet acExport, acSpreadsheetTypeExcel9, _
    "tblPublisher", "C:\My Documents\Publisher.xls"
    Exit Sub
ErrorHandler:
    strMsg = "Error number is: " & Err.Number & vbCrLf
    strMsg = strMsg & "Error message is: " & Err.Description & vbCrLf
    strMsg = strMsg & "Error source is: " & Err.Source
    MsgBox strMsg, vbOKOnly + vbCritical, "Error"
    Resume Next
End Sub
```

The message box this code creates provides you, the developer, with a lot of information about the reason that errors occur; you'll find this type of code in error handlers very useful while you're optimizing an application. However, this type of information is not meaningful to people who use your application. For those people, you need to employ a different strategy: code that identifies possible errors and suggests a remedy for each one. This involves the use of the Select Case control structure. See Appendix A, "Visual Basic for Applications Primer," for detailed information about the Select Case control structure.

The Select Case control structure allows you to identify specific errors by their error numbers and to write code that's appropriate for each type of error. Listing 13.5 is a skeleton example.

LISTING 13.5   Example of Using the Select Case Control Structure to Identify Errors

```
Private Sub cmdSpreadsheet_Click()
   On Error GoTo ErrorHandler
   DoCmd.TransferSpreadsheet acExport, acSpreadsheetTypeExcel9, _
   "tblPublisher", "C:\My Documents\Publisher.xls"
   Exit Sub
ErrorHandler:
   Select Case Err.Number
      Case 58     'File already exists
         code to solve problem
      Case 61     'Disk full
         code to solve problem
      Case 68 'Device unavailable
         code to solve problem
      Case Else 'Other errors
         Code to solve other problems
   End Select
End Sub
```

This error handler uses the Select Case control structure to look for specific error conditions recognized by their error numbers, and provides individual solutions for each type of error. You can use this type of error handler to provide specific solutions for the most likely problems and to provide a generic solution for any other problems.

Testing Your Error Handling Strategies

After you've written an error handler, you need to test it to make sure it works correctly. It's impractical to set up all possible error conditions; fortunately, you don't have to. Instead, you can temporarily modify your code to make Visual Basic think certain errors have occurred. This is known as *raising errors*. You specify which error you want to simulate by its error number.

For example, to raise error number 7 (out of memory), insert this statement

```
Err.Raise 7
```

somewhere in your code after the On Error GoTo statement and before the Exit Sub statement. When you run the code, your error handler does whatever it would do if that particular error had actually occurred.

Resuming Code Execution After an Error

With an error handler placed at the end of a procedure, immediately ahead of the End Sub statement, the procedure terminates after the code in the error handler has been processed, unless you specify otherwise.

You can use a Resume statement to control what happens after an error has been processed. A Resume statement can only occur within an error handler; an error occurs if you place it elsewhere in your code. A Resume statement can be written in the three forms shown in Table 13.4. The explanations in that table apply when an error occurs in the same procedure as the error handler.

TABLE 13.4 Action of a Resume Statement When an Error Occurs in the Same Procedure as the Error Handler

Form	Explanation
Resume	Execution resumes at the statement in which the error occurred
Resume Next	Execution resumes at the statement immediately following the statement in which the error occurred
Resume *label*	Execution resumes at the line labeled *label*

The effect of a Resume statement is somewhat different if an error trap is set in one procedure from which another procedure is called and the error occurs in the called procedure. Table 13.5 explains what happens in this case.

TABLE 13.5 Action of a Resume Statement When an Error Occurs in a Called Procedure

Form	Explanation
Resume	Execution resumes at the statement that last called out of the procedure containing the error handler
Resume Next	Execution resumes at the statement immediately following the statement that last called out of the procedure containing the error handler
Resume *label*	Execution resumes at the line labeled *label* which must be in the same procedure as the error handler

Optimizing an Access Application

Many pages have been written about optimizing an Access application. In the space available here, I can only summarize what I've personally found to be most useful. I encourage you to look in other books, magazine articles, and Web sites for more detailed information and for some ideas in addition to those mentioned here.

NOTE

These are two books that contain a lot of useful information about optimizing Access applications: *Microsoft Access 2000 Development Unleashed*, published by Sams Publishing (particularly Chapter 14, "Application Optimization") and *Access 2000 Developer's Black Book*, published by Coriolis (particularly Chapter 21, "Completing the Implementation").

Optimizing the Hardware

You may well find the applications you create work reasonably well on your computer but are much slower on other computers. If that's the case, the first place to look is at the hardware configuration.

Windows and Office applications, particularly Access, require a lot of RAM in order to run efficiently. Although Microsoft specifies a minimum of 12 megabytes of RAM to run Access under Windows 98 (16 megabytes to run under Windows NT), these figures are bare minimums. To get good performance out of Access, a realistic minimum amount of RAM is 32 megabytes (64 megabytes is even better).

When you're developing an Access application, you probably have only Access running. In contrast, people who use your application might well have other programs running at the same time, each of which requires additional RAM. If people complain that your Access application runs slowly, make sure they have enough RAM. Also discourage users from having other applications in addition to Access running at the same time, unless those other applications are absolutely necessary.

NOTE

Applications reserve memory for their own use while they're running. That memory should be released when the application closes. For various reasons, some memory reserved by applications isn't always properly released. As a result, a computer can gradually lose access to some of its memory—this is known as *memory leakage*. To recover memory that's lost in this way, you should shut down and restart Windows on a regular basis, such as once a day.

After making sure users have sufficient memory, the next thing to consider is processor power and speed. Although the most advanced and fastest processor isn't required, naturally the speed of an application depends on the power and speed of the processor.

Then there's the question of hard disk performance. Access makes intensive use of the hard disk, so it's important to have a high-performance disk that's properly maintained. For efficient use of Access, the hard disk should be regularly defragmented so that it can access data efficiently. Don't forget that the hard disk is used as virtual memory (an extension to the physical RAM) as well as for storing all the data in your tables.

Whenever you add data to your tables, or change existing data, the space occupied by the tables on your hard disk increases. Also, when you delete data, the space occupied by that data isn't necessarily recovered. For that reason, you should make sure that users regularly compact the Access application. For information about compacting an Access application, see the section "Compacting and Repairing a Database" in Chapter 16, "Maintaining a Healthy Application."

NOTE

As the Readme file that accompanies Access points out, disk compression degrades the performance of Access. If you need good performance from Access, don't compress your hard drive.

Analyzing an Application

As has been mentioned in several places in this book, the way you design your application can have a significant effect on its performance. Access has a Performance Analyzer that can help you pinpoint design problems that can result in inferior performance and, in some cases, automatically correct those problems.

To run the Performance Analyzer, open an Access application and then choose Tools, move the pointer onto Analyze, and choose Performance to display a dialog box such as the one shown in Figure 13.7.

If you elect to analyze tables, select the Tables tab to display a list of tables, select one or more tables, and then choose OK. Depending on the complexity of your tables, the analyzer might take several seconds to analyze those tables and then display either a message box or a dialog box. If you've done a good job of table design, you usually see a message box that says "The Performance Analyzer has no suggestions to improve the objects you selected." Otherwise, you see a dialog box such as the one in Figure 13.8. Although helpful, the Performance Analyzer isn't perfect. Look at its suggestions carefully and decide for yourself whether you should follow them.

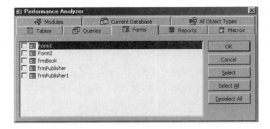

FIGURE 13.7

Use the Performance Analyzer to specify which components of the application you want to analyze.

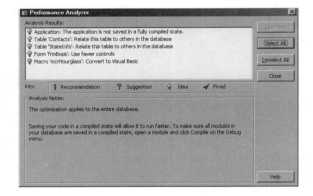

FIGURE 13.8

The Performance Analyzer lists the analysis results.

Notice that each of the analysis results is identified by an icon as Recommendation, Suggestion, Idea, or Fixed. You can select any item in the Analysis Results list to see detailed information in the Analysis Notes box below the list.

After you choose a result marked by a Recommendation or Suggestion icon, you can let Access make the optimization for you by choosing Optimize. After you do that, the result is marked with the Fixed icon. You have to follow any results marked with the Idea icon by yourself.

Choose Help in the Performance Analyzer window to display more information about using the analyzer. For addition information about improving the performance of your application, click the Help button near the bottom of the Performance Analyzer's Analysis Results page to display the Help topic shown in Figure 13.9.

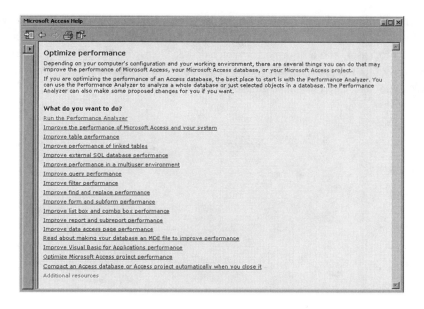

FIGURE 13.9

Help offers the topics shown here that you can access to find suggestions about optimizing your application's performance.

Summary

You can take control of Access by creating macros and by writing Visual Basic for Applications (VBA) code. Unlike other Office applications, such as Excel and Word, Access doesn't have a macro recorder you can use to create macros. Instead, you create an Access macro by selecting a sequence of predefined actions. The principal advantage of macros is that you can create them easily and quickly. Among their disadvantages are their limited capabilities and the fact that you can't control what happens when a runtime error occurs.

Access shares VBA with the other major Office applications. You can use VBA to create procedures that control almost every aspect of Access. Event procedures respond to events that occur while an application is running. These events include a form or report opening or closing, a command button on a form being clicked, text on a form being entered or changed, and a keyboard key being pressed. In addition to event procedures, you can create custom procedures that can be called from other procedures.

An important use of VBA procedures is to trap runtime errors so that a meaningful error message is displayed when a runtime error occurs and users can take whatever action is necessary to correct the error.

There are many things you can do to optimize an Access application. Primarily, you should make sure that the computer running the application has an adequate amount of memory, a sufficiently fast processor, and a high-performance disk system. You should use the Performance Analyzer utility that's supplied with Access to see suggestions about how the performance of applications you've created might be improved.

Making Access Applications Easy to Use

IN THIS CHAPTER

Most of the interaction people have with Access-based applications is by way of forms displayed on the screen. Forms display information derived from stored information and provide a way for people to enter data to be stored within the database. People can navigate within an application in several ways:

- By opening menus and choosing items in those menus
- By clicking buttons on toolbars
- By choosing buttons on forms

People can also control what an application does by opening lists and selecting items from those lists, by checking or unchecking list boxes, and by choosing option buttons on forms.

To make an application inviting, you should devote a lot of effort to making the application easy to use. One of the ways you can do that is by providing menus and toolbars that relate directly to the application. Another way is to provide informative messages to people who use the application. This chapter shows how to provide ScreenTips and ControlTips to help people understand your forms, how to customize and create menus and toolbars, and how to prevent people from changing your menus and toolbars.

Providing ScreenTips and ControlTips on Your Forms

You're probably quite familiar with ScreenTips—the small balloons that appear containing explanatory text when you move the pointer onto a toolbar button and pause for a moment. Microsoft used to call these ToolTips, but the name ScreenTips has replaced ToolTips. ScreenTips help users to be comfortable in the Access environment.

> **TIP**
>
> If a ScreenTip doesn't appear when you point onto a toolbar button, that's because the display of ScreenTips is disabled. To enable the display of ScreenTips, choose View, move the pointer onto Toolbars, and choose Customize to display the Customize dialog box. Select the Options tab and check the Show ScreenTips on Toolbars check box.

You can replace the default text for any toolbar button. You can also provide ScreenTips for buttons you add to toolbars and for buttons you place on custom toolbars.

ControlTips are similar to ScreenTips: They are balloons that pop up when you pause your cursor over a control on a form. You can make your applications friendlier for users by providing ControlTips.

The following sections first show you how to customize the ScreenTips and ControlTips that are provided with Access and then how to create your own.

Customizing ScreenTips and ControlTips

You might decide that one or more of the ScreenTips that Microsoft provides for the Access toolbar buttons are not suitable for the people who will be using your application. In that case, you can change the built-in ScreenTip, but only by using a Visual Basic for Applications (VBA) procedure to do so. The section "Changing a Toolbar Button's ScreenTip Text" later in this chapter explains how to use VBA code to change a ScreenTip.

CAUTION

If you attempt to change one of the built-in ScreenTips manually, Access appears to let you do so. In fact, after changing a ScreenTip manually in one application, Access does display the new ScreenTip while that application is open. After you close and subsequently reopen the application, Access displays the original ScreenTip, not the new one you created.

Providing ControlTips for Controls on Forms

Forms are a major component of an Access application. Each form contains controls such as command buttons, text boxes, and so on. Due to space limitations on a form, there's a limit to the amount of information you can provide with each control. A command button, for example, usually has space for only one or two words. Although these words might provide a sufficient prompt for people who are familiar with the application, people who use the application only occasionally, or who are new to it, need more help. You can provide ControlTips to make life easier for these people.

A ControlTip, like ScreenTips, are displayed when the user pauses the cursor over a control. Each ControlTip appears as text within a balloon that's superimposed over the form. You can see ControlTips by pointing onto command buttons in the Book application that accompanies this book.

The following steps describe how to create a ControlTip for a command button. You can create ControlTips for other controls in a similar manner. Each ControlTip can contain as many as 255 characters.

To see how you can provide ControlTips for controls on a form, open the Northwind application that Microsoft supplies with Access and, in the Main Switchboard, select Suppliers to display the Suppliers form. Point onto any of the controls in that form and you won't see any ControlTips. To add a ControlTip to a control on this form:

1. Choose View, Design View to display the Design view of the form.
2. If necessary, choose View, Properties to display the Property sheet.
3. Select a control on the form, such as the ReviewProducts Command Button control.
4. Select the Other tab in the Property sheet. The ControlTip Text property box is empty.
5. In the ControlTip Text property box, enter the text you want to provide as a ControlTip, such as "Display products available from this supplier."

When you return to the Form view and point onto the Review Products button, you'll see the ControlTip text you just entered displayed for a few seconds.

TIP

Sometimes, for a reason I don't understand, you can supply a ControlTip for a control but that ControlTip isn't displayed when you point onto the control in Form view. I've found a way to solve this problem. Display the form in Design view and select the control for which the ControlTip isn't displayed. Choose Format, Send to Back and then choose Format, Bring to Front. When you switch back to Form view and point onto the control, you'll find the ControlTip is displayed.

By providing ControlTip text in this way, you give people the help they might need without cluttering the form with a lot of text most people don't need. You should consistently add ControlTips to the controls on forms you create.

Customizing Menus and Toolbars

An Access application displays information to users in various windows, principally forms. Users see one menu bar and one or more toolbars whenever they display a window. The standard menus probably contain menu items that aren't appropriate for people who use your application and might not contain menu items that could be useful. Likewise, toolbars might contain buttons you don't need and might not contain buttons that would be appropriate. You can modify the standard menus, create your own menus, modify the standard toolbars, and create your own toolbars. You can also prevent people who use your application from changing the menus and toolbars you provide.

Although menus and toolbars have a different appearance, Access (and other Office 2000 applications) regards them as the same. The name *command bars* refers to both menus and toolbars.

The next few sections describe how you can change existing command bars and create new ones manually as well as under VBA control.

Manually Changing and Creating Command Bars

You're probably familiar with manually adding to command bars. Here's a quick reminder:

1. Open the form or report for which you want to change or create a command bar.
2. Choose View, move the pointer onto Toolbars, and choose Customize to display the Customize dialog box.
3. In the Toolbars tab, make sure the command bar you want to modify is selected.
4. In the Commands tab, select from the Categories list the category of the menu item or toolbar button you want to add.
5. From the Commands list, drag a command to the position where you want it to be in a menu or on a toolbar.

To remove a button from a toolbar, hold down Alt while you drag the button off the toolbar. Use the same technique to remove a menu item from a menu, with the exception that you must have the Customize dialog box open.

To create a new command bar, perform the following steps:

1. Choose New in the Customize dialog box's Toolbars tab. Access displays the New Toolbar dialog box in which it proposes a name (such as Custom 1) for the new command bar. Replace that name with something more suitable and click OK to return to the Toolbars tab.
2. Choose Properties to display the Toolbar Properties dialog box.
3. Open the drop-down Type list and select Menu Bar, Toolbar, or Popup, as appropriate. If you select Popup, a message appears stating that the toolbar will become a shortcut menu (otherwise known as a context menu).

From that point, you can drag commands onto the new menu bar or toolbar.

14

NOTE

Access can display any number of toolbars, but only one menu bar. After you create a custom menu bar, you have to set a form's or report's MenuBar property to the new menu bar's name in order to display that menu bar instead of the standard one.

The preceding procedures should remind you how easy it is to change existing menu bars and toolbars. That's the problem! If you're creating applications for other people to use, you probably don't want those people to change the command bars you've provided.

Another problem with customizing command bars in this way is that the customized bars exist only for the Access installation on the computer you used for doing the customization. Also, the customizations affect all databases you have previously, or will subsequently, create on that computer.

The solution to these problems is to use VBA to customize command bars.

Using VBA to Investigate Command Bars

You can create VBA procedures that control command bars. By making these procedures respond to a form's or report's Open event, you can be sure all the people who use your applications will have the command bars you intend. Also, you can prevent people from accessing the Customize dialog box so that they can't make their own changes to command bars.

Chapter 11, "Using Object Models Within the Office Environment," explained the concepts of objects and object models. In that chapter, the section "Displaying the Access Object Model" showed how you can display a graphical representation of the Access object model from Help. If you refer to that diagram, you see that one of the collections in Access is CommandBars; that collection contains the CommandBar objects within Access. Each CommandBar object contains controls—the menu items in a menu or the buttons on a toolbar.

Working with the CommandBars collection involves objects in the Microsoft Office 9.0 Object Library. You must set a reference to that library before you can use the VBA code described subsequently in this chapter. Refer to "Working with Object Libraries" in Chapter 11 for information about setting a reference to an object library.

To gain an initial understanding of using the CommandBars collection to work with command bars, create the event procedure in Listing 14.1, which responds to a form's open event.

LISTING 14.1   Event Procedure that Reponds to a Form's Open Event

```
Private Sub Form_Open(Cancel As Integer)
   Dim strCaption As String
   Dim strTooltipText As String

   strCaption = CommandBars("Form View").Controls(1).Caption
   strTooltipText = CommandBars("Form View").Controls(1).TooltipText

   MsgBox("Caption: " & strCaption & vbCrLf & "Tooltip: " & strTooltipText)
End Sub
```

Subsequently, when you open the form, you'll see a message box that displays the caption and ScreenTip text for the Form View toolbar's first button.

The first two statements declare string variables to which values are assigned in the next two statements. Each assignment statement refers to a specific command bar within the CommandBars collection, to a specific control on that command bar, and to a specific property of that control. The MsgBox statement displays the values of the two variables.

A specific command bar within the CommandBars collection is identified by name. To see the names of available command bars, open the form, choose View, move the pointer onto Toolbars, choose Customize, and choose the Toolbars tab, as shown in Figure 14.1.

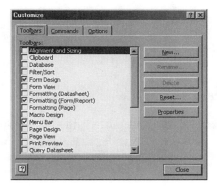

FIGURE 14.1

The list at the left side of the dialog box shows the available command bar names.

You can choose any member of the CommandBars collection by using one of the names in the list shown in Figure 14.1.

Each command bar contains one or more controls. You can choose one of these controls by using a number to specify its position. The first control is numbered 1, the second is numbered 2, and so on.

14

MAKING ACCESS
APPLICATIONS
EASY TO USE

CAUTION

VBA returns a runtime error if you attempt to access control 0 (zero).

Each control in a command bar has many properties, of which Caption and TooltipText are only two. To see a complete list of properties, open the CommandBarControl Object topic in Microsoft Visual Basic Help—not Microsoft Access Help. Refer to "Accessing Access 2000 Help" in Chapter 1, "Planning Successful Access Applications," for information about accessing Microsoft Visual Basic Help. Choose Properties to see the beginning of a list of properties as shown in Figure 14.2.

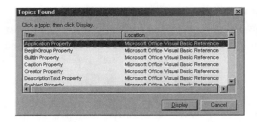

FIGURE 14.2
Scroll down the Title list to see the names of all the properties of a CommandBarControl object.

You can modify the VBA code shown previously in this chapter to examine the value of each of these properties. You can also use VBA code to change the values of some of these properties (some are read-only). The next section explains how you can change the value of CommandBarControl properties.

Changing a Toolbar Button's ScreenTip Text

As you saw in the previous section, one of the properties of a CommandBarControl object, such as a button on a toolbar, is TooltipText. You can change the value of this property, and many other properties, with the VBA code in Listing 14.2.

LISTING 14.2   VBA Code to Change a Control's ScreenTip Text

```
Private Sub Form_Open(Cancel As Integer)
   Dim strTooltipText As String

   strTooltipText = "Display"

   CommandBars("Form View").Controls(1).TooltipText = strTooltipText
End Sub
```

> **TIP**
>
> Listing 14.2 is shown as a separate event procedure that responds to a form's Open event. In practice, combine the statements in this and other examples to do whatever you need with command bars at the time a form or report opens or becomes active.

Open a form in which that event procedure responds to the Open event. Point onto the first button in the Form View toolbar. Now the word Display appears as the ScreenTip text.

Displaying and Hiding a Toolbar

Each command bar has many properties. To see these properties, open the CommandBar Object topic in Visual Basic Help and choose Properties. The list of properties is similar to that for a CommandBarControl object, shown previously in Figure 14.2. You can use the Enabled and Visible properties to control the display of a command bar, as explained in Table 14.1.

TABLE 14.1   The Enabled and Visible Properties for a Command Bar

Property	Effect
Enabled	If the property is True, the command bar appears in the list of available command bars and the command bar is displayed. If the property is False, the command bar is not listed and is not displayed.
Visible	If the Enabled property is True and the Visible property is True, the command bar is displayed. If the Visible property is False, the command bar is not displayed, even if the Enabled property is True.

You can include these statements in an event procedure to control the Enabled and Visible properties of the Form View toolbar:

```
CommandBars("Form View").Enabled = True      'Toolbar enabled

CommandBars("Form View").Enabled = False     'Toolbar disabled

CommandBars("Form View").Visible = True      'Toolbar visible

CommandBars("Form View").Visible = False     'Toolbar invisible
```

> **NOTE**
>
> You can use the same types of statements to enable and disable menu bars and to make menu bars visible or invisible. Bear in mind, though, that Access insists on displaying one and only one menu bar. Runtime errors occur if you write code that conflicts with this requirement.

Disabling and Hiding Buttons on a Toolbar

You can disable or hide buttons on a toolbar in much the same way that you can you can disable or hide toolbars—by using those buttons' Enable and Visible properties. To do this, you have to identify a toolbar button either by its position in the toolbar or by its name. Because a button's position may change, you should always identify it by name.

> **TIP**
>
> A button's name may be the same as the ScreenTip text, but isn't necessarily so.

To discover the name of a toolbar button:

1. Display a form (in Form or Design view) or a report (in Report or Design view).
2. Choose View, move the pointer onto Toolbars, choose Customize, and select the Toolbars tab. If necessary, check the name of the toolbar that contains the button you want to disable or hide.
3. With the Customize dialog box displayed, right-click the toolbar button, the name of which you want to discover, to display its context menu, as shown in Figure 14.3.

> **NOTE**
>
> The name of a toolbar button is actually its `caption` property. The ampersand (&) that precedes the first character of the name causes that character to be underlined, indicating it is the shortcut key.

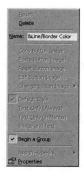

FIGURE 14.3
The third item in the context menu contains the button's name.

Knowing the button's name, you can write a statement such as

```
CommandBars("Form View").Controls("Save").Enabled = False
```

to disable the Save button in the Form View toolbar. After you do so and run the procedure containing that statement, the Form View toolbar contains a dimmed View button.

TIP

Many toolbar buttons' names contain an ampersand character. It's optional whether you include that character in the preceding statement.

A similar statement setting the Enabled property to True enables the toolbar button.

You can use a statement such as

```
CommandBars("Form View").Controls("Save").Visible = False
```

to make a toolbar button invisible. After you run a procedure containing this statement, the Save button is no longer visible in the toolbar. All buttons to the right of where that button normally is move one position to the left.

NOTE

You can also delete a button from a toolbar, as described in the section "Deleting Buttons from a Toolbar" later in this chapter.

14

MAKING ACCESS
APPLICATIONS
EASY TO USE

You can use almost the same techniques to disable or hide commands in a menu. One small difference is this: To find the name of a menu item, after you've displayed the Customize dialog box, click the menu that contains the item you want to disable or hide. When you do that, the menu opens as it normally does. Right-click a menu item to display the context menu that contains the item's name.

Creating Command Bars and Command Bar Objects

The term *command bar* includes toolbars and menu bars. You can create toolbars and add buttons to existing toolbars. You can also create new menu bars and add items to existing menu bars. The following sections are specifically about toolbars, but you can use almost the same techniques for menu bars. Remember that although Access can display as many toolbars as you have room for, it can display only one menu bar at a time.

When you're creating command bars, it's important to remember that each command bar must have a unique name. Access displays a runtime error message if you attempt to create a command bar with the same name as an existing command bar, whether or not the existing command bar is visible.

The following sections show you how to create and modify command bars, and how to prevent users from changing them.

Creating Toolbars

The event procedure in Listing 14.3 creates a toolbar named New Toolbar. This example shows an event procedure that runs in response to a form's Open event. It could, of course, respond to any other event.

> **NOTE**
>
> The Microsoft Office Object 9.0 object library must be selected as an active reference in order to use the procedures shown in Listings 14.3, 14.4, and 14.5. See "Working with Object Libraries" in Chapter 11 for information about making object libraries available.

LISTING 14.3   VBA Code to Create a Toolbar

```
Private Sub Form_Open(Cancel As Integer)
   Dim cbrToolbar As CommandBar
   Dim strCommandBarName As String

   strCommandBarName = "New Toolbar"
   Set cbrToolbar = CommandBars.Add(strCommandBarName, msoBarTop)

   cbrToolbar.Visible = True

   Set cbrToolbar = Nothing
End Sub
```

When you run this procedure for the first time, a new toolbar appears near the top of the form, immediately under any existing toolbars at the top of the form, as shown in Figure 14.4.

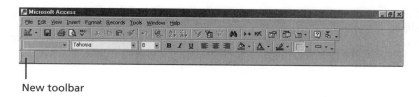

New toolbar

FIGURE 14.4
The new toolbar is empty and has space for only one button.

CAUTION

If you try to run the procedure more than once, you'll see a runtime error message because you can't create more than one command bar with the same name. Unfortunately, the error message you get refers only to an "Invalid procedure call or argument." You'll soon learn how to solve that problem but, first, make sure you understand the procedure as it stands at present.

14

MAKING ACCESS
APPLICATIONS
EASY TO USE

The first two statements in this procedure declare a variable as a CommandBar object and another variable for the new command bar's name. This is followed by two assignment statements, the first of which provides a name for the new command bar. The second assignment statement employs the Add method of the CommandBars collection. The Add method of a collection adds an object to that collection.

The complete syntax of the Add method of the CommandBars collection is

```
CommandBars.Add(Name, Position, MenuBar, Temporary)
```

The arguments of the Add method are

- Name—The name of the new command bar.
- Position—Defines the position of the toolbar. Use one of the following built-in constants:
  - msoBarFloating—Default. The new toolbar is floating.
  - msoBarBottom—The new toolbar is docked at the bottom of the form.
  - msoBarLeft—The new toolbar is docked at the left edge of the form.
  - msoBarRight—The new toolbar is docked at the right edge of the form.
  - msoBarTop—The new toolbar is docked at the top of the form.
- MenuBar—Used only for menu bars. True to replace the existing menu bar. False is the default.
- Temporary—Specifies whether the new command bar is temporary or permanent. False (default) makes the new command bar permanent. True makes the new command bar temporary so that it is automatically deleted when Access closes.

By default, a new toolbar isn't visible. The statement

```
cbrToolbar.Visible = True
```

is required to make it visible.

The final statement

```
Set cbrToolbar = Nothing
```

makes sure the memory occupied by the cbrToolbar variable is released.

It's quite easy to avoid the error message that's displayed if an attempt is made to create a command bar with the same name as a command bar that already exists. The revised procedure that does this is shown in Listing 14.4.

LISTING 14.4   VBA Code to Create a Toolbar Including Detection of Duplicate Names

```
Private Sub Form_Open(Cancel As Integer)
    Dim cbrToolbar As CommandBar
    Dim strCommandBarName As String
    Dim intCtr As Integer

    strCommandBarName = "New Toolbar"
```

```
    For intCtr = 1 To CommandBars.Count
        If CommandBars(intCtr).Name = strCommandBarName Then
            MsgBox "Command bar named '" & strCommandBarName & "' already exists."
            Exit Sub
        End If
    Next intCtr

    Set cbrToolbar = CommandBars.Add(strCommandBarName, msoBarTop)

    cbrToolbar.Visible = True

    Set cbrToolbar = Nothing
End Sub
```

This procedure contains a For loop that scans all existing command bars, checking to see whether any of them has the same name as the command bar to be added. (See Appendix A, "Visual Basic for Applications Primer," for general information about For loops.)

The For loop identifies each member of the CommandBars collection by its index number. Index numbers start at 1 (one) and end at the index number of the last member of collection. This last index number is found by using the Count property of the collection.

The Name property of each member of the CommandBars collection is compared with the name to be used for the new command bar. If any existing command bar has the same name as that, a message is displayed and the Exit Sub statement immediately terminates execution of the procedure. Only if no existing command bar has the same name as the name to be used for the new procedure does the For loop run to completion so that the Set statement that creates the command bar is executed.

As you'll discover if you run the revised procedure many times, no error message is ever displayed.

Adding Buttons to a Toolbar

As you saw in the preceding section, a new toolbar contains no buttons. In this section, you'll learn how to add buttons to an existing toolbar.

The event procedure in Listing 14.5 runs when a command button named cmdNewButton is clicked on a form. The procedure adds a button to a toolbar named New Toolbar.

LISTING 14.5   VBA Code to Add a Button to a Toolbar

```
'Add button to toolbar
Private Sub cmdNewButton_Click()
    Dim cbrToolbar As CommandBar
    Dim cmdToolbar As CommandBarControl

    Set cbrToolbar = Commandbars.Item("New Toolbar")
    Set cmdToolbar = cbrToolbar.Controls.Add(msoControlButton)
    With cmdToolbar
        .FaceId = 59
        .Caption = "Happy Face"
        .TooltipText = "Happy Face"
        .OnAction = "=MsgBox(""You pressed the Happy Face button!"")"
    End With
End Sub
```

The first two statements in the procedure declare a CommandBar variable and a CommandBarControl variable. The first Set statement assigns the CommandBar variable to the specific toolbar named New Toolbar. The second Set statement adds a control button to the toolbar's Controls collection (this statement is explained in more detail a little later). The next statements set four properties of the new button:

- FaceId—Identifies the image displayed on the button's face

- Caption—Provides a name by which the button can subsequently be referred to in VBA code

- TooltipText—Is the text displayed in a ScreenTip when you point onto the button and pause

- OnAction—Defines what happens then the button is clicked

When you run this procedure, you see the new control button, as shown in Figure 14.5.

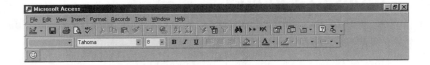

FIGURE 14.5

The toolbar now contains a button with the happy face icon on its face.

The new button has the happy face icon on its face because the event procedure just displayed set the button's FaceId property to 59. You'll learn about setting the FaceId property a little later in this section.

If you move the pointer onto the new button and pause, the ScreenTip text Happy Face is displayed because the procedure sets the `TooltipText` property to "Happy Face".

If you click the new toolbar button, a message box appears because the procedure sets the `OnAction` property to call the MsgBox function.

> **NOTE**
>
> You might be curious about the double quotation marks in the statement that sets the `OnAction` property. The value of the `OnAction` property must be a string—that's why the entire text at the right of the equals sign is enclosed within quotation marks. In this case, the `OnAction` property calls the MsgBox function, the argument of which contains quotation marks. For a quotation mark within a string to be regarded as a literal quotation mark, rather than as a character that terminates the string, you must use double quotation marks. Regard that as a quirk of VBA if you like, but it's one of the rules you must follow.

This basic example of placing a button in a toolbar should give you the general idea. Now, look at the process in a little more detail. The fourth statement in the previous procedure

```
Set CmdToolbar = cbrToolbar.Controls.Add(msoControlButton)
```

uses the Add method to add a control to the Controls collection. The general syntax for the Add method is

```
expression.Add(Type, Id, Parameter, Before, Temporary)
```

in which

- *expression* returns a CommandBarControls object.
- *Type* specifies the type of control to be added. Use one of the constants msoControlButton, msoControlComboBox, msoControlDropdown, msoControlEdit, or msoControlPopup.
- *Id* is an integer that specifies a built-in control. If this argument is omitted or has the value of 1 (one), a blank custom control is added to the toolbar.
- *Parameter* is used to send information to VBA procedures.
- *Before* is an integer that defines the position of the new control in the toolbar. If this argument is specified, the new control is inserted at the left of the control in the specified position. If this argument is omitted, the new control is added at the right of the existing controls.
- *Temporary* determines whether the new control is temporary or permanent. If True, the control is automatically deleted when Access closes; if False, the control is permanent.

14

MAKING ACCESS APPLICATIONS EASY TO USE

A toolbar button has quite a long list of properties, some of which are defined in Table 14.2.

TABLE 14.2   Frequently Used Toolbar Button Properties

Property	Description
BeginGroup	True if command bar control is at the beginning of a group of controls on command bar. Otherwise, this property is False.
Caption	Caption text. Also default ScreenTip text.
Enabled	True if control is enabled.
FaceId	ID number of control's face.
Height	Height of control in pixels.
Index	Position of control in toolbar.
Left	Position of control's left edge in pixels.
OnAction	Name of procedure that runs when button is clicked.
Position	Position of or type of control. Can be msoBarBottom, msoBarLeft, msoBarRight, msoBarTop, msoBarFloating, msoBarPopup, or msoBarMenuBar.
TooltipText	Text displayed in ScreenTip.
Top	Position of control's top edge in pixels.
Visible	True if control is visible.
Width	Width of control in pixels.

Most of these properties are fairly self-explanatory. One that requires explanation, though, is the FaceId property. How did I know when I wrote the preceding procedure to specify the value of the FaceId property to be 59 in order to place a Happy Face image on the button? The answer to that question is that I had to do some work to find out.

Microsoft supplies with Office several thousand images, each identified by a number (the FaceId property), for use on button faces. Office leaves it to you to find out what images are available and which number identifies each image. With such a large number of images, it's obviously impractical to create a button separately with each image to find out what they all look like. What you can do, though, is to create a procedure that creates a very large toolbar and automatically places several hundred buttons, each with a different image, on that toolbar. The procedure can set the TooltipText property of each button to show the value of the FaceId property. The event procedure in Listing 14.6 does just that. The procedure runs when a command button named cmdShowFace is clicked.

> **NOTE**
>
> The procedure in Listing 14.6 only displays buttons so that you can discover the value of each button's FaceId property. The buttons created by this procedure don't do anything because no OnAction properties are defined.

LISTING 14.6   Procedure to Display FaceID Properties for Buttons

```
'Display toolbar buttons with tooltips containing FaceID properties
Private Sub cmdShowFace_Click()
   Dim intFirstID As Integer
   Dim intLastID As Integer
   Dim cbrToolbar As CommandBar
   Dim cmdButton As CommandBarButton
   Dim intCtr As Integer
   Dim strCommandBarName As String

   intFirstID = 1
   intLastID = 500
   strCommandBarName = "FaceID"

   'Delete FaceID toolbar if it already exists
   On Error Resume Next
   CommandBars(strCommandBarName).Delete
   On Error GoTo 0

   'Create FaceID toolbar
   Set cbrToolbar = CommandBars.Add(strCommandBarName)

   'Add toolbar buttons
   For intCtr = intFirstID To intLastID
      Set cmdButton = cbrToolbar.Controls.Add(msoControlButton)
      With cmdButton
         .FaceID = intCtr
         .TooltipText = "FaceID: " & intCtr
      End With
   Next intCtr

   'Show toolbar
   With cbrToolbar
      .Width = 600
      .Left = 100
      .Top = 50
      .Visible = True
   End With
End Sub
```

As shown here, the procedure displays toolbar buttons with `FaceId` properties in the range 1 through 500 as shown in Figure 14.6. Be patient after you start the procedure. Depending on the speed of your computer, it can take several tens of seconds for the images to be displayed.

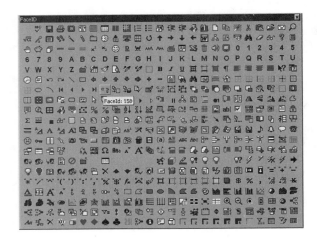

FIGURE 14.6
With the pointer resting on an image, the Tooltip displays that image's FaceId number.

If your screen displays 800×600 pixels, five hundred images is about as many as you can display at one time. You can display a different range of images by changing the values of the `intFirstID` and `intLastID` variables near the beginning of the preceding procedure.

This procedure is not explained in detail because it's shown here principally to give you a way to find out the `FaceId` property of images you might want to use. However, if you look carefully at the procedure, you'll find most of the statements it contains are similar to statements in procedures you've previously seen.

The procedure for adding a button to a toolbar (shown previously in this section) allows duplicate buttons to be added to a toolbar. You could add code to the procedure that would allow a button to be added only if that button didn't already exist. The next section describes a procedure in which code looks to see if a button already exists.

Deleting Buttons from a Toolbar

You can delete a button from a toolbar by using a procedure such as that shown in Listing 14.7.

LISTING 14.7   VBA Code to Delete a Button from a Toolbar

```
'Delete toolbar button
Private Sub cmdDeleteButton_Click()
   Dim cbrToolbar As CommandBar
   Dim cmdToolbar as CommandBarControl

   Set cbrToolbar = CommandBars.Item("New Toolbar")
   Set cmdToolbar = cbrToolbar.Controls("Happy Face")

   cmdToolbar.Delete
End Sub
```

The first two statements in this event procedure declare a CommandBar variable and a CommandBarControl variable. The first Set statement assigns the CommandBar variable to a toolbar named New Toolbar. The second Set statement assigns the CommandBarControl variable to the Happy Face button on the New Toolbar. The final statement deletes the button.

This procedures works fine if the toolbar named New Toolbar exists and if that toolbar contains a button named Happy Face. However, if the toolbar doesn't exist, or if the toolbar does exist but doesn't contain a button named Happy Face, VBA generates an error message when the procedure runs.

To avoid the possibility of getting error messages (something you should always endeavor to do), modify the procedure as shown in Listing 14.8.

LISTING 14.8   VBA Code to Delete a Button from a Toolbar Including Code to Avoid an Error Message if the Named Button Doesn't Exist

```
'Delete toolbar button
Private Sub cmdDeleteButton_Click()
   Dim cbrToolbar As CommandBar
   Dim cmdToolbar As CommandBarControl
   Dim intCtr1 As Integer    Dim intCtr2 As Integer
   Dim strCommandBarName As String
   Dim strControlCaption As String

   strCommandBarName = "New Toolbar"
   strControlCaption = "Happy Face"

   For intCtr1 = 1 To CommandBars.Count
      If CommandBars(intCtr1).Name = strCommandBarName Then
         Set cbrToolbar = CommandBars.Item(strCommandBarName)
         For intCtr2 = 1 To cbrToolbar.Controls.Count
```

continues

14

MAKING ACCESS
APPLICATIONS
EASY TO USE

LISTING 14.8   Continued

```
            If cbrToolbar.Controls(intCtr2).Caption = strControlCaption Then
                Set cmdToolbar = cbrToolbar.Controls(strControlCaption)
                cmdToolbar.Delete
                Exit For
            End If
        Next intCtr2
    End If
  Next intCtr1
End Sub
```

Notice these points about the expanded procedure:

- Two addition variables are declared for the names of the toolbar and the button to be deleted. The actual names of the toolbar and button are assigned to these variables. The variables are used within the remainder of the procedure instead of using the actual toolbar and button names there.

- The procedure contains one For loop nested within another. The outer For loop looks for a specific named toolbar so that the code within that loop runs only if the named toolbar exists.

- The inner For loop looks for a specific named button so that the code within that loop runs only if the named button exists.

Securing Your Customized Toolbars and Menus

So far in this chapter, you've learned how to modify the toolbars and menus supplied with Access and how to create custom toolbars and menus. After you've done that, you probably want to make sure people who use your applications don't make changes to the toolbars and menus.

As you know, Access users can make changes to toolbars and menus by way of the Customize dialog box. This dialog box can be accessed by

- Choosing View, moving the pointer onto Toolbars, and choosing Customize

- Right-clicking the menu bar or a toolbar and then choosing Customize in the context menu

- Choosing Tools, Customize

You can prevent people from making changes to toolbars and menus by denying access to the Customize dialog box. You can use the procedure in Listing 14.9 to do that.

LISTING 14.9   VBA Code to Prevent People from Making Changes to Toolbars and Menus

```
'Deny access to toolbar and menu customization
Private Sub cmdDenyCustomize_Click()
    CommandBars("Toolbar List").Enabled = False
    CommandBars("Tools").Controls("Customize...").Enabled = False
End Sub
```

The first statement in this procedure makes Toolbars in the View menu unavailable and also turns off the context menu for toolbars and the menu bar. The second statement makes Customize unavailable in the Tools menu.

You can restore access to toolbar and menu customization by running a similar procedure, this time with the Enabled properties in the third and fourth lines set to True.

Summary

You can make your applications easy for people to use by customizing and supplementing the menus and toolbars Access provides. For example, you can remove unneeded menus from the menu bar and add menus. You can also remove items from menus and add items to menus. Similarly, you can remove buttons from the standard Access toolbars and add buttons to those toolbars.

You can even replace standard Access menu bars with customized menu bars, each with its own set of menu items. Also, you can create toolbars, each with its own set of buttons.

Another way to make your applications easy to use is to provide ScreenTips, which provide information to people as they work with your application.

The main purpose of all of this is to make your programs user friendly.

14

MAKING ACCESS
APPLICATIONS
EASY TO USE

Calculating Values and Making Decisions

IN THIS CHAPTER

The more you want to become an expert in creating Access applications, the more thoroughly do you have to become familiar with the tools at your disposal. Among these tools is a rich set of operators, and that's the subject of this chapter.

Many of the things you need to do when dealing with data involve making calculations of one type or another. Among the available operators are those that perform arithmetic operations. You can use these to calculate values.

When designing applications, you often need to include decision-making, such as which information to include in a report. The comparison operators enable you to do that.

Although less frequently used than arithmetic and comparison operators, logical operators greatly extend what you can do. These operators provide the capability to combine conditions.

Whether you're using Access at a quite basic level or are developing complex applications, you need to become skilled in the use of operators. This chapter provides detailed information about

- The arithmetic, relational, logical, concatenation, comparison, and identity operators available in Access
- Using operators in queries and filters
- Using operators in macros
- Using operators in VBA code

Understanding Operators

In general, an *operator* is a code name or symbol used to prescribe a command or function. For example, the plus (+) operator adds one value to another, the equal (=) operator compares one value with another, and so on. The values on which an operator performs operations are known as *operands*. When an operation occurs, a value is returned.

The subsequent sections that define individual operators contain basic examples of operands. In practice, operands are usually single variables or can be expressions that combine variables and other elements.

Arithmetic Operators

With the single exception of the unary minus operator, arithmetic operators perform mathematical operations between two numeric operands, returning a numeric value. The unary minus operator changes the sign of a numeric operand from positive to negative, or from negative to positive. The arithmetic operators are listed in Table 15.1. The following statement shows a typical use of arithmetic operators:

```
intCounter = intCounter + 1
```

In this statement, intCounter is a variable of type Integer. The expression on the right of the equals sign uses the addition operator (+) to add 1 to the previous value of intCounter. The complete statement replaces the original value of intCounter with the new value.

TABLE 15.1 Arithmetic Operators

Operator	Symbol	Purpose
Addition	+	Adds one operand to another. Example: 5 + 2 returns 7.
Subtraction	–	Subtracts one operand from another. Example: 5 - 2 returns 3.
Unary Minus	–	Changes the sign of an operand. Example -5 returns –5.
Multiplication	*	Multiplies one operand by another. Example: 5 * 2 returns 10.
Division	/	Divides one operand by another. Example: 5 / 2 returns 2.5.
Integer Division	\	Divides one operand by another, rounding off the result to an integer. Example: 5 \ 2 returns 2.
Integer Modulus	Mod	Divides one operand by another, returning only the remainder. Example: 5 Mod 2 returns 1.
Exponentiation	^	Raises first operand to power of the second operand. Example: 5 ^ 2 returns 25.

Relational Operators

Relational operators compare the relationship of one operand with that of another, and, with one exception, return the value True if the comparison is satisfied; otherwise, they return the value False. The exception is if either of the values being compared is Null (an undefined value), a comparison returns the value Null. The relational operators are listed in Table 15.2.

The following statements show a typical use of a relational operator.

```
If intCounter > 10 Then
    ...
End If
```

The first statement in this example begins an If...End If control structure. The ellipsis in the second line represents some statements that are executed if the condition in the first statement is satisfied. The condition, which employs the more positive than operator (>), ensures that the statements within the control structure are executed only if the value of the variable intCounter is greater than 10.

TABLE 15.2   Relational Operators

Operator	Symbol	Purpose
Equal to	=	Tests one operand for equality with another. Example: `5 = 2` returns False.
Not equal to	<>	Tests one operand for inequality with another. Example: `5 <> 2` returns True.
More negative than	<	Tests whether one operand is more negative than another. Example: `5 < 2` returns False.
More positive than	>	Tests whether one operand is more positive than another. Example: `5 > 2` returns True.
More negative than or equal to	<=	Tests whether one operand is more negative than, or equal to, another. Example: `5 <= 2` returns False.
More positive than or equal to	>=	Tests whether one operand is more positive than, or equal to, another. Example: `5 >= 2` returns True.

> **NOTE**
>
> Table 15.2 lists = as a relational operator. As explained in the section "Using Operators in Other VBA Statements" later in this chapter, = is also used as an assignment operator.

Logical Operators

Logical operators (also known as Boolean operators) operate on operators that have logical values of True or False and, with one exception, return a value of True or False. If one or both of the operands has a value of Null (an unknown value), the logical operators return a value of Null. Table 15.3 lists the logical operators.

The following statements illustrate the use of a logical operator.

```
If (strFname = "John") And (strLname = "Freeman") Then
   ...
End If
```

In this case, the statements represented by the ellipsis in the `If...End If` control structure are executed only if both the expressions in the `If` statement are true.

TABLE 15.3   Logical Operators

Operator	Symbol	Purpose
Negation	Not	Negates the logical value of an operand. Example: Not (5 > 2) returns False.
Conjunction	And	Returns True only if two operands are both True; otherwise, returns False. Examples: (5 > 2) And (2 < 5) returns True, whereas (5 > 2) And (2 > 5) returns False.
Disjunction	Or	Returns True if one or both of two operands are True; otherwise, returns False. Examples: (5 > 2) Or (2 > 5) returns True, whereas (5 < 2) Or (2 > 5) returns False.
Exclusion	Xor	Returns True if only one of two operands is True; returns False if both operands are True or if both operands are False. Examples: (5 > 2) Xor (2 > 5) returns True, whereas (5 > 2) Xor (2 < 5) returns False.
Equivalence	Equ	Performs logical equivalence on two expressions. See explanation later in the text.
Implication	Imp	Performs logical implication on two expressions. See explanation later in the text.

NOTE

You're unlikely to have a need to use the Equivalence and Implication operators. They are included in Table 15.3 only for the sake of completeness.

The Equivalence operator is used in the syntax

Expression1 Equ *Expression2*

and returns True or False according to Table 15.4 unless either expression is Null, in which case the value returned is Null.

TABLE 15.4   Value Returned by Equivalence Operator

Expression1	Expression2	Value Returned
True	True	True
True	False	False
False	True	False
False	False	True

The Implication operator is used in the syntax

Expression1 Imp *Expression2*

and returns True or False according to Table 15.5.

TABLE 15.5 Value Returned by Implication Operator

Expression1	Expression2	Value Returned
True	True	True
True	False	False
True	Null	Null
False	True	False
False	False	True
False	Null	True
Null	True	True
Null	False	Null
Null	Null	Null

Concatenation Operator

The concatenation operator (&) creates a single text string from two separate text strings. For example, "Out" & "look" returns "Outlook".

In some circumstances, the plus sign (+) can be used instead of the ampersand (&) as the symbol for this operator; however, this usage is discouraged because it can lead to unpredictable results. This use of the plus sign is mentioned here because you might come across it in applications other people have written. Refer to the later section "Concatenating Strings" for more information about this point.

Comparison Operators

Comparison operators ascertain whether the content of a field satisfies certain conditions. Table 15.6 lists the comparison operators.

TABLE 15.6 Comparison Operators for Queries and Validation Rules

Operator	Purpose
Is Null	Determines whether value of a field is Null. Enter Is Null into the Criteria cell in the QBE grid.
Is Not Null	Determines whether value of a field is not Null. Enter Is Not Null into the Criteria cell in the QBE grid.

Operator	Purpose
Like	Determines whether a string value begins with specified characters. Enter Like followed by one or more characters, using the wildcard characters * or ? for unspecified characters into the Criteria cell of the QBE grid. Example: Like R* to find fields starting with R.
In	Determines whether a string value is a member of a list of string values. Enter In followed by a list of possible values, enclosed within parentheses, into the Criteria cell of the QBE grid. Example: In("Red", "Blue", "White") to find fields containing one of the strings.
Between	Determines whether a numeric or date value is within a specified range. Enter Between and then the range of values into the Criteria cell of the QBE grid. Examples: Between 5 And 10 and Between #1/1/2000# And #1/31/2000#.

See the section "Using Operators in Queries" subsequently in this chapter for more detailed information about these operators and more examples of using them. See the section "Comparing Dates" later in this chapter for an explanation of the way dates are formatted in the last example in Table 15.6.

Identity Operators

Identity operators are used in VBA code and queries to identify objects, properties, and methods.

The bang operator (!) identifies a member, as in these examples:

- A member of a class within a class. For example, if a form named frmPublisher exists within the Forms collection, that form is identified as Forms!frmPublisher.
- A field within a table. For example, if a field named strTitle exists within a table named tblBook, that field is identified as tblBook!strTitle.

The dot operator (.) separates a property or method name from an object name, as in these examples:

- A property of an object. For example, txtTitle.Visible identifies the Visible property of a control named txtTitle.
- A method of an object. For example, mrstBook.MoveNext calls the MoveNext method of the mrstBook object.

15

CALCULATING VALUES

Controlling Operator Precedence

Quite often, two or more operators occur within a single statement. When that's the case, the order in which operations occur affects the result. Take this statement for example

```
Result = 3 + 4 * 5
```

Without knowing any better, you might take this to mean add 3 to 4 and multiply the result by 5 to give a result of 35. In fact, you probably know that multiplication takes precedence over addition so that what really happens is that 4 is multiplied by 5 and then 3 is added so that the result is 23. This simple example illustrates the fact that it's important to be able to control the order in which operations occur.

Operators have a built-in order of precedence as shown in Table 15.7.

TABLE 15.7   Operator Precedence

Precedence Order	Operators
1	Exponentiation (^)
2	Unary minus (−)
3	Multiplication (*) and division (/)
4	Integer division (\)
5	Integer modulus (Mod)
6	Addition (+) and subtraction (−)
7	Relational (=, <>, <, >, <=, and >=)
8	Negation (Not)
9	Conjunction (And)
10	Disjunction (Or)
11	Exclusion (Xor)
12	Equivalence (Eqv)
13	Implication (Imp)

As Table 15.7 shows, multiplication is higher in the order of precedence than addition. That's why, in the example shown previously, multiplication occurs before addition.

Although the built-in order of precedence defines the order in which operations occur so that guesswork is eliminated, this order doesn't always achieve the result you want. You can take control of precedence by the use of parentheses. For example

```
Result = (3 + 4) * 5
```

forces the addition to occur first.

You're not limited to one pair of parentheses. When you use multiple pairs of parentheses, the operation within the innermost pair occurs first, and then the operation within the next pair of parentheses, and so on. For example, in the statement

```
Result = 72\((3 + 4) * 5)
```

the operation (3 + 4) within the innermost pair of parentheses occurs first, resulting in a value of 7. Then the operation within the next set of parentheses multiplies that value by 5, resulting in 35. Finally, the integer division operation divides 72 by 35, resulting in a final value of 2. If all the parentheses were removed, the multiplication would occur first, the integer division next, and then the addition, resulting in a value of 44. Precedence matters!

> **TIP**
>
> When you write statements that include two or more operators, pay particular attention to precedence. Even if you're relying on the natural precedence, it's a good idea to include parentheses so that other people who read your code can easily understand your intentions.

Using Operators in Queries

Chapter 4, "Creating Information Out of Data," introduced you to some examples of using operators within queries. For example, the section "Combining Table Fields into Recordset Fields" contained an example of using the concatenation operator. You'll often find it beneficial to use operators within queries, particularly when defining criteria.

Pause for a query refresher here (summarized from Chapter 4). A select query creates a recordset (a temporary table) that contains data from one or more tables (or other recordsets). You can use the QBE grid to specify the fields to be contained in the recordset and to specify criteria for records to be included in the recordset. The following sections suggest some ways in which you can use operators to construct queries.

Concatenating Strings

As you learned in Chapter 4, a field in a recordset can be identical to a field in a table, or can be constructed from two or more fields in a table. For example, if the table being used as the basis for a recordset contains the two fields strName and strImprint, you can create a single field named strNameImprint in the recordset created by a query by entering the following line in the Field row of the QBE grid:

```
strNameImprint: [strName] & ", " & [strImprint]
```

This line uses the concatenation operator (&) twice. Let's suppose the recordset displays a record for a publisher named Macmillan and an imprint named Sams. In that case, the value in the strNameImprint field is Macmillan, Sams. The concatenation operators create a string that combines the value of the strName field with a comma and a space and then the value of the strImprint field, such as Macmillan, Sams. You can combine as many field values from tables into one recordset field as you like using this method.

> **TIP**
>
> You can use the + operator as a concatenation character but, sometimes, this leads to problems. If both the fields being concatenated contain characters, & and + work satisfactorily to concatenate the fields. However, if one or both fields being concatenated contain Null, only & works satisfactorily; in this case, + returns Null.
>
> You should always use &, not +, as the concatenation operator.

Calculating Values

Chapter 3, "Storing Your Data Efficiently," explained why a table shouldn't contain fields that depend on other fields. Instead, if you need to have a value that's calculated from other fields, you should use a query to do that.

The classic example of this is a table that contains information about orders for an item. Such a table probably contains a field for the unit price of the item (curItem) and another field for the number of items ordered (intItems). That table shouldn't contain a field that contains the cost of the items ordered. Instead, you should use a query to calculate the total cost. That query should contain a calculated field that multiplies the unit price by the number of items. To do that, create a column in the QBE grid in which the field is named

```
curTotalCost: curItem*intItems.
```

By doing that, the name of the field in the recordset is curTotalCost. The values in that field are calculated by multiplying the cost of each item by the number of items.

You can, of course, create fields in a recordset based on fields in tables using various operators, usually arithmetic operators.

Setting Criteria

The section "Setting Criteria for a Recordset" in Chapter 4 introduced you to using operators for setting criteria in a query's QBE grid. That chapter contained the example of having "IN" in the Criteria row of a field that contained state abbreviations to create a recordset containing only records in which the state field contained IN. The chapter also mentioned using Not "IN" to create a recordset containing all records except those in which the state field contained IN. This is an example of using the negation operator Not.

> **NOTE**
>
> When you use text in a criterion, place that text within quotation marks just in case that text is an Access or VBA reserved word. If you omit the quotation marks and the text happens to be a reserved word, Access interprets the text as a reserved word instead of a criterion, usually resulting in a runtime error message.

Here are some more examples of using operators when setting criteria.

Multiple Strings

To specify a criterion so that a recordset contains records in which the state field is one of several states, you can use the disjunction (Or) operator, as in

```
"IN" Or "OR" Or "WA"
```

Alternatively, you can use the In operator, as in

```
In("IN", "OR", "WA")
```

Partial Matching of Strings

You can use the Like operator to specify a criterion for a field value that contains certain specified characters. For example

```
Like "M*"
```

specifies a field that starts with M followed by any other characters. This illustrates the use of * as a wild card that represents any number of characters. You can also use ? as a wild card representing any single character or # as a wild card representing a single numeric digit. Table 15.8 shows some examples of using wild-card characters.

TABLE 15.8 Examples of Using Wild-Card Characters

Example	Interpretation
Like "M*"	String starting with M (such as Macmillan or Microsoft)
Like "M*t"	String starting with M and ending with t (such as Microsoft)

continues

TABLE 15.8 Continued

Example	Interpretation
Like "M???t"	String starting with M, and then any three characters, ending with t (such as Monet)
Like "?a*r?"	String starting with any character, and then a, and then any number of characters, with r as the second from last character (such as Masters)
Like "#####"	String containing five digits (such as a five-digit ZIP code in the United States)
Like "#####-####"	String containing five digits, a hyphen, and then four digits (such as a five-plus-four ZIP code in the United States)
Like "??# #??"	String containing two characters, a digit, a space, a digit, and then two more characters (such as a postal code in the United Kingdom)

TIP

You can use the Customers table in the Northwind database to create some queries containing criteria such as those described in this section.

Comparing Numbers and Currency

Relational operators are often used to establish criteria based on numbers and currency. For example, if you have a table that lists orders received, that table probably has fields for Unit Price and Quantity. To create a query that produces a list of orders for quantities of 100 or more, use the criterion

```
>=100
```

Likewise, to create a query that produces a list of orders for items with a unit price of $50 or more, use the criterion

```
>=50
```

Notice that the criterion for a currency value doesn't include the currency symbol.

To create a query that has a range criterion, such as quantities in the range 100 through 150, you can use the criterion

```
Between 100 And 150
```

Although the operator is named Between, the records produced by the criterion include the limiting values; in this case, those records in which the quantity is 100 and those in which the quantity is 150.

Alternatively, you can use the criterion

```
>=100 And <=150
```

to achieve the same result.

Use the same types of criteria with currency values.

TIP

You can use the Order Details table in the Northwind database to experiment with these types of criteria.

Comparing Dates

You can use the same types of criteria for dates as those described for numbers and currency in the preceding section. The important difference is that dates in criteria must be enclosed within # characters. For example, to look for orders received on or after January 2, 2000, you would use the criterion

```
>=#1/2/2000#
```

NOTE

The preceding information about enclosing a date within # symbols is based on Microsoft documentation. In fact, if the # symbols are omitted, Access inserts them automatically, at least in the examples I've looked at. Until such time as Microsoft documents the automatic insertion of the # symbols, I suggest you insert them yourself in case there are circumstances in which automatic insertion doesn't occur.

You can use the same techniques for ranges of dates as described in the preceding section for numbers and currency.

15

CALCULATING
VALUES

> **TIP**
>
> You can use the Orders table in the Northwind database to experiment with dates in queries.

Creating Complex Query Criteria

Many of the criteria you create in the query's QBE grid are relatively simple. You can easily enter them in the space provided in the grid. Sometimes, though, you need more space than is available, and perhaps you'd like some help.

To gain more space for creating a criterion, right-click in a criterion cell in the QBE grid to display its context menu and then choose Zoom to display the Zoom dialog box in which you can enter your criterion. After you've finished entering your criterion, choose OK to dismiss the dialog box and return to the QBE grid, which now contains the criterion. You can also use the Zoom dialog box to edit an existing criterion.

To gain some help in creating a criterion, choose Build in the context menu mentioned in the preceding paragraph to display the Expression Builder, as shown in Figure 15.1.

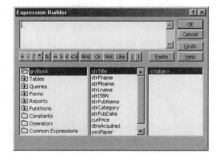

FIGURE 15.1

The Expression Builder dialog box helps you remember which operators are available.

Like the Zoom dialog box, the Expression Builder dialog box provides much more space for creating a criterion than is available in the QBE grid. You can, if you like, enter a criterion in the large box in the top part of the dialog box, and then choose OK to copy that expression into the QBE grid.

Instead of entering an operator from the keyboard, you can enter many of them by clicking the appropriate button on the dialog box. For example, to enter &, click the button that has & as its caption.

The dialog box has buttons only for the more commonly used operators. To see a complete list of operators, select Operators in the list at the bottom-left. Then, in the center list, select All, Arithmetic, Comparison, or Logical according to which list of operators you want to display in the right list. Double-click an operator in the right list to copy that operator into the expression box at the top.

Whichever way you use to create an expression in the Expression Builder dialog box, when you're finished, choose OK to copy the expression into the QBE grid.

Using Operators in Filters

As you should recall from Chapter 4, a filter can be used to limit the records displayed in a datasheet, form, or report to those that satisfy certain criteria. The section "Using Advanced Filter/Search" in that chapter introduced you to using the Design grid for creating a filter. Figure 4.23 shows an example of a Design grid.

A Design grid is very similar to a query's QBE grid. You can use expressions containing operators in the Criteria rows of the Design grid to define a filter.

To see how this works, follow these steps:

1. Open a table such as tblBook in the Book application.

2. Choose Records, move the pointer onto Filter, and choose Advanced Filter/Sort to display the Filter window shown in Figure 15.2.

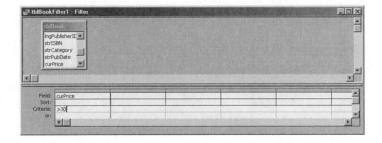

FIGURE 15.2

The Filter window contains a list of fields in the open table in its upper pane and a Design grid in its lower pane.

3. Drag one of the fields (such as the curPrice field) from the upper pane into the first column of the Design grid.

4. Enter an expression that defines a criterion into the Criteria row. If you chose the curPrice field in step 3, you could enter a criterion such as >30 to create a filter that looks for books with a cover price greater than $30.

5. Choose Filter, Apply Filter/Sort to display the result of applying the filter. Access displays a datasheet containing records that satisfy the filter criterion.

You can, of course, create much more complex criteria as described previously in this chapter. Access doesn't let you save a filter. You have to create a filter every time you want to use it. If you do want to be able to display the results of a filter in the future, you should create that filter as a query.

Controlling the Flow of a Macro

This book doesn't have much to say about macros primarily because most people who develop Access-based applications prefer using VBA code rather than macros. However, you might find it beneficial to use macros, particularly when you need to get an application up and running quickly. After you've developed an application in this way, you'll probably want to convert the macros to VBA code.

> **TIP**
>
> To automatically convert macros to VBA code, choose Tools, move the pointer onto Macro, and choose Convert Macros to Visual Basic.

The section "Making the Buttons Work" in Chapter 5, "Making Your Forms Smarter," contains some preliminary information about macros, but the macros shown there didn't have any flow control. Without flow control, the actions in a macro take place one after the other. You can use expressions containing operators to provide conditions that control whether each action takes place.

To add conditions to a macro, display either a new or an existing macro, and then choose View, Conditions to display the Condition column, as shown in Figure 15.3.

You create a condition for an action by entering an expression in the Condition column adjacent to any action by

- Entering the expression directly into the Condition column.
- Right-clicking in the Condition column to display a context menu, and then choosing Zoom to display the Zoom dialog box. Enter the expression into the dialog box, and then press OK.

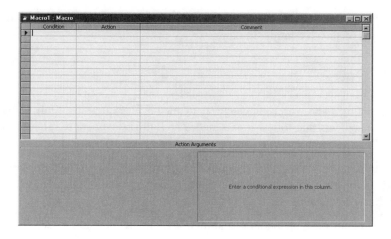

FIGURE 15.3
You can use the Condition column in a Macro window to enter a logical expression that determines whether each action runs.

- Right-clicking in the Condition column to display a context menu, and then choosing Build to display the Expression Builder. Create the expression in the manner described in the section "Creating Complex Query Criteria" previously in this chapter.

Refer to "Using Operators in Queries" earlier in this chapter for detailed information about creating expressions.

Using Operators in VBA Code

You'll make frequent use of operators, particularly arithmetic and relational operators, in VBA code. Control structures rely heavily on operators. Refer to Appendix A, "Visual Basic for Applications Primer," for detailed information about control structures.

Using Operators in Control Structures

Control structures are the means of controlling the execution of code within VBA procedures. You can use control structures for such purposes as

- Determining whether certain statements are executed
- Having a sequence of statements repeat a certain number of times
- Having a sequence of statements repeat until a certain condition occurs
- Determining which of several sequences of statements are used

Operators play a key role in control structures.

One of the most common control structures used in VBA code is `If...End If`. Here's a skeleton example of such a control structure:

```
If Price > 50 Then
   <statements>
End If
```

The control structure starts with a statement that contains an expression. Only if that statement is true are the statements that follow it executed. The End If statement terminates the statements affected by the condition.

The expression in the first line of the If control structure can be anything that returns a value of True or False. In most cases, the expression contains one or more of the relational operators defined previously in this chapter.

Other control structures use operators in a similar manner, as shown in Appendix A.

Using Operators in Other VBA Statements

Many times within VBA code you need to make calculations or manipulate text. You use operators to do so, as the following examples show.

Suppose you have a form or report based on a query that has separate Cost and Quantity fields, and you want to display the product of those two fields in a text box named TotalCost. The statement

```
TotalCost = Cost * Quantity
```

does that.

This simple statement brings to light the dual personality of =. Previously in this chapter, = is presented as one of the relational operators. In this statement, though, = is used as an assignment operator. The value on the right of the assignment operator is assigned to the variable on the left. VBA is smart enough to know by context when = is an assignment operator and when it's a relational operator.

The expression on the right of the assignment statement makes use of the multiplication operator (*) to multiply the value of the Cost field by the value of the Quantity field. After that multiplication occurs, the result is assigned to the TotalCost variable and is displayed on the form or printed in the report.

The need to increment a variable frequently occurs in VBA code. For example, you might want to increase the value of a variable named intCtr by 1 (one). To do so, use the statement

```
intCtr = intCtr + 1
```

As before, = in this statement is used as an assignment operator. It might seem strange at first to see the same variable on both sides of an assignment statement. One of VBA's precedence rules controls what happens in this type of circumstance: The expression on the right in an assignment statement is evaluated before the assignment occurs. In this case, if intCtr initially has a value of 8, 1 is added to it, resulting in 9, which is temporarily saved. Then the temporarily saved value is assigned to intCtr, with the result that intCtr now has a value of 9.

Another common example of using operators within VBA code is for the manipulation of text. Suppose you have a form based on a query that contains FirstName and LastName fields, and you want to display a person's name in a text box named txtFullName. To do so, use a statement such as

```
txtFullName = [FirstName] & " " & [LastName]
```

that uses the concatenation operator (&) to assemble a string from two other strings and places a space between the two strings. If you want the name on the form to be displayed with the last name first, use the statement

```
txtFullName = [LastName] & ", " & [FirstName]
```

in which a comma and a space separate the last name from the first name.

In both these examples, the names of the fields in the query are enclosed within brackets. It's not strictly necessary to enclose these names within brackets unless the field names contain spaces, but it's good practice to do so. If you omit the brackets when the field names don't contain spaces, VBA automatically inserts the brackets. If you omit the brackets when the field names do contain spaces, VBA gets confused and displays error messages.

Summary

A rich assortment of operators is available for your use while you're creating Access applications. Some of these operators perform arithmetic, logical, and comparison operations; others are useful when you're working with text. A thorough understanding of operators is essential for you to become successful in developing applications.

You can use operators at all levels of working with Access. You can, for example, use comparison operators to establish criteria in queries to extract data that satisfies certain conditions from your tables. You can use arithmetic operators in queries to create new fields based on values in existing fields, and you can use the concatenation operator to combine text from two or more existing fields into a new field. Operators are also a key component of creating filters.

When developing macros, you can use operators to create conditions that determine whether specific actions take place. Operators are also used to specify conditions in certain action arguments.

VBA code relies heavily on operators. Control structures use operators to control the flow of program execution. Operators are also used in many VBA statements to calculate values, to make decisions, and to compare values.

Maintaining a Healthy Application

IN THIS CHAPTER

After you've spent a lot of time and energy in creating an application, it's important to keep it healthy—that means keeping it working efficiently and not losing data.

The size of Access files increases quite rapidly. To keep an application working efficiently, you should regularly compact all your files. You should also keep your data files as small as possible by archiving data you're not using to a separate medium.

Despite your best efforts, files can become corrupted. The process of compacting Access files includes an attempt to repair corrupted files. In some cases, corruption is more than can be handled in this way. For that reason, you should make regular backup copies of all your files so that you can restore corrupted files. All these issues are addressed in this chapter.

Compacting and Repairing a Database

Left to their own devices, Access files tend to grow quite rapidly. When you delete records from Access tables, the disk space previously occupied by those records isn't automatically recovered. Likewise, when you edit records, Access might delete the original records and create completely new ones, without recovering the disk space occupied by the original records. The same type of behavior occurs when you modify objects within the front end. You can use the Compact utility that's part of Access to recover unused disk space.

Here's a specific example to show what can happen. I have a small database I've been using to develop examples for this book over the last few weeks. Before compacting, Windows showed the size of the .mdb file to be 3,056 kilobytes. After compacting, the file occupied 480 kilobytes. I've noticed that Access 97 and Access 2000 files seem to increase in size significantly faster than was the case with Access 95 and earlier versions of Access.

In order to conserve disk space and to optimize the performance of Access, users should make a habit of regularly compacting their Access files. To be more specific:

- People who use an Access application without frequently deleting or modifying data should probably compact their files weekly.

- People who frequently delete or modify data should probably compact their files every day.

- While you're creating an Access application and making frequent changes to objects as you develop forms, queries, and reports, consider compacting your files several times a day.

> **TIP**
>
> The best way to judge how often you need to compact your Access files is to pick a schedule based on the preceding suggestions. Before you start compacting, use Find from the Windows desktop to find your .mdb files and make a note of their size. After compacting, look again at the size of the files. The before and after sizes show the effect of compacting. Adjust your schedule accordingly.

Access offers two ways for you to compact files. You can

- Save the compacted file with the same name as the original file
- Save the compacted file with a name that's different from that of the original file

Being a cautious soul, I recommend the second approach. Although I've never experienced a problem with a compacted file, that doesn't guarantee a problem will never happen. It's possible, for example, that a power failure could occur during compaction. By saving the compacted file with a different name, you can return to the original file if necessary. Both techniques, along with repairing damaged files, are described in the following sections.

Saving a Compacted File with the Same Name as the Original

When you compact a file with the same name as the original, you're placing a lot of faith in the integrity of the procedure because the new file replaces the original. If something should go wrong, such as a power failure occurring while you're compacting, you'll probably lose everything. For that reason, I strongly recommend backing up a file before you attempt to compact it in this way. The section "Backing Up Your Application," later in this chapter, contains information about backing up Access files.

To compact an .mdb file and save it with the same name as the original file

1. Open the database you want to compact.
2. With the Database window displayed, choose Tools, move the pointer onto Database Utilities, and choose Compact and Repair Database. Access immediately compacts the open database and returns you to the Database window.

If you have the entire database—tables, queries, forms, reports, macros, and modules—within a single .mdb file, everything in that file is compacted. However, if the tables in another database file are linked to your database (as recommended in Chapter 3, "Storing Your Data Efficiently"), those tables are not compacted. To compact linked tables, you must open the database that contains those tables and separately compact that database.

Saving a Compacted File with a Name That's Different from the Original

To compact an .mdb file and save it with a name that's different from the original file

1. Close any open database so that the Database window isn't displayed.

2. Choose Tools, move the pointer onto Database Utilities, and choose Compact and Repair Database. Access displays a window such as the one shown in Figure 16.1.

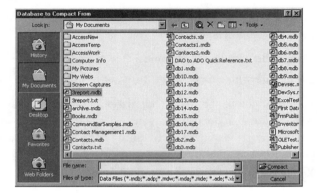

FIGURE 16.1

This window displays the names of data files in your default folder.

3. If necessary, navigate to the folder that contains the .mdb file you want to compact. Select that file and then choose Compact. Access displays the window shown in Figure 16.2.

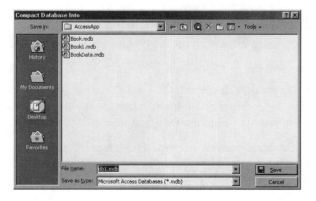

FIGURE 16.2

Use this window to provide a name for the compacted file.

4. Enter a name for the compacted file in the File Name box, and then choose Save. Access compacts the file and saves it with the new name.

Repairing an Access File

Versions of Access prior to Access 2000 contained separate Compact and Repair utilities, whereas Access 2000 has a combined Compact and Repair utility. This utility compacts and repairs Access databases, but only compacts Access projects. According to Microsoft, in most cases Access detects that a database is damaged when you try to open it, and gives you the option of compacting it at that time. I'm one of those fortunate people who haven't experienced a damaged Access database, so I can't comment on that procedure.

In any case, if a database does become damaged, there's no guarantee that the Compact and Repair utility will be able to recover the database. For this reason, you should be meticulous about making regular backups of all your database files. If a database is damaged but can be opened, you can attempt a repair by creating a new, empty database, and then copying elements from the damaged database into the new one.

You can find suggestions about repairing a damaged database in the Microsoft Knowledge Base article Q209137 "How to Repair a Damaged Database." Go to the Web site `http://search.support.microsoft.com/kb/c.asp` to find this and other Microsoft Knowledge Base articles.

Cleaning Up Your Application

An Access application consists of the front end (the user interface) and data, both of which can, if you're not careful, contain unnecessary and unused elements. For example:

- While you're creating an application, you might sometimes create temporary forms, queries, reports, macros, and modules that aren't used in the finished application.
- Standard modules and class modules might contain VBA procedures that aren't used in the finished application.
- Your tables might contain obsolete or redundant records.

Any of these wastefully consumes disk space and might contribute to degraded performance of your application.

As an application developer, it's your responsibility to eliminate all unnecessary and unused elements. Access can't do that for you automatically. You have to meticulously weed out what's not required. The following sections describe procedures for cleaning up your Access application.

> **CAUTION**
>
> Make sure that you create a backup copy of your entire application before deleting anything. That's to ensure you can restore anything you delete by mistake.

Cleaning Up the User Interface

With the Database window displayed, look carefully through the lists of queries, forms, reports, macros, and modules. You might find it helpful to click the Details button in the Database window's toolbar to see the dates on which each listed item was last modified. Those items that have been recently modified are probably used in your application, whereas items that haven't been modified for a long time might well be no longer used.

Class modules behind forms and reports quite often contain unused event procedures. This can happen, for example, when you place a control on a form or report and create event procedures for that control. Subsequently, you might decide you don't need that control, so you delete it. Deleting a control from a form or report doesn't delete the event procedures for it. Consequently, you're left with unused event procedures in class modules. You should look for such procedures and delete those you're sure aren't being used.

Standard modules are quite likely to contain unused procedures. To ascertain whether a procedure is used, select that procedure's name in the VBE window, and then choose Edit, Find. The Find dialog box opens with the procedure name you selected in the Find What box. Under Search, select Current Project, and then choose Find Next. If that procedure is referred to anywhere else in your project, including the class modules behind forms and reports, the reference will be located. If you don't find a reference to the procedure in this way, the procedure is a candidate for being deleted.

It's important to realize that the SQL code that defines queries can contain references to function procedures. Using Find in the manner described in the preceding paragraph doesn't find procedures referred to in that SQL code. Before you delete a function procedure in a standard module, make sure that procedure isn't used in a query.

Cleaning Up Your Data

Depending on the nature of your application, your tables might contain data that's no longer needed. For example, the Book database used as an example in this book might contain data about books you have discarded or given away. There's probably no need to keep records for those books, so you can delete them. On the other hand, if your database contains business information, such as the Northwind database does, you probably want to keep all your records except, perhaps, those entered in error.

CAUTION

When you manually delete records from a table, Access gives you one chance to confirm that you want to delete those records. If you go ahead, Access permanently deletes records. Be quite sure you really do want to delete records before you do so.

In most cases, instead of permanently deleting records, you should archive the records you don't need in your current tables. After you've archived the records, you can safely delete them from your current tables. The section "Archiving Your Data" later in this chapter explains how to archive records.

Backing Up Your Application

Backing up an application is quite different from archiving, the subject of the next section. You back up your application so that you can recover data and the front end if disaster strikes. Archiving, on the other hand, copies data that's not currently required in order for that data to be available should it be needed in the future.

An Access-based application can be organized in several ways, some of which are

- Having the entire application, including its data, in a single .mdb file
- Having the application's data in one or more .mdb files with the front end in a separate .mdb file
- Having the application's data on a server with the front end in an .mdb file on the local computer

Whichever way your application is organized, you should regularly make backup copies of all the files. In a large organization, backing up is a task for the system administrator, so that's not covered in this chapter. In a smaller organization, backing up is often the responsibility of individual users.

The easiest way to back up your .mdb files is to use Windows Explorer, the Backup utility supplied with Windows, or another backup utility. Although you can use these methods to copy files onto your local hard disk, it's not a good idea to do so. That's because one reason you might need the backup files is that something goes wrong with that disk. Another possibility, if your computer is on a network, is to back up the files to a network disk, although I don't recommend that for security reasons. My recommendation is that you back up your files onto a removable disk, magnetic tape, or a writable CD-ROM disc so that you can store your backup data in a safe place. You can find detailed information about these media in *Upgrading and Repairing PCs*, published by Que, Chapters 12, "Magnetic Storage," and 13, "Optical Storage."

Whichever backup medium you use, you should adopt a rotation strategy. Suppose you decide to back up your data on a daily basis using magnetic tape. You should have five tapes, each of sufficient capacity for all your data. Label these tapes Monday, Tuesday, Wednesday, Thursday, and Friday. Each day, back up onto the appropriate tape. By doing that, you always have several backup tapes from which you can recover data should something go wrong with one of the tapes or during the process of backing up.

While you're developing an application, it's important to back up the .mdb file that contains your queries, forms, reports, macros, and modules. Do so regularly, perhaps several times a day, so that there's no danger of losing your work.

Before you back up any .mdb file, make sure that file isn't being accessed by anyone. In the case of a single-user application, close down Access before you start the back up. In a multi-user situation, make sure all users are logged off from the application. If you do attempt a back up of a file that's in use, the backup file is likely to become corrupted and not completely repairable.

TIP

You can schedule back up to occur during the night providing no one uses the application at night. The Microsoft Knowledge Base article Q125772, "Overnight Batch Considerations and Sample Code," suggests how this can be done.

Unfortunately, backing up data to a disk or tape is no guarantee the data can be restored from that medium. A problem with the backup device or medium can make it seem that a backup has been created when, in fact, it hasn't. You'll be unhappy, to put it mildly, if you have a problem with the files you're using, attempt to restore those files from a backup, and find the backup is unreadable. To prevent this problem, you should regularly test backups to make sure they're good. The only way to do that is to attempt to restore data from a backup medium.

Don't forget to take care of the security of your backup copies. You should store those in a location separate from your computer.

Archiving Your Data

Archiving data is a three-step process for each table. First you use a Make-table query to copy specified records from a current table into an archive table. Then use a Delete query to delete the same records from the current table. Finally, export the archive table to a separate database.

Maintaining a Healthy Application

CHAPTER 16

409

16

MAINTAINING A
HEALTHY
APPLICATION

The following steps illustrate how you can archive records from the Orders table in the Northwind database.

1. With the Northwind Database window open, create a new query based on the Orders table.

2. Drag each of the fields in the Orders table into the QBE grid.

3. Choose Query, Make-Table Query to convert the Select query into a Make-table query.

4. Add a criterion into the query. For example, in the OrderDate column of the QBE grid, enter a criterion of <=#12/31/1996# to select records for orders dated 12/31/1996 or earlier.

NOTE

See the section "Setting Criteria" in Chapter 15, "Calculating Values and Making Decisions," for information about using date expressions in query criteria.

5. Choose View, Datasheet View to display the records selected by the criterion so that you can verify the correct records are selected.

6. Return to the Design view of the query. Assuming the correct records were displayed in the preceding step, choose Query, Run. A dialog box asks you to enter a name for the new table.

7. Enter a name for the archive table and choose OK. The query creates the new table and copies the selected records into it.

That completes the first part of the task, creating the archive table. It remains now to delete the records from the original table. Proceed as follows:

1. With the Make-table query still displayed, choose Query, Delete Query to convert the query to a Delete query.

2. Choose Query, Run. Access displays a message stating that you are about to delete rows from the table.

3. Choose Yes if you want to go ahead and delete the records, or choose No if you don't want to delete the records.

Now the original table contains all the records except those archived.

Although what you've done so far has separated the original table into two tables, one containing current records and the other containing old records, both tables are in the same .mdb file. To make a separate archive, you have to export the archive table. The following steps export the file to another .mdb file. You can, though, export the table to a file in any of the formats Access supports.

1. Create a new Access database.

2. Open the database for which you created an archive table, such as the Northwind database, and in the Database window, select the archive table.

3. Choose File, Export to display the Export Table dialog box. If necessary, navigate to the folder that contains the .mdb file to which you want export the archive table.

4. Select the .mdb file to which you want to export. Access displays the Export dialog box in which you can confirm the name of the file to which you want to export. The dialog box has Definition and Data already selected in the Export Tables section.

5. Choose OK to export the table.

Now you have your archive table in a separate database that you can copy to a removable storage medium.

> **Tip**
>
> You can automate the process of backing up and archiving a database. Refer to the Microsoft Knowledge Base article Q125772, "Overnight Batch Considerations and Sample Code," for some suggestions.

The same considerations apply to archives as to backup copies, as explained in the preceding section. Test your archives regularly and store them in a secure location.

Summary

To make your Access-based application reliable and efficient, you should regularly compact its files. Not only does this make efficient use of disk space, it also improves the performance of the application.

Furthermore, you should clean up your application by removing temporary items, unused VBA procedures, and obsolete or redundant records instead of allowing data to accumulate on your disk. You should also archive data that isn't in regular use. That means copying data to another medium and deleting that data from your working files.

Most important, to prepare for the inevitable day when data becomes corrupted, it's important to make regular backup copies of all your files. You should store the media used for archive and backup copies in a secure location that's separate from your working area.

Extending Access to the Web

IN THIS CHAPTER

In common with other Office 2000 applications, Access is integrated with the World Wide Web and the technologies associated with it. This chapter describes some of the ways your Access applications can take advantage of Web technologies.

Tables contain the raw data that's the basis of all Access applications. One of the data types available for fields in Access tables is Hyperlink. You can use this type of field to store URLs that can access files, folders, and pages to which you have access. These URLs can connect to locations on your local computer, your LAN or intranet, or to anywhere on the Internet.

Within Access, you can save data stored in tables or data that queries derive from tables as HTML files that you can distribute to people who don't have Access. People who receive those files can view your Access data in a browser. You can also use technologies such as Data Access Pages that provide a means for people who don't use Access to interact with your Access data.

Using Hyperlink Fields

One of the simplest ways to extend Access into the Web is to make use of Hyperlink fields. Hyperlink fields give you the ability to provide a connection between your Access-based application and many other information sources, including

- Files on your own computer
- Files to which you have access on your local area network
- Information available on the Internet or your intranet

Access 97 and Access 2000 make Hyperlink available as a data type in tables. In reality, the Hyperlink data type isn't a distinct data type; it's a special use of the Memo data type. When you create a field of Hyperlink data type, you're really creating a field of Memo data type with instructions to interpret values in that field as a hyperlink.

Seeing Hyperlinks at Work

The Northwind database supplied with Access contains examples of using a Hyperlink field in the Suppliers table and the Suppliers form. Open the Suppliers table in Design view to see a list of the fields it contains. The last field in the list, named HomePage, is of Hyperlink data type. This field is used to access suppliers' home pages on the Web.

If you switch to the Datasheet view of the table and scroll to the right, you'll see that a few of the suppliers listed in the table have entries in the Home Page field. Notice that some of the entries contain the name of an .htm file and others contain descriptive text. This is explained in the subsequent section, "Specifying Hyperlinks." Although you can click any entry in the Home Page field to open the referenced page in your browser, you probably want to open a supplier's home page from a form.

A control on a form can be bound to a Hyperlink field in a table or query. The Suppliers form in the Northwind database, shown in Figure 17.1, provides an example of this.

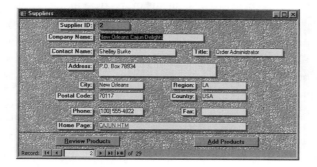

FIGURE 17.1

The Suppliers form contains a Home Page control near the bottom.

When you first display the Suppliers form, the Home Page control is empty because there isn't a Home Page entry for the first supplier in the Suppliers table. If you move to the second supplier, as shown in Figure 17.1, a filename is displayed. Click that filename to open and display the corresponding page.

> **NOTE**
>
> Microsoft provides dummy home pages, some of which are installed as .htm files in your Program File\Microsoft Office\Office\Samples folder. Others are on the Microsoft site at http://www.Microsoft.com/accessdev/sampleapps/.

Specifying Hyperlinks

A complete hyperlink has three components, with one component separated from the next with a pound sign (#). The second component is required; the other two are optional. The three components are

- Display Text—A description of the hyperlinked page or file
- Address—The address of the page or file to be displayed
- Subaddress—A location within the address, such as a bookmark within a Word or HTML document, a specific cell or a named range in an Excel worksheet, or a slide number in a PowerPoint presentation

Here are some examples of hyperlinks:

- `Macmillan Home Page#http://www.mcp.com` creates a hyperlink to the Macmillan home page at `http://www.mcp.com`. The contents of the field in a table and control on a form are shown as `Macmillan Home Page`.

- `http://www.mcp.com` also creates a hyperlink to the Macmillan home page. In this case, the contents of the field in a table and control on a form are shown as `http://www.mcp.com`.

- C:\Program Files\Microsoft Office\Office\Samples\Cajun.htm opens the Cajun.htm file.

- C:\Program Files\Microsoft Office\Office\Samples\Samples.xls opens the Samples.xls file.

- States#C:\My Documents\States.xls#StateInfo creates a hyperlink named States to the States.xls file and displays the range named StateInfo.

Use these examples as models for entering hyperlinks.

If you omit the Display Text component of a hyperlink, the Table and Form views show the Hyperlink address. On the other hand, if you provide a Display Text component, the Table and Form views show that text.

Editing a Hyperlink

After you've created a hyperlink, only the display text (if it exists) or the Address component is displayed in a table, query, or form. To make changes to the hyperlink, right-click it in the table, query, or form, to display a context menu. In the context menu, move the pointer onto Hyperlink to display another menu. In that menu, choose Edit Hyperlink to display a dialog box such as the one shown in Figure 17.2.

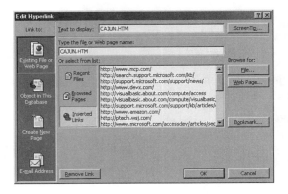

FIGURE 17.2

You can use this dialog box to change the hyperlink's displayed text and the address to which the hyperlink refers.

There's more you can do in the Edit Hyperlink dialog box, but that's beyond what this chapter can cover.

Exporting to a Web Page

You can make the contents of an Access table or a recordset created by a query available to people who don't have Access by exporting to a Web page. Access creates a file in HTML format that can be displayed by a browser such as Internet Explorer.

After you've created a Web page, you can distribute it to other people by making it available on your LAN, or on an Internet or intranet server. You can also send it to other people as an attachment to an email message.

Exporting an Access Table

The following steps illustrate the process of creating an HTML file that contains the contents of an Access table. These steps export the entire contents of the selected table.

1. In the Access Database window, select a table such as the Suppliers table in the Northwind database. Alternatively, open the table in Datasheet view.
2. Choose File, Export to display the Export Table dialog box shown in Figure 17.3.

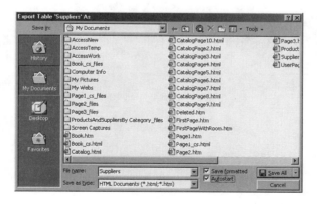

FIGURE 17.3
The Export Table dialog box is shown here after you've followed the next three steps.

3. Open the Save As Type drop-down list at the bottom of the dialog box and select HTML Documents. When you do so, the Save Formatted check box becomes available.
4. Check Save Formatted. When you do so, the Autostart check box becomes available.

5. Check Autostart. This causes your default browser to open automatically when the HTML file is created.

6. If you want to change the default name for the HTML file, change the name in the File Name box.

7. Choose Save All to start the export process. Access displays the HTML Options dialog box in which you can specify an HTML template. See the subsequent section "Creating an HTML File Based on a Template" for information about using templates.

> **NOTE**
>
> The button is labeled Save All to remind you that all records in the Access table are saved, even if you've selected specific records.

8. Choose OK in the HTML Output Options dialog box to signify that no template is to be used. The table is exported and the browser opens showing the exported file, as shown in Figure 17.4.

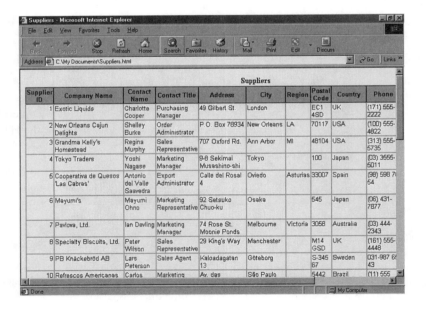

FIGURE 17.4

This is the table as displayed by Internet Explorer.

You can, if you like, display the HTML code that Access generates automatically. With the table displayed in Internet Explorer, choose View, Source to display the code in Notepad. Although there's quite a lot of code, it's quite simple and you'll recognize its structure if you have some previous experience with HTML.

If, in step 4, you didn't check Save Formatted, the browser displays the data in the table but not as well formatted. An advantage of creating an HTML file in this way is that the file contains much less formatting code and is, consequently, much smaller. After saving an unformatted table, you can insert HTML code to modify the table's appearance.

Selecting What's to Be Exported

The procedure explained in the preceding section creates an HTML file containing the entire contents of a table. Many times, though, you want to create an HTML file that contains only some of what's in a table—only some of the fields and only some of the records. You can use a query to do that.

Create a query that contains only the fields you want to export and has criteria to select specific records. After creating a query, open that query in Datasheet view, and then follow the steps in the preceding section.

You can also use a query to create an HTML file containing data from related tables.

Creating an HTML File Based on a Template

As you saw previously in the section "Exporting an Access Table," after you check the Save Formatted check box and then choose Save All in the Export Table dialog box, Access displays the HTML Output Options dialog box. If you choose OK in that dialog box, Access creates an HTML file formatted much like a table in Datasheet view. You can enter the complete path name of an HTML template in the HTML Template box if you want to format the HTML file according to an existing template.

Microsoft supplies one sample template with Access 2000. You should be able to find that template in your C:\Program Files\Microsoft Office\Office\Samples folder; its name is Nwindtem.htm. Although this is a very simple template, you can use it to get an idea of how templates work.

You can, of course, create your own templates, but it's beyond the scope of this book to describe the process. One way to create templates by using FrontPage 2000 is described in Chapter 10, "Creating Pages with FrontPage Templates," in the book *Special Edition Using Microsoft FrontPage 2000*, published by Que. Refer to the section "Creating Custom Templates."

Exporting Reports to HTML Files

You can also export an Access report to an HTML file. If the report consists of two or more pages, a separate HTML file is created for each page. Each HTML file contains a set of navigation buttons at the bottom that you can use to move from one page to another.

The procedure for exporting a report is almost identical to that for exporting a table. Follow the steps in the section "Exporting an Access Table" earlier in this chapter. Some differences are

- The Save Formatted check box in the Export Report dialog box isn't available.
- The button labeled Save All in the Export Table dialog box is labeled Save in the Export Report dialog box.

Each HTML file generated from an Access report is automatically formatted to somewhat reproduce the appearance of the report when displayed in Preview view by Access. Because Access reports are normally formatted ready for printing, it's not usually a good idea to export those reports to HTML files to be displayed by your browser. You should normally create reports specially formatted for display by a browser and export those reports.

Importing Data from HTML Files

In addition to exporting from Access to HTML files, you can also import data from HTML files to Access tables. I'll not explain the first process in detail because it doesn't seem to have much practical use.

In outline, you start by choosing File, moving the pointer onto Get External Data, and choosing Import to open the Import dialog box. In that dialog box, select HTML documents in the Files of Type drop-down list and navigate to the folder that contains the HTML file from which you want to import data. Select the HTML file and choose Import. This opens the Import HTML Wizard. Follow through the wizard to complete importing the data.

Creating Active Web Pages

The previous sections of this chapter describe how you can create HTML files that people can use under a browser to display static Web pages. People can read this data but can't interact with it. You can also create active Web pages with which people can interact.

Microsoft offers three ways for you to create active Web pages:

- Active Server Pages—This is Microsoft's recommended technology for creating active Web pages in a client/server environment. Changes that users make to a page are sent to the server for processing. The server sends an updated version back to the user. For introductory information about Active Server Pages, see *Sams Teach Yourself Active Server Pages in 21 Days*. For more complete information, see *Active Server Pages 2.0 Unleashed*. Both books are published by Sams.

- Data Access Pages—This technology is the subject of the remaining pages of this chapter.

- Internet Database Connector—This was Microsoft's initial approach to creating active Web pages and is no longer widely used. The subject isn't covered in this book.

Introducing Data Access Pages

New in Access 2000, you can provide access to your Access-based applications by way of LAN or an intranet by using Data Access Pages. Data Access Pages are Dynamic Hypertext Markup Language (DHTML) documents that contain HTML code, HTML controls, and ActiveX controls. These files have .htm as their filename extension.

NOTE

By exporting data to a Web page, as described in the section "Exporting to a Web Page" previously in this chapter, you create a static image that can't be changed. In contrast, a Data Access Page is dynamic and can be used to edit existing data to create new data, just as you can use an Access form.

You can create Data Access Pages to be used as front ends for Access or SQL Server databases, although only Access databases are considered in this chapter. People can view Data Access Pages in Internet Explorer using a LAN or an intranet to connect to the database. A Data Access Page, often referred to simply as a Page or a DAP, is a file that's separate from but linked to Access or SQL Server data. In many ways, a Page is quite similar to an Access form.

NOTE

You can use Web browsers other than Internet Explorer to display Data Access Pages, but with limited functionality. Internet Explorer 5 or later is required to have full access to Data Access Pages.

One advantage of creating Pages is that you can make your Access or SQL Server data available to people who don't have Access. Those people must have Internet Explorer 5 installed on their computers and each must have a license for Office 2000. You can use a Page to

- Display data
- Analyze data
- Edit data
- Delete data
- Enter new data

NOTE

Although Pages can certainly be used to edit and delete existing data, as well as to add new data to databases, Pages are not well-suited for use by people who spend a large amount of time doing so. Those people should use Access forms, rather than Pages.

The use of Data Access Pages is limited to within an intranet. This is because many Data Access Pages employ Office Web components that are available only if Office 2000 is installed. Within an intranet in which all users have Outlook 2000 installed, Data Access Pages provide a convenient way for people who don't use Access to interact with information in Access databases.

Getting Acquainted with Data Access Pages

An easy way to begin to understand Pages is to see some in action, something you can easily do if you have the Northwind database that comes with Access installed on your computer. You must also have Internet Explorer 5.0 or later installed.

The Northwind application has five Page files:

- Analyze Sales.htm
- Review Orders.htm
- Review Products.htm
- Sales.htm
- View Products.htm

All these files are probably in your C:\Program Files\Microsoft Office\Office\Samples folder.

In the next two sections, you'll take a quick look at the Review Products Page, first in Internet Explorer and then in Access.

Viewing a Data Access Page in Internet Explorer

To view one of the Northwind files listed in the previous section, display the filenames in Windows Explorer and double-click one of them. That should open the file under Windows Explorer, as shown in Figure 17.5.

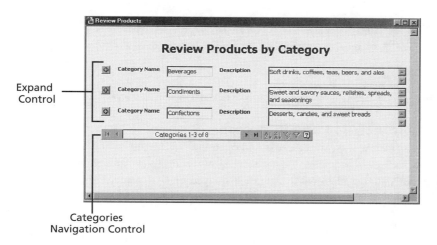

Expand Control

Categories Navigation Control

FIGURE 17.5

This is what you see when you open the Review Products Page under Internet Explorer.

This is an example of a read-only Page. It initially shows the names of three of the eight product categories in the Northwind database. You can use the buttons in the Categories Navigation control to display the remaining product categories.

Click the Expand button at the left of a category name to display the first three products in that category, as shown in Figure 17.6.

You can use the buttons in the Products Navigation control to display information about other products in the selected category.

What you're seeing here is an .htm file that's linked to an Access Page. To verify that statement, choose View, Source to display the file's source code displayed in Notepad. Don't be concerned about the complexity of this code. The code is generated automatically by Access—you don't have to work with this code yourself.

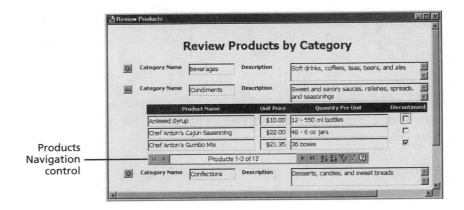

Products
Navigation
control

FIGURE 17.6

With the Condiments category expanded, the information about the first three products in that category is displayed.

Viewing a Data Access Page in Access

To see the same Page in Access, start Access and open the Northwind database. In the Database window's Objects bar, select Pages, select Review Products, and choose Open. This displays a page that's almost identical to the one displayed under Internet Explorer, as previously shown in Figure 17.5.

With the Page displayed under Access, you can switch to the Design view to investigate and modify the design of the page, something you can't do when displaying the Page under Internet Explorer.

Creating a Data Access Page

There are several ways to create a Page. Three of them are by

- Using AutoPage
- Using the Page Wizard
- Creating the Page sfrom scratch

Each of these methods is described in the next few sections.

Using AutoPage to Create a Data Access Page

AutoPage makes it easy to create a Page. In the Database window's Objects bar, select Pages, and then choose New to display the dialog box shown in Figure 17.7.

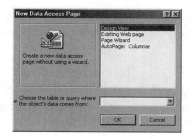

FIGURE 17.7

The New Data Access Page dialog box offers four ways to create a new Page.

Select AutoPage: Columnar, and then open the drop-down list of tables and queries, select the table or query on which you want to base the new Page, and choose OK. After a few seconds delay, Access displays the Page, such as the one shown in Figure 17.8.

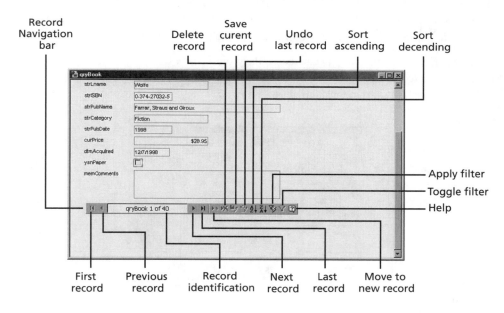

FIGURE 17.8

This Page is based on the qryBook query in the sample application.

This automatically created Page looks quite similar to an Access form. One difference to notice is that labels for text boxes on the Page contain the original field names from the underlying tables, not any alias names you might have provided. Another difference is the inclusion of the Record Navigation toolbar at the bottom of the page.

AutoPage creates a page using your current default theme which, if you haven't changed it, is the Straight Edge theme. See "Setting Themes" later in this chapter for information about themes.

After you've created a Page in this way, you can save it by choosing File, Save. If this is the first Page you've created, Access proposes to save the page in your default folder with the name Page1.htm. You can, of course, change the filename, but it always has .htm as its file-name extension.

Subsequently, when you select Pages in the Database window's Objects bar, you'll see the name of the Page you saved listed in the right pane. That name is actually a shortcut to the .htm file. If you point onto the Page name and pause, a ScreenTip reveals the path to the .htm file.

To reopen the Page, select its name in the Database window, and choose Open.

Using the Page Wizard to Create a Data Access Page

As an alternative to using AutoPage, you can use the Page Wizard to create a Page. The wizard gives you much more control than AutoPage over the resulting Page.

Select Page Wizard in the New Data Access Page dialog box (shown previously in Figure 17.7), select a table or query on which to base the new page, and choose OK. Access displays the first wizard window, shown in Figure 17.9.

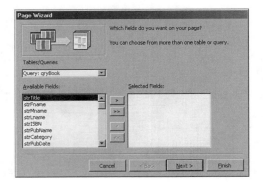

FIGURE 17.9

Use this wizard window to select the fields you want to appear on the Page.

Select the fields you want to appear on the page in the left list and click the > button to move those fields into the right list. Choose Next > to display the second wizard window. This and subsequent wizard windows provide the opportunity to

- Group records in the Page based on one or more fields
- Define a sort order based on up to four fields
- Provide a title for the page
- Apply a theme to a page

Subsequent sections in this chapter provide detailed information about all these points.

Creating a Data Access Page from Scratch

A third way to create a Page is to do so from scratch. This is more work than using AutoPage or the Page Wizard, but it gives you complete control over the Page design.

To create a Page from scratch, follow these steps:

1. Open a database, such as the Northwind database, and display the Database window.
2. Select Pages in the Objects bar and choose New to display the New Data Access Page dialog box.
3. Select Design View and then, in the drop-down list, select the table or query on which you want to base the Page, and choose OK. After several seconds, Access displays a blank Page in Design view with a Field List superimposed, as shown in Figure 17.10.

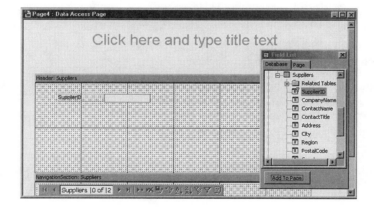

FIGURE 17.10

This is the Design view of a Page on which you can construct a Page, shown here with one field placed on it.

4. Drag fields from the Field List onto the Page. Alternatively, select one field at a time in the Field List and click Add to Page. The Record Navigation toolbar at the bottom appears automatically as soon as the Page contains one field.

Using this method, you can create a Page that exactly suits your requirements.

In addition to adding fields onto a Page from the Field List, you can place other controls onto a Page.

Choose View, Toolbox to display the toolbox. You can select an icon in the toolbox and then place the corresponding tool on the page. Refer to "Working with Controls" later in this chapter for more information about the tools available in the toolbox.

Displaying Information in a Page

The left part of the Record Navigation toolbar at the bottom of the page shown in Figure 17.10 contains buttons you can click to display one record after another.

To create a title for the Page, click and type, as the onscreen instruction suggests.

The Design view opens with a single section named Section: Unbound. The Field List contains the names of the fields in the table or query on which you're basing the Page.

In the Field List, select the first field you want to display on the Page, and then choose Add To Page. Access

- Places the selected field with its label on the Page in the section previously called Section: Unbound

- Changes the name of the section to Header:, followed by the name of the table or query on which you're basing the Page

- Adds a section named NavigationSection below the Header section and places a Navigation Toolbar control in that section

Now, select other fields in the Field List and choose Add To Page to add those fields to the Page. Access automatically aligns those fields and their labels on the Page.

Modifying the Design of a Page

To modify the design of a Page that's already displayed, choose View, Design View. If the Page isn't already displayed, select the Page in the Database window and choose Design. In either case, the Page is displayed in Design view, as shown in Figure 17.11.

This Page has two sections, with a section selector at the top of each. Other Pages can have more than two sections.

Examining and Setting Properties

To examine and set the properties of a Page, its sections, and the controls in those sections, choose View, Properties to display a Property sheet, as shown in Figure 17.12.

Title Bar

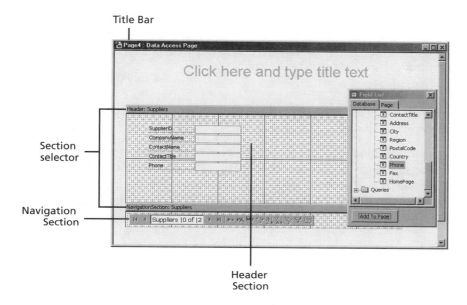
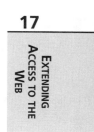

Section selector

Navigation Section

Header Section

FIGURE 17.11

A Page in Design view is quite similar to a form in Design view.

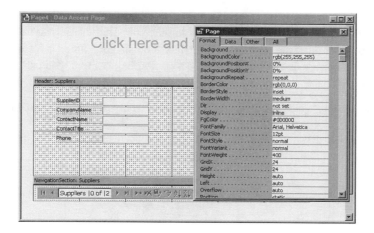

FIGURE 17.12

The Property sheet for a Page is similar to the Property sheet for a form, but many of the individual properties are different.

To access properties

- Of a Page, click the Page's title bar
- Of a section, click the section's section selector
- Of a control, select the control

Working with properties for a Page is similar to working with properties for a form, so there's no need to go into details about that.

Although you're probably familiar with many of the properties for forms and controls on those forms, you won't recognize many of the properties for Pages. To get information about any property, select that property and press F1. Access displays a Help topic that contains an alphabetical list of properties. Select the property you want to know about to see detailed information about that property.

Working with Controls

You can work with controls interactively in much the same way that you work with controls on a form, using such techniques as

- Dragging to move a control or change its size
- Using the Alignment and Sizing tools available in the Format menu to position and adjust controls

One significant difference between working with controls on a Page and on a form is that you can select only one control at a time on a Page. Another important difference is that you can't convert a control from one type to another type on a Page as you can on a form. For example, on a form, you can convert a text box control to a combo box control; you can't do that on a Page.

To add controls onto a Page, choose View, Toolbox to display the toolbox shown in Figure 17.13.

FIGURE 17.13

Several of the icons in the Page toolbox are different from those in the form toolbox (encountered in Chapter 5, "Making Your Forms Smarter."

Table 17.1 compares toolbox icons in a form with those available on a Page. Notice that some of the icons in the form toolbox are unavailable in the Page toolbox, and that the Page toolbox has icons that aren't in the form toolbox. Refer to Figure 5.5 in Chapter 5 for an illustration of the form toolbox.

TABLE 17.1   Toolbox Contents for Forms and Pages

Form	Page	Purpose
Label	Label	Displays descriptive text
	Bound HTML	Displays text stored as HTML code in a field
Text Box	Text Box	Displays data from a record source
	Scrolling Text	Displays text that moves or scrolls
Option Group	Option Group	Contains option buttons (or other controls), of which only one can be selected at a time
Toggle Button		Displays one of two values
Option Button	Option Button	Displays one of two values
Check Box	Check Box	Displays one of two values
Combo Box		Combines the functionalities of a text box and a list box
	Dropdown List	Can be opened to display a list of values
List Box	List Box	Displays a list of values
Command Button	Command Button	Can be clicked to initiate an action
	Expand	Expands or collapses grouped records
	Record Navigation	Provides facilities for navigating among records
	Office PivotTable	Displays a PivotTable
	Office Chart	Displays a chart
	Office Spreadsheet	Displays a spreadsheet
	Bound Hyperlink	Binds to a field containing an Internet address
	Hyperlink	Contains a link to a file or Web page
	Hotspot Image	Contains an image that, when clicked, opens another Web page
	Movie	Displays audio and video content

continues

TABLE 17.1 Continued

Form	Page	Purpose
Image	Image	Provides a container for a graphic image that's not bound to a field
Unbound Object Frame		Provides a container for a graphic image that's not bound to a field
Bound Object Frame		Provides a container for a graphic image that is bound to a field
Page Break		Defines a page break on a form
Tab Control		Provides a choice among several pages
Subform/ Subreport		Displays a subform or subreport
Line	Line	Displays a straight line
Rectangle	Rectangle	Displays a rectangle
More Controls	More Controls	Adds more controls to the toolbox

You place controls on a Page in the same way you place controls on a form.

Setting Themes

A theme is a unified design for all the elements on a Page. Among other things, themes define fonts and colors. By applying a theme to a Page, you set

- Body and heading styles
- Background color and design
- Fonts
- Colors for table borders, lines, bullets, and controls

NOTE

Themes are installed with Office 2000. If you chose not to install themes, you won't have themes available for your Pages.

Unless you have chosen differently, your default theme is the one named Straight Edge. Pages you create with AutoPage have this theme.

If you use the Page Wizard to create a page, you have the opportunity to apply any available theme to your Page. If you create a Page from scratch, no theme is initially applied to the Page.

To apply a theme to a Page, open that Page in Design view and choose Format, Theme to display the dialog box shown in Figure 17.14.

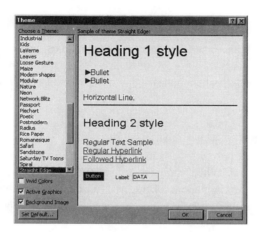

FIGURE 17.14

The list on the left contains the names of themes available on your computer.

The right pane of the Theme dialog box displays a preview of the selected theme. Select any theme in the list to preview it. If you're satisfied with the theme, choose OK to apply that theme to your Page.

With the Theme dialog box open, you can check three check boxes:

- Vivid Colors—To have brighter colors for table borders and background colors.
- Active Graphics—To display animated graphics when the Page is displayed in Internet Explorer (if the theme contains animation). Graphics are not animated when the Page is displayed by Access.
- Background Image—To use the background image included in the theme. Clear this check box if you want to provide a solid background color.

You can select any available theme to be your default theme. To do so, select the theme and then choose Set Default.

> **TIP**
>
> You're not limited to using themes supplied with Office 2000. For example, if you have FrontPage 2000 installed, you can use the themes it provides.

Automating a Data Access Page

Other chapters in this book have made frequent references to using Visual Basic for Applications (VBA) as a means of automating Access objects. You can't use VBA to automate Pages and the objects on those pages. Instead, you have to use Visual Basic Scripting Edition (VBScript).

VBA and VBScript are both dialects (derivatives) of Visual Basic, and each focuses on specific objectives. The VBA dialect provides maximum functionality within a secure environment. In contrast, the VBScript dialect provides adequate functionality within the exposed environment of the Internet and an intranet. When you have to use VBScript, as when automating Pages, you might be tempted to complain about VBScript's limitations. However, you should understand that most of those limitations help to ensure the security and stability of your application.

You can find detailed information about VBScript at the Web site http://msdn.microsoft.com/scripting/.

The book *Sams Teach Yourself VBScript in 21 Days*, published by Sams, provides a good, although not entirely up-to-date, introduction to VBScript. Another good book to refer to is *VBScript Programmer's Reference*, published by Wrox. Be aware, though, that the information published in these sources about VBScript focuses on using the language in the environment of Web pages. Some of the information in those books doesn't directly apply to Data Access Pages. Appendix C of *Active Server Pages 2.0 Unleashed*, published by Sams, is an excellent reference for VBScript.

Viewing a Data Access Page

You can view a Page using Access or using Internet Explorer.

To view a Page in Access, select that Page in the Database window and choose Open. What you see is an emulation of how the Page appears when viewed using Internet Explorer.

To view a Page using Internet Explorer 5.0 or later, first save the page as an .htm file. Then, within Access, choose File, Web Page Preview. That opens Internet Explorer, and displays the Page.

To convince yourself that Access isn't required to display the Page, close Access, and then use Windows Explorer to locate the .htm file. Double-click that file to open Internet Explorer and display the Page.

Having reached this stage, you should feel confident about creating Data Access Pages. For additional information about Data Access Pages, open Help and, in the Index box, enter **data_access_page** and choose Search. Access responds by listing 213 Help topics relating to Data Access Pages. You can open these topics to get detailed information.

You can find additional information about Data Access Pages in Microsoft's Technet site. One particularly informative article is available at `http://www.microsoft.com/TechNet/office/trdhtml.asp`.

Summary

Like other Office applications, Access provides integration with Internet technologies. You can include a Hyperlink field in any table and use that field to store a URL that gives direct access to a file, folder, or site.

You can save data stored in an Access table, or data derived from Access tables by a query, as an HTML file. You can make that file available to other people who don't necessarily have Access installed on their computers to let them see the data by using a browser.

Within an intranet environment, you can create Data Access Pages that people who don't have Access installed can use to interact with Access data.

Making Your Application Secure

IN THIS CHAPTER

The subject of security is important and complex, and it deals with many issues. Basically, you need to ensure that a database system remains intact and usable, and that only specific people can access the database, read the data it contains, make changes to existing data, and add and delete data.

Much more is involved in all this than can be covered in a single chapter. Chapter 16 of this book, "Maintaining a Healthy Application," covers some of the issues involved in ensuring a database system remains intact and usable. This chapter deals with what you can do within Access to control who can access the database and what each of those people can do. For more detailed information about security issues as they apply to Access, you can't do better than refer to Chapter 33, "Database Security Made Easy," and Chapter 34, "Advanced Security Techniques," in *Mastering Microsoft Access 2000 Development*, published by Sams Publishing.

If you don't take advantage of the security capabilities built into Access, people who have access to your files can do whatever they want with them. Some of the ways you can protect your Access files are by requiring a password for each file, defining which users have access to each file, and defining what each user has permission to do with each file. These aspects of Access security are covered in this chapter.

Protecting a Database File with a Password

An easy way to protect a database is to require entry of a password before the database can be opened. A password can consist of up to 14 characters and is case-sensitive. Any characters except the Null character (ASCII 0) can be used.

Follow these steps to provide a password.

1. If the database is open, close it but leave Access open.
2. Choose File, Open to display the Open dialog box.
3. Navigate to the folder that contains the database file you want to protect and select that file.
4. Click the triangle at the right end of the Open button (near the bottom-left of the dialog box) to display a menu.
5. Choose Open Exclusive to display the Database window.
6. Choose Tools, move the pointer onto Security, and choose Set Database Password to display the Set Database Password dialog box.
7. Enter a password into the Password box, and then enter the password again into the Verify box.
8. Choose OK to set the password.

The next time you attempt to open the database, Access asks you to enter the password.

To remove a password

1. Open the password-protected database.

2. Choose Tools, move the pointer onto Security, and choose Unset Database Password to display the Unset Database Password dialog box.

3. Enter the password into the Password box and choose OK.

Establishing Yourself as a Database Administrator

By default, every Access user is designated to be an administrator. That means all users can administer every database. That might be okay if you have your own computer that's not on a network and you are the only person who uses that computer. It's definitely not okay if you share your computer with other people or if other people have access to your files by way of a network.

In this section, you learn how you can make yourself the sole administrator of specific database files.

Understanding the System.mdw File

Access maintains a master database file named System.mdw that contains

- Names of users and groups of users who have permissions to open Access. (User groups are described in the section "Controlling Access to Data with Groups" later in this chapter.)

- User passwords.

- A unique binary value, known as a System ID (SID) that identifies the current user.

- Access options selected in the Options dialog box.

- Definitions of custom toolbars.

> **NOTE**
>
> Access calculates the System ID from the User ID, password, and Personal Identification (PID).

You'll probably find your System.mdw file in the C:\Program Files\Microsoft Office\Office folder.

> **CAUTION**
>
> The procedures subsequently described make changes to your System.mdw file. If you make an error in these procedures, you might not be able to open Access or any of the databases you've previously created. For that reason, make a copy of your System.mdw file before you follow these procedures. Then, if you make a mistake, you can restore the original file.

If you want to restore Access to its original condition with no security, you can delete the System.mdw file. Subsequently, when you open Access and attempt to open a database, the message "An error occurred and this feature is no longer functioning properly. Would you like to repair this feature now?" is displayed. Choose Yes. You are then prompted to insert your Microsoft Office 2000 CD-ROM into the drive. Do so, and then choose OK. This causes the Office Installer to replace the missing System.mdw file. The database you tried to open opens with no security. From this point, you can recreate the security environment you need.

Changing the Default Administrator Name

By default, Access uses the name Admin as the name of each database administrator's account and doesn't provide password protection for that name. This section shows how you can change the name of the administrator's account and provide it with a password.

The steps described here might seem somewhat circuitous. The reason for this is that only an administrator's account can create, and make changes to, other accounts.

The first step is to provide a password for the default Admin account.

1. With Access running but with no databases open, choose Tools, move the pointer onto Security, and choose User and Group Accounts to display the dialog box shown in Figure 18.1.
2. Select the Change Logon Password tab shown in Figure 18.2.
3. At this time you don't have an old password, so press Tab to move the insertion point into the New Password box and enter a password. Enter the same password in the Verify box and choose OK to close the dialog box. Access saves the password in the System.mdw file.

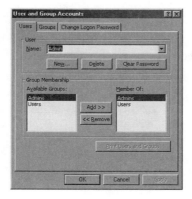

FIGURE 18.1
By default, your initial username is Admin.

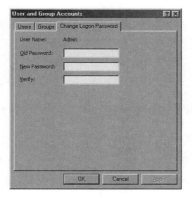

FIGURE 18.2
This is where you create your new password.

NOTE

Remember that passwords are case-sensitive.

4. Close Access.

The next time you attempt to start Access and open a database, the Logon dialog box is displayed. In this dialog box, enter Admin in the Name box and the password you created in the previous procedure in the Password box. Click OK to proceed.

Now you can create a new account that will subsequently become the administrator's account.

1. Choose Tools, move the pointer onto Security, and choose User and Group Accounts to display the dialog box shown previously in Figure 18.1.

2. Choose New to open the dialog box shown in Figure 18.3.

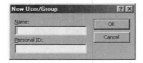

FIGURE 18.3
Use this dialog box to identify yourself.

3. Enter a name for yourself in the Name box and a personal identification in the Personal ID box. The personal identification must consist of at least four characters.

NOTE

The combination of a name and personal ID (PID) uniquely identifies each person who uses Access. The personal ID is required to overcome the problem that two or more people might have the same name.

4. Choose OK to return to the Users tab of the User and Group Accounts dialog box.

5. Select Admins in the Available Groups list and choose Add >> to make yourself a member of the Admins group.

6. Choose OK to close the dialog box and then close Access.

Now that you've established yourself as a member of the Admins group, you can password-protect the name you use as an administrator.

1. Start Access and open a database. Access displays the Logon dialog box.

2. Enter your new username in the Name box. Leave the Password box empty because you haven't provided a password for that name yet. Choose OK to proceed.

3. Choose Tools, move the pointer onto Security, and choose User and Group Accounts.

4. Open the Name drop-down list and select your new username.

5. Select the Change Logon Password tab. Leave the Old Password box empty. Enter a password for your account in the New Password box and again in the Verify box. Remember that passwords are case-sensitive. Choose OK.

6. Close Access.

The steps in the next procedure verify that you have correctly created a new username and password.

1. Start Access and open a database.

2. In the Logon dialog box, enter your new name in the Name box and the password for that name in the Password box.

3. Choose OK to open the database.

Now you can remove the original Admin account.

1. Choose Tools, move the pointer onto Security, and choose User and Group Accounts.

2. With the Users tab displayed, open the Name drop-down list and select your username. Look in the Member Of list to verify you are a member of the Admins and Users groups.

3. Open the Name drop-down list and, this time, select Admin.

4. Select Admins in the Member Of list, and then choose << Remove so that the Admin user is no longer a member of the Admins group.

5. Choose OK and then close Access.

Controlling Access to Data with Groups

One of the duties of an administrator is to give specific people access to a database. Each person has a unique username and password. In addition, each person has specific permissions, such as permission only to read data, permission to create new records, permission to change existing records, and so on. See "Assigning Permissions" later in this chapter for more detailed information about permissions.

If you're dealing with only a very small group of people, it's relatively easy to assign permissions to individual people. However, if you're dealing with more than just a few people, assigning individual permissions is a time-consuming process. To solve this problem, you can create groups and assign permissions to each group. Subsequently, you can assign people to groups; each person in a group automatically receives the permissions assigned to that group. If you subsequently change the permissions assigned to a group, all the members of the group have the changed permissions.

The next section explains how you add users to groups.

Adding Users to Groups

As an administrator, you can add new members to existing groups by following these steps.

1. Start Access and, using your administrator account, open a database.

2. Choose Tools, move the pointer onto Security, and choose User and Group Accounts.

3. With the Users tab displayed, choose New to display the dialog box previously shown in Figure 18.3.

4. Enter a name and Personal ID for the new user. Usernames can consist of up to 20 characters, must not contain punctuation characters, but can contain spaces. A username can't be the same as a group name. Choose OK to return to the User and Group Accounts dialog box.

5. By default, Access makes the new user a member of the Users group. If you want to make the new user a member of the Admins group, select Admins in the Available Groups list and then choose Add >>.

6. Choose OK to close the dialog box.

You should immediately contact the new user, saying that you have created the account with a blank password. Instruct the user to open the account and provide a password. Alternatively, close Access and restart it using the account you have just created. In that account, provide a temporary password, and close Access. Then tell the new user to open the account and immediately change the temporary password you've provided to a password chosen by that user.

From your Admin account, you can delete user accounts. Open the Users tab of the User and Group Accounts dialog box. Enter the name of the user account to delete in the Name box and choose Delete. Access doesn't let you delete the Admin account.

Creating New Groups

As you've seen, Access initially provides two groups: Admins and Users. Accounts you create in the Admins group have certain permissions, including creating new accounts. Accounts you create in the Users group have a different set of permissions that doesn't include creating new accounts. See "Assigning Permissions" later in this chapter for more information about permissions.

In many cases, the Admins and Users accounts are all you need. You can, as a member of the Admins group, create additional groups, each group having a different set of permissions.

To create a new group:

1. Open Access in your Admins account.

2. Choose Tools, move the pointer onto Security, and choose User and Group Accounts.

3. Select the Groups tab and choose New to open the dialog box shown previously in Figure 18.3.

4. Enter a name, such as Supervisors, for the new group in the Name box. Group names can consist of up to 20 characters, must not contain punctuation characters, but can contain spaces. A group name can't be the same as a username.

5. Enter a personal identification for the group in the Personal ID box.

6. Choose OK to return to the Users tab of the User and Group Accounts dialog box.

7. Choose OK to close the dialog box.

After Step 6, if you select the Users tab, you'll see the new group name listed in the Available Groups list.

Having created a new group, you have to assign permissions for that group so that all members of that group have those permissions. See "Assigning Permissions" subsequently in this chapter for information about permissions.

After you've created a new group, you can subsequently delete that group by choosing Delete in the Groups tab of the User and Group Accounts dialog box. Access displays a message asking you to confirm that you want to delete the group. Access doesn't let you delete the Admins and Users groups.

Printing a Summary of Users and Groups

After you've created user accounts and, perhaps, added new groups, you can print a list of those accounts and groups. To do so, open the Users tab of the User and Group Accounts dialog box and choose Print Users and Groups. That opens the Print Security dialog box in which you can choose to list

- Users and groups
- Only users
- Only groups

After making your choice, choose OK. Access prints the list on your default printer.

Assigning Permissions

Permissions determine what type of access a user has for objects. The Read permission by itself, for example, makes it possible for a user to see an object, but not to change it or delete it. You can assign permissions to a group, in which case all users who are members of that group have those permissions. You can also assign permissions to individual users. Table 18.1 lists the permissions you can assign.

TABLE 18.1   Permissions Available in Access

Permission	Explanation
Administer	Can create a database password and change start-up properties. Full access to other objects.
Delete Data	Can delete records.
Insert Data	Can add new records.
Modify Design	Can change and delete objects.
Open Exclusive	Can open a database and prevent other users from having it open at the same time.
Open/Run	Can run VBA procedures and macros.
Read Data	Can view data but not change it.
Read Design	Can open objects in Design view.
Update Data	Can view and change records.

Every object is owned by the person who created it. An object's owner has full permissions for that object.

You should normally assign permissions to groups, rather than to individual users. The easiest way to change an individual user's permissions is to make that person a member of a group to which the necessary permissions have already assigned.

Assigning Permissions to a Group

By default, the Users group has full permissions. You probably want to limit the permissions for that group. Follow these steps:

1. Open the database for which you want to assign permissions.
2. Choose Tools, move the pointer onto Security, and choose User and Group Permissions to open the dialog box shown in Figure 18.4.
3. Choose Groups so that the User/Group Names list contains group names. Select Users in that list.
4. Open the drop-down Object Type list and select Database.
5. You probably want users to have only Open/Run permission for the Database, so remove the check marks from Open Exclusive and Administer. Choose Apply to set your changes.
6. Successively, open Table, Form, Report, and Macro in the Object Type drop-down list, modify the permissions for each, and choose Apply.

You can assign permissions to other groups in the same way.

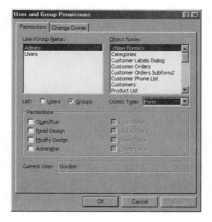

FIGURE 18.4
You can use this dialog box to change permissions and also to change ownership.

Assigning Permissions to Individual Users

You can assign permissions to individual users in the same way that you assign permissions to groups. The only difference is that you start by choosing Users so that the User/Group Name list contains the names of users.

Summary

The simplest way to provide some level of security to a database is to assign a password to it. Then, only those people who know the password have access to that database. The potential problem with this is that everyone who knows the password has full access to the database; everyone can add, change, and delete records and even make changes to the design of the database.

A more sophisticated approach to database security is to create individual users, each of whom has a password, and to create groups. You can assign specific permissions to each group and make specific people members of one or more groups. The people who are members of a group have the permissions assigned to that group. You can also assign permissions to individual users. By this means, you have detailed control over what each person can do.

Increasing the Capabilities of an Access Application

IN THIS CHAPTER

Access consists of two major components. One is a database front end that provides what you need to interact with a database engine. The other is the database engine itself. Versions of Access prior to Access 2000 used Jet as the database engine.

Whether you know so or not, you've probably been using Jet as a database engine in your work with Access. Jet provides all the services you need to work with data in the native Access format. In addition, you can use Jet to work with data in many other databases, including SQL Server databases.

Access 2000 offers you the choice of using an improved version of Jet (the default data engine) or the new Microsoft Data Engine (MSDE). Whereas SQL Server runs under Windows NT Server, MSDE runs on your local computer under Windows 98, Windows 2000, or Windows NT Client. You can use MSDE as a database engine for a small workgroup; you can also use it as a means to develop a database front end for SQL Server without needing access to SQL Server during the development process. For a detailed comparison of Jet and MSDE, see the article "Microsoft SQL Server: Microsoft Access 2000 Data Engine Options" that you can download from `http://msdn.microsoft.com/library/backgrnd/html/acmsdeop.htm`.

You can use Access to create a front end in Access Data Projects (ADP) format to interact with an MSDE database on your local computer or a networked computer. That front end can also interact with SQL Server versions 6.5 and 7.0 databases without incurring the overhead of doing so by using Jet.

This chapter

- Introduces the Microsoft Data Engine and describes how to install it
- Tells you about Access Data Projects—the front end for the Microsoft Data Engine and for SQL Server
- Describes how to upsize an Access application that uses Jet as its data engine to use the Microsoft Data Engine or SQL Server as its data engine
- Describes how to downsize an application that depends on the Microsoft Data Engine or SQL Server to use Jet as its data engine

Installing the Microsoft Data Engine

To work with a Microsoft Data Engine (MSDE) database, you first have to install the MSDE database engine. It's not automatically installed when you install Office 2000.

To install MSDE, follow these steps. The steps described here apply if you're installing MSDE under Windows 98 or Windows 2000. You'll see some additional steps if you're installing under Windows NT.

1. Insert the Office 2000 CD-ROM (Disk 1) into your drive.

2. Using Windows Explorer, navigate to the SQL\X86\Setup folder on the CD-ROM.

3. Double-click Setupsql.exe to display the Microsoft Data Engine (MSDE) Welcome dialog box.

4. Choose Next > to display the User Information dialog box. If necessary, change the default information in the Name and Company boxes.

5. Choose Next > to display the Setup Type dialog box in which you can specify the folder in which you want to install program files and data files. By default, the setup program installs program and data files on your C: drive. If you specify a different drive, the setup program still installs files on your system drive that occupy somewhat more than 10 megabytes.

6. Choose Next > to display the Character Set/Sort Order/Unicode Collation dialog box. You should normally accept the defaults unless you have a particular reason for choosing otherwise.

7. Choose Next > to display the Network Libraries dialog box. You should accept the defaults unless you have a particular reason for choosing otherwise.

8. Choose Next > to display the Start Copying Files dialog box.

9. Choose Next > to begin copying files and initiating MSDE, a process that takes several minutes. When the process is complete, the Setup Complete dialog box is displayed.

10. Choose Finish. Then close Windows Explorer.

After you've installed MSDE, choose Start in the Windows taskbar, and then choose Programs. The list of programs includes MSDE. Move the pointer onto MSDE to see these program names:

- Client Network Utility—A utility for setting up aliases and connection protocols to remote Microsoft Data Engines and to SQL Server databases.

- Import and Export Data—Opens the Data Transformation Services Wizard you can use to import data from, and export data to, other formats including databases, spreadsheets, and text files.

- Server Network Utility—A utility you can use to examine, modify, and add to server network libraries.

- Service Manager—Gives you the ability to start, pause, and stop MSDE. You should normally check Auto-start Service When OS Starts so that MSDE starts when you boot your computer.

- Uninstall MSDE—Starts the process of uninstalling MSDE.

19

INCREASING THE
CAPABILITIES OF
AN APPLICAITON

The MSDE installation procedure adds an icon to the Windows taskbar. This icon is added immediately when you install MSDE under Windows 98 or Windows 2000. If you install MSDE under Windows NT, the icon appears after you reboot your computer. Double-click the icon to display the SQL Server Service Manager dialog box in which you can start, pause, or stop MSDE, and in which you can check or uncheck the Auto-start Service When OS Starts check box.

With MSDE installed, you're ready to work with MSDE databases. The easiest way to become familiar with MSDE is to look at the sample that's supplied with Access.

Running a Sample MSDE Project

The file NwindCS.adp is copied to your hard drive when you install Access 2000, normally in the C:\Program Files\Microsoft Office\Office\Samples folder. This is an Access project that's similar to the Northwind database. You must have installed the Microsoft Data Engine, as described in the preceding section, before you can work with the NwindCS database.

To install the NwindCS database, follow these steps:

1. Use Windows Explorer to locate the NwindCS.adp file.
2. Double-click NwindCS.adp. The startup process automatically starts MSDE. After a few seconds, the Database window is displayed. The first time you run NwindCS.adp, a message box is superimposed on the Database window in which you are asked if you want to install the sample database.
3. Choose Yes to install the database. Installation takes a minute or so. When installation is complete, a message states that the database has been created. Choose OK. When a Welcome screen appears, choose OK to continue so that you can see the Database window shown in Figure 19.1.

Familiarize yourself with the Access Data Project (ADP) Database window by selecting in turn each type of object in the Objects bar. For typical objects, choose Design, Open, and New. Although the layout of the windows is different from what you're used to seeing, you'll easily understand most of what you see.

Some of the significant differences between this Database window and the Access Database window you're accustomed to seeing are

- Fewer choices are available in the right pane.
- The names of linked tables are shown without an arrow as though they're local tables.
- Views as stored queries. Views are saved in the MSDE database. Figure 19.2 shows a View in Design view.

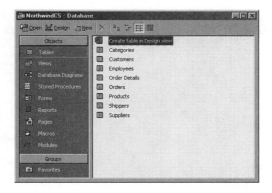

FIGURE 19.1
The Access Data Project Database window is somewhat different from the Access Database window.

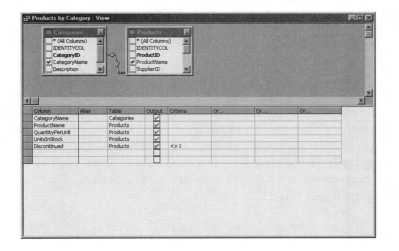

FIGURE 19.2
Although the format is different, you can see the similarity between this Design view of a View and the Access Query window.

- Database diagrams display relationships between tables. Figure 19.3 shows the relationships in the NorthwindCS database.

- Stored procedures are precompiled scripts that run significantly faster than SQL statements.

You can work with forms and reports in this MSDE database in the same way you work with them in an Access database.

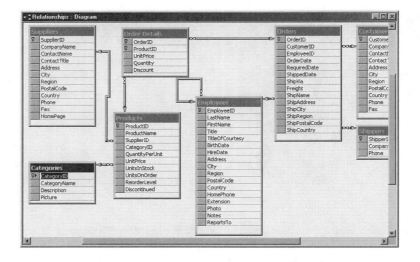

FIGURE 19.3
You can drag the tables in this window to show some of the relationships more clearly.

Upsizing and Downsizing Applications

A common scenario is to develop a new Access application on a local computer using Jet as the database engine. After the new application has been put into service, usage might grow and the amount of data to be handled might increase to an extent that Jet can't handle. When that happens, you need to upsize the application to use SQL Server as the database engine. Table 19.1 compares some of the capabilities of Jet and SQL Server so that you can see why you might want to upsize to SQL Server.

TABLE 19.1   Comparison of Jet and SQL Server

Capability	Jet	SQL Server
Concurrent Users	255 maximum	Virtually unlimited
Maximum Data Size	2 gigabytes	Terabytes
Transaction Logging	No	Yes
Security Integration	No	Yes

The Upsizing Wizard included with Access 2000 provides a fairly smooth transition from Jet to SQL Server. This wizard converts your Access tables in the Jet environment to SQL Server tables. It also converts the application's front end from queries, forms, and reports that interact with Jet to a Access Data Project (ADP) that interacts with SQL Server.

The Microsoft Data Engine (MSDE) helps the transition process. MSDE is a limited version of SQL Server that runs on your local computer. You can use MSDE to upsize an Access application on your local computer where you can optimize that application without having access to SQL Server.

> **NOTE**
>
> You can also use MSDE and ADP to develop SQL Server applications from scratch, but that's beyond the scope of this book.

You can also downsize an application from SQL Server to Jet, providing, of course, the downsized application doesn't exceed Jet's capabilities.

The next two sections provide information about upsizing and downsizing applications. Upsizing is described in detail because it's something you might often need to do. Downsizing is covered only briefly because it's not often used.

Upsizing an Access Application

The Upsizing Wizard in Access automates most of the process of converting an Access database to SQL Server or to MSDE. The wizard converts a Jet database to an equivalent MSDE or SQL Server database with the same table structure, data, and many of the original database attributes. The wizard also converts your Access front end to an Access Data Project. Follow these steps to convert a database:

1. Point onto the MSDE icon in the Windows taskbar to see whether MSDE is running. If the ScreenTip states that MSDE is paused or stopped, double-click the icon to display the SQL Server Service Manager dialog box, choose Start/Continue, and then close the dialog box.

2. Open the Access database you want to convert to display its Database window. The Upsizing Wizard can't run if any of the database's objects are open.

3. Choose Tools, move the pointer onto Database Utilities, and choose Upsizing Wizard to display the first wizard window.

> **NOTE**
>
> Each wizard window provides online help. Click the Help button at the bottom left to access help.

4. Choose Create New Database and then choose Next > to display the dialog box shown in Figure 19.4.

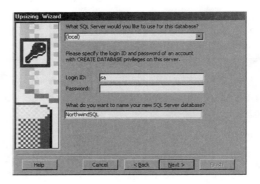

Figure 19.4

You must supply information in all the boxes, with the exception of the Password box in this window.

5. Enter (local) in the What SQL Server Would You Like to Use for This Database box. Note that the work must be enclosed in parentheses.

6. Enter sa in the Login ID box. (sa is an abbreviation for system administrator.) Leave the Password box empty.

7. Accept the default name in the What Do You Want to Name Your New SQL Server Database box. The default name provided is the name of your open database with the letters SQL appended.

8. Choose Next > to connect to MSDE and to display the next wizard window in which you identify the tables you want to export to SQL Server (meaning MSDE).

9. After selecting tables, choose Next > to display the next wizard window shown in Figure 19.5.

10. Accept the defaults in this window, at least the first time you convert a database.

11. Choose Next > to display the next wizard window. In this window, select Create a New Access Client/Server Application. The wizard automatically provides an ADP filename. Check the Save Password and User ID box.

12. Choose Next > to display the final wizard window, and then choose Finish. The wizard displays a progress bar while the conversion takes place. When the conversion is complete, the wizard displays an Upsizing Wizard Report that lists what has been accomplished and notifies you of any problems. You can print this report.

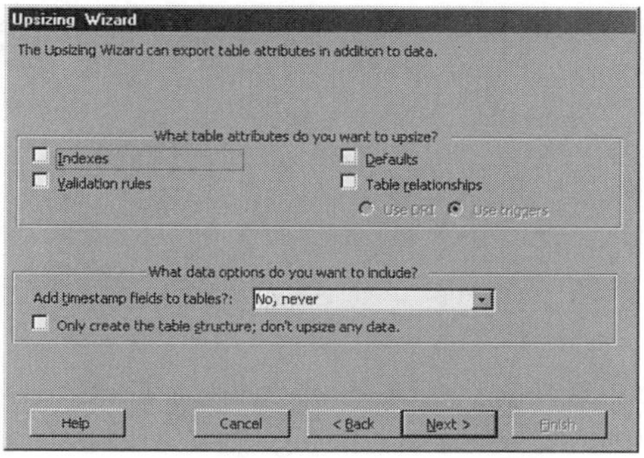

FIGURE 19.5
Use this window to select which of the table attributes you want to include in your MSDE database.

When you close the report, the Database window for the new Data Access Project is displayed. At this point, you can see the results of upsizing your original Access database:

- Open each of your tables in MSDE to verify it has been properly converted.
- Look to see whether queries in the original database have been properly converted to views or stored procedures. The Upsizing Wizard isn't able to convert all queries, so you'll probably have to manually create some views or stored procedures.
- Verify that forms and reports are properly converted. You should be able to see all forms and reports in Design view, but you won't be able to open forms and reports that require queries that haven't been converted.

What remains to be done is to construct the views and stored procedures that the wizard couldn't handle.

Downsizing an MSDE or SQL Server Application

Just as you can upsize an Access database to MSDE or SQL Server, so you can downsize an MSDE or SQL Server database to an Access database, providing Access can support the requirements. When you install MSDE, the Data Transformation Services (DTS) Wizard is automatically installed. You can use that wizard to convert an MSDE or SQL Server database to Access or into several other formats.

To downsize an MSDE or SQL Server database:

1. Create and save an empty Access database.
2. In the Windows taskbar, choose Start, move the pointer onto Programs, move the pointer onto MSDE, and choose Import and Export Data to open the DTS Wizard's first window.

From there, follow through the various wizard windows in much the same way that's described in the preceding section for upsizing a database.

Summary

You can greatly increase the capabilities of an Access-based application by upsizing from the Jet data engine to the SQL Server data engine. An interim step is to upsize to the Microsoft Data Engine.

The Microsoft Data Engine, supplied with Access 2000, is a limited version of SQL Server than runs on your local computer. You can use it to upsize Access applications and to design SQL Server applications without having access to SQL Server.

The Upsizing Wizard in Access leads you through the process of upsizing an Access application that uses the Jet data engine to one that uses the Microsoft Data Engine or SQL Server as a data engine. The Data Transformation Services Wizard, automatically installed with the Microsoft Data Engine, leads you through the process of downsizing an application based on the Microsoft Data Engine or SQL Server to use the Jet data engine.

Sharing an Application with Other People

IN THIS CHAPTER

It would take many chapters, perhaps a whole book, to address thoroughly the subject of sharing Access applications with other people. Instead of attempting to cover the whole subject, this chapter focuses on just two issues:

- Sharing an application on a network with other people who have Access installed on their computers

- Distributing copies of your application for use by people who don't have Access installed on their computers

The recommended way to share an application on a network is to split the application into a front end and a back end. The front end is installed individually on all computers. The back end, which consists of the data tables, is installed on the server. When creating an application for use in this way, it's particularly important to set up the appropriate permissions to avoid conflicts.

There are two ways to make an Access application available to people who don't have Access installed on their computers. One of these is to make use of Data Access Pages, as described in Chapter 17, "Extending Access to the Web." By doing that, people can use Internet Explorer to work with your Access application. Another way is to create a runtime version of your application. To do so, you must have Microsoft Office Developer (MOD) installed on your computer so that you can use the Package and Deployment Wizard that's included in MOD. After you've created a runtime version of your application, people who don't have Access installed can run the application on their computers.

Sharing an Access Application on a Network

This section covers sharing an Access application on a small network in which relatively few users need to access the application simultaneously—the type of problem readers of this book are quite likely to face. The problem of sharing an Access application on a large network with many users is way beyond the scope of this book. If that's your problem, you need the services of a network specialist.

Defining the Problem

Two important factors to consider before getting into details about sharing your application are the number of people who will use it, and the amount of data to be handled. Your answers to these questions provide the basis for how the application should be designed and how it will be shared.

How Many Users?

How many people will simultaneously use the application? Consider not only the number of people who will initially use the application, but how many people will eventually use it. The specification for the Jet data engine allows for a maximum of 255 simultaneous users, but the practical limit is much smaller than that.

If you expect the application to be used by more than about 50 simultaneous users, you should plan to use the Microsoft Data Engine (MSDE) so that you can easily upsize to SQL Server, which can support a virtually unlimited number of users.

How Much Data?

If you're using Jet as your data engine, bear these two considerations in mind:

- The maximum size of an Access (.mdb) file is two gigabytes.
- The maximum size of a table is one gigabyte.

You can use multiple files for tables, so the significant limitation is the maximum size of each table.

In practice, databases tend to fall into one of two categories: those that have tables considerably smaller than one gigabyte, and those that have very much larger tables. It shouldn't be difficult to decide which category applies to your application.

If the one-gigabyte limit is acceptable, you should use Jet as your data engine. Otherwise, use the Microsoft Data Engine so that you can easily upsize to SQL Server.

Subsequent sections of this chapter assume the limitations of Jet are not a problem, and are based on an application that uses Jet as its data engine.

Splitting the Application

Several chapters in this book have pointed out the advantages of splitting a database into at least two Access files. Use one or more files for tables (the back end) and use one file for the front end (everything except the tables). There are two important reasons for adopting this approach:

- When you make changes to the front end, you can distribute the file containing the updated front end to people without affecting the data in tables.
- People who have access to data in the tables can have a separate copy of the front end on their local computers so that only the file or files that contain tables are shared. The purpose of this to minimize network traffic.

Access contains the Database Splitter Wizard, a tool you can use to split an Access database into front end and table files. To use this wizard:

1. Make a backup copy of the database you intend to split.

2. Open the database, choose Tools, move the pointer onto Database Utilities, and choose Database Splitter to display the first Database Splitter window.

3. Choose Split Database. The wizard displays the Create Back-end Database dialog box in which it proposes to create the back-end (tables) file in your default folder and with a name that appends "_be" to the original database name. You can navigate to a different folder and change the proposed name if you want.

TIP

It's a good idea to save the back end at this time on the server so that links to that location will be automatically created in the front end.

4. Choose Split. The process starts and might take several minutes. A message box stating the database has been successfully split appears when the new back end has been created. Choose OK to return to the Database window.

The Database Splitter Wizard creates a new .mdb file and moves all the tables in the current database, together with their properties and relationships, into the new database. It also creates links from the original database to the tables in the new database. When the Database window reappears, notice that all the tables are marked with arrows to indicate that they are linked to another file.

You now have two Access files. One is the original file, now no longer containing the tables. The other is a new file that contains only the tables. The first is the front end to install on all users' computers. The second is the back end, the one to be shared.

Verifying and Changing Table Links

After you've used the Database Splitter Wizard, the front-end database contains links to tables in the back end, as shown by the arrows at the left of table names in the front-end Database window. To verify these links are correct

1. Open the front-end database, display its Database window, and select Tables in the Objects bar.

2. Choose Tools, move the pointer onto Database Utilities, and choose Linked Table Manager to display the dialog box shown in Figure 20.1.

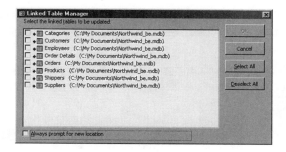

FIGURE 20.1
The Linked Table Manager displays a list of the linked tables with the path of each table.

3. If the links to all tables are correct, choose Cancel to close the dialog box. Otherwise, continue with the following steps.

4. Select the names of one or more tables for which you want to change the path to the same new path, and then choose OK to display the Select New Location dialog box that names the first selected table.

5. Navigate to the folder that contains the correct path for the table, select that folder, and choose Open. The table manager updates the links for the selected tables.

6. Repeat Steps 4 and 5 if you need to change the paths for other tables.

Setting Record-Locking Properties

Record locking provides the ability to control what happens in a shared application when two or more people try to modify a record at the same time. You don't have to be concerned with that while you're developing an application because only you have access to the data. You need to be very much concerned with record locking when you distribute an application for use by two or more simultaneous users.

Record locking is of significance for forms that people can use to edit existing data. It is not of significance for forms used only for viewing data or for switchboard forms. Record locking can also be used to prevent data being changed while a report is being printed or while a query is running.

Access provides three levels of record locking. No Locks is the default. The three levels are

- No Locks—Two or more users can use a form to edit a record at the same time. Data can be changed while a report is being printed or previewed, or while a query is running. With this level of record locking, Access locks records only while it is writing changed data to the disk. This is also known as "optimistic locking."

- All Records—All records in the underlying table or query are locked while one user has a form open in Form or Datasheet view, while one user is printing or previewing a report, and while one user is running a query.
- Edit Record—This applies only to forms and queries. A page of records is locked while one user is editing a record on that page. This is also known as "pessimistic locking."

NOTE

A page, in this context, is a four-kilobyte portion of a .mdb file in which records are stored. A page may contain several records, depending on the size of those records.

To set the record-locking property of a form, open that form in Design view, display the Property sheet, and select the Data tab. Open the Record Locks drop-down list and select No Locks, All Records, or Edit Record. Set the record-locking property for reports in a similar manner, with the exceptions that the property is in the Other tab and only No Locks and All Records are available. Set the record-lock property for queries in the General tab of the Property sheet.

Securing the Front End

Having split the database as described in the previous section, you have a front end that users can install on their computers. As things stand, a potential problem is that each user can modify the front end, something that can cause you headaches because, undoubtedly, some people will make changes that don't work.

The solution to this problem is to distribute a version of the front end that users can't modify. You can do so by creating and distributing an MDE file, instead of a normal Access (.mdb) file, to people who will access the database. People who use the MDE file are prevented from using Design view to view, modify, and create forms, reports, pages, and modules.

CAUTION

Save the original .mdb file from which you create an MDE file. Just as people to whom you distribute an MDE file can't change it, neither can you. If you need to make changes to the front end, you must do so in the original .mdb file and then create a new MDE file from the updated .mdb file.

For more information about MDE files, see the topic "About MDE Files" in Microsoft Access Help.

To create an MDE file

1. Open the database on which you want to base the MDE file.
2. Choose Tools, move the pointer onto Database Utilities, and choose Make MDE File to open the Make MDE As dialog box. This dialog box proposes to save the MDE file in the same folder as the original database and to save it with the same filename as the original database, but with .mde as the extension.
3. Choose Save to save the file.

After creating an MDE file in this way, you can see how it works by following these steps:

1. Close the original database and close Access.
2. Use Windows Explorer or Find to locate the MDE file.
3. Double-click the name of the MDE file to start Access and open the MDE file.
4. In the Database window, select each object name in turn in the Objects bar and notice the commands at the left end of the toolbar.

You'll see

- With Tables or Queries selected, Open, Design, and New are all available. Users have full access to tables and can create their own queries.
- With Forms, Reports, or Pages selected, only Open is available. Users can open these objects, but can't access their design or create new ones.
- With Macros selected, Run, Design, and New are available. Users have full access to macros.
- With Modules selected, no commands are available. Users have no access to modules.

Distributing the Front End to Users

Having completed creating the front end on your computer either as a normal Access .mdb file or as an MDE file, you're ready to distribute that file to other people. The easiest way to do that is to make the file available on a shared drive and invite people to download it. Providing those people have Access 2000 installed, they'll be able to start working with the database.

Sharing Access Applications with People Who Don't Have Access Installed

People don't necessarily need to have Access installed on their computers in order to run Access-based applications. You can develop an Access-based application on your computer, create a runtime version of that application, and freely distribute that version to other people. To be able to do that, you must have Microsoft Office 2000 Developer installed on your computer. That version of MS Office and the runtime version of Access, as well as the procedure for using them to deploy your application, are described in the following sections.

Introducing Microsoft Office 2000 Developer

Microsoft Office 2000 Developer, often referred to as MOD, is the top-of-the-line edition of Microsoft Office. In addition to containing everything in the Premium edition of Office 2000, MOD contains many tools of great value to developers of Access and other Office applications. Among these tools is the Package and Deployment Wizard that you can use to create runtime versions of Access-based applications.

Although MOD is quite expensive, it can save your organization a lot of money if you need to develop Access-based applications for several people to use. That's because those people don't need to have editions of Office that contain Access in order to work with runtime versions of Access applications.

Comparing Standard and Runtime Access

Whereas you can use standard Access to develop databases and applications based on databases, as described in the previous chapters of this book, people can use runtime Access only for running Access-based applications. The things not available in runtime Access include

- Database, Macro, and Module windows
- All Design views
- Built-in toolbars
- Various menu commands
- Built-in Help
- Some keys and key combinations

> **NOTE**
>
> As stated in the preceding paragraph, the Database window is not available in runtime Access. In fact, it's there but is not visible because its colors are set to the Windows background color. As a result of this, you can include VBA code that interacts with the Database window in your application.

These limitations mainly protect an application from being changed by users. The limitations do mean, though, that you can't just take any Access application and use the Package and Deployment Wizard to convert it into runtime. You have to keep the runtime environment in mind while you develop the application.

Preparing an Application for Conversion to Runtime

The absence of a Database window in runtime Access makes it necessary to base an application on forms. When the application starts, a switchboard or another type of form must be displayed on which users can click buttons to navigate to other forms. You can specify the form that's displayed when an application starts in the Startup dialog box, as described in the section "Displaying a Startup Form When an Application Starts" in Chapter 5, "Making Your Forms Smarter."

The standard toolbars in Access aren't available in a runtime version of an application. Also, most menus aren't available and many of the commands in the menus that are available are disabled. For that reason, you have to create your own toolbars and menus in any application that you plan to convert to runtime.

Microsoft Access Help isn't available in runtime. The reason for that is the majority of help topics deal with design issues. If you're creating a fairly straightforward application, you can probably provide enough help for users by providing ControlTips for the controls on your forms and Description text for fields in tables. You can also create a custom Help file, although that takes considerable time and effort.

It's particularly important to include error handling in an application you intend to convert to runtime. If you don't include error handling, a person using an application converted to runtime will see only one of the built-in Access error messages when an error occurs. The only option the person has at that time is to choose OK, and that causes the application to quit. On the other hand, by including custom error handling in your application, you can ensure that any errors are handled in a manner that's meaningful to users. The section "Responding to Runtime Errors" in Chapter 13, "Taking More Control of Access," explains how to include error handling in an application.

Security is just as important in a runtime application as it is in a normal Access application. Although you may distribute an application as a runtime version, intending it to be used by people who don't have Access installed on their computers, some of the people who use the application may have Access installed. Those people can open your application under Access and use its tools to modify the application. Chapter 18, "Making Your Application Secure," contains information about making an application secure.

Checking a Runtime Application

You can simulate how an application will be seen in the runtime environment before you convert it to a runtime version by using the Runtime switch to start the application under Access. You can use the Runtime switch only if you have MOD installed on your computer. One way to simulate a runtime version of your application is to create an icon on the Windows desktop, as described in the section "Starting an Application Automatically" in Chapter 5.

Step 6 in the procedure in that section shows the text to provide to start the Northwind database. By appending a space, a forward slash, and the word Runtime to that text, as in

```
"C:\Program Files\Microsoft Office\Office\MSACCESS.EXE "
➥"C:\Program Files\Microsoft Office\Office\Samples\Northwind.mdb" /Runtime
```

the icon on the Windows desktop starts Access in a simulated runtime mode and opens the Northwind application in that mode.

> **NOTE**
>
> The command line is split into two lines here so that it fits within the width of this page. The command line you enter must be all on a single line.

You can create a similar icon to test applications you create before you convert them to runtime.

You can also start an Access application in runtime mode by choosing Start, Run from the Windows taskbar and entering the text shown previously in the Open box.

Installing the Package and Deployment Wizard

After installing Office 2000 Developer on your computer, proceed as follows to install the
Developer tools:

1. Start Access and open an application.

2. Choose Tools, move the pointer onto Macro, and choose Visual Basic Editor to display
   the VBE window.

3. Choose Add-Ins, Add-In Manager to display the dialog box shown in Figure 20.2.

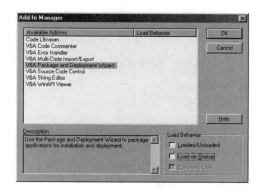

FIGURE 20.2

*The Add-In Manager dialog box lists the add-ins available in MOD, together with any other add-ins you may have
installed.*

4. Select VBA Package and Deployment Wizard, and then check Loaded/Unloaded at the
   bottom right of the dialog box. The word Loaded appears in the column at the right of
   that add-in.

5. If you want the selected add-in to load automatically each time you start Access, check
   Load on Startup.

6. Choose OK to close the dialog box.

After loading an add-in in this manner, that add-in's name appears in the Add-Ins menu.

Installing Access Runtime

The required installation process is somewhat less than intuitive. Follow these steps carefully.

1. With the MOD CD-ROM inserted in your drive, open Windows Explorer and open the
   folder Mod2000\Odetools\V9\Accessrt.

2. Double-click Setup.exe to open the Access Runtime Setup window.

3. Select Customize to specify the folder in which Runtime is to be installed.

4. In the Microsoft Access 2000 Runtime Installation Location dialog box, navigate to the C:\Program Files\ODETools\V9 folder.

5. In that folder, create a new folder named Runtime and choose OK. It's necessary to do this because, when you subsequently create a runtime package, the Package and Employment Wizard expects to find Access Runtime in the C:\Program Files\ODETools\V9\Runtime folder.

6. Choose OK to display the Microsoft Access 2000 Runtime: Ready to Install dialog box.

7. Choose Install Now. The installation process takes several minutes. During the process you have to restart your computer.

Preparing an Application for Distribution

With an application ready to be packaged for distribution, and with the Package and Deployment Wizard loaded, you're ready to use the wizard. Follow these steps:

1. Open the Access application you want to distribute.

2. Choose Tools, move the pointer onto Macro, and choose Visual Basic Editor to open the VBE window.

3. Choose Add-Ins, Package and Deployment Wizard to display the first wizard window shown in Figure 20.3.

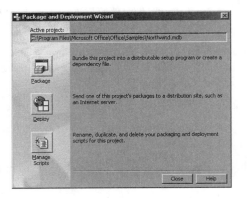

FIGURE 20.3

You can use the Package and Deployment Wizard to package or deploy an application, as well as to manage scripts.

4. Select Package to provide a name for your packaging script, as shown in Figure 20.4.

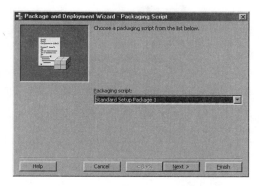

FIGURE 20.4

The wizard proposes a name for your packaging script.

The wizard proposes a name for the script, but you can change that name. The script is a program that controls how the package is assembled. Choose Next > to display the next wizard window, shown in Figure 20.5.

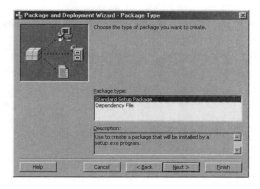

FIGURE 20.5

Use this wizard window to select the type of package you want to create.

5. Select Standard Setup Package in the Package Type list, and then choose Next > to display the next wizard window, shown in Figure 20.6.

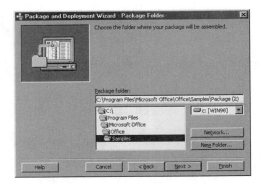

FIGURE 20.6

This wizard window is where you select a folder in which to assemble your package.

6. The wizard proposes to assemble the package in a new folder named Package under the folder that contains your application. You can change this name or choose New Folder to create a new folder in a different place. Choose Next >. If the folder you've chosen doesn't exist, a message appears asking whether you want to create the new folder. Choose Yes.

7. At this point, you might see a dialog box stating that some dependencies—files your application depends on—are missing. If there are no missing dependencies, the wizard window shown in Figure 20.7 is displayed.

8. Choose Scan to locate missing dependencies. When the wizard locates the missing dependencies, the wizard window shown in Figure 20.7 is displayed.

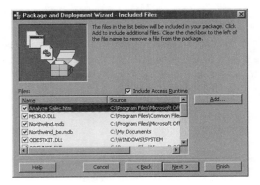

FIGURE 20.7

The window displays a list of files to be included in your package.

NOTE

By default, every file in the list is checked. If you don't want a specific file to be included in the package, uncheck that file. If you want to add more files to the package, choose Add to display the Add File dialog box in which you navigate to a specific folder, select one or more files in that folder, and choose Open to add the file to the package.

9. If it's not already checked, check Include Access Runtime. At this point, you might see a message about locating Access Runtime files. Choose OK to display the Locate Data1.msi dialog box. In this dialog box, navigate to the folder in which you installed Access Runtime, usually C:\Program Files\Microsoft Office\ODETools\V9\Runtime, and choose Open to return to the wizard window. Choose Next > to display the dialog box shown in Figure 20.8.

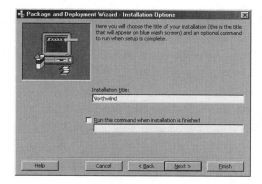

FIGURE 20.8
This is where you provide a title for the package.

10. By default, the wizard proposes to use the name of your application as the name of the package. You can change the name in the Installation Title box. The name is displayed when the package is subsequently installed.

11. If you want a command to run when the installation is complete, check the Run This Command When Installation Is Finished box and enter the command in the adjoining text box. Choose Next > to display the window shown in Figure 20.9.

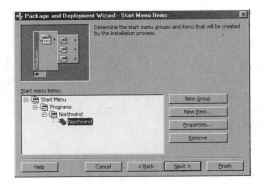

FIGURE 20.9
Use this window to define the menus to be created by the installation process.

12. You can add groups only to the Start and Program menus. Select either the Start or Program menu in the diagram at the left and then choose New Group to add a group. The wizard adds the group to the diagram. Edit the new group's name. Repeat this step to create more groups.

13. Select a group and then choose New Item to display the Menu Item Properties dialog box in which you can define the properties of the new item. Repeat this step to create more items.

14. Choose Properties to display the Menu Properties dialog box. You can use this dialog box to select group properties if the application is to be installed under Windows NT.

15. Choose Next > to display the window shown in Figure 20.10.

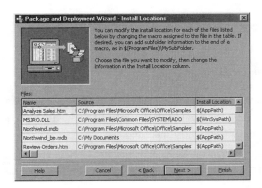

FIGURE 20.10
Use this window to specify the folders into which the application's components will be installed.

16. Normally, accept the default folders in this window; select other folders only if you have a specific reason for doing so. Select an Install Location for any file listed in this window, open the drop-down list of available locations, and select the one you want to use. Repeat this step to change the install locations for additional files. Choose Next > to display the window shown in Figure 20.11.

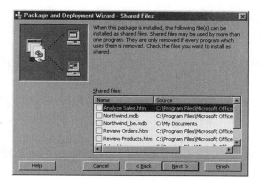

FIGURE 20.11

This window lists the files to be installed; no file is shared.

17. If you want any file to be shared after it is installed, check the box adjacent to its name.

18. Choose Next > to display the final wizard window, shown in Figure 20.12, and enter the name under which you want the package to be saved in the Script Name box.

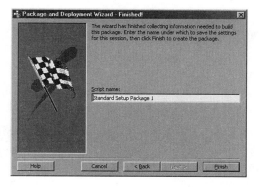

FIGURE 20.12

This is the final wizard window.

19. Choose Finish to begin building the package.

When the process of building the package is complete, the wizard displays a window that reports to that effect. Choose Save Report, and then choose Close to close the window and return to the first Package and Deployment Wizard window.

Deploying Your Application

Deploying an application means placing the package in a location from which it can be installed on workstations. The Package and Deployment Wizard guides you through the process.

1. In the first Package and Deployment Wizard window, choose Deploy. This displays a window that lists packages available for deployment.

2. Select the package you want to deploy and choose Next > to display a wizard window that offers you the option of deploying to a folder or by way of the Web.

3. Select the method of deployment you want to use. The following steps are based on deployment to a folder; the steps for deploying by way of the Web are somewhat different. Choose Next > to display the next wizard window.

4. Use this window to select whether you want to deploy the application locally or to a network. In most cases, you'll want to deploy to a network. Choose Next > to display the final wizard window.

5. Provide a name for the deployment script, and then choose Finish to begin the deployment.

A deployment report appears when the deployment process is complete. Choose Save Report and then choose Close to return to the first Package and Deployment Wizard window.

Testing Your Packaged Application

The last thing you want to happen is that people install your application on their computers, only to find it doesn't work. For that reason, it's vitally important to test your packaged application before anyone installs it. You must test the package using a computer on which the full version of Access, or another packaged runtime Access application, has never been installed.

Here's an explanation of why proper testing is so important. A packaged application consists of Cab files that contain the application itself; the application also contains many support files. For the application to run successfully, all the support files must be present. The point of testing is to make sure that all the required support files are installed when a person installs your application.

Suppose, for one reason or another, some of the support files are missing from the package. If you attempt to test the application by installing it on your computer, or on another computer on which the full version of Access is or has been installed, chances are the support files are already present, so it doesn't matter that they're missing from your package. The same could be true if you install your package on a computer on which another packaged runtime application has previously been installed.

So, what do you do? There's no one-hundred-percent answer to that question. Even all the resources of Microsoft, with the cooperation of many thousands of beta testers, don't result in software that runs on every computer. There are, however, things you can do make it likely your application will run properly on most computers.

The best approach is to have a computer used only for testing purposes. When the time comes to test your ready-for-distribution application, reformat the test computer's hard drive and install on it only the version of Windows people who will be using your application have. Don't install Office. Then install and test your packaged application. If it works correctly, you know it contains all the required support files.

Even that method doesn't ensure no hardware or software conflicts will arise when people install your packaged application on their computers. Be prepared for problems.

Whatever you do, don't make your packaged application available for a large number of people to install at one time. Have a few people install it and check for problems. If problems arise, correct them, and have a few more people install the application. Proceed incrementally in this way until everyone has the application up and running.

Installing a Packaged Application

Follow these steps to install a packaged application on a computer.

1. Choose Start in the Windows taskbar, and then choose Run.
2. In the Open box, enter the path to Setup file in the deployment folder, and choose OK. After some while, a Welcome message box appears.
3. Choose OK to continue. A dialog box appears that shows the location in which the application will be installed.
4. Choose the button at the top left of the dialog box to install the application.

After the application is installed, it's ready for use.

Summary

Creating an Access application to be shared by other people is not easy. But why should it be? The whole idea of databases is quite complex.

You can create an Access-based application that can share information by way of a local area network, an intranet, or the Internet. To do that effectively and reliably, you have to carefully design the structure of the database and pay attention to security issues.

You can also create Access-based applications that people who don't have Access installed on their computers can use. To do that, you have to use Microsoft Office 2000 Developer to create runtime versions of your applications.

Visual Basic for Applications Primer

IN THIS APPENDIX

If you want to go beyond using what Access provides on the surface, you have to delve into what's beneath the surface. What's beneath the surface is a programming language known as Visual Basic for Applications (VBA). You don't want to be a programmer? That's okay. Nevertheless, if you want to be able to control Access, you have to be prepared to get, at least somewhat, involved with what lies behind Access—that's VBA.

English is a language, as are Greek, Latin, French, Spanish, and many more. All these are spoken and written languages that people use to communicate with one another. Visual Basic, Pascal, C, FORTRAN, and others are also languages you can use, not to communicate with other people, but to communicate with computers. To communicate effectively with people or computers, you have to use a language those people or computers can understand. Like other languages, VBA has a vocabulary—words that have meaning—and also has syntax rules— ways you can put words and groups of words together so that they can be understood.

There's nothing mysterious about a programming language. It's just a list of instructions. Like any language, the VBA language Access uses requires you to follow rules so that your intentions are understood.

This appendix introduces you only to the basics of using the VBA language—its vocabulary and its syntax rules—so that you can control what Access does, rather than have Access limit what you can do. (For further reading, see Appendix C, "Information Resources for Access 2000.") It does this by first creating a laboratory in which you can work with VBA, and then suggesting experiments you can use within that laboratory.

Setting Up Your VBA Laboratory

Follow these steps to set up a laboratory in which you can experiment with VBA.

1. Open Access and, in the Microsoft Access window, choose Blank Access Database.
2. Choose OK to display the File New Database dialog box in which the File Name box proposes a name for the new database. Accept that name.
3. Choose Create to display the Database window.
4. Select Forms in the Objects bar and then choose New to display the New Forms dialog box.
5. Select Design View and choose OK to display a new form in Design view.
6. If the Design view of the form doesn't contain the Toolbox, choose View, Toolbox.
7. Click the Command Button icon in the toolbox, and then use the mouse to outline a small rectangle on the form. That rectangle becomes a command button. Access automatically gives that command button the name Command0, as shown in Figure A.1.

Visual Basic for Applications Primer

APPENDIX A

481

A

VISUAL BASIC FOR
APPLICATIONS
PRIMER

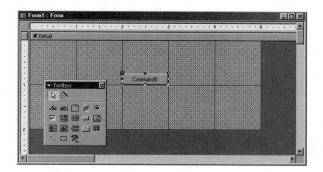

FIGURE A.1

This is a form with a command button on it.

8. Choose View, Properties to display the Property sheet for the command button you just created and select the Event tab.

9. Click the On Click property and then click the button with three dots at the right of that property's value to display the Choose Builder dialog box.

10. Select Code Builder and choose OK. Access displays a Visual Basic Editor (VBE) window, shown in Figure A.2. This window contains several panes, the largest of which is the one in which you can create VBA code that runs when you click the command button on your form.

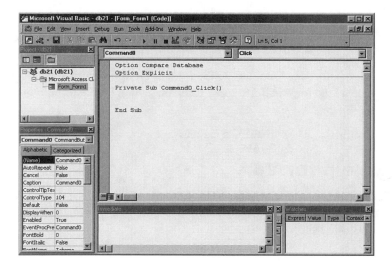

FIGURE A.2

This is the window in which you can create VBA code.

Now you have set up your laboratory. The door into your laboratory is the statement Private Sub Command0_Click(). The door out of your laboratory is the statement End Sub. Whatever statements you write between those two statements determine what happens within the laboratory. The beginning and ending statements shown here are known as a *stub*.

To see how this works, insert two statements, such as those shown in Figure A.3, within the stub.

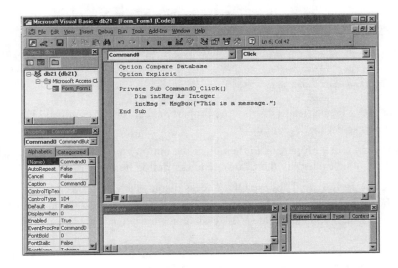

FIGURE A.3
This VBA code displays a message on your form.

Choose View, Microsoft Access to return to the form in Design view, and then choose View, Form View to display the form in Form view. Click the button on the form to display the message as shown in Figure A.4.

Choose OK in the message box to dismiss the message.

Getting Help for VBA

Access contains extensive online help for VBA in Microsoft Visual Basic Help. To access this help, display the VBE window shown previously in Figure A.2, and then choose Help, Microsoft Visual Basic Help.

Visual Basic for Applications Primer

APPENDIX A

483

A

VISUAL BASIC FOR
APPLICATIONS
PRIMER

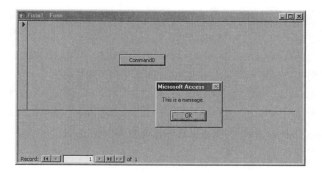

FIGURE A.4

This is the message displayed on the form.

Understanding VBA Modules

All VBA code exists in containers known as modules. Code that extends the functionality of a form exists in a form module that's part of that form. Code that extends the functionality of a report exists in a report module that's part of the report. Modules of this type are collectively known as class modules.

Some code is independent of a specific form or report. That code exists in one or more separate modules, which are known as standard modules. The set of standard modules in an application is known as a project.

Understanding VBA Structure

VBA code consists of a series of statements, each on a single line. Most statements are within procedures.

NOTE

VBA is not case sensitive. The conventional capitalization throughout this book is used to help people understand code. Capitalization has no effect on how the code runs.

The example in Figure A.2 shows a small procedure containing two statements. Until you get into quite advanced programming, you'll deal with two types of procedures:

- Sub Procedure—A sequence of statements that makes something happen. Figure A.2 shows a sub procedure that makes a message appear on a form.
- Function Procedure—Similar to a sub procedure, but with the additional capability of returning a value.

There can be any number of procedures of either type within a module.

Sub procedures are declared by a statement such as

```
Private Sub CountBooks()
```

in which CountBooks is the name of the procedure. The end of a sub procedure is marked by the statement

```
End Sub
```

Function procedures are declared by a statement such as

```
Private Function CountBooks()
```

in which CountBooks is the name of the procedure. The end of a function procedure is marked by the statement

```
End Function
```

See the subsequent section "Scope of Procedures" for information about the significance of the keyword Private in the preceding examples of procedure declarations.

You'll often encounter event procedures, which are a particular type of sub procedure. Event procedures run when an event, such as clicking a button on a form, occurs. The procedure shown in Figure A.2 is an event procedure of this type. Event procedures are automatically named according to the event they respond to. Each name has two parts separated by an underscore character. The first part is the name of the object experiencing the event; the second part is the name of the event.

Statements can contain various types of things combined together in a way that follows VBA syntax rules. Some of the contents of statements are introduced in the next few sections.

Data Types

Many VBA statements contain data. Each item of data is of a specific type so that VBA knows how to handle it. The available data types are Byte, Boolean, Currency, Date, Decimal, Double, Integer, Long, Single, Object, String, and Variant. The String data type normally has variable length, but a fixed-length String data type is also available.

Detailed information about each of these data types is available in Microsoft Visual Basic Help.

Constants

A constant is a value (usually a number or text) that never changes. VBA contains many built-in (intrinsic) constants you can use within your code. All these constants are defined in Microsoft Visual Basic Help. To see these definitions, select the Contents tab and open the Visual Basic Language Reference book. Within that book, open the Constants book. There you see a list of topics, each of which contains information about a related group of constants. If, for example, you open the Color Constants topic, you see definitions of those constants, as shown in Figure A.5.

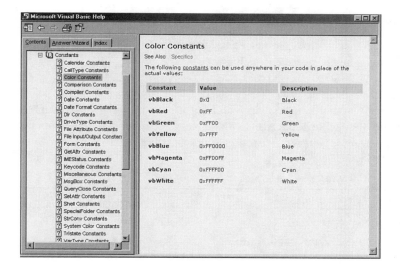

FIGURE A.5

Each of the VBA constants has a name starting with vb.

Each constant has a value that's meaningful to VBA. Instead of having to remember values, it's easier to use the names of constants within statements.

You can also create your own constants by writing a declaration statement such as

```
Const TAXRATE As Single = .07
```

This declaration creates the constant named TAXRATE as a Single data type and assigns a value to it. You can use any of the data types listed in the preceding section, "Data Types." If you omit the data type, VBA automatically uses Variant as the data type.

Constant declarations like this are normally placed so that they apply throughout an application, but that's not necessarily the case. See "Scope and Lifetime of Variables and Constants" subsequently in this appendix for more information on this point. By convention, all the characters in constant names are capitalized.

Variables

A variable is a named value that can change while a program runs. Variables are created in declaration statements such as

```
Dim intCounter As Integer
```

This statement creates a variable named `intCounter` as Integer data type. You can use any of the data types listed in the preceding section "Data Types." If you omit the data type, VBA automatically uses Variant as the data type.

Unlike in constant declarations, you can't assign a value in a variable declaration. Instead, you use a separate assignment statement such as

```
intCounter = 5
```

VBA automatically initializes variables with a specific value when you declare them. These initial values are defined in Table A.1. In that table, the Numeric variable type includes the Byte, Currency, Double, Integer, Long, and Single data types.

TABLE A.1 Initial Values of Variables

Variable Type	Initial Value
Numeric	0 (zero)
String	Zero-length string
Boolean	False
Object	Space reserved in memory and value set to Nothing

NOTE

A variable of variable-length string type is initialized as a zero-length string. A variable of fixed-length string type is filled with characters represented by the ASCII character code 0 (zero).

A variable is normally declared within a procedure and is available only within that procedure. See the subsequent section "Scope and Lifetime of Variables and Constants."

Visual Basic for Applications Primer

APPENDIX A

487

A

VISUAL BASIC FOR
APPLICATIONS
PRIMER

You don't necessarily have to declare variables, although there are several reasons why you should always do so. The code example shown in Figure A.2 contains the statement `Option Explicit` near the top of the module. When that statement is present, as it always should be, VBA insists that you declare all variables before you use them. If you omit Option Explicit, you can use variables without declaring them. This type of variable is known as an implicit variable, whereas declared variables are known as explicit variables. All variables implicitly declared are of type Variant.

Scope and Lifetime of Variables and Constants

The scope of a variable defines the places from which it is available. There are three levels of scope: procedure-level, private module-level, and public module-level. A variable that's available is said to be visible; a variable that's not available is said to be invisible.

A variable declared within a procedure has procedure-level (local) scope. That variable is visible only within the procedure in which it is declared. The statement

```
Dim intCounter As Integer
```

within a procedure declares a procedure-level variable.

A variable declared within a module, but not within one of that module's procedures, has private module-level scope by default. That variable is visible in any of the procedures in that module, but not in procedures in other modules. The declaration of that variable can begin with the keyword Private, but that isn't necessary. The statements

```
Dim intCounter As Integer
```

```
Private intCounter As Integer
```

are equivalent. Written within a module, but not within one of that module's procedures, these statements declare private module-level variables.

> **NOTE**
>
> Each module begins with a General Declarations section that can contain module-level variables.

A variable declared within a module, but not within one of that module's procedures, and with the keyword Public at the beginning of the declaration, has public module-level scope. That variable is visible in all procedures in all modules of the project. The statement

```
Public intCounter As Integer
```

written within a module, but not within one of that module's procedures, declares a public module-level variable.

It's good programming practice to give procedure-level scope to as many variables as possible.

The scope of constants is defined in the same manner as the scope of variables. Unlike variables, though, most constants are declared with public module-level scope.

The lifetime of a variable is the period during which it retains its value. Lifetime depends on the scope of a variable. Whenever a variable loses scope, it no longer has a value.

A procedure-level variable retains its value while the procedure running. Normally, a procedure-level variable loses its value at the end of that procedure. An exception to this is if the variable is declared with the keyword Static, as in

```
Static intCounter As Integer
```

In this case, the variable retains its value after the end of the procedure and while code in any module is running.

A module-level variable retains its value while any code is running.

Scope of Procedures

The section "Understanding VBA Structure," previously in this appendix, shows two examples of procedure declarations, each starting with the keyword Private. The use of this keyword makes a procedure available only in the module in which it is declared.

Instead of Private, a procedure declaration can start with the keyword Public. This makes the procedure available from all modules.

Understanding Functions

Some of the preceding sections of this appendix contain information about function procedures. These are procedures you write to provide the capabilities you need. Many times, though, you don't need to write function procedures because VBA has many built-in functions available for your use. By using these functions, you can greatly reduce the amount of VBA code you have to write.

Microsoft Visual Basic Help contains detailed information about all the built-in functions, as well as many examples of their use. To access this information, select the Contents tab, open the Visual Basic Language Reference book and, within that, open the Functions book. There, five books list the built-in functions alphabetically. Open one of these five books to see a list of functions. Select a function name to see information about that function. In most cases, you can choose Example just under a topic's heading to see one or more examples of how to use the function.

Visual Basic for Applications Primer

APPENDIX A

489

A

VISUAL BASIC FOR
APPLICATIONS
PRIMER

Many functions require some information in order to work. Consider the Len function, for example. This function finds the length of a string—how many characters it contains.

Using a Built-in Function

Let's put your laboratory to work to learn some things about functions in general and the Len function in particular. Proceed as follows:

1. Open the VBE window with the original procedure displayed.

2. Replace the original two statements within the procedure with six statements so that the complete procedure looks like this:

```
Private Sub Command0_Click
    Dim intReply As Integer
    Dim intLength As Integer
    Dim strText As String

    strText = "Charlie"
    intLength = Len(strText)
    intReply = MsgBox("Length of the text is " & intLength & "
➥characters.")
End Sub
```

The first three statements declare variables. The fourth statement assigns a value to the strText variable. Because this is a variable of type String, the value assigned to it must be a string. The quotation marks that enclose the value tell VBA that the value is a string.

The fifth statement demonstrates the use of the Len function. Clearly, the function needs to know what it's to find the length of. This information is known as an argument of the function. The argument is enclosed in parentheses after the function name. In this case, the argument is the name of the variable that contains text.

When the Len function runs, it finds the number of characters in the text and assigns that number to the variable intLength. Programmers refer to a function returning a value.

The final statement is merely a way to display the result of running the function. It's similar to the second statement in the original procedure.

This short procedure demonstrates several things, perhaps the most important of which is the value of VBA's built-in functions. Suppose the Len function didn't exist and you needed to include in your application a way to count the number of characters in some element of text. What would you do? You'd have to write your own function procedure to do that, something that would take some considerable effort. The lesson to be learned is, before writing a procedure, make sure that VBA doesn't already contain a function that does what you want to do.

Something else to understand is that you don't need to be concerned about how a function works. Just accept it and use it.

One more thing. Because a function returns a value, you must provide a variable to which the value is returned. That's even the case if you don't use the returned value value.

More About Arguments

The Len function that you used in the preceding section requires only one argument. Other functions require two or more arguments, some of which may be optional. When an argument is optional, VBA provides a default value for that argument if you don't provide a value.

Take the MsgBox function as an example. This function can have as many as five arguments, but only the first three of them are considered here. These three arguments define

- The message that appears in the message box
- The appearance of the message box, including the icon that's displayed
- Text that's displayed in the message box's title bar

Here's an example of a MsgBox function that has these three arguments :

```
intMsg = MsgBox("Hello!", vbInformation, "Sample")
```

Notice these points:

- All the arguments are enclosed within one pair of parentheses
- One argument is separated from the next by a comma
- The arguments must occur in the correct order

Just as many built-in functions have arguments, so can the procedures you write have arguments. For example, you could create a function that adds two numbers, although you should not do that because you can achieve the same objective by using an expression without placing that expression within a function. Here is such a function:

```
Private Function Adder(Value1, Value2)
    Adder = Value1 + Value2
End Function
```

The function declaration shows it requires two arguments—the two numbers to be added. The body of the function contains a single statement in which the value created by an expression is returned to a variable that is the name of the function.

You can call this function—that is, make it run—from within another procedure by using either of these statements

```
Adder intValA intValB
```

```
Call Adder(intValA, intValB)
```

Both statements have exactly the same effect. They both assume the variables intValA and IntValB are declared and have values assigned to them.

Visual Basic for Applications Primer

APPENDIX A

491

A

VISUAL BASIC FOR
APPLICATIONS
PRIMER

Expressions

An expression is a combination of variables, constants, functions, and operators that return a value. Chapter 15, "Calculating Values and Making Decisions," contains detailed information about expressions.

Controlling Program Flow

The statements in a procedure execute one after another unless you do something to control the order of statement execution. VBA provides several ways for you to control which statements are executed and the order in which those statements are executed. These are known as control structures or, colloquially, as constructs.

The next few sections provide basic information about some commonly used VBA control structures.

Controlling Which Statements Are Used

Quite frequently, you want some statements to run only if a certain condition is true. For example, you might want VBA to display a message box only in certain circumstances. You can use the If...End If control structure to do that. Here's an example:

```
If curBalance > 100 Then
    intMsg = MsgBox("You are delinquent.")
End If
```

This short example assumes the existence of a variable named curBalance that contains the value of an outstanding balance on an account. The first statement contains an expression that is either true or false. If that expression is true, the subsequent statements, as far as End If, are executed. If the expression is false, those statements aren't executed.

You can extend the If...End If control structure to provide an alternative, as shown in this example.

```
If curBalance > 100 Then
    intMsg = MsgBox("You are delinquent.")
Else
    intMsg = MsgBox("Your account is in good shape.")
End If
```

In this case, the first message is displayed if the condition in the first statement is true; the second message is displayed if the condition is false.

Although the preceding two examples show only one statement that gets executed, any number of statements can be executed if the condition is true, and another set of statements can be executed if the condition is false.

You can expand the If...End If control structure even more. For information about that, see the topic "If...Then...Else Statement" in Microsoft Visual Basic Help.

In circumstances where you want to take some action according to various values of a variable, you can use the Select Case control structure. Here's an example.

```
Select Case curBalance
    Case Is >200
        intMsg = MsgBox("You are very delinquent.")
    Case 100 To 200
        intMsg = MsgBox("You are delinquent.")
    Case 1 To 100
        intMsg = MsgBox("Please pay what you owe.")
    Case 0
        intMsg = MsgBox("You owe nothing.")
    Case Else
        intMsg = MsgBox("You have overpaid.")
End Select
```

The Select Case control structure begins with the Select Case statement that names a variable; curBalance, in the example. The structure ends with the End Select statement. Within the structure, there can be as many Case statements as needed, each one identifying a value for the variable. The value can be expressed in several ways, including

- Case followed by a value, such as Case 0
- Case followed by a range of values, such as Case 100 To 200
- Case Is followed a relational operator and a value, such as Case Is >200
- Case Else without a value

The example here shows numerical values. The structure can also evaluate other types of values such as strings and dates. There can be as many statements under each Case statement as required.

When a Select Case control structure is encountered, VBA scans down the Case statements until it finds one that matches the value of the variable. It then executes the statements under that value up to, but not including, the next Case statement. At that point, the statement following the End Select statement is executed.

The Case Else statement isn't required, but usually is included. Statements under Case Else are executed only if the variable doesn't match the condition in all the preceding Case statements.

For more information about the Select Case...End Select control structure, see the topic "Select Case Statement" in Microsoft Visual Basic Help.

Visual Basic for Applications Primer

APPENDIX A

493

A

VISUAL BASIC FOR
APPLICATIONS
PRIMER

Repeating Statements with a `For...Next` Structure

It's often necessary to repeat consecutive statements several or many times. VBA provides several ways to do so, one of which is the For...Next control structure. Here's an example.

```
Dim intCounter As Integer
Dim intSum As Integer
Dim intMsg As Integer

For intCounter = 1 To 50
    intSum = intSum + intCounter
Next intCounter

intMsg = MsgBox("The sum is " & intSum)
```

This For...Next structure calculates the sum of the numbers in the range 1 through 50. The first three statements declare three variables. The fourth, fifth, and sixth statements form a For...Next control structure. The last statement displays the result in a message box.

A For...Next structure starts with a For statement and ends with a Next statement. The For statement contains a variable (intCounter in this example) that controls the number of times the statements between the For and Next statements are executed. The variable is defined to have a range of values.

The first time the statements are executed, the variable in the For statement has the first value in the range; the second time the statements are executed, the variable has the second value in the range, and so on. The statements are executed with each value in the range specified for the variable.

By default, the variable in the For statement increases by one at a time. You can specify a different increment by writing a statement such as

```
For intCounter = 1 To 50 Step 3
```

which causes the variable to increment by three. In this case, the statements between the For and Next statements are executed with the variable having values of 1, 4, 7, and so on, up to a maximum value of 49. Execution stops at that point because the next increment gives the variable a value of 52, which is greater than the maximum value in the specified range.

You can specify a negative step value, but in that case take care to make the beginning value in the range more positive than the ending value. If you don't do that, you'll get an invalid result.

Interrupting a `For...Next` Structure

A For...Next structure doesn't have to run to completion. You can interrupt it using an Exit For statement, as in this example:

```
Dim intCounter As Integer
Dim intSum As Integer
Dim intMsg As Integer

For intCounter = 1 To 50
    intSum = intSum + intCounter
    If intSum > 200 Then
        Exit For
    End If
Next intCounter

intMsg = MsgBox("The sum is " & intSum)
```

In this case, the If...End If structure repeatedly tests the value of intSum and, when that value exceeds 200, immediately executes Exit For, so that the statement after the Next statement is executed.

In addition to showing how you can prematurely exit from a For...Next structure, this example illustrates nesting one control structure within another.

Repeating Statements with a Do While...Loop Structure

Another way to repeat a block of statements until a specific condition occurs is to use a Do While...Loop control structure, as in this example:

```
Dim intSum As Integer
Dim intCount As Integer
Dim intMsg As Integer

Do While intSum < 200
    intSum = intSum + intCount
    intCount = intCount + 1
Loop

intMsg = MsgBox("The sum is " & intSum)
```

This example produces the same result as the preceding For...Next structure and has the advantage of being somewhat simpler.

The structure starts with a Do While statement and ends with a Loop statement. The first time the structure is encountered, the value of intSum is evaluated and if it is less than 200, the block of statements as far as the Loop statements is executed. Notice that the first of these statements increases the value of intSum. The Loop statement causes execution to loop back to the Do While statement, where the intSum is again evaluated. This process continues until the condition in the Do While statement is false, at which time the statement after the Loop statement is executed.

Visual Basic for Applications Primer

APPENDIX A

495

A

VISUAL BASIC FOR
APPLICATIONS
PRIMER

It's possible to prematurely execute from the structure by including an Exit Do statement within the block of statements. This is similar to including an Exit For statement in a For...Next structure, as explained in the preceding section.

Repeating Statements with a `Do Until...Loop` Structure

A Do Until...Look structure is similar to a Do While...Loop structure, as shown in this example.

```
Dim intSum As Integer
Dim intCount As Integer
Dim intMsg As Integer

Do Until intSum > 200
    intSum = intSum + intCount
    intCount = intCount + 1
Loop

intMsg = MsgBox("The sum is " & intSum)
```

Whereas a Do While statement states a condition that must be true in order for the block of statements to run, a Do Until statement states a condition that must be false for the block of statements to run. Otherwise, Do While...Loop and Do Until...Loop structures are identical.

Repeating Statements with `Do...Loop While` and `Do...Loop Until` Structures

One of the things to notice about a Do While...Loop structure is that it's possible for the block of statements never to run. This occurs when the condition in the Do While statement is false the first time that statement is executed. You'll come across occasions when you want a block of statements always to be executed at least once. In these cases, you can use a Do...Loop While structure, such as

```
Dim intSum As Integer
Dim intCount As Integer
Dim intMsg As Integer

Do
    intSum = intSum + intCount
    intCount = intCount + 1
Loop While intSum < 200

intMsg = MsgBox("The sum is " & intSum)
```

In this case, the intSum isn't evaluated until after the block of statements has been executed. For that reason, the block of statements is always executed at least once, even if the condition in the Loop While statement is initially false.

The Do...Loop Until structure is similar, as in

```
Dim intSum As Integer
Dim intCount As Integer
Dim intMsg As Integer

Do
    intSum = intSum + intCount
    intCount = intCount + 1
Loop Until intSum > 200

intMsg = MsgBox("The sum is " & intSum)
```

Making Your VBA Code Easy to Understand

The examples of VBA code in this section are short and, I hope, fairly easy to understand. Inevitably, code you write in your applications will contain several or many procedures, most containing many more statements than in these examples. It's very important you do everything you can to make your code as easy as possible for people to understand. That's because, in all probability, requirements will change so that you or someone else will have to modify the code at some time in the future.

Commenting Your Code

There are several techniques you can use to make your code easy to read, one of the most important being the proper use of comments (sometimes called remarks). Comments are text that explains the purpose of sections of code and individual statements. Comments have no effect on how the code runs; they are there only for the benefit of people who need to understand the code.

With one exception, VBA regards all text to the right of a single quotation mark as a comment. The exception is when a single quotation mark occurs within a string. In that case, the single quotation mark is understood to be a character within the string.

Some comments are on lines by themselves. These lines start with a single quotation mark. Other comments occur to the right of a statement. After the last character of a statement, enter a few spaces (or one or more tabs), enter a single quotation mark, and then type your comment.

Some of the uses of comments are

- To identify the person who wrote the code and the date the code was written
- To identify the person who made any change to the code, the date that change was made, and the reason for the change
- To explain the overall purpose of each module

Visual Basic for Applications Primer

APPENDIX A

497

A

VISUAL BASIC FOR
APPLICATIONS
PRIMER

- To explain the purpose of each procedure
- To explain the significance of each declared constant
- To explain the purpose of each declared variable
- To explain the purpose of blocks of code where that purpose might not be self-evident

It's not necessary or advisable to provide comments for every statement. For example, you shouldn't write comments to explain your use of built-in constants, built-in functions, control structures, and so on, unless you've used them in some way that might not be apparent.

The time to write comments is while you're writing the code. When you're writing code, it's often tempting to put off providing comments until the code is complete. You shouldn't do that, for at least two reasons:

- When the code is complete, in all probability you'll be too busy starting on another project to have time to go back and insert comments. The result is that comments don't get written.
- By the time you finish the code, you're likely to have forgotten reasons for some of that code. As a result, your comments will miss some important points.

Indenting and Spacing Your Code

The code examples throughout this book make use of indenting code from the left margin so that it's easy to see what belongs together.

All lines of code within a control structure should be indented so what is within that structure is obvious at a glance.

SQL Primer

IN THIS APPENDIX

SQL (pronounced as the letters S Q L, or as the word "sequel") stands for *Structured Query Language*, a language that interacts with relational databases. SQL is used by Access to control the Jet data engine and the Microsoft Data Engine (MSDE). Jet provides access to native Access and other databases. MSDE provides access to SQL Server databases as well as to a simulated SQL Server database on the local computer.

SQL is the language of relational databases. You can do a lot of work in Access without knowing anything about SQL, but SQL is there in the background. Access automatically creates SQL code from all the queries you create. It is the SQL code that does the work, not the actual query.

You need to become familiar with SQL for two reasons:

- You sometimes need to interact with a database in ways that are beyond the capabilities of queries, but can be achieved by writing SQL code.
- When working with large databases with many tables, you can eliminate the need for a large number of queries by incorporating SQL code within VBA.

Each SQL statement consists of several clauses, and each clause is introduced by a keyword. Although clauses are quite simple in concept, their interaction provides a powerful means of working with databases.

When you create a query within Access, you are, in fact, constructing SQL code. It's the SQL code that controls how Access interacts with the database. The QBE grid provides an easy-to-understand picture of how Access interacts with the database. The SQL code that the QBE grid represents actually controls the interaction.

In many cases, you don't need to be concerned with SQL code because the QBE grid is sufficient. However, the further you get into developing Access-based applications, the more likely it is you'll have to become involved with SQL code. This occurs when

- The QBE grid can't provide the interaction with data you need
- You want to create union queries
- You want to create subqueries
- You need to construct SQL code programmatically to avoid creating a large number of queries

This appendix provides the basic knowledge of SQL code you need to deal with these situations. In addition, the more you know about SQL, the better you'll understand queries in Access.

SQL is defined by the ANSI standard X3.135-1992 (often referred to as ANSI SQL92). SQL, as used in Access, closely but not completely, follows this standard. This appendix describes SQL as used in Access.

This appendix provides only an initial glimpse at SQL, but is probably enough to make you comfortable in understanding how SQL works. You can find more information about SQL in Access Help topics, and many articles about SQL are available in the Microsoft Knowledge Base. For further reading, see Appendix C, "Information Resources for Access 2000."

SQL Statements for Select Queries

The fastest way to learn SQL is to create simple, then increasingly complex, queries in Access and then choose View, SQL View to display the equivalent SQL code. Access doesn't provide any direct way to print SQL code, but you can copy SQL code to the Clipboard and then paste it into a text editor or word processor from which you can print it.

Selecting Fields

Each Access query creates a SQL statement. For example, if you create a Query window, place a single table in the upper pane, drag one field from that table onto the QBE grid, and choose View, SQL View, you'll see an SQL statement such as

```
SELECT tblBook.strTitle
FROM tblBook;
```

that illustrates some facets of SQL syntax.

- A SQL statement consists of clauses, and each clause begins with a keyword. This example contains the keywords SELECT and FROM. The SQL language is not case-sensitive, but it is conventional to make keywords all uppercase. SQL statements generated by Access from queries adhere to this convention.

- A clause contains one or more items known as parameters. Both clauses in this example contain a single parameter.

- Each clause is separated from the next by one or more spaces.

- An entire SQL statement is terminated by a semicolon.

Access usually starts each clause in a SQL statement on a new line, but line breaks have no significance within a SQL statement. The previous SQL statement could just as well be written as

```
SELECT tblBook.strTitle FROM tblBook;
```

A SQL statement created by Access shows the source of each field together with the field name, with the source separated from the field name by a period. SQL doesn't require you to include the source in the SELECT parameters because the source is defined in the FROM clause. The previous SQL statement could be

```
SELECT strTitle FROM tblBook;
```

It's usually good practice to include the sources of fields in SELECT clause parameters to avoid any chance of ambiguity.

Even though the source of a field is included in SELECT clause parameters, SQL requires a FROM clause. The FROM clause is, in effect, defining what's in the upper pane of the Query window. Just as you can't create a query without a table in the upper pane of the Query window, so you can't create a SQL SELECT statement without a FROM clause.

> **NOTE**
>
> You might often see field names and table names in SQL statements enclosed within brackets. Brackets are required if a field name includes spaces, punctuation marks, and other symbols. Access automatically encloses field names within brackets when they are required and often when they are not required. It is never wrong to enclose field names and table names within brackets, even when the brackets are not required.

If you add more fields to the QBE grid and look again at the equivalent SQL statement, you'll see a SELECT clause that contains several parameters, such as

```
SELECT tblBook.strTitle, tblBook.strFname, tblBook.strLname
FROM tblBook;
```

This illustrates that one parameter is separated from the next by a comma. Note that the final parameter in a clause is not followed by a comma.

The SELECT clause contains the names of the fields in the QBE grid for which Show is checked. If you uncheck Show for a field in the QBE grid and look again at the SQL statement, you'll see the SELECT clause no longer contains that field.

Aliasing Fields

An aliased field is a field in the QBE grid or in a SQL statement that has a name that's not in the underlying table. This happens when you create a field in the QBE grid by combining two or more fields from a table. For example a Field cell in the QBE grid could contain

```
Author: strLname & ", " & strFname
```

to combine two fields. Notice that the alias is a name at the beginning of the cell followed by a colon.

The corresponding SQL format

```
Select tblBook.strLname & "," & tblBook.strFname AS Author
```

uses the AS keyword to indicate the alias.

When Access converts an aliased field to SQL code, it creates

```
Select [tblBook].[strLname] & "," & [tblBook].[strFname] AS Author
```

although the brackets are not strictly required.

Sorting Fields

A SQL statement can contain an ORDER BY clause to control the order in which the statement sorts fields. If you mark one field in the QBE grid for ascending sort order and another field for descending sort order and switch to SQL View, you'll see something like

```
SELECT tblBook.strTitle, tblBook.strFname, tblBook.strLname
FROM tblBook
ORDER BY tblBook.strTitle, tblBook.strLname DESC;
```

The ORDER BY clause contains one or more parameters that determine the sort order, with the parameters listed in priority order. Each parameter in an ORDER BY clause can be followed by one of these keywords:

- ASC   Sort in ascending order
- DESC   Sort in descending order

If a parameter is followed by neither of these keywords, ascending order is assumed.

Setting Criteria

A SQL statement can contain a WHERE clause that contains a criterion, as shown in this example:

```
SELECT tblBook.strTitle, tblBook.strFname, tblBook.strLname
FROM tblBook
WHERE tblBook.curPrice<30
ORDER BY tblBook.strTitle, tblBook.strLname DESC;
```

The WHERE clause in this example defines the criterion in which the tblBook.curPrice field contains a value less than 30.

For some reason, WHERE clauses created by Access contain unnecessary parentheses. For example, the WHERE clause as created by Access in this example appears as

```
WHERE (((tblBook.curPrice)<30))
```

You can delete these parentheses by editing the SQL code.

Joining Tables

In the QBE grid, you can join tables by dragging from a field in one table to a related field in another table. Most joins are equi joins in which the related fields in the two tables must have the same value. SQL refers to these as inner joins.

A typical inner join, as created by Access, is

```
SELECT tblBook.strTitle, tblPublisher.strName
FROM tblBook INNER JOIN tblPublisher
ON tblBook.lngPublisherID = tblPublisher.lngPubID;
```

NOTE

The SQL code created by Access combines the second and third lines of this statement into one line. As previously mentioned, line breaks have no significance within a SQL statement. I've split the single line into two lines to clarify the structure.

In this statement, the SELECT clause names two fields, each in a different table.

The FROM clause is somewhat more complex than what you saw before in this appendix. The clause names two tables and shows they are connected by an inner join. The part of the clause after the ON keyword defines the condition for the join; in this case, the condition for the join is that the value in the lngPublisherID field in the tblBook table is equal to the value of the lngPubID field in the tblPublisher table. In other words, the statement matches the value of a record's lngPublisherID field (a foreign key) in the tblBook table to the value of the lngPubID field (the primary key) in the tblPublisher table.

SQL Statements for Action Queries

Access can create four types of action queries: Append, Delete, Make-Table, and Update. Each of these creates SQL statements similar to those created by Select queries.

Make-Table Queries

A Make-Table query creates a new table containing some data from an existing table. A typical query of this type identifies some fields in the existing table to be copied to the new table and specifies a criterion for selecting records.

A SQL statement for a typical Make-Table query that creates a new table in the current database is

```
SELECT tblPublisher.strName, tblPublisher.strPhone INTO tblNew
FROM tblPublisher
WHERE tblPublisher.strCountry="USA";
```

The only difference between this statement and a SELECT statement is the addition of the INTO keyword in the SELECT clause. The INTO keyword is followed by the name of the new table.

A typical SQL statement that creates a new table in another database is

```
SELECT tblPublisher.strName, tblPublisher.strPhone INTO tblNew IN 'db12.mdb'
FROM tblPublisher
WHERE tblPublisher.strCountry="USA";
```

Here, the IN keyword is followed by the name of the other existing database in which the new table is to be created. Notice that the name of the database is enclosed in single quotation marks. The database must already exist. If the target database is in a different folder from the source, the IN clause must contain the full pathname of the target folder.

Append Queries

An Append query adds records from one or more tables into one or more other tables.

A typical SQL statement that appends fields from one table to another within the same database is

```
INSERT INTO tblNew (strName, strPhone, strWeb)
SELECT tblPublisher.strName, tblPublisher.strPhone, tblPublisher.strWeb
FROM tblPublisher;
```

The INSERT INTO clause specifies the name of the table into which records are to be appended. The names of the fields in that table are listed after the table name. Notice that the list of field names is enclosed within parentheses.

The SELECT clause specifies the source of the fields to be appended. The number of fields in the INSERT INTO and SELECT clauses must be the same; the names of the fields can be different. The order of the field names in both clauses is important. The first field in the SELECT clause is appended into the first field in the INSERT INTO clause without regard to field names; the second field in the SELECT clause is appended into the second field in the INSERT INTO clause, and so on.

If the records are to be appended into a database other than the current database, the INTO keyword is added to the INSERT INTO clause in a manner similar to that described in the preceding section for a Make-Table statement.

Delete Queries

A Delete query deletes specified records from a table. A typical SQL statement that deletes records is

```
DELETE tblPublisher.*, tblPublisher.strCountry
FROM tblPublisher
WHERE tblPublisher.strCountry="UK";
```

This statement deletes all records from the tblPublisher table in which the strCountry field has the value UK.

The DELETE clause contains tblPublisher.* to include all fields. The clause also contains the name of the field used in the WHERE clause.

Update Queries

An Update query changes the data in specific records. A typical SQL statement that updates records is

```
UPDATE tblPublisher SET tblPublisher.strPhone = "317-581-3500"
WHERE tblPublisher.strName="Macmillan USA";
```

This statement updates the strPhone field in the tblPublisher table for all records in which the value in the strName field is Macmillan USA.

The UPDATE clause specifies the name of the table to be updated. In this clause, the SET keyword is followed by an expression that states the new value of a specific field. The WHERE clause specifies which records in the table are to be updated.

SQL Statements for Union Queries

The preceding sections in this appendix contain examples of SQL statements that correspond to Access queries defined in the QBE grid. However, the QBE grid allows you to create only commonly used SQL statements. SQL is capable of doing much more than that. One example of that is the creation of Union queries.

You can use a Union query to combine one or more Select queries. Here's an example of a Union query:

```
SELECT tblBook.strTitle, tblBook.strCategory, tblBook.strLname
FROM tblBook
WHERE tblBook.strCategory Like "Biography"
UNION
SELECT tblBook.strTitle, tblBook.strCategory, tblBook.strLname
FROM tblBook
WHERE tblBook.strLname="Michener";
```

As you can see, this Union query uses the UNION keyword to combine two separate Select statements. The terminating semicolon occurs only at the end of the complete statement.

Information Resources for Access 2000

IN THIS APPENDIX

There are many sources of information available to you to find out more about Access and creating applications based on Access. These include books, the Microsoft Knowledge Base, Web sites supported by other companies and individuals, magazines, and newsgroups.

Books

The following is a list of books, arranged in alphabetical order by title, that contain additional information about using Access 2000 and creating applications based on Access 2000. I'm certainly not recommending you buy all these books. Some of them might be too elementary for your needs and others might be too advanced. You'll find some recommendations after the list.

Access 2000 Developer's Black Book. Technology Press, 1999. ISBN 1-57610-349-8.

Access 2000 Developer's Handbook. Sybex, 1999. ISBN 0-7821-2370-8.

Access 2000 Programming Blue Book. Technology Press, 1999. ISBN 11-57610-328-5.

Access 2000 Programming from the Ground Up. Osborne, 1999. ISBN 0-70-882575-X.

Designing Relational Database Systems. Microsoft Press, 1999. ISBN 0-7356-0634-X.

How to Use Microsoft Access 2000. Sams, 1999. ISBN 0-672-31491-2.

Mastering Microsoft Access 2000 Development. Sams, 1999. ISBN 0-672-31484-3.

Microsoft Office 2000 Visual Basic Programmer's Guide. Microsoft Press, 1999. ISBN 1-57231-952-6.

Programming Microsoft Access 2000. Microsoft Press, 1999. ISBN 0-7356-0500-9.

Sams Teach Yourself Microsoft Access 2000 in 21 Days. Sams, 1999. ISBN 0-672-31292-1.

Sams Teach Yourself Microsoft Access 2000 in 24 Hours. Sams, 1999. ISBN 0-672-31289-1.

Sams Teach Yourself Microsoft Access 2000 Programming in 24 Hours. Sams, 1999. ISBN 0-672-31661-7.

Sams Teach Yourself SQL in 10 Minutes. Sams, 2000. ISBN 0-672-31664-1.

Sams Teach Yourself SQL in 21 Days, Third Edition. Sams, 1999. ISBN 0-672-31674-9.

Sams Teach Yourself SQL in 24 Hours. Sams, 1998. ISBN 0-672-31245-X.

Sams Teach Yourself VBScript in 21 Days. Sams, 1996. ISBN 0-57521-120-3.

Special Edition Using Microsoft Access 2000. Que, 1999. ISBN 0-7897-1606-2.

VBA for Microsoft Office 2000 Unleashed. Sams, 1999. ISBN 0-672-31567-X.

VBScript Programmer's Reference. Wrox, 1999. ISBN 1-8610-0271-8.

Recommendations

This book assumes you are fairly familiar with using Access. If you need to fill in some of the details, *Special Edition Using Microsoft Access 2000* is a good resource, although it's somewhat overwhelming. If you need a book to recommend to beginning Access users, you can't do better than suggest *How to Use Microsoft Access 2000*.

If you're new to Access 2000 programming, *Access 2000 Programming from the Ground Up* will get you started. After that, if you really want to become an expert, take a look at *Programming Microsoft Access 2000*. If you want to expand your knowledge of VBA programming to cover not just Access, but all the Office applications, you can't do better than to put aside many hours to read *VBA for Microsoft Office 2000 Unleashed*.

Designing all but the simplest Access-based applications requires at least some understanding of relational databases. I've found *Designing Relational Database Systems* to be very readable and practical. What's more, most of that book is written with Access in mind.

The World Wide Web and Periodicals

There are many other sources of information about Access besides published books. One of the best is Microsoft's Knowledge Base, which you can access on the Web at `http://search.support.microsoft.com/kb/c.asp`. There, you can select Access 2000 (or another Microsoft product) and ask a question. The site returns a list of Knowledge Base articles from which you can select, view on your screen, and print. There are hundreds of articles about Access 2000 available, and more are added almost daily. Each article is identified by a sequential number.

TIP

If you don't find what you want for Access 2000 in the Microsoft Knowledge Base, try looking for Access 97 articles. Many of those articles apply also to Access 2000.

Another good source of information on the Web is `http://visualbasic.about.com/compute/visualbasic/`. That site contains many references to information about Access, database development, VBA, and VBScript.

Take a look at the monthly magazine *Visual Basic Programmer's Journal*. Don't be put off by its name. Each issue contains articles of interest to beginning, intermediate, advanced, and expert programmers who use Visual Basic and its dialects, such as VBA. The magazine's publisher, Fawcette Technical Publications, maintains the Web site `http://www.devx.com` that contains a wealth of information that could be of use to you.

Don't forget your friendly search engine. When I'm looking for technical information, my first choice is AltaVista (`http://www.altavista.com`). While writing this page, I opened AltaVista and submitted a search request for "Microsoft Access 2000". The engine told me it found 6,600 pages! Of course, only a few of these are of interest to me, but it's worth taking a look. There's a lot of free information available on the Web. You just have to find it.

Newsgroups

Newsgroups you can access on the Internet are discussion areas in which you can ask questions and receive answers to those questions from whomever feels like responding. If you haven't already used newsgroups, you'll be surprised how quickly you receive useful answers, often several, to the questions you ask.

Most newsgroups are supported by volunteers. If you ask a question about Access, for example, the replies you receive come from people like yourself. The people who answer your questions are mostly not Microsoft employees. Even if they are Microsoft employees, they're acting on their own behalf, not as Microsoft employees.

Here, I'll cover only the newsgroups sponsored by Microsoft. Many other newsgroups sponsored by other companies and individuals are available.

To get information about the Microsoft-sponsored newsgroups, go to `http://support.microsoft.com/support/news/`. There, you find a list of subjects, one of which is Microsoft Office Family of Products. Click that subject to display a subordinate list of topics, one of which is Access. Click that to display a list of newsgroups, each of which focuses on a specific aspect of Access. At the time I wrote this, 22 newsgroups were available. By the time you read this, there are probably more.

If you have Office 2000 installed on your computer, click any newsgroup. Outlook Express opens and downloads recent messages in that newsgroup. You can learn a lot by looking at the questions people have recently asked and the replies they've received. You can ask your own question by choosing New Post. Out of courtesy to the people who answer questions, please review the existing questions and answers before you ask a question. As one of the people who answer questions on newsgroups, I don't appreciate receiving a question to which I posted an answer a couple of days ago. Try to spend 30 minutes each day scanning the newsgroups that interest you. You'll be amazed at what you learn.

Glossary

This glossary contains definitions of words and abbreviations as used throughout this book and in other sources of information about databases and database applications. Italicized words and phrases within definitions are defined in this glossary.

You can find additional definitions of terms in the Microsoft Access 2000 Glossary topic in Microsoft Access Help.

Access Data Project (ADP)   A front-end for SQL Server databases. See *front end*.

Access Run Time   A component of Microsoft Office Developer (MOD) you can use to enable people who don't have Access installed on their computers to run Access applications.

action query   A query that copies or changes data in one or more tables. Action queries can append records to tables, delete records from tables, and update records in tables.

ActiveX   A set of technologies that enables software components to interact with one another.

ActiveX Data Object (ADO)   An object that represents the structure of a database and the data contained in that database.

ad hoc report   A report created by an application user, rather than a report that's built into the application.

ADO   See *ActiveX Data Object*.

ADP   See *Access Data Project*.

alias   An alternative name assigned to an object.

application   Software that's used to achieve a specific objective or set of related objectives.

archive   Data not currently in use that's copied to a separate medium for safe storage.

argument   Data supplied to a procedure.

arithmetic operator   A symbol representing an elementary arithmetic operation such as addition, subtraction, multiplication, division, and exponentiation.

assign   To give a value to a variable.

assignment   A statement that gives a value to a variable.

attribute   A fact about an entity. For example, one of the attributes of the Book entity is Publication Date. See *entity*.

Automation   The ability of applications to expose their object libraries for use by other applications. Previously known as OLE Automation.

Automation controller   An application that can use objects in an object library exposed by another application.

Automation server   An application that exposes its object library for use by other applications.

AutoNumber data dype   A field data type that automatically assigns a unique number to a record.

backup   Data copied to a medium from which it can be recovered if the working data becomes corrupted.

bind   To connect a form or report to data in a table or data resulting from a query. Also, to connect a control on a form or report to a field in a table or recordset.

Bookmark   A long integer that references a record in a recordset.

Boolean operator   See *logical operator*.

breakpoint   An executable statement within VBA code that's marked to pause execution. When the code is displayed, the current status can be examined and that status can be modified.

call   To cause a procedure to execute.

cardinality   The number of tuples in a relation. More colloquially, the number of records in a table. See *tuple* and *relation*.

Check Box control   A control that can be placed on a form to provide a choice between two values.

check digit   A digit in a field that provides some verification that other characters in the field are valid.

class   A model that defines all the properties, methods, and responses to events for a data type.

class module   A code module containing the VBA code that responds to form or report events, or containing a definition of a new object.

code   One or more statements in a programming language such as Visual Basic for Applications.

coercion   Changing data from one data type to another.

collection   A group of objects of the same class.

column   In a table, the values of a specific field.

COM   See *Component Object Model*.

Combo Box control   A control that can be placed on a form to provide a choice between preset values and, optionally, the creation of a new value.

Command Button control   A control that can be placed on a form to trigger the execution of a procedure.

comment   Explanatory text within code. Comments have no effect on the execution of the code. VBA interprets all text to the right of a single quotation mark (') on a line as a comment.

Comparison operator   An operator that compares one value with another.

Component Object Model (COM)   A specification for building software components that can be assembled into programs running under Windows.

concatenate   To combine two or more elements of text.

connection   The operation of connecting Access to a specific set of tables.

constant   A named memory location used to store a value that cannot change during the execution of code. Also a value built into Access. Each constant is used for a value of a specific data type.

construct   See *control structure*.

control   An object on a form, report, or data access page that's used to enter or display information.

control structure   In the Visual Basic for Applications language and other languages, a method for controlling the flow of program execution.

Currency field   A field that contains a monetary value in a table.

cursor   A mechanism that returns records and defines how those records can be used.

DAO   See *Data Access Object*.

data   Raw facts and figures that can processed to provide information.

Data Access Object (DAO)   An object that represents the structure of a database and the data it contains. Data Access Objects interact with the Jet database engine. See *Jet*.

Data Access Page   An HTML document that can be directly bound to an Access table or recordset.

data dictionary   A definition of a database that describes tables and the fields within those tables. A data dictionary may also contain more detailed information about a database.

data model   A conceptual description of the data contained in, and manipulated by, a database application.

data type   The type of data that a variable or field can contain. Within the Access environment, the available data types include Text, Number, Currency, and Yes/No.

database   An application used to store and retrieve data. A database consists of one or more tables, a mechanism to add data, edit data, and display or print information derived from data in the tables.

database diagram   A visual representation of a database.

database engine   A software component that manipulates data. Jet and SQL Server are examples of database engines.

datasheet   Data displayed in a row and column format.

Date/Time field   A field that contains dates, times, or both.

declaration   A statement that names a variable or constant and, optionally, assigns a data type to it. A declaration can also create a custom data type.

declare   To create a variable, give it a name, and optionally define a data type for it.

debug   The process of examining the functionality of an application and correcting errors in that functionality.

default   A value or option Access assumes if a user hasn't chosen a specific value or option.

degree   The number of attributes in a relation. More colloquially, the number of columns in a table. See *attribute* and *relation*.

design time   The time during which an application is being created. Contrast with *run time*.

Design view   The image Access displays while you're creating (designing) an application, as opposed to while you're using an application. In the Design view of a table, you can create and modify fields in that table. In the Design view of a form, you can designate the controls that appear on the form.

domain   All possible values an attribute may have. See *attribute*. Domain, used in this context, has nothing to do with the use of the same word within the context of a Windows NT Server environment.

dynaset   A recordset that's dynamically linked to underlying tables. Any changes made to fields in a dynaset affect the fields in the underlying tables. See *recordset*.

empty   The condition of a VBA variable that has been declared but to which a value has not been assigned. See *null* and *zero-length string*.

entity   A thing about which a database stores data. In an application that manages a collection of books, Book and Publisher are entities. Each entity has data items known as attributes. See *attribute*.

enumerate   To list the members of a collection. See *collection*.

equi-join   A join between tables in which the values in the related fields are compared for equality and in which all records in both tables are displayed. See *join*.

Err object   An object that defines the nature of a run-time error. See *run-time error*.

error   See *syntax error*, *logic error*, and *run-time error*.

error handler   Program code that runs when a run-time error occurs. See *run-time error*.

error trap   Program code that detects a run-time error. See *run-time error*.

event   Something that happens and is recognized by an application such as Access so that an appropriate action can be taken. Typical events are a key being pressed, a button being clicked, and an object being activated.

event procedure   A *procedure* that runs when an *event* occurs. For example, when a command button on a form is clicked, the procedure for that button's click event runs.

expression   A combination of constants, variables, operators, and functions that, when evaluated, results in a value.

Expression Builder   A component of Access that provides help in creating expressions. See *expression*.

field   A component of a *table* that contains data of a specific type. Tables usually contain many fields.

field type   The type of data that a field or a database *table* can contain. The field types in Access are *Text*, *Memo*, *Number*, *Date/Time*, *Currency*, *AutoNumber*, *Yes/No*, *OLE Object*, and *Hyperlink*.

focus   The ability of an object to receive input from a user. Only one object at a time can have the focus.

footer   Text that appears at the bottom of every page of a report. See *header*.

Form   A database object, usually displayed on the screen, containing controls used to initiate actions, display information, or enter information.

foreign key   A field in a table, or set of fields, the value of which must match a primary key in another table to which the table is related. See *key* and *primary key*.

front end   An application that enables users to interact with a database.

function   A procedure that returns a value. See *function procedure* and *procedure*. Access includes built-in functions that can be supplemented by user-defined functions written as function procedures.

function procedure   A user-defined procedure that returns a value. Function procedures can be used in other procedures and in expressions. Contrast with *sub procedure*.

global   Something accessible from anywhere within an application, as contrasted with *local*. A global variable or constant is available throughout an application, whereas a local variable or constant is available only within the environment in which it's declared.

header   Text that appears at the top of every page of a report. See *footer*.

hyperlink   Text on a form that can be clicked to jump to a file, a location in a file, or an HTML page on the Web or an intranet.

Hyperlink field   In an Access database, a field of Hyperlink data type used to store hyperlink addresses. In an Access project, a field of Char, Nchar, Nvarchar, or Varchar data type used to store hyperlink addresses.

Immediate window   A Visual Basic Editor window that can display values of variables and be used to run Visual Basic for Applications code.

Indexed Sequential Access Method (ISAM)   A method of minimizing the time required to locate records in a database. Databases that use this method are known as ISAM databases. dBASE, FoxPro, and Paradox are examples of ISAM databases.

instance   An object created from a class. The class defines the object. Multiple instances of a class can be created from the same class.

intrinsic   Something that's defined within Access and, therefore, can be used without being defined within an application. Access has intrinsic constants and intrinsic functions.

ISAM   See *Indexed Sequential Access Method*.

Jet   See *Joint Engine Technology*.

join   The process of establishing a relationship between tables.

Joint Engine Technology (Jet)   A data store used by Access and other Microsoft applications. The Jet data store can be accessed by *DAO* and *ADO*.

junction table   A table that's joined to two other tables by one-to-many relationships to create a many-to-many relationship.

key   A field that identifies a complete record by the value of that field. See *foreign key* and *primary key*.

keyword   A word that has a specific meaning within the Access environment. You cannot use a keyword as a variable or constant name. Also known as a reserved word.

Label control   A control that places specific text on a form or report.

library   A collection of functions often associated with a specific application. A library that's part of one application can be referenced by another application.

lifetime   The period during which a variable exists.

Line control   A control that places a straight line on a form or report.

link   To enable Access to use information in an external file. The external file may be another Access file or may be a file in another format.

List Box control   A control on a form or report that contains a list of values.

local   Existing only within a procedure. A variable declared within a procedure is local.

Locals window   A Visual Basic Editor window that automatically displays the values of all declared variables in the current procedure.

logic error   An error in program code that results in an incorrect calculation or decision.

logical operator A symbol representing an elementary logical operation such as And, Or, and Not. Also known as a Boolean operator.

macro A set of actions, each of which performs a specific operation.

many-to-many A relationship between two tables in which each record in the first table can be related to many records in the second table, and in which each record in the second table can be related to many records in the first table. For example, one teacher can have many students and one student can have many teachers. See *junction table*.

Memo field A data type that can contain up to 65,535 characters.

method A built-in procedure that can operate on specific objects.

Microsoft Data Engine (MSDE) A technology that provides local data storage that's compatible with SQL Server.

Microsoft Office Developer (MOD) The top-of-the-line edition of Office 2000 that contains tools and utilities for developing Office-based applications.

MOD See *Microsoft Office Developer*.

modal An object, usually a dialog box, that must be closed before a user can take further action. The opposite of modal is modeless. See *modeless*.

modeless An object that can remain open while a user takes further action. The opposite of modeless is modal. See *modal*.

MSDE See *Microsoft Data Engine*.

naming convention A standardized method of naming objects, variables, and constants so that the nature and purpose of each is apparent by its name.

normalization The process of refining one or more tables in a relational database to avoid unnecessary duplication of data and to simplify access to data.

non-equi join A join between tables in which field values are not equal.

Nothing The value of an object variable to which no assignment is made. Also the value of a Variant subtype variable that hasn't been initialized.

Null The value Access assigns to a field until a specific value is entered by a user.

Number field A field that can contain a numeric value.

object An instance of a class. An object inherits the properties, methods, and responses to events defined in the class.

Object Browser A dialog box that displays information about objects, properties, methods, and constants in current referenced object libraries and in the current project.

object library A file containing definitions of objects together with their properties and methods.

object model A definition of the objects within an application and the relationships between those objects.

ODBC See *Open Database Connectivity*.

Office Developer   See *Microsoft Office Developer*.

OLE object   An object that supports the OLE protocol for linking and embedding.

one-to-many   A relationship between two tables in which a record in one table can be linked to many records in another table.

One-to-one   A relationship between two tables in which a record in one table can be linked to only one record in another table.

Open Database Connectivity (ODBC) A protocol used to access data in SQL Server and other database servers.

operand   A data value on which an operator operates. See *operator*.

operator   An agent that affects data values. The principal types of operators are arithmetic, comparison, logical, and relational. See *arithmetic operator*, *comparison operator*, *logical operator*, and *relational operator*.

Option Button control   A control used on forms to indicate or set one of two states. Option buttons are usually within an option group control. See *option group control*.

Option Group control   A control that contains a group of option buttons, check boxes, or toggle buttons. Only one of the controls within an option group control can be set at a time. See *option button control*, *check box control*, and *toggle button control*.

Performance Analyzer   A tool that analyzes the performance of an Access database and suggests ways to improve that performance.

permission   Something that defines what kind of access a user has to data or objects.

precedence   The order in which the operations performed by operators occur.

primary key   The field (or set of fields) whose value uniquely identifies a record.

private   A variable that exists only within the procedure in which it's declared. Also a procedure that's available only within the module in which it's declared. Contrast with *public*.

procedure   A named sequence of declarations and statements in a module that performs a specific task.

project   All the code modules in a database.

Project Explorer   A Visual Basic Editor window that displays a list of modules in a project.

property   One of the characteristics of a control, field, or object.

Property sheet   A window in which many of the properties of an object are displayed and can be set.

property procedure   A procedure in which custom properties can be defined.

protocol   A set of rules that define how data is transmitted from one device to another.

public   A variable that can be shared with procedures in all modules within a database. Also a procedure that's available within all the modules in a database. Contrast with *private*.

query   A question that is addressed to a table or related tables that results in presentation of information or an action. See *select query* and *action query*.

QueryDef   An object that defines a query.

record   Data about a single item. A Datasheet view of a table, query, or form displays a record as a single row. A record is also known as a *row* or *tuple*.

recordset   A temporary table in memory that contains fields derived from one or more tables, or from other recordsets. Also known as a result set.

Rectangle control   A control that displays a rectangle on a form or report.

referential integrity   A set of rules that define relationships between tables.

relation   In formal database terminology, a relation is what you probably think of as a table. For a table to qualify as a relation, it must contain zero or more records, none of which are duplicates. More colloquially, a relation is the way one table is connected to another.

relational database   A database based on relations. In this context, the word "relations" refers to tables that satisfy certain criteria not to what, in everyday English, we think of as relationships. See *relation*.

relational operator   A symbol representing an elementary relational operation such as equal to, not equal to, greater than, or less than. A relational operation returns True or False.

replica   A complete copy of a database, including its tables, queries, forms, reports, macros, and modules.

replicate   To update two or more copies of a database so that each copy contains the most recent data and objects.

report   Printed information based on data in tables and elsewhere.

reserved word   A word that has a special meaning within Access or Visual Basic for Applications. Reserved words can't be used to name objects.

result set   See *recordset*.

return   To provide a value or object. Functions can return a value or object. Expressions can return a value.

Rich Text Format (RTF)   A file format for text that preserves the appearance of the text as well as the actual text characters. Text saved in rich text format can be transferred between applications running on the same or different platforms.

row   All the data about a single item in a table. Also known as a *record* or *tuple*.

RTF   See *rich text format*.

run-time   The time during which an application is running, as opposed to design time. Contrast with *design time*.

run-time Error   An error that's detected while an application is running.

schema   The organization of the physical tables in a database.

scope   The availability of a variable, constant, or procedure.

ScreenTip   A small window displayed when the pointer pauses over a menu item, toolbar button, or other element. The small window contains a short description of the element.

select query   A query that asks a question about data in one or more tables and returns a set of records in response to that query.

self join   A relationship between two fields in the same table.

snapshot   A static recordset. Unlike in a dynaset, the data displayed in a snapshot can't be changed.

SQL   See *Structured Query Language*.

standard module   A set of VBA declarations and procedures not associated with a specific form or report. The public declarations and procedures in a module can be accessed from any form or report.

statement   In Visual Basic for Applications or other code, a unit that expresses an operation or declaration.

static   Unless declared static, variables declared within a procedure disappear at the end of the procedure. A variable declared static remains in existence after the procedure closes.

Structured Query Language (SQL) A programming language used to interact with database tables.

stub   The first and last statements in a procedure.

sub procedure   A user-defined procedure that doesn't return a value. Contrast with *function procedure*.

subform   A form contained within another form.

subreport   A report contained within another report.

switchboard   A form containing buttons that can be clicked to switch from one part of an application to another. The switchboard is usually the first form that appears when an application is opened.

synchronize   To update a database and a replica of that database so that both contain the most recent changes to data and objects.

syntax   The grammatical structure of a statement or series of statements.

syntax error   An error in the grammatical structure of a statement. The Visual Basic Editor can automatically detect syntax errors.

tab order   The order in which controls on a form receive the focus when the Tab key is pressed repeatedly. See *focus*.

table   An object that stores data items in records (rows) and fields (columns).

Text Box control   A control on a form or report that displays text and can, in the case of a form, be used to enter text.

Text field   A field in a table that can be used to store up to 255 text characters.

theme   A set of formats that determine the appearance of a Data Access Page.

Toolbox   A box that can be superimposed on a form or report at design time. The toolbox contains icons representing controls that can be placed on the form or report.

transaction   A logical unit of work. A transaction may consist of several actions. Within a transaction, all actions must be completed successfully; otherwise, all data is restored to the values before the transaction started.

tuple   A row in a relation. You can think of a tuple as a record in a table. To be considered a database expert, pronounce the word so that it rhymes with "couple." Each column in a tuple is an attribute. See *attribute*.

Unicode   A method of digitally representing characters in which each character occupies two bytes. Unicode can be used to store characters in all languages.

UNC   See *Universal Naming Convention*.

Universal Naming Convention (UNC)
A machine-independent naming convention for files.

validation   The process of checking whether entered data complies with defined conditions or limitations.

variable   A named memory location used to store a value or object that can change during the execution of VBA code. Most variables are used for a value or object of a specific data type. An exception to this is a variable of Variant type, which can be used for values of many different types.

VB   See *Visual Basic*.

VBA   See *Visual Basic for Applications*.

VBE   See *Visual Basic Editor*.

view   The way in which data is displayed. You can change the view of data in a table by sorting the data based on a specific field. Changing the view like this doesn't affect the order in which records are stored. Another definition of view is the window that allows working in a particular way. For example, a form can be displayed in Design view or Form view.

Visual Basic (VB)   An object-based programming language.

Visual Basic Editor (VBE)   A set of tools used for creating Visual Basic code.

Visual Basic for Applications (VBA)
A programming language derived from Visual Basic for creating enhancements to Office and Office-compatible applications.

Watch window   A Visual Basic Editor window that displays the values of specified variables while a procedure runs.

Yes/No field   A field in a table that contain either one value or another. Fields of this type are used to save such pairs of values as Yes or No, or True or False.

zero-length string   A string that contains no characters. A zero-length string is represented by a pair of adjacent quotation marks.

INDEX

SYMBOLS

A

Q

q (symbol), 173
QBE dialog box, 104
QBE grid (Query By Example grid), 38, 93
queries, 36, 91, 521
  action, 179, 513
    append, 37
    delete, 37
    make-table, 37
    update, 37
  append, 179
    SQL, 505
  comparison operators, 386-387
  creating
    related tables, 102
    select, 37
    several tables, 102
    single tables, 91-94
    to base forms on, 143
    unbound charts, 219-220
    unrelated tables, 103
  crosstab, 37
    controlling column order, 112
  Crosstab, in charts, 226-227
  Datasheet view, 101
  delete, 179
  displaying, 36
    information on forms, 143
  joining with tables, 113-114
  make-table, 179

minimizing number, 106
modifying, 38
operators, 389-390
  calculating values, 390
  creating criteria, 394
  setting criteria, 391-393
parameters, 108
performance, 107
properties, 38
  setting, 98
QBE grid, 38
relationships, 38
reports, creating, 205
select, 91
  organizing data, 90-91
SQL view, 104-105
Union
  creating, 113
  SQL, 506
update, 179
Query By Example grid. *See* QBE grid
Query Design window, 36
Query menu, Crosstab Query command, 226
Query window, 93
QueryDef, 521
question mark (?), 161
quotation marks ("), 171, 174

R

raising errors, 351
RAM, optimizing hardware, 352
readable VBA code, displaying messages, 187-188
records, 8521
  archiving, 408-410
  changing order in recordsets, 96
  counting, 318-320
  displaying
    forms, 234-239
    specific information, 239
  filtering, 87
    by form, 87-89
    by selections, 90
    excluding selections, 90
  finding, 85, 240-241
  Keep Together property, 215
  locking, 463-464
  navigating, 314-316
  order, changing, 84
  pictures
    displaying in forms, 197
    displaying in reports, 197
  reports, counting, 215
recordsets, 521
  adding fields, 95
  changing record order, 96